D1130650

Language and
Cultural Description

Language and Cultural Description

Essays by Charles O. Frake

**Selected and Introduced
by Anwar S. Dil**

Stanford University Press, Stanford, California   1980

Language Science and National Development

A Series Sponsored by the
Linguistic Research Group of Pakistan

General Editor: Anwar S. Dil

Stanford University Press
Stanford, California
© 1980 by Charles O. Frake
Introduction and compilation © 1980 by the
Board of Trustees of the
Leland Stanford Junior University
Printed in the United States of America
ISBN 0-8047-1074-0
LC 79-67771

Contents

Acknowledgments

The Linguistic Research Group of Pakistan and the General Editor of the Language Science and National Development Series are deeply grateful to Professor Charles O. Frake for giving us the privilege of presenting his selected writings as the fifteenth volume in our series established in 1970 to commemorate the International Education Year.

We are indebted to the editors and publishers of the following publications. The ready permission on the part of the holders of the copyrights, acknowledged in each case, is a proof of the existing international cooperation and goodwill that gives hope for better collaboration among scholars of all nations for international exchange of knowledge.

The Ethnographic Study of Cognitive Systems. Anthropology and Human Behavior, ed. by T. Gladwin and W. Sturtevant (Washington, D.C.: Anthropological Society of Washington, 1962), pp. 72–85, with permission of the publisher.

Cultural Ecology and Ethnography. American Anthropologist 64. 53–59 (1962), with permission of the American Anthropological Association.

Notes on Queries in Ethnography. American Anthropologist 66(No. 3, Part 2). 132–45 (1964), with permission of the American Anthropological Association.

Plying Frames Can Be Dangerous: Some Reflections on Methodology in Cognitive Anthropology. [Originally subtitled "An

Assessment of Methodology in Cognitive Anthropology."] The Quarterly Newsletter of the Institute for Comparative Human Development (The Rockefeller University) 1(No. 3). 1-7 (1977).

The Eastern Subanun of Mindanao. Social Structure in Southeast Asia, ed. by George Peter Murdock (Viking Fund Publications in Anthropology No. 29, 1960), pp. 51-64. Copyrighted 1960 by the Wenner-Gren Foundation for Anthropological Research, Incorporated, New York.

The Diagnosis of Disease among the Subanun of Mindanao. American Anthropologist 63. 113-32 (1961), with permission of the American Anthropological Association.

Litigation in Lipay: A Study in Subanun Law. Proceedings of the Ninth Pacific Science Congress (Bangkok) 3. 217-22 (1957).

A Structural Description of Subanun "Religious Behavior." Explorations in Cultural Anthropology: Essays in Honor of George Peter Murdock, ed. by Ward Goodenough (New York: McGraw-Hill Book Company, 1964), pp. 111-30, with permission of the publisher.

How to Ask for a Drink in Subanun. American Anthropologist 66(No. 6, Part 2). 127-32 (1964), with permission of the American Anthropological Association.

Struck by Speech: The Yakan Concept of Litigation. Law in Culture and Society, ed. by Laura Nader (Chicago: Aldine, 1969), pp. 147-67, with permission of the editor.

How to Enter a Yakan House. Sociocultural Dimensions of Language Use, ed. by M. Sanches and B. Blount (New York: Academic Press, Inc., 1975), pp. 25-40, with permission of the publisher.

Lexical Origins and Semantic Structure in Philippine Creole Spanish. Pidginization and Creolization of Languages, ed. by Dell Hymes (Cambridge: Cambridge University Press, 1971), pp. 223-42, with permission of the publisher.

Dedicated with affectionate gratitude
to the people of the Philippines,
whose wisdom, patience, and kindness
have made possible the work
represented in this book

EDITOR'S NOTE

These essays have been reprinted from the originals with only minor changes made in the interest of uniformity of style and appearance. In cases where substantive revisions have been made proper notation has been added. Misprints and mistakes appearing in the originals have been corrected in consultation with the author. In some cases references, notes, and bibliographical entries have been updated. Footnotes marked by asterisks have been added by the Editor.

Introduction

Charles Oliver Frake was born in Laramie, Wyoming, on May 9, 1930. When he was in high school in Salt Lake City, his father, then a U.S. Army officer serving in the Philippines, sent him a Tagalog grammar that first aroused his interest in the culture of that region. In 1951, after graduating from Stanford University, Frake went to Yale for graduate work in anthropology with George P. Murdock and Floyd G. Lounsbury, among others. He earned his Ph.D. degree in 1955 with a dissertation on the Subanun culture of Mindanao. In 1958, after two years of military service and a year of postdoctoral research in the Philippines, he was appointed instructor in anthropology at Harvard. Two years later he moved to Stanford as Assistant Professor of Anthropology, and since 1969 he has been Professor of Anthropology at Stanford.

Beginning in 1953, when he first went to the Philippines as a graduate student for a year of field research among the Subanun, Frake has had a fruitful career as an ethnographer. In 1957 he returned to the Philippines to spend a year studying Subanun linguistics and ethnobotany, and to conduct a general ethnographic exploration of the area. He pursued his cultural linguistic studies among California Filipinos in 1961, and subsequently for some ten years among the Yakan and other peoples in the Philippines and Indonesia.

Frake's work among the Subanun involved learning the language and culture of a people about whom very little was known. As a starter he collected and published in 1954 a word list based on Harold Conklin's Test Vocabulary for Philippine Languages (1953). Next he made extensive collections of plants with a view to understanding the people's agricultural system. This led him to studying the use of plants in curing illness, which led to a study of the medical system; and this in turn led to a study of the Subanun system of litigation, on which Frake presented a paper at the Pacific Science Conference in Bangkok in 1957. It became his characteristic method to get at the workings of a people's law or religion, say, through a study of their language and speech behavior rather than starting with a preconceived notion of law or religion and looking for examples that supported or modified this notion. In 1958 he completed his well-known paper on the concept of disease among the Subanun, which was published in 1961.

The first study Frake completed after moving to Stanford in 1960, on cognitive systems, opens this volume; it remains perhaps the most celebrated of his works to date. Though his approach to culture does not sound radical today, when the paper appeared in 1962 it was widely criticized as an assault on the typological approach to cultural description that was current at the time. In essence, Frake's concern is to find out how people organize their lives by exploring what they are thinking and talking about. His method requires the careful formulation of precise strategic questions designed to discover how particular concepts are related in a culture; a sharp sensitivity to what people are doing when they are talking, and what they think they are doing; and a scientific rigor in description. Such methods may not be for everyone, yet all can learn from the theory and methodology section that opens this volume.

In 1962 Frake developed an interest in the Yakan people of Basilan Island, whom he continued to visit annually until 1972, when political conditions made a further visit impossible. Once again he started by learning a new language on which almost no work had been done, and once again he methodically proceeded to investigate a culture and describe it in its own terms. Soon he was making comparisons between the Subanun and Yakan cultures, notably in his well-known paper "Struck by Speech: The Yakan Concept of Litigation" (1968). Though the Yakan culture is in fact considerably more complex and aggressive than the Subanun, this paper shows the two legal systems to be remarkably similar. Frake's findings in this study encouraged him to broaden his focus and examine cross-cultural and universal dimensions of concepts like formality and informality; his current work is in this area.

Frake's relaxed enjoyment of his work as an ethnographer is perhaps most evident in "How to Enter a Yakan House" (1975). The Yakan have a vivacious sense of humor and tell lots of jokes and stories about themselves. They have an elaborate set of rules on how to enter a house, and often amuse themselves by deliberately breaking these rules; but to understand what is funny one must understand what rule or rules have been broken. This essay is a notable contribution to the study of speech acts and people's interpretations of their own behavior.

The major focus in Charles Frake's work to date has been on describing people's ways of life. He sees in the ethnography of language and communication a means to revealing the essential humanness shared by all human beings across languages, cultures, and social boundaries. His central questions are: What does it mean to be doing ethnography? What is it that one describes in describing a culture? And what are the best methods of doing ethnography? Frake feels strongly that talking with people is at the heart of describing a culture, and not just the kind of talking that leads to taking factual notes. Even an ethnographer who knows all the words cannot take for granted that he understands what people are saying: he must keep asking, keep listening, keep refining his sense of what is going on. Frake is a master of this art, and that is why the importance of his explorations in the Philippines goes far beyond their locale.

The fruitfulness of Frake's ideas is apparent from the work of a number of young researchers who are following his lead in investigating other societies, some of them urban. It is a pleasure indeed to present this volume of Frake's distinguished essays in ethnographic theory and method to readers across the world.

Anwar S. Dil

United States International University
San Diego, California
May 9, 1980

**Language and
Cultural Description**

Part I. Language and Ethnography: Theory and Methodology

1 | The Ethnographic Study of Cognitive Systems

<u>Words for Things</u>

A relatively simple task commonly performed by ethnographers is that of getting names for things.[1] The ethnographer typically performs this task by pointing to or holding up the apparent constituent objects of an event he is describing, eliciting the native names for the objects, and then matching each native name with the investigator's own word for the object. The logic of the operation is: if the informant calls object X a <u>mbubu</u> and I call object X a <u>rock</u>, then <u>mbubu</u> means <u>rock</u>. In this way are compiled the ordinary ethnobotanical monographs with their lists of matched native and scientific names for plant specimens. This operation probably also accounts for a good share of the native names parenthetically inserted in so many monograph texts: "Among the grasses (<u>sigbet</u>) whose grains (<u>bunga nen</u>) are used for beads (<u>bitekel</u>) none is more highly prized than Job's tears (<u>glias</u>)." Unless the reader is a comparative linguist of the languages concerned, he may well ask what interest these parenthetical insertions contain other than demonstrating that the ethnographer has discharged a minimal obligation toward collecting linguistic data. This procedure for obtaining words for things, as well as the "so-what" response it so often evokes, assumes the objective identifiability of discrete "things" apart from a particular culture. It construes the name-getting task as one of simply matching verbal labels for "things" in two languages. Accordingly, the "problem-oriented" anthropologist, with a broad, cross-cultural perspective, may disclaim any interest in these labels; all that concerns him is the presence or absence of a particular "thing" in a given culture.

If, however, instead of "getting words for things," we redefine the task as one of finding the "things" that go with the words, the eliciting of terminologies acquires a more general interest. In actuality not even the most concrete, objectively apparent physical object can be identified apart from some culturally defined system of concepts (Boas 1911: 24-25; Bruner et al. 1946; Goodenough 1957). An ethnographer should strive to define objects[2] according to the conceptual system of the people he is studying. Let me suggest, then, that one look upon the task of getting names for things not as an exercise in linguistic recording, but as a way of finding out what are in fact the "things" in the environment of the people being studied. This paper consists of some suggestions toward the formulation of an operationally explicit methodology for discerning how people construe their world of experience from the way they talk about it. Specifically these suggestions concern the analysis of terminological systems in a way which reveals the conceptual principles that generate them.

In a few fields, notably in kinship studies, anthropologists have already successfully pushed an interest in terminological systems beyond a matching of translation labels. Since Morgan's day no competent student of kinship has looked upon his task as one of simply finding a tribe's words for "uncle," "nephew," or "cousin." The recognition that the denotative range of kinship categories must be determined empirically in each case, that the categories form a system, and that the semantic contrasts underlying the system are amenable to formal analysis has imparted to kinship studies a methodological rigor and theoretical productivity rare among etnnographic endeavors. Yet all peoples are vitally concerned with kinds of phenomena other than genealogical relations; consequently there is no reason why the study of a people's concepts of these other phenomena should not offer a theoretical interest comparable to that of kinship studies.

Even with reference to quite obvious kinds of material objects, it has long been noted that many people do not see "things" quite the way we do. However, anthropologists in spite of their now well-established psychological interests have notably ignored the cognition of their subjects. Consequently other investigators still rely on stock anecdotes of "primitive thinking" handed down by explorers, philologists, and psychologists since the nineteenth century (Brown 1958: 256; Hill 1952; Jespersen 1923: 429; Ullman 1957: 95, 308). Commonly these anecdotes have been cited as examples of early stages in the evolution of human thought—which, depending on the anecdote selected,

may be either from blindly concrete to profoundly abstract or from
hopelessly vague to scientifically precise. A typical citation, purporting to illustrate the primitive's deficient abstractive ability, concerns
a Brazilian Indian tribe which allegedly has no word for "parrot" but
only words for "kinds of parrots" (Jespersen 1934: 429ff). The people
of such a tribe undoubtedly classify the birds of their environment in
some fashion; certainly they do not bestow a unique personal name on
each individual bird specimen they encounter. Classification means
that individual bird specimens must be matched against the defining
attributes of conceptual categories and thereby judged to be equivalent
for certain purposes to some other specimens but different from still
others. Since no two birds are alike in every discernible feature, any
grouping into sets implies a selection of only a limited number of features as significant for contrasting kinds of birds. A person learns
which features are significant from his fellows as part of his cultural
equipment. He does not receive this information from the birds. Consequently there is no necessary reason that a Brazilian Indian should
heed those particular attributes which, for the English-speaker, make
equivalent all the diverse individual organisms he labels "parrots."
Some of this Indian's categories may seem quite specific, and others
quite general, when compared to our grouping of the same speciments.
But learning that it takes the Indian many words to name the objects we
happen to group together in one set is trivial information compared to
knowing how the Indian himself groups these objects and which attributes he selects as dimensions to generate a taxonomy of avifauna.
With the latter knowledge we learn what these people regard as significant about birds. If we can arrive at comparable knowledge about
their concepts of land animals, plants, soils, weather, social relations,
personalities, and supernaturals, we have at least a sketch map of the
world in the image of the tribe.

     The analysis of a culture's terminological systems will not,
of course, exhaustively reveal the cognitive world of its members, but
it will certainly tap a central portion of it. Culturally significant cognitive features must be communicable between persons in one of the
standard symbolic systems of the culture. A major share of these
features will undoubtedly be codable in a society's most flexible and
productive communication device, its language. Evidence also seems
to indicate that those cognitive features requiring most frequent communication will tend to have standard and relatively short linguistic

labels (Brown 1958: 235–41; Brown and Lenneberg 1954). Accordingly, a commonly distinguished category of trees is more likely to be called something like "elm" by almost all speakers rather than labeled with an ad hoc, non-standardized construction like "You know, those tall trees with asymmetrical, serrated-edged leaves." To the extent that cognitive coding tends to be linguistic and tends to be efficient, the study of the referential use of standard, readily elicitable linguistic responses—or terms—should provide a fruitful beginning point for mapping a cognitive system. And with verbal behavior we know how to begin.

The beginning of an ethnographic task is the recording of what is seen and heard, the segmenting of the behavior stream in such a way that culturally significant noises and movements are coded while the irrelevant is discarded. Descriptive linguistics provides a methodology for segmenting the stream of speech into units relevant to the structure of the speaker's language. I assume that any verbal response which conforms to the phonology and grammar of a language is necessarily a culturally significant unit of behavior. Methodologies for the structural description of non-verbal behavior are not correspondingly adequate in spite of important contributions in this direction by such persons as Pike and Barker and Wright (Barker and Wright 1955; Pike 1954; cf. Miller et al. 1960: 13–14). By pushing forward the analysis of units we know to be culturally relevant, we can, I think, more satisfactorily arrive at procedures for isolating the significant constituents of analogous and interrelated structures. The basic methodological concept advocated here—the determination of the set of contrasting responses appropriate to a given, culturally valid, eliciting context—should ultimately be applicable to the "semantic" analysis of any culturally meaningful behavior.

Segregates

A terminologically distinguished array of objects is a segregate (Conklin 1954, 2962; cf. Lounsbury 1956). Segregates are categories, but not all categories known or knowable to an individual are segregates by this definition. Operationally, this definition of a segregate leaves a problem: how do we recognize a "term" when we hear one? How do we segment the stream of speech into category-designating units?

The segmentation of speech into the grammatically functioning units revealed by linguistic analysis is a necessary, but not sufficient, condition for terminological analysis. Clearly no speech segment smaller than the minimal grammatical unit, the morpheme, need
be considered. However, the task requires more than simply a search
for the meanings of morphemes or other grammatical units. The items
and arrangements of a structural description of the language code need
not be isomorphic with the categories and propositions of the message.
Linguistic forms, whether morphemes or larger constructions, are
not each tied to unique chunks of semantic reference like baggage tags;
rather it is the use of speech, the selection of one statement over
another in a particular sociolinguistic context, that points to the category boundaries on a culture's cognitive map (Chomsky 1955; Haugen
1957; Hymes 1961; Joos 1958; Lounsbury 1956; Nida 1951).

Suppose we have been studying the verbal behavior accompanying the selection and ordering of items at an American lunch counter.[3]
The following text might be typical of those overhead and recorded:

"What ya going to have, Mac? Something to eat?"

"Yeah. What kind of sandwiches ya got besides hamburgers
and hot dogs?"

"How about a ham 'n cheese sandwich?"

"Nah ... I guess I'll take a hamburger again. "
* * *
"Hey, that's no hamburger; that's a cheeseburger!"

The problem is to isolate and relate these speech forms according to
their use in naming objects. Some, but apparently not all, orderable
items at a lunch counter are distinguished by the term something to
eat. A possibility within the range of 'something to eat' seems to be
a set of objects labeled sandwiches. The forms hamburger, hot dog,
ham 'n cheese sandwich, and cheeseburger clearly designate alternative choices in lunch-counter contexts. A customer determined to
have a 'sandwich' must select one of these alternatives when he orders,
and upon receipt of the order, he must satisfy himself that the object
thrust before him—which he has never seen before—meets the criteria

for membership in the segregate he designated. The counterman must decide on actions that will produce an object acceptable to the customer as a member of the designated segregate. The terminological status of these forms can be confirmed by analysis of further speech situations, by eliciting utterances with question frames suggested to the investigator by the data, and by observing non-verbal features of the situation, especially correlations between terms used in ordering and objects received.

In isolating these terms no appeal has been made to analysis of their linguistic structure or their signification. Sandwich is a single morpheme. Some linguists, at any rate, would analyze hot dog and even hamburger as each containing two morphemes, but, since the meaning of the constructions cannot be predicted from a knowledge of the meaning of their morphological constituents, they are single "lexemes" (Goodenough 1956) or "idioms" (Hockett 1958: 303-18). Ham 'n cheese sandwich would not, I think, qualify as a single lexeme; nevertheless it is a standard segregate label whose function in naming objects cannot be distinguished from that of forms like hot dog. Suppose further utterances from lunch-counter speech show that the lexically complex term something to eat distinguishes the same array of objects as do the single morphemes food and chow. In such a case, a choice among these three terms would perhaps say something about the social status of the lunch counter and its patrons, but it says nothing distinctive about the objects designated. As segregate labels, these three frequently heard terms would be equivalent.

Although not operationally relevant at this point, the lexemic status of terms bears on later analysis of the productivity of a terminological system. In contrast, say, to our kinship terminology, American lunch-counter terminology is highly productive. The existence of productive, polylexemic models such as ham 'n cheese sandwich permits the generation and labeling of new segregates to accommodate the latest lunch-counter creations. However, the non-intuitive determination of the lexemic status of a term requires a thorough analysis of the distinctive features of meaning of the term and its constituents (Goodenough 1956; Lounsbury 1956). Such an analysis of the criteria for placing objects into categories can come only after the term, together with those contrasting terms relevant to its use, has been isolated as a segregate label.

Contrast Sets

In a situation in which a person is making a public decision about the category membership of an object by giving the object a verbal label, he is selecting a term out of a set of alternatives, each with classificatory import. When he asserts "This is an X, " he is also stating that it is not specific other things, these other things being not everything else conceivable, but only the alternatives among which a decision was made (Kelly 1955). In lunch-counter ordering, 'hamburger, ' 'hot dog, ' 'cheeseburger, ' and 'ham and cheese sandwich' are such alternatives. Any object placed in one of these segregates cannot at the same time belong to another. Those culturally appropriate responses which are distinctive alternatives in the same kinds of situations—or, in linguistic parlance, which occur in the same "environment"—can be said to contrast. A series of terminologically contrasted segregates forms a contrast set.

Note that the cognitive relation of contrast is not equivalent to the relation of class exclusion in formal logic and set theory. The three categories 'hamburger, ' 'hot dog, ' and 'rainbow' are mutually exclusive in membership. But in writing rules for classifying hamburgers I must say something about hot dogs, whereas I can ignore rainbows. Two categories contrast only when the difference between them is significant for defining their use. The segregates 'hamburger' and 'rainbow, ' even though they have no members in common, do not function as distinctive alternatives in any uncontrived classifying context familiar to me.

Taxonomies

The notion of contrast cannot account for all the significant relations among these lunch-counter segregates. Although no object can be both a hamburger and a hot dog, an object can very well be both a hot dog and a sandwich or a hamburger and a sandwich. By recording complementary names applied to the same objects (and eliminating referential synonyms such as something to eat and food), the following series might result:

Object A is named: something to eat, sandwich, hamburger
Object B is named: something to eat, sandwich, ham sandwich

Object C is named: <u>something to eat</u>, <u>pie</u>, <u>apple pie</u>
Object D is named: <u>something to eat</u>, <u>pie</u>, <u>cherry pie</u>
Object E is named: <u>something to eat</u>, <u>ice cream bar</u>, <u>Eskimo pie</u>

Some segregates include a wider range of objects than others and are subpartitioned by a contrast set. The segregate 'pie' <u>includes</u> the contrast set 'apple pie,' 'cherry pie,' etc. For me, the segregate 'apple pie' is, in turn, subpartitioned by 'French apple pie' and 'plain (or 'ordinary') apple pie.' Figure 1 diagrams the subpartitioning of the segregate 'something to eat' as revealed by naming responses to objects A-E.[4]

Again it is the use of terms, not their linguistic structure, that provides evidence of inclusion. We cannot consider 'Eskimo pie' to be included in the category 'pie,' for we cannot discover a natural situation in which an object labeled <u>Eskimo pie</u> can be labeled simply <u>pie</u>. Thus the utterance "That's not a sandwich; that's a pie" cannot refer to an Eskimo pie. Similar examples are common in English. The utterance "Look at that oak" may refer to a 'white oak' but never to a 'poison oak.' A 'blackbird' is a kind of 'bird,' but a 'redcap' is not a kind of 'cap.' For many English speakers, the unqualified use of <u>American</u> invariably designates a resident or citizen of the United States; consequently, for such speakers, an 'American' is a kind of 'North American' rather than the converse. One cannot depend on a particular grammatical construction, such as one of the English phrasal compounds, to differentiate consistently a single cognitive relation, such as that of inclusion (cf. Hockett 1958: 316-17). Because English is not unique in this respect (Frake 1961), the practice of arguing from morphological and syntactic analysis directly to cognitive relations must be considered methodologically unsound.

Segregates in different contrast sets, then, may be related by inclusion. A system of contrast sets so related is a <u>taxonomy</u> (Conklin 1962; Gregg 1954; Woodger 1952). This definition does not require a taxonomy to have a unique beginner, i. e. a segregate which includes all other segregates in the system. It requires only that the segregates at the most inclusive level form a demonstrable contrast set.

Something to eat				
Sandwich		Pie		Ice cream bar
ham-burger	ham sandwich	apple pie	cherry pie	Eskimo pie
A	B	C	D	E

Objects placed before the final row: A, B, C, D, E

Figure 1. Subpartitioning of the segregate 'something to eat' as revealed by naming responses to objects A-E.

Taxonomies make possible a regulation of the amount of information communicated about an object in a given situation (compare "Give me something to eat" with "Give me a French apple pie a la mode"), and they provide a hierarchal ordering of categories, allowing an efficient program for the identification, filing, and retrieving of significant information (Herdan 1960: 210-11). The use of taxonomic systems is not confined to librarians and biologists; it is a fundamental principle of human thinking. The elaboration of taxonomies along vertical dimensions of generalization and horizontal dimensions of discrimination probably depends on factors such as the variety of cultural settings within which one talks about the objects being classified (Frake 1961: 121-22), the importance of the objects to the way of life of the classifiers (Brown 1958; Nida 1958), and general properties of human thinking with regard to the number of items that the mind can cope with at a given time (Miller 1956; Yngve 1960).[5] Determining the precise correlates of variations in taxonomic structure, both intraculturally and cross-culturally, is, of course, one of the objectives of this methodology.

In order to describe the use of taxonomic systems and to work out their behavioral correlates, evidence of complementary naming must be supplemented by observations on the sociolinguistic contexts that call for contrasts at particular levels. One could, for example, present a choice between objects whose segregates appear to contrast at different levels and ask an informant to complete the frame: "Pick up that ——." Suppose we have an apple pie on the counter next to a ham sandwich. The frame would probably be completed as "Pick up that pie." If, however, we substitute a cherry pie for the ham sandwich, we would expect to hear "Pick up that apple pie." Variations on this device of having informants contrast particular objects can be worked out depending on the kind of phenomena being classified. Some objects, such as pies and plants, are easier to bring together for visual comparison than others, such as diseases and deities.

Another device for eliciting taxonomic structures is simply to ask directly about relations of inclusion: "Is X a kind of Y?" Since in many speech situations even a native fails to elicit a term at the level of specification he requires, most, if not all, languages probably provide explicit methods for moving up and down a taxonomic hierarchy:

"Give me some of that pie." "What kind of pie d'ya want, Mac?"

"What's this 'submarine' thing on the menu?" "That's a kind of sandwich."

Once a taxonomic partitioning has been worked out it can be tested systematically for terminological contrast with frames such as "Is that an X?" with an expectation of a negative reply. For example, we could point to an apple pie and ask a counterman:

1. "Is that something to drink?"
2. "Is that a sandwich?"
3. "Is that a cherry pie?"

We would expect the respective replies to reflect the taxonomy of lunch-counter foods:

1. "No, it's something to eat."
2. "No, it's a pie."
3. "No, it's an apple pie."

(Admittedly it is easier to do this kind of questioning in a culture where one can assume the role of a naive learner.)

In employing these various operations for exploring taxonomic structures, the investigator must be prepared for cases when the same linguistic form designates segregates at different levels of contrast within the same system ('man' vs. 'animal,' 'man' vs. 'woman,' 'man' vs. 'boy') (Frake 1961: 119); when a single unpartitioned segregate contrasts with two or more other segregates which are themselves at different levels of contrast ("That's not a coin; it's a token." "That's not a dime; it's a token."); and when incongruities occur in the results of the several operations (terminological contrasts may cut across subhierarchies revealed by complementary naming; explicit statements of inclusion may be less consistent than complementary naming).

Attributes

Our task up to this point has been to reveal the structure of the system from which a selection is made when categorizing an object. When you hand a Navajo a plant specimen, or an American a sandwich, what is the available range of culturally defined arrays into which this object can be categorized? Methodological notions of contrast and inclusion have enabled us to discern some structure in this domain of cognitive choices, but we still have not faced the problem of how a person decides which out of a set of alternative categorizations is the correct one in a given instance. How does one in fact distinguish a hamburger from a cheeseburger, a chair from a stool, a tree from a shrub, an uncle from a cousin, a jerk from a slob?

A mere list of known members of a category—however an investigator identifies these objects cross-culturally—does not answer this question. Categorization, in essence, is a device for treating new experience as though it were equivalent to something already familiar (Brown 1958; Bruner 1957; Bruner et al. 1956; Sapir 1949). The hamburger I get tomorrow may be a quite different object in terms of size, kind of bun, and lack of tomatoes from the hamburger I had today. But it will still be a hamburger—unless it has a slice of cheese in it! To define 'hamburger' one must know, not just what objects it includes, but with what it contrasts. In this way we learn that a slice of cheese makes a difference, whereas a slice of tomato does not. In the context of different cultures the task is to state what one must know in order to categorize objects correctly. A definition of a Navajo plant category is not given by a list of botanical species it contains but by a rule for distinguishing newly encountered specimens of that category from contrasting alternatives.

Table 1. Defining Attributes of the Contrast Set of Stem
Habit in the Subanun Plant Taxonomy

Contrast Set	Dimensions of Contrast	
	Woodiness	Rigidity
gayu 'woody plants'	W	R
sigbet 'herbaceous plants'	W̄	R
belagen 'vines'		R̄

Ideally the criterial attributes which generate a contrast set
fall along a limited number of dimensions of contrast, each with two
or more contrasting values or "components." Each segregate can be
defined as a distinctive bundle of components. For example, the plant
taxonomy of the Eastern Subanun, a Philippine people, has as its beginner a contrast set of three segregates which together include almost all of the more than 1,400 segregates at the most specific level
of contrast within the taxonomy. This three-member contrast set can
be generated by binary contrasts along two dimensions pertaining to
habit of stem growth (see Table 1). Applications of componential analysis to pronominal systems and kinship terminologies have made this
method of definition familiar (Austerlitz 1959; Conklin 1962; Goodenough
1956; Lounsbury 1956; McKaughan 1959; Thomas 1955; Wallace and
Atkins 1960). The problem remains of demonstrating the cognitive
saliency of componential solutions—to what extent are they models of
how a person decides which term to use?—and of relating terminological attributes to actual perceptual discriminations (Frake 1961; Wallace and Atkins 1960). As a case of the latter problem, suppose we
learn that informants distinguish two contrasting plant segregates by
calling the fruit of one 'red' and that of the other 'green.' We set up
'color' as a dimension of contrast with values of 'red' and 'green.'
But the terminology of 'color' is itself a system of segregates whose
contrastive structure must be analyzed before color terms can serve
as useful defining attributes of other segregates. Ultimately one is
faced with defining color categories by referring to the actual perceptual dimensions along which informants make differential categorization
These dimensions must be determined empirically and not prescribed
by the investigator using stimulus materials from his own culture. By

careful observation one might discover that visual evaluation of an object's succulence, or other unexpected dimensions, as well as the traditional dimensions of hue, brightness, and saturation, are criterial to the use of "color" terms in a particular culture (Conklin 1955).

Whether aimed directly at perceptual qualities of phenomena or at informants' descriptions of pertinent attributes (Frake 1961: 122–25), any method for determining the distinctive and probabilistic attributes of a segregate must depend, first, on knowing the contrast set within which the segregate is participating, and, second, on careful observations of verbal and non-verbal features of the cultural situations to which this contrast set provides an appropriate response.

This formulation has important implications for the role of eliciting in ethnography. The distinctive "situations," or "eliciting frames," or "stimuli," which evoke and define a set of contrasting responses are cultural data to be discovered, not prescribed, by the ethnographer. This stricture does not limit the use of preconceived eliciting devices to prod an informant into action or speech without any intent of defining the response by what evoked it in this instance. But the formulation—prior to observation—of response-defining eliciting devices is ruled out by the logic of this methodology which insists that any eliciting conditions not themselves part of the cultural-ecological system being investigated cannot be used to define categories purporting to be those of the people under study. It is those elements of our informants' experience, which they heed in selecting appropriate actions and utterances, that this methodology seeks to discover.

Objectives

The methodological suggestions proposed in this paper, as they stand, are clearly awkward and incomplete. They must be made more rigorous and expanded to include analyses of longer utterance sequences, to consider non-verbal behavior systematically, and to explore the other types of cognitive relations, such as sequential stage relations (Frake 1961) and part-whole relations, that may pertain between contrast sets. Focusing on the linguistic code, clearer operational procedures are needed for delimiting semantically exocentric

units ("lexemes" or "idioms") (Goodenough 1956; Nida 1951), for discerning synonomy, homonymy, and polysemy (Ullman 1947; 63), and
for distinguishing between utterance grammaticalness (correctly constructed code) and utterance congruence (meaningfully constructed
message) (Chomsky 1957; Joos 1958). In their present form, however,
these suggestions have come out of efforts to describe behavior in the
field, and their further development can come only from continuing
efforts to apply and test them in ethnographic field situations.

The intended objective of these efforts is eventually to provide the ethnographer with public, non-intuitive procedures for ordering his presentation of observed and elicited events according to the
principles of classification of the people he is studying. To order
ethnographic observations solely according to an investigator's preconceived categories obscures the real content of culture: how people
organize their experience conceptually so that it can be transmitted
as knowledge from person to person and from generation to generation.
As Goodenough advocates in a classic paper, culture "does not consist
of things, people, behavior, or emotions," but the forms or organization of these things in the minds of people (Goodenough 1957). The
principles by which people in a culture construe their world reveal
how they segregate the pertinent from the insignificant, how they code
and retrieve information, how they anticipate events (Kelly 1955), how
they define alternative courses of action and make decisions among then
Consequently a strategy of ethnographic description that gives a central
place to the cognitive processes of the actors involved will contribute
reliable cultural data to problems of the relations between language,
cognition, and behavior; it will point up critical dimensions for meaningful cross-cultural comparison; and, finally, it will give us productive descriptions of cultural behavior, descriptions which like the
linguists' grammar, succinctly state what one must know in order to
generate culturally acceptable acts and utterances appropriate to a
given socioecological context (Goodenough 1947).

NOTES

[1] In preparing this paper I have especially benefited from suggestions by Harold C. Conklin, Thomas Gladwin, Volney Stefflre, and
William C. Sturtevant.

[2] In this paper the term <u>object</u> designates anything construed
as a member of a category (Bruner et al. 1956: 231), whether perceptible or not.

[3] Because this is a short, orally presented paper, suggested
procedures are illustrated with rather simple examples from a familiar
language and culture. A serious analysis would require much larger
quantities of speech data presented in phonemic transcription. For a
more complex example, intended as an ethnographic statement, see
Frake 1961.

[4] This example is, of course, considerably oversimplified.
If the reader does not relate these segregates in the same way as our
hypothetical lunch-counter speakers, he is not alone. Shortly after
I completed the manuscript of this paper, a small boy approached me
in a park and, without any eliciting remark whatsoever on my part,
announced: "Hamburgers are more gooder than sandwiches." One
could not ask for better evidence of contrast.

[5] At least in formal, highly partitioned taxonomic systems an
ordering of superordinates according to the number of their subordinates appears to yield a stable statistical distribution (the Willis distribution) regardless of what is being classified or who is doing the
classifying (Herdan 1960: 211-25; Mandelbrot 1946).

REFERENCES

Austerlitz, Robert. 1959. Semantic components of pronoun systems:
        Gilyak. Word 15 (1): 102-9.
Barker, Roger G., and Herbert F. Wright.   1955. Midwest and its
        children, the psychological ecology of an American town.
        Evanston: Row, Peterson.
Boas, Franz. 1911. Introduction. In Handbook of American Indian
        languages. Bureau of American Ethnology Bulletin 40, Pt.
        1, 1-83.
Brown, Roger. 1958. Words and things. Glencoe: Free Press.
Brown, Roger, and Eric H. Lenneberg. 1954. A study in language
        and cognition. Journal of Abnormal and Social Psychology
        49(3): 454-62.
Bruner, Jerome S. 1957. Going beyond the information given. In
        Contemporary Approaches to Cognition; a Symposium Held
        at the University of Colorado. Cambridge: Harvard Univer-
        sity Press, pp. 41-70.

Bruner, Jerome S., J. J. Goodnow, and G. A. Austin. 1956. A
        study of thinking. With an appendix on language by Roger W.
        Brown. New York: Wiley.
Chomsky, Noam. 1955. Semantic considerations in grammar. George-
        town University Monograph Series on Language and Linguistics,
        no. 8, pp. 141-50.
_____. 1957. Syntactic structures. The Hague: Mouton.
Conklin, Harold C. 1954. The relation of Hanunóo culture to the plant
        world. Unpublished Ph.D. dissertation. New Haven: Yale
        University.
_____. 1955. Hanunóo color categories. Southwestern Journal of
        Anthropology 11(4): 339-44.
_____. 1962. Lexicographical treatment of folk taxonomies. Work
        paper for Conference on Lexicography, Indiana University,
        Nov. 11-12, 1960. In Fred W. Householder and Sol Saporta,
        eds., Problems in lexicography. Supplement to International
        Journal of American Linguistics 28, no. 2. Indiana Univer-
        sity Research Center in Anthropology, Folklore and Linguis-
        tics, Publication 21, Bloomington.
Frake, Charles O. 1961. The diagnosis of disease among the Subanun
        of Mindanao. American Anthropologist 63(1): 113-32.
Goodenough, Ward H. 1956. Componential analysis and the study of
        meaning. Language 32(1): 195-216.
_____. 1957. Cultural anthropology and linguistics. Georgetown
        University Monograph Series on Language and Linguistics,
        no. 9, pp. 167-73.
Gregg, John R. 1954. The language of taxonomy, an application of
        symbolic logic to the study of classificatory systems. New
        York: Columbia University Press.
Haugen, Einar. 1957. The semantics of Icelandic orientation. Word
        13(3): 447-59.
Herdan, Gustav. 1960. Type-token mathematics, a textbook of math-
        ematical linguistics. The Hague: Mouton.
Hill, A. A. 1952. A note on primitive languages. International
        Journal of American Linguistics 18(3): 172-77.
Hockett, Charles F. 1958. A course in modern linguistics. New
        York: Macmillan.
Hymes, Dell H. 1961. On typology of cognitive styles in language
        (with examples from Chinookan). Anthropological Linguis-
        tics 3(1): 22-54.

Jespersen, Otto. 1934. Language: its nature, development, and origin. London: Allen & Unwin.

Joos, Martin. 1958. Semology: a linguistic theory of meaning. Studies in Linguistics 13(3): 53-70.

Kelly, George. 1955. The psychology of personal constructs. New York: Norton.

Lounsbury, Floyd G. 1956. A semantic analysis of the Pawnee kinship usage. Language 32(1): 158-94.

Mandelbrot, Benoit. 1956. On the language of taxonomy. In Colin Cherry, ed., Information theory. New York: Academic Press, pp. 135-45.

McKaughan, Howard. 1959. Semantic components of pronoun systems: Maranao. Word 15(1): 101-2.

Miller, George. 1956. Human memory and the storage of information. IRE Transactions on Information Theory IT 2: 129-37. New York: Institute of Radio Engineers.

Miller, George, Eugene Galanter, and Karl Pribram. 1960. Plans and the structure of behavior. New York: Holt-Dryden.

Nida, Eugene. 1951. A system for the description of semantic elements. Word 7(1): 1-14.

_____. 1958. Analysis of meaning and dictionary making. International Journal of American Linguistics 24(4): 279-92.

Pike, Kenneth. 1954. Language in relation to a unified theory of the structure of human behavior. Part 1. Glendale: Summer Institute of Linguistics.

Sapir, Edward. 1949. The psychological reality of phonemes. In David G. Mandelbaum, ed., Selected writings of Edward Sapir in language, culture, and personality. Berkeley and Los Angeles: University of California Press, pp. 46-60.

Thomas, David. 1955. Three analyses of the Ilocano pronoun system. Word 11(2): 204-8.

Ullman, Stephen. 1957. The principles of semantics. New York: Philosophical Library.

Wallace, Anthony, and J. Atkins. 1960. The meaning of kinship terms. American Anthropologist 62(1): 58-80.

Woodger, J. H. 1952. Biology and language, an introduction to the methodology of the biological sciences including medicine. Cambridge: The University Press.

Yngve, Victor H. 1960. A model and an hypothesis for language structure. Proceedings of the American Philosophical Society 104(5): 444-66.

2 | Cultural Ecology and Ethnography

Ecology is the study of the workings of ecosystems, of the behavioral interdependences of different kinds of organisms with respect to one another and to their non-biotic environment. Cultural ecology is the study of the role of culture as a dynamic component of any ecosystem of which man is a part. Unique among organisms, man carves his ecological niches primarily with cultural tools of his own invention rather than with biological specializations. This niche-carving activity of man not only remolds existing biotic communities but also has a shaping effect on the tools—that is on man's cultural knowledge and equipment—themselves. In addition, man constantly devises new tools for carving out more effective places in the ecosystem surrounding him. Because of this progressive cultural adaptation and specialization to environmental conditions, the study of cultural ecology, under one name or another, has been closely linked with theoretical interest in culture history and culture evolution. Steward, who framed the present designation of the subject, construes cultural ecology largely as a methodology for building evolutionary theory (Steward 1955: 30–42).

Although the utility of ecological studies for such pursuits is undeniable, it is not necessary to regard cultural ecology simply as a methodological adjust to nobler tasks. Cultural ecology, in that it refers to a delimitable system of phenomena, is a legitimate field of anthropological interests in its own right, as legitimate as the study of social systems which has so absorbed the efforts of many of us. If the social system be envisioned as a network of relationships among persons of a social community, then the ecological system is a network of relationships between man, the other organisms of his biotic community, and the constituents of his physical environment. In both cases the net is woven of cultural threads, and the two networks are, of course, interconnected at many points.

But before the possibilities for general theory inherent in a study of cultural ecological systems are fully realized, the problem of describing these systems, the ethnographic problem, must, I think, be taken more seriously. As Hymes (1960: 343) has remarked of linguistics, "One need not stop with the individual systems, but one must pass through them. " The comparative method, whether on the scale of a Murdock (1949), a Steward (1955), or a Gulliver (1955), cannot yield results of greater validity than that of the data being compared. This paper has the purpose of assessing cultural ecology as an ethnographic endeavor. First, I will present some notions of what constitutes an ethnographic description, then I will suggest some ways in which ecological studies might be encompassed within the framework of these notions, giving a brief example from my field work.

Following Goodenough (1957), this paper proposes that a description of cultural behavior is attained by a formulation of what one must know in order to respond in a culturally appropriate manner in a given socioecological context. Such a description, like a linguist's grammar, is productive in that it can generate new acts which will be considered appropriate responses by the members of the society being described. A successful strategy for writing productive ethnographies must tap the cognitive world of one's informants. It must discover those features of objects and events which they regard as significant for defining concepts, formulating propositions, and making decisions. This conception of an ethnography requires that the units by which the data of observation are segmented, ordered, and interrelated by delimited and defined according to contrasts inherent in the data themselves and not according to a priori notions of pertinent descriptive categories.

The necessity of coming to terms with one's informants' concepts is well recognized in some ethnographic endeavors, kinship studies providing the most notable example. No ethnographer describes social relations in an alien society by referring to the doings of "uncles, " "aunts, " and "cousins. " Many ethnographers do, however, describe the pots and pans, the trees and shrubs, the soils and rocks of a culture's environment solely in terms of categories projected from the

investigator's culture. In comparison with studying religious conceptions or kinship relations, the description of the tangible objects of
a culture's ecosystem is usually regarded as one of the ethnographer's
simpler tasks. If he does not know a word for a specimen of fauna,
flora, or soil, he can always ship it off to a specialist for "identification." However, if one insists that no specimen has been described
ethnographically until one has stated the rules for its identification
in the culture being studied, then the problem of describing a tangible
object such as a plant may become rather more complex than the relatively simple task of defining contrasts between categories of kinsmen.
Consider, for example, the problem of identifying plants according to
the Hanunóo system of folk botany (Conklin 1954, 1957). The Hanunóo
tropical-forest agriculturists of the central Philippines, exhaustively
partition their plant world into more than 1,600 categories, whereas
systematic botanists classify the same flora into less than 1,200
species. To place correctly, by Hanunóo standards, a newly encountered plant specimen in the appropriate one of the 1,600 categories
requires rather fine discriminations among plants—and these discriminations rely on features generally remote from the botanist's count
of stamens and carpels. By discovering what one must know in order
to classify plants and other ecological components in Hanunóo fashion,
one learns what the Hanunóo consider worth attending to when making
decisions or how to behave within their ecosystem.

An ethnographer, then, cannot be satisfied with a mere cata-
loguing of the components of a cultural ecosystem according to the
categories of Western science. He must also describe the environment as the people themselves construe it according to the categories
of their ethnoscience. From a presentation of the rules by which
people decide upon the category membership of objects in their experience, an ethnographic ecology can proceed to rules for more complex
kinds of behavior: killing game, clearing fields, building houses, etc.
Determining the requisite knowledge for such behavior shows the ethnographer the extent to which ecological considerations, in contrast,
say, to sociological ones, center into a person's decision of what to
do. The ethnographer learns, in a rather meaningful and precise
sense, what role the environment in fact plays in the cultural behavior
of the members of a particular society.

A partial description of the settlement pattern of the Eastern
Subanun, a Philippine people, will illustrate the notions of cultural

ecological description advanced here. This analysis would ideally
rest upon a presentation of the pertinent Subanun ethnoscience relating
to agriculture and vegetation types. Limitations of time force a rather
inadequate and simplified description, but one, which if not a contribution to ethnography, may at least point up some of the desirable features of a legitimate ethnographic contribution to cultural ecology.

The Subanun have carved a niche for themselves in the tropical rain forests of Zamboanga Peninsula, on the island of Mindanao,
by swidden agriculture (or "shifting cultivation, " Frake 1955, 1960; cf.
Conklin 1957). The tropical forest agriculturist must establish a controlled biotic community of sun-loving annuals and perennials in a
climatic region whose natural climax community, the tropical rain
forest, is radically different in almost every respect from the community agricultural man seeks to foster. The swidden farmer meets
this problem by periodically putting the forest through its successional
paces. He modifies and operates on an existing ecosystem rather than
permanently replacing it with an utterly different kind of biotic and
edaphic world, such as that of the wet-rice paddy.

The Subanun settlement pattern is one of clustered new,
secondary, and fallow swiddens with individual nuclear family households dispersed within these swidden clusters. This pattern contrasts
with that of many other Southeast Asian shifting cultivators who dis-
perse their swiddens around relatively fixed and nucleated settlements.

The Subanun themselves do not have a notion of "settlement
pattern" in the sense of an image of spatial relationships among households and settlements to which they must conform. Rather their settlement pattern as seen by an ethnographer is, like their "rule of postmarital residence, " the outcome of a large number of individual decisions. These decisions are not made at random, say by flipping a
coin, but by evaluation of the immediate circumstances in terms of
a set of quite explicit principles about the desirable relations among
houses and fields. An ethnographic description of the Subanun settlement pattern as part of their ecological adaptation must consist of
more than a map locating house sites and more than a characterization as "neighborhood, " "hamlet, " or "village. " It should comprise
a set of rules which state what one must know in order to decide where
to live. Ideally the description should be a set of rules which will gen-

erate the Subanun settlement pattern appropriate to any given set of conditions.

To simplify the discussion I will take three features of the Subanun ecological adaptation as given, although they too could be derived from further rules of individual decision. The givens are:

1) Swidden agriculture with grain-crop staples, requiring an annual shift in locus of primary agricultural effort.

2) Organization of production and consumption is assigned to the nuclear family. Each family has the responsibility for clearing and cultivating its own swidden and enjoys joint and exclusive control over the distribution of its produce. No social group larger than a nuclear family cultivates a single swidden. Any individual who is not currently a member of a nuclear family is responsible for his or her own support by swidden agriculture (see Frake 1960).

3) Division of the population at any one time into discrete social groups, here termed settlements. Settlements are local groups emerging from alliances formed by a half-dozen or so related families for cooperation in agriculture and other activities. (One basis for settlement groupings, that of swidden clustering, derives from the rules that follow. But this rule, in itself, is not sufficient to account for the division of the population into settlement groups. Here we take these social groups to be given and concern ourselves only with the spatial arrangement of households within a settlement.)

With these givens in mind any arrangement of households found among the Subanun derives from the application of the following rules to particular ecological and sociological situations:

1) Minimum number of "wild-vegetation boundaries" (gelunan "to-be watched") of a swidden consistent with other swidden-site requirements.

2) Minimum house to swidden distance ("house" means the residence of those persons responsible for cultivating a swidden).

3) Maximum house to house distance consistent with the above rules.

These rules are explicit in that they are based on informants' discussions of actual and potential residence-site choices as well as on observations of settlement and swidden patterns. Many other factors, of course, enter into individual decisions of where to live—house-site auguries, access to water, relations with neighbors, kinship obligations such as bride service, etc.—but these do not affect, in any systematic way, the spacing of households with respect to each other.

In most situations, settlement members can feasible reduce exposed swidden boundaries by clustering all or almost all of their swiddens and by making new swidden clusters adjacent to previous years' clusters. The first rule, then, has the normal consequence of clustering the fields of a settlement.

Since a swidden work group normally consists of a nuclear family (and is never a larger social group) the second rule, by demanding that each group live as close as possible to its own swidden, yields a norm of nuclear family households. It furthermore requires that new houses must be constructed periodically at new locations. A distance from house to swidden such that a separate field-house would be required as a base for agricultural operations is considered beyond the maximum limits. When this point is reached, if not sooner, a new residence is always constructed. When new houses are constructed they are invariably located at the absolute minimum distance from the current grain swidden; that is, they are placed inside it, situated to overlook as much of current and prospective swidden sites as possible. When a prospective swidden site is too far away to be cleared from one's existing household, cultivators must temporarily reside in someone else's house (since all houses are built within swiddens, and a new house cannot be constructed in a swidden before the swidden has been cleared and burned).

Within the restraints imposed by swidden clustering and location of houses with respect to swiddens, the Subanun explicitly endeavor to maximize the distance between households. Two households are never, for example, placed adjacent to one another across a swidden boundary, though such an arrangement would often be consistent with ecological considerations. Temporary compound households are maintained only so long as ecologically necessary to gain access to a new swidden. Once it is feasible to build a new house of its own, a family

will always do so. This rule of household dispersal derives from the
sociological facts of Subanun life which make it prudent to live sufficiently far from one's nearest neighbor so that family conversations
and arguments cannot be overheard (see Frake 1960).

The ecological rules (i.e. Nos. 1 and 2) which determine
Subanun swidden and household arrangements are explicitly geared to
protection of swiddens from animal pests with a minimum expenditure
of time and energy in such tasks as fence building, field-house construction, and travel to fields for daily watching. Yet the practice of
clearing large areas adjacent to previously cleared areas increases,
under certain conditions, the probabilities of succession to grassland
instead of forest, thus removing the land from future swidden cycles.
The Subanun emphasize the immediate returns of increased swidden
protection and accessibility at the cost of some loss of control over
the fallowing stages of the swidden cycle. Other swidden farmers of
the same part of the world weigh the advantages and disadvantages of
alternative techniques for controlling faunal and floral enemies differently with different consequences for swidden arrangements and settlement patterns (cf. Frake 1954; Freeman 1955; Conklin 1957; Izikowitz
1951). The contrasts among the remarkably different settlement patterns exhibited by Southeast Asian swidden farmers will become ecologically interpretable when one compares the factors which generate
these patterns in each case rather than forcing ethnographic observations directly into a priori comparative categories. The full ecological and sociological implications of this analysis of Subanun settlement
pattern for both internal and cross-cultural studies cannot be explored
here. Hopefully, however, this incomplete account has revealed some
of the advantages for the study of cultural ecology derivable from ethnographic description ordered according to the principles by which
one's informants interpret their environment and make behavioral decisions. We were able to specify to what extent ecological factors
determine settlement pattern, to point out significant general features
of the Subanun ecological adaptation, and to discover some meaningful
dimensions for cross-cultural comparison. These methodological suggestions are not, of course, intended to replace the analysis of an ecosystem that Western biological science can provide. A scientific knowledge of the climate, soils, plants, and animals of a culture's environment is an essential foundation for ecological ethnography—but it does
not, of itself, constitute ethnography.

REFERENCES

Conklin, H. C. 1954. The relation of Hanunóo culture to the plant
world. Doctoral dissertation, Yale University, New Haven.
_____. 1957. Hanunóo agriculture. A report on an integral sys-
tem of shifting cultivation in the Philippines. Rome: Food
and agricultural Organization of the United Nations.
Frake, C. O. 1955. Social organization and shifting cultivation among
the Sindangan Subanun. Doctoral dissertation, Yale University, New Haven.
_____. 1960. Family and kinship among the eastern Subanun. In
G. P. Murdock, ed., Social structure in Southeast Asia.
New York: Viking Fund Publications in Anthropology 29.
Freeman, J. D. 1955. Iban agriculture: a report on the shifting cul-
tivation of hill rice by the Iban of Sarawak. Colonial Research
Studies 18. London: Her Majesty's Stationery Office.
Goodenough, W. H. 1957. Cultural anthropology and linguistics. In
P. L. Garvin, Ed., Report of the Seventh Annual Round Table
Meeting on Linguistics and Language Study. Monograph Ser-
ies on Languages and Linguistics 9. Washington, D.C.:
Georgetown University Press.
Gulliver, P. H. 1955. The family herds: a study of two pastoral
tribes in East Africa, the Jie and the Turkana. London:
Routledge and Kegan Paul.
Hymes, D. H. 1960. More on lexicostatistics. Current Anthropology
1(4): 338-45.
Izikowitz, K. G. 1951. Lamet: hill peasants in French Indochina.
Etnologiska Studier 17. Göteburg.
Murdock, G. P. 1949. Social structure. New York: Macmillan.
Steward, J. H. 1955. Theory of culture change: the methodology of
multilinear evolution. Urbana: University of Illinois Press.

3 | Notes on Queries in Ethnography

The only existing field manual for ethnographers, Notes and Queries on Anthropology (Royal Anthropological Institute, 1951,[1] presents a list of queries that an investigator can take to the field, present to his informants, and thereby produce a set of responses.[2] His ethnographic record, then, is a list of questions and answers. (The tradition in modern anthropology, however, is not to make such a record public but to publish an essay about it.) The image of an ethnography we have in mind also includes lists of queries and responses, but with this difference: both the queries and their responses are to be discovered in the culture of the people being studied. The problem is not simply to find answers to questions the ethnographer brings into the field, but also to find the questions that go with the responses he observes after his arrival.

Ethnography, according to this image, is a discipline which seeks to account for the behavior of a people by describing the socially acquired and shared knowledge, or culture, that enables members of the society to behave in ways deemed appropriate by their fellows. The discipline is akin to linguistics; indeed, descriptive linguistics is but a special case of ethnography since its domain of study, speech messages, is an integral part of a larger domain of socially interpretable acts and artifacts. It is this total domain of "messages" (including speech) that is the concern of the ethnographer. The ethnographer, like the linguist, seeks to describe an infinite set of variable messages as manifestations of a finite shared code, the code being a set of rules for the socially appropriate construction and interpretation of messages.

Accounting for socially meaningful behavior within a given society is not the sole aim of ethnography. By developing methods for the demonstrably successful description of messages as manifestations of a code, one is furthermore seeking to build a theory of codes—a theory of culture. Since the code is construed as knowledge in people's heads, such a theory should say something of general relevance about cognition and behavior.

A familiar model for behavior is the stimulus-response frame: if a person encounters stimulus X, he will do Y. To account for behavior we need only observe the input and the output. We can ignore whatever might be going on inside the actor's head. This model has had some success under conditions in which the investigator defines the stimulus beforehand and strives to eliminate from the situation anything else that might impinge on the subject as a stimulus. The model is somewhat less successful in accounting for what people do during those intervals of life spent outside the psychologist's laboratory. In the natural settings of behavior, it is difficult to determine which of a multitude of potential stimuli confronting a subject evoke a particular response and which portion of the subject's behavior is a response to some stimulus (Chomsky 1959). If we want to account for behavior by relating it to the conditions under which it normally occurs, we require procedures for discovering what people are attending to, what information they are processing, when they reach decisions which lead to culturally appropriate behavior. We must get inside our subjects' heads. This should not be an impossible feat: our subjects themselves accomplished it when they learned their culture and became "native actors." They had no mysterious avenues of perception not available to us as investigators.

The aims of ethnography, then, differ from those of stimulus-response psychology in at least two respects. First, it is not, I think, the ethnographer's task to predict behavior per se, but rather to state rules of culturally appropriate behavior (Frake 1964). In this respect the ethnographer is again akin to the linguist who does not attempt to predict what people will say but to state rules for constructing utterances which native speakers will judge as grammatically appropriate. The model of an ethnographic statement is not "if a person is confronted with stimulus X, he will do Y," but "if a person is in situation X, performance Y will be judged appropriate by native actors." The second difference is that the ethnographer seeks to discover, not prescribe, the significant stimuli in the subject's world. He attempts to

describe each act in terms of the cultural situations which appropriately
evoke it and each situation in terms of the acts it appropriately evokes.

There are a variety of methods one might use to discover those
aspects of cultural situations relevant to rendering appropriate performances—many more, I am sure, than I am concerned with here.[3] The
method considered here attends to the way people talk about what they
do. Since the knowledge that enables one to behave appropriately is
acquired from other people, it must be communicable in some symbolic
system which can travel between one mind and another as code signals
in a physical channel. The procedures of this paper seek to reveal the
knowledge that is communicated by talking. This may not include everything a person knows which is relevant to his cultural performances,
but it will certainly include a sizable chunk of it. Actually, I find it
difficult to conceive of any act, object, or event which can be described
as a cultural artifact, a manifestation of a code, without some reference to the way people talk about it. This is the case because the informants' interpretation of a socially meaningful act (a message) is
the key to the discovery of code rules. An informant makes an interpretation by applying code rules to the observable message. Therefore, if one knows the message and the interpretation, one can infer
the relevant code rules (Ebeling 1962: 13). (Let me emphasize, however,
that I do not believe an adequate ethnography can be produced from a
record only of what people say, most especially it cannot be produced
from a record only of what people say in artificial interviewing contexts
removed from the scene of their ordinary cultural performances.)

What we want to do, then, is to discover how a person in a
given society finds out from one of his fellows what he knows. In general, if you want to find out what someone knows, you ask him. This
suggests that the informative utterances produced by native actors be
matched with the inquiries which elicit them. For every response,
discover the set of inquiries which appropriately evokes it; and for
every inquiry, discover a set of responses it appropriately evokes.

By presenting an inquiry (e.g. "What kind of tree is that?"),
a native inquirer seeks to restrict the appropriate responses to a given
set of responses (e.g. tree names), so that the selection of a particular
response (e.g. "elm tree") by alter from the set conveys information
significant to the inquirer. A description organized by linked queries

Chinese jars, is prepared for consumption by adding water to a wort which has fermented aerobically for several hours and anaerobically in the sealed jar for at least several weeks, generally much longer. The wort is prepared by adding rice chaff and powder from pulverized 'yeast cakes' to a mash of cooked rice, manioc, maize, and/or Job's tears. The 'yeast cakes,' prepared in advance and stored for use as necessary, are made by mixing an assortment of 'spices' with a dough of uncooked rice flour and an infection of old yeast. We will focus the present description on these yeast cakes, ignoring the complex routines of processing the ingredients and attending only to a relatively simple and, at first sight, trivial little problem: the selection of 'spices' to add to the other yeast ingredients.

One task is to specify operationally the relations among 'spices,' 'yeast,' and 'beer.' That there is some relation seems apparent from observation. Fig. 1a shows that beginning with a term for some item (Sk) used for 'spice,' the successive application of query ? u 'what is X used for' will link any Sk with 'yeast,' 'yeast' with 'beer,' and 'beer' with 'drinks.' (The arrow travels from topic to response.) Next we seek to discover the reciprocals of ? u in each case, e.g. if 'yeast' is the response to 'what are spices used for,' then what can be asked about 'yeast' to elicit 'spices' as a response? Interlinking queries, displayed in Fig. 1b, enable one to proceed by queries from any item in the chain to any other item. In traveling down the chain, three noteworthy things happen. First, the reciprocals of ? u are not all the same. Thus 'beer' will be included in the response to query ? kD 'what kinds of drinks are there,' but 'yeast' will not occur as a response when the same question is asked of 'beer' (? kB); instead there will occur the names of the plants that provide starch for the mash. A different query, ? i 'what are the ingredients of X,' is required to get from 'beer' to 'yeast.' Our operations demonstrate that each of the pairs in the chain are not linked by equivalent relations as appeared at first sight. A second event in downward querying in this chain is that ? i asked of 'yeast' (? iY) may yield List Sk instead of 'spices' as a response. The reasons for this will be apparent shortly, but had we proceeded in one direction only, we might have missed one link in the chain (especially if we were interviewing an informant outside the context of using the referents of these terms). Third, downward queries in this chain produce responses other than those shown in Figs. 1a and 1b; they produce lists. (The

Table 1. Queries and Interlinkages

Queries

?u: ditaq ig baalan dun X?	'What is X used for?'
?k: ditaq X ai run ma iin?	'What kind of X is it?'
ditaq dega X ai run?	'What all kinds of X are there?'
?i: ditaq ma kig baalan X-en kin?	'What is that ingredient of X?'
ditaq dega ig baalan X-en?	'What all are the ingredients of X?'
ditaq ig baalan mu rin X-en?	'What are you using there for making X?'
?w: ditaq alandun ma X?	'What is X (a kind of)?'
?p: ditaq ginalapan dun X ma iin?	'What (separated) part of X is it?'
ditaq kaqalapan dun X ma iin?	'What (separable) part of X is it?'
ditaq dega i kaqalapan dun X?	'What are the (potentially separable) parts of X?'
?s: ditaq ma bwat kini?	'What does this come from?'

Interlinkages

?k/?w	species—genus
?k/?u	species—use
?i/?u	ingredient—use
?p/?s	part—source
?u/?s	use—source

list may be elicited by a single query such as 'what kinds of X are there' or by successive applications of a query such as 'what kind of X is that' (Table 1). (The notation of Fig. 1 does not distinguish list-eliciting from item-eliciting queries.) Fig. 1c displays the lists and the queries that interlink an item in a given list with the list below it. Colons separate <u>contrasting</u> items in a list (Frake 1961, 1962; Conklin 1962). The parsing of lists into contrast sets (see 'mash' in Fig. 1c) must be performed by further inquiries; it cannot be assumed that all responses elicited by a given inquiry contrast at the same level (Frake 1961).

The list (Sk) of items used for 'spices' presented in Table 2 is a composite list produced by asking ?iY and ?kS of all available

Table 2. Yeast Spice Ingredients

List Sk	Botanical identification of at least three specimens of the equivalently named plant category (List Pk)[5]
1. belili	Eleusine indica, (L.) Gaertn. (Gram.)
2. belurus	Ficus saherthwaitei, Elm. (Mor.)
3. bilaw	? (Zingiber.)
4. busyuŋ	Ficus botryocarpa, Miq. (Mor.)
5. deluyut	Saurania glabrifolia, Merr. (Dillen.)
6. gebul	Solanum ferox, L. (Solan.)
7. geleŋug	Champereia manillana, (Blm.) Merr. (Opil.)
8. gimit	Ficus minahassae, (Teysm. and De Vr.) Miq. (Mor.)
9. glabana	Anona muricata, L. (Apon.)
10. gleknu	Cyclosorus unitus, Ching. (Aspid.)
11. glempiq	Vernonia cinerea, (L.) Less. (Composit.)
12. glimbuŋa	Macaranga tanarius, (L.) Muell.-Arg. (Euphor.)
13. glinda	Macaranga hispida, (Blume) Muell.-Arg. (Euphor.)
14. glumbilan	Leucosyke capitellata, (Poir.) Wedd. (Urt.)
15. gluntud-ulaŋan	Buddleia asiatica, Lour. (Logan.)
16. gluya	Zingiber officinale, Roscoe (Zingiber.)
17. guburubud	Oreocnide rubescens, (Blume) Miq. (Urt.)
18. guleŋkem	Mismosa pudica, L. (Legum.)
19. gupa	Litsea garciae, Vidal. (Laur.)
20. mendyabaw	Wendlandia luzoniensis, DC. (Rub.)
21. naŋka	Artocarpus heterophyllus, Lam. (Mor.)
22. niup	Callicarpa sp. (Verben.)
23. palay	Oryza sativa, L. (Gram.)
24. payaw	Homalomena philippinensis, Engl. (Ar.)
25. peŋgya	Ananas comosus, (L.) Merr. (Bromel.)
26. sagiŋ tubali	Musa sp. (Musac.)
27. sili	Capsicum sp. (Solan.)
28. tebu belekbut	Saccharum officinarum, L. (Gram.)
29. tetibeg	Ficus carpentariana, Elm. (Mor.)
30. tuba	Derris elliptica, (Roxb.) Benth. (Legum.)
31. tubayag	Piper umbellatum, L. (Piper.)
32. tuyabaŋ	Spathoglottis plicata, Blume. (Orchid.)

yeast makers (a subset of women) and by recording actual recipes of
items used as spices on given occasions. The complete list was then
cross-checked with informants to determine which items, if any, were
consistently judged as unfamiliar, idiosyncratic, or inappropriate by
informants other than the original respondee. Idiosyncratic items are
enclosed by parentheses in Table 3. Certain items occur in every
recipe, and some of these are consistently regarded as necessary
(starred items in Table 3). One item, palay 'rice,' is always used if
the appropriate parts ('roots') are available (they are available in the
post-harvest season, the usual time for yeast making). Note that,
for a Subanun, the identification of an item in List Sk is, because of
the length of the list and the unpredictability of the constituents of a
given recipe, generally much more informative than the identification
of an item in List Yi. It is apparently for this reason that in many
contexts ? iY elicits an item in Sk, skipping List Yi (see Fig. 1).

Since a particular recipe contains only about half the number
of items included in the composite List Sk, the next task of description
is to specify how, and from what set of objects, a particular selection
of 'spices' is made. What information about the items in List Sk is
relevant to this decision? Of the many information-probing questions
entertainable about an item in List Sk, we will describe the results of
applying a few general queries: ? w, ? k, ? p, and ? s (Table 1).

The query ? w, 'what is X (a kind of),' will yield for any
Sk(x): gayu 'tree' (rigid-stemmed woody plant); sigbet 'herb' (rigid-
stemmed non-woody plant); or belagen 'vine' (non-rigid-stemmed
plant). The reciprocal link is ? k, 'what kind of X is it (are there)':

List Sk   ? w/? k   List Pt, gayu : sigbet : belagen

(In this representation of an interlinkage, the query symbol (e.g. ? w)
appears on the same side of the slash as its topic and on the opposite
side from its response.)

Query ? k, asked about items in List Pt, yields (eventually)
a 1,500+ member list, Pk. List Sk is a subset of List Pk. One can
infer, then, that List Pk represents the universe of objects from which
a particular spice recipe is selected.

One thing apparent from observation, however, is that objects represented by forms in List Sk differ radically in appearance

Table 3. Intersection of List Sk (Kinds of Yeast Species)
with List Pt (Plant Types), List Pp (Plant Parts),
and Category C 'Cultigens'

	'Young leaves'	'Underground parts'	Other
'trees'	belurus busyuŋ deluyut gimit glimbuŋa glindaŋ glumbilan guburubud gupa mendyabaw tetibeg tubayag	gluntud–ulaŋan (geleŋug) (glabana) C (naŋka) C	*sili C (niup)
'herbs'	(gebul) (guleŋkem) gleknu	(guleŋkem) belili bilaw glempiq *gluya C palay C payaw peŋgya C sagiₙtubali C tuyabaŋ	*tebu belekbut C
'vines'		(tuba)	

from other things called by the same terms, objects pointed out as
examples of Pk. Forms in List Sk denote bits and pieces of things
that can be picked up by the handfuls; forms in List Pk denote entire
plants, including large trees. This observation suggests a 'part of'
question. The appropriate Subanun question in this case is ? p which
inquires about the 'separable' or 'separated' constituents of an object:

List Pk   ?p/?s   List Pp (a long list of plant parts)

If we restrict ourselves to those Pk occurring also in List Sk, then
we elicit a much reduced subset of Pp: gekbus 'young leaves'; ganet
'root'; gabi 'corm'; guned 'tuber'; buna 'fruit'; gayu 'stem.' Further
querying, which we will not display here, will reveal that not all of
these terms for plant parts contrast as different parts of a single plant.
Thus a given plant may have both 'fruit' and 'stem,' but it has either
a 'root' or a 'tuber' or a 'corm.' In contexts involving the selection
of a part from a given plant, there can be no choice among the last
three items. Consequently, we can rewrite the portion of List Pp
that concerns this description (List Pp(Sk)) as follows:

> List Pp(Sk), gekbus 'young leaves': (ganet : guned : gabi)
> 'underground parts': buna 'fruit': gayu 'stem

Table 3 displays the intersection of List Sk with Lists Pp and
Pt, showing what parts of what type of plants are selected as yeast
spices. It reveals sufficient patterning to suggest some preliminary
rules of selection:

To construct a 'yeast spice' recipe, select a subset of plant
parts which include (1) the 'fruits' of sili 'chili,' (2) 'stem' pieces of
tebu 'sugar cane,' (3) 'young leaves' of selected 'trees,' (4) 'underground parts' of selected 'herbs' (including gluya 'ginger' and, if
available, palay 'rice'). If these rules do not perfectly determine a
recipe selection, they at least predict idiosyncratic responses with
considerable accuracy, e.g. tuba 'Derris,' a 'vine'; nanka 'jackfruit,'
a 'tree' whose roots are used.

To improve these rules many further questions could be
asked, questions of treatment, habitat, properties. etc. For example,
items marked C in Table 3 are those that receive the response pemul-
anan 'cultigen' in answer to a query about treatment. All items considered necessary (starred in Table 3) are 'cultigens.' If List Sk is
divided into three groups, 'cultigens,' 'wild trees,' and 'wild herbs,'
then it is the case that any given recipe will contain at least three but
not more than nine items from each group. The following diagram
displays the appropriate combinations, for all but a few items, of
plant type (T 'tree,' H 'herb'), treatment (C 'cultigen,' W 'wild'), and
part used (L 'young leaves,' R 'underground parts'): (Read across.)

```
┌───────┬─────┬───────┐
│   T   │     │   L   │
│       │  W  ├───────┤
├───────┤     │   R   │
│   H   ├─────┴───────┤
│       │      C      │
└───────┴─────────────┘
```

A habitat query reveals that all source plants grow in secondary forest, fallow fields, or cultivated fields; none are primary forest
plants. Consequently an appropriate selection of ingredients (always
picked fresh before use) can be made within close range of a household. In contrast to the case of 'medicines,' for example, no value is
placed on rare, unusual, or difficult-to-obtain items in the selection
of yeast ingredients. Questions about the desirable properties of
yeast spices would point up attributes such as 'sweetness,' 'piquancy,'
'flossiness,' 'milky sap,' and, for one idiosyncratic maker, 'toxicity'
(tuba and niup are fish poisons). Continued questioning would reveal
that yeast making is considered to be the critical stage of brewing and
that the selection of ingredients properly combined under a set of com-
pulsively observed routines and taboos is essential to the desired
strength and flavor of the final product. Still other questions would
lead into social structure (e.g. the social relations among yeast makers and users), religion (gods as well as men are inveterate drinkers),
and magic (yeast is a ritual object of considerable potency; its improper
handling can cause grave misfortune).

One does not have to attempt very many descriptive statements
of this type to realize that any concept is interlinked by a variety of
relationships to a large number of other concepts, which, in turn, are
interlinked with still other concepts. If a semantic domain is a set of
related concepts, then it is clear that there is no one way to separate
the conceptual structure of a people into a finite number of discrete,
clearly delimited, domains. Rather, we have a network of relations
whose links enable us to travel along a variety of paths from one concept to another.

The utility of the exercise in description, however, goes beyond explicating the ramifications of Subanun yeast making. We have
succeeded in isolating some of the basic types of relationships linking

concepts among the Subanun. Each pair of interlinking queries defines such a relationship. These relationships are of interest because of their applicability throughout many domains of the culture and because of the implications they have for the ways people talk about the things so interlinked. The interlinkages isolated thus far and some of their implications are:

1. X ?k/?w Z 'X is a kind of Z.' Implication: Any object, a, called X can also be called Z, and there is some object, b, which can be called Z but which cannot be called X. Z is the head term for List Zk (produced by ?kZ), that is, the items of List Zk, considered collectively as well as individually, can be called Z.

2. X ?i/?u Z 'X is an ingredient of Z.' Implication: An object called X cannot be called Z, nor can List Zi taken as a collectivity be called Z. Thus List Bi (Figure 1) is not equivalent to 'beer,' for 'beer' results only after the items named in List Bi have been subjected to processing whereby they lose their identify. In the case of Bi, Yi, and most ingredient lists, the head term for the list depends on the stage of processing, revealing another type of relationship, 'X is a stage of Z' (cf. Frake 1961).

3. X ?k/?u Z 'X is something used for Z.' Implication: Similar to that of ?k/?w rather than of ?i/?u. (?k/?w appears generally, perhaps always, substitutable for ?k/?u, but the converse is not true.)

4. X ?p/?sZ 'X is a part of Z.' Implication: X is 'separable' or 'separated' from Z at some conventional point. List Zp, if separated parts, cannot collectively be called Z and there is no processing by which they can become Z. An object named X cannot be called Z.

One of the practical problems to which this approach can contribute is that of sorting out the different but related concepts which a single linguistic form can represent without relying on the number of equivalents required to translate the form into some other language. In a previous paper (Frake 1961: 120-21), I discussed a case in which a single Subanun disease term, nuka, labels three concepts, X, Y, Z, where Y is a kind of X, and Z is an initial stage of some but not all

X. The following is a somewhat more complex example involving the use of the Subanun form buŋa to mean:

B1. A kind of 'tree,' the 'areca palm.'
B2. A plant part, 'fruit.'
B3. A category of betel quid constituents.
B4. A kind of 'fruit,' the 'areca nut.'
B5. One member of category B3, the 'areca nut.'

Fig. 2 displays the queries that interlink these concepts. (Note a new interlinkage of familiar queries, ?u/?s.) If the full lists, rather than single responses, generated by these queries were displayed, then each occurrence of buŋa would be as a member of a different list. Thus although B4 and B5 denote the same objects, 'areca nuts,' they have different meanings in that the contrasting categories are different: other 'fruits' in one case and other substances used for constituent category B3 in the other.

Fig. 2 also suggests the possibility of formulating logical rules of interlinkage general for the culture. It appears to be the case, for example, that

if A is interlinked with B by some query pair ?x/?y
and A is interlinked with C by ?k/?w,
and B is interlinked with D by ?k/?w,
then C is interlinked with D by ?x/?y.

(Compare 'tree,' B2, B1, and B4 in Fig. 2.) This example is a demonstration of one of the semantic properties of a 'kind of' (?k/?w) relation, namely any property of a superordinate will also be held by its subordinates (but not the converse).

Because of inadequacies in the ethnographic record (obtained before these analyses were attempted), both the descriptive examples in this paper may contain errors. However, the errors could be easily discovered and corrected by testing the description with informants. To produce ethnographic statements that can be demonstrated to be wrong, and not simply judged to be unpersuasively written, is, I think, some advance over the production of most current statements. Also, the probable deficiencies in the present examples demonstrate

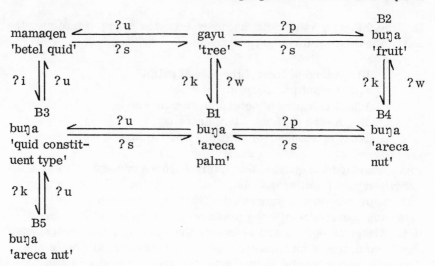

Fig. 2. Interlinkages of categories labeled buŋa (for queries see Table 1

the need to carry out and test analyses as part of data collecting procedures. Only in this way can errors be detected, gaps filled, and,
through successively better approximations, an adequate descriptive
statement be produced.

These procedures are intended not only to be replicable and
testable, but also perfectly general. They are procedures for describing anything people talk about, be it plants, kinsmen, or gods. There
is no argument that any one aspect of culture should be selected as the
focus of a description. Indeed, short of a "complete" description of
a culture, the preferable strategy is probably to focus in depth on a
variety of domains in order to reveal the kinds and range of patterns
in the culture for construing the world. No one working with procedures
similar in intent to these has yet described a complete culture, but
some have succeeded in producing descriptions of a remarkable variety
of cultural manifestations. Metzger and Williams, for example,
emerged from one field session with descriptions of firewood (1963b),
terms of personal reference (1962), curers (1963c), and weddings
(1963a). Conklin has described ethnobotanical systems, agriculture,
betel chewing, pottery, verbal play, color, kinship, and water (see

Conklin 1962 for methodological statement). None of these descriptions, whatever its faults, can be called superficial, and each says a great deal not only about the topics at hand but also about the cultures being investigated and about culture in general.

At this point the reader himself may have a query: "All this is fine, but how do I go about finding appropriate queries?" Even though it is somewhat fashionable these days to dismiss "discovery procedures" as something not amenable to statement, we consider such a query appropriate and will attempt a response.

Two tasks are assumed to be completed or at least well under way: an analysis of the phonology and grammar of the language being investigated, and an ability of the ethnographer to produce utterances that are phonologically and grammatically acceptable. In the course of language learning and analysis, the ethnographer will learn some basic query frames which can be checked for appropriateness with specific topics. The ethnographer can listen for queries in use in the cultural scenes he observes, giving special attention to query-rich settings, e.g. children querying parents, medical specialists querying patients, legal authorities querying witnesses, priests querying the gods. He can take advantage of the power of language to construe settings: hypothetical information-eliciting situations can be described or even staged with native actors, a technique especially useful when working with informants removed from their society. When using interpreters, instead of relying on contact-language questions to elicit native equivalents, one can describe situations in the contact language and inquire how one would ask questions about features of the situation. Once a few general queries such as "What is it called?" or "What kind of X is it?" are discovered, these can be used to elicit lists which in turn can be used in the search for other queries to which items in the list are topics and responses.

Discovered queries must be tested for appropriateness with respect to particular topics. To learn to distinguish appropriate from inappropriate queries, the ethnographer can try apparently inappropriate questions on informants to determine the pattern of their response. Typical cues of appropriateness are length of response (in number of forms and/or elapsed time), consistency of response across informants or across time, and non-verbal aspects of the response

such as laughter, frowning, or raised eyebrows. As a test, the
reader with a chair and an English-speaking informant handy might
try to detect which of the following queries are inappropriate:

> What kind of chair is it?
> What does a chair taste like?
> What is a chair used for?
> What sex is that chair?
> What part of a chair is this?
> How fast is this chair?
> Is that a couch?

One can, of course, contrive to evoke concise responses to inappropriate questions: "This is a psychological test; answer 'yes' or 'no':
Is a chair sexy?" A response to such a query may be revealing to
some investigations (any selection of alternative responses is presumably informative of something), but not to what the ethnographer seeks
to describe: the relations between appropriate behavior and the cultural settings for such behavior.

NOTES

[1] These procedures are an outgrowth of those employed in
Frake 1961. The present formulation owes a great deal to discussions
with Duane Metzger and Gerald Williams, whose writings exemplify
intensive application of similar methodological notions (Metzger and
Williams). I am also indebted to the editor of this volume, Roy
D'Andrade. This paper was written with the support of USPHS Grant
M-6187, under the direction of the National Institute of Mental Health.
   [2] This characterization of Notes and Queries is more apropos
of earlier editions (1874, 1892, 1899, 1912, 1929) than of the sixth
edition (1951).
   [3] Any representation of an object or an event by an informant,
for example, can be useful (for use of native drawings and models by
Harold Conklin, see Rockefeller Institute 1961). In this paper we are
concerned with verbal descriptions as representations of objects and
events.
   [4] English forms enclosed by single quotation marks are
glosses, devices to enable talking about Subanun concepts without

using the Subanun forms that represent them. They are selected for
their mnemonic, not their defining, value. Thus 'beer' represents
the Subanun concept labeled gasi, not the English concept labeled beer.
    [5] Identifications by the Philippine National Museum from speci-
mens collected by the writer. Listing partially matching botanical
identifications is the only way the referents of plant categories can be
identified with any accuracy. Although there are many reasons why
botanical identifications are necessary in ethnobotanical descriptions,
it should be emphasized that they do not provide definitions of Subanun
categories, nor can defining features of Subanun categories be extracted from matched botanical identifications with procedures analogous
to those used in performing componential analyses of kinship categories from matched lists and kin terms and kin types (Frake 1961).

                            REFERENCES

Burkill, I. H. 1935. A dictionary of the economic products of the
        Malay Peninsula. London: Crown Agents for the Colonies.
        2 vols.
Chomsky, Noam. 1959. Review of B. F. Skinner, ed., Verbal
        behavior. Language 35.1: 26-58.
Conklin, H. C. 1962. Lexicographical treatment of folk taxonomies.
        In F. W. Householder and Sol Saporta, eds., Problems in
        lexicography. International Journal of American Linguistics
        28.2, Part IV.
Ebeling, C. L. 1962. Linguistic units. Janua Linguarum 12.
        's-Gravenhage: Mouton & Co.
Frake, C. O. 1960. The Eastern Subanun of Mindanao. In G. P.
        Murdock, ed., Social structure in Southeast Asia. Chicago:
        Quadrangle Books, pp. 51-64.
_____. 1961. The diagnosis of disease among the Subanun of
        Mindanao. American Anthropologist 63.1: 113-32.
_____. 1962. The ethnographic study of cognitive systems. In
        Thomas Gladwin and William C. Sturtevant, eds., Anthro-
        pology and human behavior. Washington, D.C.: Anthropo-
        logical Society of Washington.
_____. 1964. A structural description of Subanun "religious be-
        havior." In Ward Goodenough, ed., Explorations in cultural
        anthropology in honor of George Peter Murdock. New York:
        McGraw-Hill.

Metzger, Duane, and Gerald E. Williams. 1962. Patterns of primary
    personal reference in a Tzeltal community. Anthropology
    Research Projects: Preliminary Report no. 10. Stanford.
_____. 1963a. A formal ethnographic analysis of Tenejapa Ladino
    weddings. American Anthropologist 65.4.
_____. 1963b. Procedures and results in the study of native cate-
    gories: Tzeltal firewood. Anthropology Research Projects:
    Preliminary Report no. 12. Stanford.
_____. 1963c. Tenejapa medicine I: the curer. Southwestern
    Journal of Anthropology 19: 216-34.
Rockefeller Institute. 1961. Visiting anthropologist shows drawings
    clue to form of culture. The Rockefeller Institute Quarterly
    5.4.
Royal Anthropological Institute. 1951. Notes and queries on anthropol-
    ogy. 6th ed. London: Routledge & Kegan Paul.

4 | Plying Frames Can Be Dangerous: Some Reflections on Methodology in Cognitive Anthropology

(What is written here is not so much a "paper" addressed to a reader as it is a representation of a "talk" presented to an audience. Some of the discussion refers to the audience's shared experience as listeners to the talk. It would be helpful if the reader could imagine that he or she were a member of that audience. Accordingly, he or she will henceforth be addressed in the second person. Remarks addressed to you as a "reader" rather than as an "audience member" will be set off by dots and placed in parentheses.)

* * *

Cognitive anthropoligists,[1] sometimes known as "ethnoscientists," are said to be people who listen to what the natives have to say. I do not claim to be one of the experts among cognitive anthropologists, but I do claim to be a native. This occasion, then, can be taken as an opportunity to assess the interest of listening to a native's point of view about the activities of his own group.

The research tradition that has come to be known as "cognitive anthropology," like most labeled schools of thought, includes such a diversity of approaches and perspectives that it is difficult to find much, apart from the label itself (and, maybe, the attacks of Marvin Harris), that holds the tradition together. Probably the most apparent common theme has been a concern for methodology, inspired by an admiration for the supposedly greater rigor of sister sciences, either psychology or linguistics. The value of the various methods proposed may be debatable, but the effort of pursuing them has succeeded in giving the field of cognitive anthropology a bag-of-tricks image among both adherents and critics. Some adherents seem to feel that the problems of the field, problems of lack of coherent theory or of substantial descriptive accounts, can be solved by ever more diligent pursuit of new methods. Somehow, with tighter frames, more dimensional scales, and more flawless flow charts, the cognitive maps of our informants will be brought into focus. Critics, on the other hand have pointed to the danger of this kind of excessive methodological tinkering. The scope of the data narrows to accommodate the methods. A pursuit of methods that work for something—anything—replaces the search for a theory that explicates what we want to know.

I am not about to suggest that cognitive anthropology abandon its methodological concerns. I do not recommend following the route of some linguists, freeing oneself for theoretical flights by cutting off ties with empirically grounded data. Nor do I advocate joining the hermeneutic circle, burying data under repetitive interpretations of "what it means (to me)," a tactic that produces thick books, but does not necessarily deepen understanding.

Methodology, some theoretically motivated notions of what to do when faced with the real world, is as necessary in science as it is in everyday life. Methods link data—what we construe to be observations of some particular reality—with theory, our proposals for understanding reality in general. When methods fail, the answer may be not only to tinker some more with the methods, but also to rethink the theory. My purpose here is to reflect upon some of the methodological successes and failures of cognitive anthropology in terms of their implications for general conceptions of the relations among behavior, verbal descriptions of behavior, cognition, and culture.

I will focus on what is certainly one of the best-known items in the cognitive anthropologist's bag of tricks: the frame. This methodological device was lifted out of the distributional model of structural linguistics, and shares kinships with similar notions of the same ancestry: paradigmatic/syntagmatic, slot-filler, contrast/contiguity, alternation/co-occurrence. Some element, A, is specified by its contextual constraints, X—Y, and by its relation to other elements, B, that can occur in the same context, $X\left|\genfrac{}{}{0pt}{}{A}{B}\right|Y$. The unique, and still poorly appreciated, contribution that the cognitive anthropologist made to this contextual model was that the context was not limited to portions of single, isolated sentences. A frame was construed as an inquiry matched with a set of responses. The unit of analysis was a question-answer sequence, a conversational exchange.

This extension of the range of linguistic context beyond single speakers uttering isolated sentences was made in an effort to find a context that would frame semantic, rather than grammatical, relations (the latter being the sole concern of both structural and transformational linguists at that time). Inquiries specify informational contexts, constraining the semantic domain of the response. Speakers of language were seen as question askers and answerers, not simply as sentence producers. This pursuit of meaning by relating sentences produced by different speakers together as part of a discourse was an advance over the sentence-bound semantics practiced until recently by linguists. (Compare the analysis of "bachelor" in Katz and Fodor's much-heralded 1963 paper on linguistic semantics with what was being done at that time in ethnographic semantics. Katz and Fodor's analysis would have allowed a married man to answer a woman's question "Are you a bachelor?" by "Yes," on the grounds that he was a holder of a B.A. degree.

The notion of frames proved to be a powerful and useful methodological tool. It provided ways of obtaining and organizing certain kinds of data so that they made certain kinds of sense in convincing ways. But, as critics have been quick to point out, not all kinds of data proved to be equally tractable and, more significantly, the results, while they may have made some kind of sense, often did not seem to answer very interesting or important questions. In contrast to the essays of symbolic anthropologists, not so hampered by methodological constraints, the output of cognitive anthropology often seemed compartmentalized and trivial. One might counter that one person's trivia is another's eureka, and, moreover, a secure little truth is as useful as a wobbly grand theory. Nevertheless, cognitive anthropology ought to aspire to bigger truths, to go beyond offering tiny fragments of cognitive maps from here and there, to offer an overall view of the landscape.

More upsetting to cognitive anthropologists than the triviality issue have been problems of inducing people to verbalize in consistent question-response fashion about many topics of interest to the investigator and of obvious relevance to the people being studied. Why is it easier to get a taxonomy of birds than of social roles?

The other problem that has arisen from applying frames and other, more experimental, methods in cognitive anthropology has been the high degree of informant variability that is so often manifest. This result, to my mind, reveals a strength, not a weakness, of the method. It reflects the way the world is, a reality less methodologically oriented approaches in anthropology have obscured. The last thing we should do is to flee from this reality or to tinker with our methods to eliminate it. But there remains the question of how to account for variability. The traditional use of the frame as a question-response device leads to what I think is the wrong answer: that we each go around with unique cognitive ideolects in our heads, each of which must be separately described and somehow summed up to equal culture.

These methodological difficulties have arisen from a failure to exploit fully the interactive aspects of the frame model, to widen the frame so as to capture a context that more fully specifies how human behavior comes to have meaning. Instead, attention was focused on questions and responses as chunks of verbiage isolated from their settings and their speakers. The specter of the stimulus-response model of behavior hung over many early programmatic statements. Some investigators emphasized that the idea was to discover the questions (stimuli) that evoked the answers (responses) we were trying to describe. But this notion that the answers are there, that the job is to find the questions, while often cited, did not seem really to take hold. Frames began to be called eliciting frames, to be thought of not as contexts for behavior but as prods to behavior. The ethnographer, rather than the informant, thus becomes the questioner.

Of course, one tries to elicit the questions from the informant, but this process can amount to little more than finding out how to translate into the informant's language the questions the ethnographer wants to ask. Both the prevalence and the hopelessness of this procedure have become apparent to me in classroom informant-eliciting exercises, both those I have staged and those I have witnessed. In cases where I had some knowledge of the language and culture (and I quickly restricted this game to such cases), it was clear that the only way to discover useful questions was to specify inquiry contexts within which such questions could be asked. Doing this in English without a knowledge of the culture is nearly impossible for most domains. But it does show, more clearly than actual ethnography (where the context is more likely to be taken for granted because it is there) that questions have to be related to larger contexts.

Apart from the distortion of frames into probes, there are certain technical difficulties with the notion of a "question." An inquiry for information (a query) is a kind of speech act that must be distinguished from a question, a grammatical interrogative. An interrogative can, and perhaps most often does, represent such speech acts as summons and greetings, which are not queries. The ethnographer of American disease who goes around our society asking "How are you?" is not likely to elicit a very large inventory of disease terms. In Yakan (a Philippine language), a frequent question is "Who is your companion there?," an ideal question, one might think, for eliciting terms of social identity. Yet, the question is most appropriately posed to someone who is alone. The only appropriate answer is "nobody." This question is, in most contexts, a greeting. The Yakan question "What are you carrying there?" is typically a greeting if what is being carried is easily visible, a query if it is not (Frake 1975). The status of a question as a query is dependent on the context in which it was uttered. Formal eliciting—so-called white-room ethnography—is an attempt to circumvent this problem by removing all previously relevant context, training the informant to see the white room as an interrogation chamber. This is an excellent methodological strategy—if what we want to know is how people behave in white rooms.

Even when we have a context in which we know that a given question is a query, we still can't be certain what query the question represents. A single question (a given surface-structure form) can represent a variety of queries for different kinds of information. The form of the question constrains the grammatical form of the response, but it does not, in itself, necessarily constrain the semantic domain of information. In Yakan, the common question "X is Y's what?" represents any query, the answer to which can be given in the genitive (surface) case: X is Y's grandfather; X is Y's rice field; X is Y's roof; X is Y's fate; etc. The answer to this kind of problem is not to search for more specific and necessarily highly artificial questions that, it is hoped, will sort out these different semantic relations, but to attend to the wider contexts of questioning that accomplish this sorting for the Yakan.

If one takes seriously the admonition to go out into the real world and look for queries, to seek "query-rich settings," as I once put it, one finds that people talk all the time and ask each other a lot of questions, but disappointingly few of the questions represent queries about the overt topics of the questions. Even children, the champion questioners, use this grammatical form in subtle ways. The child's stock question, "Mommy, you know what?" is not a request for information, but a clever use of sociolinguistic rules to acquire speaking rights (Sacks 1972).

Perhaps instead of trying to devise provocative questions and other instruments to persuade people to talk about things they do not ordinarily talk about in that way, we should take as a serious topic of investigation what people in fact talk about, or, better, what they are in fact doing when they talk. When we look at talk, we find that people do not so much ask and answer inquiries; they propose, defend, and negotiate interpretations of what is happening. Because what is happening is what we are interested in explicating, these interpretations provide the key to understanding. Viewing informants not just as question-answerers, but also as interpreters of their lives, provides not only a sounder perspective for handling problems of informant variability and reticence, but also a more realistic notion of the relation of cognitive systems to behavior.

It is not so much that some things are hard to talk about. People can and do talk about anything. But some questions, if taken seriously as inquiries, are hard to answer. What kinds of sounds are there in your language? This is obviously a ridiculous question to pose to an informant if what you want to know are his phonological concepts; yet it can be answered, not by asking it, but by attending to interpretations of sounds made by speakers of the language. The problem with verbalized interpretations is not a difficulty in eliciting them but in locating what cues are being responded to in formulating a particular interpretation. Cues of sound, appearance, expression, body stance, and movement often cannot easily be explicitly identified by those who use them. Careful observation of the behavior, object, or event being interpreted is required. Simply recording what people say about things is no more adequate than simply recording what one sees. The informant's interpretations must be linked with the investigator's observations.

Attending to interpretations will not eliminate variation, but it will help to explicate it. Of course, people vary in behavior because they have different life experiences, different childhood traumas, different mental capacities, different hormonal balances, and so on. But this is only part of the story. Informants vary in what they say and do because interpretation itself is problematic. (It can be especially problematic when an informant is confronted with an ethnographer across a tape recorder.) An interpretation is not an answer to a question automatically produced in the mind by a cultural computer program as a result of proper input. It is a proposal, a theory to be tested, tested not only against the reality it covers, but (like scientific theory) also against its reception by one's fellows (or by the ethnographer).

Construing talk about things (including responses to the investigator's queries and tests) as proposals for interpreting not only what is being talked about, but also what is going on now, makes variability in verbal responses much more understandable. Where we must seek underlying cultural constants is not in the content of the talk, but in the principles for formulating interpretations, for making sense of life. It is when things do not make sense that you know you have wandered off the edge of your cognitive map.

My arguments thus far all point to the necessity of expanding our frames to encompass the wider social context that makes interpretation possible. Calls for considering wider context, for defining behavior in terms of the situations in which it occurs, are certainly not new. Malinowski made them, ethnoscientists and ethnomethodologists have made them, sociolinguists have made them. Even straight linguists have begun to make some moves in this direction. Appeals are made, but it is rarely very clear how one specifies and delimits relevant context. All that is clear is that specification of relevant context is problematic, not only for investigators, but also for natives. It is itself, as ethnomethodologists are fond of telling us, a matter of interpretation. Context is not there to be seen. Its specification is a social accomplishment.

One way to begin a search for the units by which the specification of context is accomplished is to track a bit of meaningful behavior through a variety of native interpretations. Take one of the more secure findings of cognitive anthropology: that the English word for mother is "mother" (sometimes pronounced "muh-thuh"). Cognitive anthropologists have learned this by asking a query equivalent to

"How are you related to so-and-so?," where the so-and-so's are named individuals in the informant's social world. This frame serves to sort out a domain of "relatives" ("We're not related; we're just friends"), and also to distinguish real "mothers" from such metaphorical mothers as mother superiors, mother tongues, and mother nature—the kinds of mothers who attract symbolic anthropologists.

Componential analysis permits us to define real kinship mothers as female, first ascending generation, lineal ($♀G^{+1}$ L). Whenever you encounter a $♀G^{+1}$ L, you have found yourself a real mother. But even real $♀G^{+1}$ L kinship mothers can suffer a variety of interpretive fates. Here are some recorded comments on mothers, made by a native—an American-English-speaking informant of Irish-Catholic background. The informant begins by describing his home community.

*   *   *

(In the oral presentation of this talk, I play here a few excerpts from a phonograph record by the comedian George Carlin [1973]. He does a routine on his neighborhood, "White Harlem" [Morningside Heights], then one on verbal dueling, "slip-fights," in the parlance of his group. He notes that some groups have a rule for slip-fights: "No mothers, man; no mothers." His group didn't have that rule. They started right in with mothers:

"Hey, where'd yuh go last night?"

"I was out with yuh muh-thuh, man."

He then notes that it is a cause of some embarrassment if the mother of the addressee turns out to be dead:

"I forgot, man."

Carlin goes on to acknowledge the origin of slip-fights in such Black street games as "the dozens." He recites an example of the dozens, in which the reference to what the speaker does with the addressee's mother is rather more graphic than in the white, Irish-Catholic slip-fight example.

The recording includes the laughter of Carlin's audience.)
* * *

The slip-fight exchange is ostensibly rather innocent. It is
not difficult to imagine contexts in which it could so be taken: if the
respondent, for example, were the questioner's father. There could
also easily be contexts in which this exchange could be a grievous insult: if, for example, there were good reason to believe that the
respondent really had been out with the questioner's mother. But what
we have is not a real insult, but a ritual insult as part of a game of
verbal dueling. But if the target's mother happens to be dead, then
the insult can no longer be taken ritually. An apology is called for.
So, even though participants clearly take the depicted event as mythical, it is a real kinship mother, not a mythical or metaphorical mother,
who is being referred to.

But, of course, what you (the member of the audience) heard
was not the mention of "mother" in a slip-fight. Nor did you really
hear an informant describing a slip-fight for the enlightenment of an
ethnographer. I am sure you quickly saw through that fabrication and
realized you were hearing a performance intended to entertain an audience. So you knew you were not being insulted, not even ritually. But
you were not being entertained, either. For you are not an audience of
a "show" but of a "talk." And, although the audience of a talk is
allowed to laugh, too, we would all agree that reference to mothers in
this talk would be a failure if it could not somehow be interpreted as
a reasonably apt illustration of some serious, scholarly point.

The point here is not so much to characterize varieties of
such speech acts as insults and invitations. This is an active enterprise
now in several scholarly fields. Nor is the real point even that of
Goffmanesque frames (Goffman 1974): how to distinguish real insults
from ritual ones in slip-fights; real slip-fight ritual insults from performances of them in a show; and real show performances of ritual
insults from illustrative use of them in a talk. These matters are
very relevant. But my focus here is not on the kinds of acts that can
be discerned within contextual frames, nor on the human capacity to
reframe reality repeatedly, but rather on the shape of the contextual
frames themselves, frames within which people organize their conceptions of what, basically, is happening at a given time.

It is easy to argue for the indeterminability of specifying what is really happening at any given here and now. What is the spatial extent of here? What is the time span of now? Which of the multitude of detectable motions and changes surrounding us and within us constitute what is really happening here and now? Are we scratching our heads? Feeling hungry? Worrying about taxes? Watching a fly on the wall? Breathing in our neighbor's cold germs? being bombarded by cosmic rays? Suffering through a drought? Being watched over by the gods? Traveling around the sun on a whirling ball? Actually, we all know very well what is happening now: this is a talk. That this is a talk structures the time and space of what's happening. Within these boundaries of here and now, whatever transpires is interpreted in relation to our shared awareness of what we are doing. You may not be paying attention to the talk—your thoughts may be far away from this time and place—but what you are doing is not paying attention to the talk. And it is only by knowing that this is a talk that you know what you are doing.

A talk, like a slip-fight and a show, represents the kind of thing we are looking for, a basic unit of interpretive context. At a rather immediate level, the kind of thing a talk is might be termed a social occasion. Social occasions are relatively easy to recognize. They are where ethnographers go for their data: to weddings, parties, ceremonies, legal cases, etc. Typically, investigators intrude upon an occasion, a religious ceremony for example, collect samples of behavior within it, and then go home, examine the samples, and write a monograph on religion. But the nature of the occasion that made the behavior "religious" for the participants is often ignored. Making the nature of occasions themselves an object of study has not been entirely neglected, however. A number of studies in anthropology, sociology, and sociolinguistics could be cited.[2]

Some of my work in this area has been guided by an image of a society as an organization for the production of social occasions, or "scenes," as I have called them, and of a culture as a script for planning, staging, and performing scenes. The major chunks of society, institutions like "religion" and "education," can be discerned and defined with respect to particular social systems—"emically," if I dare use that word anymore—by viewing them as organizations for the production of scenes of the same type. In our society, "education" can be seen as a complex of buildings, teachers, bureaucrats, procedures, values, etc., which have the purpose of assuring that classes and such related occasions as office hours and academic talks take place.

Of more interest for cognitive studies, however, is that by attending to the way occasions are contrastively defined, classified, distributed among settings, scheduled, and linked by planning sequences, this and related approaches have begun to reveal dimensions of cultural structure that do promise to give overall views of a culture's conceptual landscape, tying together the fragments of cognitive maps left behind by previous studies. These dimensions provide an alternative to the traditional institutional rubrics of religion, education, economics, politics, law, etc., which serve to divide up the academic world and organize monographs, but, perhaps, do not always reflect how people divide up and organize their own cultural worlds.

Such dimensions of cultural structure begin to emerge when one considers what makes a talk a talk and not, say, a class, or a speech, or a show. We can note that what goes on in talks and classes is to be taken as instructive, whereas shows are entertaining and speeches are persuasive. Talks can be distinguished from classes by (among other things) role structure: talks have a "speaker" and an "audience"; classes have a "teacher" and "students." The differences are more than terminological. For one thing, speakers get introduced. And that little difference is a marker of a very important dimension of cultural structure found, I would argue, in all societies: the dimension along which some occasions are marked as more special than others, as requiring more planning, as having explicit signals of beginning and ending, as entailing elaborate and explicit rules of procedure, and as demanding marked behavioral displays—dressing up, sitting straight, and speaking in elevated style. This is the dimension of formality, the dimension that occurs so often as a context for linguistic variation.

This dimension has interesting links with social stratification, in that everywhere displays of formality, like a necktie, erect posture, long sentences, Latin words, titles before names, and, among New Yorkers, postvocalic r's are also emblems of high status and, at the same time, a display of deference. So my necktie may be taken as a tribute to this occasion, or a badge of my middle-class standing, or a sign that I have just come from the Dean's office. (Then, again, I may

have worn a necktie, a very unusual garment for me, simply to illustrate this point.) Cultures differ, of course, in how they range social
occasions along the dimension of formality. Classes and talks are
probably more formal in France than in California.[3] These differences
can have important implications for the investigator's interpretation of
what a particular kind of activity, say litigation, does in a given society (cf. Frake 1972).

Societies also differ in the value they place on formality itself as a symbol of identity and differentiation. Some peoples think
of themselves as refined and civilized, rather than crude and vulgar;
others, like Americans, and especially like western Americans, pride
themselves in being natural and casual, rather than artificial and
stuffy. These kinds of differences are not limited to the Western
world. The Batak and Javanese of Indonesia provide a classic case
(Bruner 1974). In our own society, we also think of previous eras as
being more formal than our own. Things seem to get more informal
all the time (I can remember when I wore neckties to classes, as well
as to talks). Why does formality become a symbol of ethnic and historical differentiation? I do not intend to pursue such questions here, but
wish only to indicate some of the directions in which the study of social
occasions in their own right has led.

There are other general dimensions like formality—"risk, "
for example. Assessment of risk can operate in rather subtle ways,
even in relatively non-risky situations. One way in which talks differ
from classes is that, in a talk, the speaker faces some risk, a similar risk to that confronting a performer in a show; whereas the audience, you people, can relax. In a class, on the other hand, it is the
students who typically face the risk. Facing risk is a test of character. Colloquial English provides a rich vocabulary for evaluating performance in this test: he kept his cool, he pulled it off, he got by, he
blew it. Many societies stage risky social occasions for this purpose,
for providing some "action" (Goffman 1967). Among many groups—
Chicago street gangs, for example—the assessment of risk provides
the primary dimension for distinguishing social occasions, for differentiating "humbugging, " "gang-banging, " "wolf-packing, " and "hustling"
from "gigs, " "games, " "sets, " and "pulling jive" (Keiser 1969). It is
in the former set of risky activities that one earns "rep, " displays
"heart, " and shows he is no "punk. "

Now let me move on from dimensions revealed by contrasting types of social occasions to the kind of thing a social occasion is. Consider again this talk. What most of you probably planned to do this evening was to come to a talk rather than, say, to go to a show, watch TV, read a book, kill time, or find some action. You probably did not plan to "do education." Nor, at the other end of this continuum, did you plan to sit in a chair in this lecture hall—although that is what a camera would reveal you are doing. But it is not what's happening. Later, if asked what you did this evening, saying you "went to a talk" is an appropriate account. To say that what you did was to sit in a chair in a lecture hall would sound odd, unless you could propose a context, a happening, within which sitting in a chair becomes eventful. "I was sitting in this chair and suddenly the roof collapsed over my head." What is happening is no longer a talk, but an earthquake.

A talk, then, exemplifies a conceptual unit whereby we organize our strips of experience in formulating accounts of what is happening, our memories of what has happened, and our predictions and plans for what will happen. Let me call such units "events." Note that "events," in this sense, are not occurrences out there in the world capturable by a camera, tape recorder, or behaviorist observer. They are proposed interpretations of what is happening at some time and place.

A talk is a social event, an occasion. But there are other kinds of events. Some things are not planned for and staged; they happen to one: earthquakes, droughts, illnesses, wars, gas crises, flat tires. Of course, in many societies it is a matter for some discussion whether such things just happen or are the deeds of motivated agents, but, in any case, unless one is a malicious god, a witch, or a plotting general, such things are not, for most of us, social occasions that we plan and stage. They are happenings that befall us. Like social occasions, happenings provide interpretive contexts for behavior and units for formulating accounts. Ordinarily, in the polite society of Marin County, California, it would be unthinkably crude for a dinner guest to ask his host if he should flush the toilet. Now, in the context of what's happening being a severe drought, such a question is a sign of gracious consideration. Toilet-flushing and other ordinarily mundane hydraulic tasks have become eminently reportable topics of conversation and favorite subjects for newspaper columnists.[4]

Every situation in life, as it is experienced, can be defined
by reference to one or more events that can be construed to encompass
it and to lend meaning to what occurs within it. We account for our
lives as sequences of eventful chunks of experience. Of course, not
all experience is equally eventful. Sometimes nothing much happens.
There are occasions when one is hard put to think of interestingly
reportable occurrences to fill in conversations, letters, diaries, and
field notes. To assert the occurrence of a particular event is to propose something significant and reportable about the experience it encompasses. As a proposal, it is subject to test not only against the
reality it covers, but also against its reception by one's fellows.

The view proposed earlier, of culture as a script for the production of social occasions, should be recast a bit into one that sees
it as a set of principles for creating dramas, for writing scripts, and,
of course, for recruiting players and audiences. Culture provides
principles for framing experience as eventful in particular ways, but
it does not provide one with a neat set of event-types to map onto the
world. Culture is not simply a cognitive map that people acquire, in
whole or in part, more or less accurately, and then learn to read.
People are cast out into the imperfectly charted, continually shifting
seas of everyday life. Mapping them out is a constant process resulting not in an individual cognitive map, but in a whole chart case of
rough, improvised, continually revised sketch maps. Culture does
not provide a cognitive map, but rather a set of principles for map-
making and navigation. Different cultures are like different schools
of navigation designed to cope with different terrains and seas. In
this school, one must learn not only how to map out everyday life, but
also how to fix one's position, determine a destination, and plot a
course. And because people do not voyage alone, one must recruit a
crew. Maps, positions, and courses must be communicated and sold.
The last time—on a real boat in a real sea—I tried to sell a position
and course to my crew (which included a distinguished cognitive anthropologist), I won the argument but promptly ran the boat aground.

NOTES

[1] Presented as a talk to the Institute of Human Learning, University of California, Berkeley, April 1977. The talk was a revision
and expansion of a presentation made under the same main title to a

Conference on Cognitive Anthropology at Duke University, 1974, organized by Naomi Quinn and Ronald Casson. The appearance of this version in print owes much to the prodding and encouragement of Ray McDermott.

[2] See especially the works of Erving Goffman and of the ethnomethodological sociologists. Useful recent studies by anthropologists include Agar (1974, 1975) and McDermott (1976).

[3] Even French elementary school classes strike Americans as rather formal; see the classes so remarkably portrayed in Truffaut's movie "Small Change."

[4] In the 1974 version of this talk, I used the then ongoing gas crisis to make this point. In the current era, there always seems to be some ambient crisis we can orient to.

REFERENCES

Agar, M. 1974. Talking about doing: lexicon and event. Language and Society 3.83–89.

_____. 1975. Cognition and events. In M. Sanches and B. Blount, eds., Sociocultural dimensions of language use. New York: Academic Press, pp. 41–56.

Bruner, E. 1974. The expression of ethnicity in Indonesia. In A. Cohen, ed., Urban ethnicity. London: Tavistock, pp. 251–80.

Carlin, G. 1973. Occupation Foole (a phonograph record). New York: Little David Records.

Frake, C. 1972. Struck by speech: the Yakan concept of litigation. In J. Gumperz and D. Hymes, eds., Directions in sociolinguistics. New York: Holt, Rinehart & Winston, pp. 106–29.

_____. 1975. How to enter a Yakan house. In M. Sanches and B. Blount, eds., Sociocultural dimensions of language use. New York: Academic Press, pp. 25–40.

Goffman, E. 1967. Where the action is. In E. Goffman, ed., Interaction ritual. Garden City, N.Y.: Doubleday, pp. 149–270.

_____. 1974. Frame analysis. New York: Harper & Row.

Katz, J., and J. Fodor. 1963. The structure of a semantic theory. Language 39.170–210.

Keiser, L. 1969. The vice lords: warriors of the streets. New York: Holt, Rinehart & Winston.

McDermott, R. 1976. Kids make sense: an ethnographic account of

the interactional management of success and failure in one
first-grade classroom. Ph. D. thesis, Stanford University.
Sacks, H. 1972. On the analyzability of stories by children. In J.
Gumperz and D. Hymes, eds., Directions in sociolinguistics.
New York: Holt, Rinehart & Winston, pp. 325-45.

5 | Interpretations of Illness: An Ethnographic Perspective on Events and Their Causes

> Someday we must diagram our con-
> temporary inexplicability, as it is
> represented to us not by science but
> by common sense; ...
> —Roland Barthes[1]

Beliefs about illness, one of life's most inexplicable happenings, provide useful substance upon which to begin sketching the diagram called for by Barthes, a diagram for reading the eventfulness
of experience, for determining what's happening and what to do about
it.[2]

The beliefs being considered are those commonly called "folk"
beliefs. The qualifier "folk" serves to exclude the ideology of modern
scientific medicine, though not necessarily ruling out beliefs entertained by those who benefit from it. By "folk" I mean here simply the
ordinary person leading his everyday life out there on the streets, in
the jungle, or in a lecture hall. I purport to be talking at a level of
generality applicable to folk everywhere, but will refer principally to
systems of medical belief in simpler societies not yet fully engulfed
by the traditions of Western civilization.

Viewed cross-culturally, medical belief systems exhibit fascinating variety in content. There seems to be little constraint on the
imagination when conjuring up extraordinary agents and powers responsible for disease. Yet the broad, structural patterns of these systems
appear similar everywhere—I cannot say "remarkably" similar, as I
was about to, because, when one enumerates these patterns, they seem

rather unremarkable. They are not particularly surprising precisely because knowledge of them, among anthropologists at any rate, is so commonplace. But, as Joseph Greenberg is fond of advising: "Whenever you are not surprised, stop and ask yourself: 'Why am I not surprised?'"[3]

The first unsurprising, but for our purposes critical, thing to note is that sickness is everywhere recognized as an event; it is not an experience to be ignored. It is furthermore a happening that is sufficiently problematic and consequential to command social attention. In no society does one suffer alone. The interpretation and treatment of illness is accomplished as social behavior. Medical systems in even the most primitive of societies are social systems. Another characteristic, important to us, is that notions of causation are central to folk systems of medical belief. Cause is critical, but the etiological question is not the same one ordinarily posed by medical science. In folk medicine the response to an occurrence of illness is closely linked to the attribution of a cause to that occurrence. What is being queried is not the pathogenesis of one kind of disease, but the cause of a particular event. It is a query for which modern science has few fully satisfactory answers, a query which at least one noted philosopher, Bertrand Russell (1929: 180), discards as meaningless: "The law of causality, I believe, like much that passes muster among philosophers, is a relic of a bygone age, surviving, like the monarchy, only because it is erroneously supposed to do no harm." Folk beliefs give answers. They attribute causes to events, and everywhere attribute the same kinds of causes to illness. Everywhere some illnesses are dismissed as natural, the consequence of ordinary causal processes, whereas other illnesses (or the same illness later on) are blamed on the supernatural, on extraordinary causal powers and agents. The supernatural always looms large in folk medical systems, and everywhere seems to emerge in much the same places. Diverse explanations have been offered for the prominence of supernatural beliefs in the interpretation of such a grimly real phenomenon: psychological projections, social functions, even adaptive efficacy.[4] What is offered here in no way challenges any of these lines of explanation. My purpose is different. I am not seeking the "cause" of people's beliefs, but diagraming people's beliefs about cause. The argument is that people's beliefs about cause derive from a framework of ordinary expectations, against which the unexpected—the informative—can be

discerned, and its signification deciphered. The aim is to understand
how people make sense of their experience.

      Sickness is an event. To say one is sick is to propose a par-
ticular interpretation of experience. Whatever actual and perceived
realities may be, we generally account for our experience as sequences of occurrences, each grounded in some situation. Such occurrences are events, conceptual units for framing current, past, or prospective strips of experience.[5] The identification of events is usually
taken for granted in both scientific practice and in everyday life.
Events appear to be "out there" where they can be observed, recorded,
and explained. The proper criteria for identifying an event, for determining what's really happening, are generally held to inhere in happening itself and not in the social and mental worlds of observers. But
the answer to the question "What's happening?" is never completely
unproblematic. Often it is vexingly obscure. Try listing all the argu-
ably legitimate ways you could answer that question right now where
you are. (Try first to specify where it is exactly you are at, and what
is the time span of "now.") Any strip of experience can be interpreted
as exhibiting a practically unlimited number of happenings. To assert
the occurrence of a particular event is to propose what is significant
and reportable about the experience it encompasses. As a proposal it
is subject to test not only against the reality it covers, but also against
its reception by one's fellows.

      Every situation in life, as it is experienced, can be defined
by reference to one or more events that can be construed to encompass
it, events whose scope could range from an eye twitch to a war. We
tend to account for our lives as a sequence of such happenings. We
even give eventful descriptions when they are not logically called for.
New Yorkers, when asked to describe the layout of their apartments,
do not draw verbal maps; they conduct imaginary tours (Linde and
Labov 1975). But not all experience is equally eventful. Sometimes
nothing much happens. There are occasions when one is hard put to
think of interestingly reportable occurrences to fill in conversations,
letters, diaries, and field notes. What is eventful about the past and
the future depends, of course, on the situation during which accounts
of them are proposed. A trivial incident in the past may become quite
eventful should it prove to provide a needed alibi in a murder case.[6]

An anticipatable future incident, like getting gas next week, could become eventful should another gas crisis occur. An event is an account of experience that can be warranted as a report in the situation of its telling. Sickness has the property of being eminently reportable in almost any situation. Even minor ailments are good fillers for gaps in conversations and letters. A good case of malaria provides a lifetime of anecdotes. The threat of sickness is that it can become the event, perhaps the ultimate event, of one's life.

Insisting that events are concepts for interpreting experience, that interpretation is problematic and socially negotiable, does not, of course, deny that there is a reality out there, an unfolding, firmly irreversible one. There is a sense in which things happened the way they did, a sense in which history can be true or false, experience real or imagined. Among the realities that everyone must come to terms with, few are more real than sickness and death.

Sickness is real. Everyone believes that. Wherever reality is conceived to be, there sickness is. If one conceives of multiple realities, realities like those of the Faiwol of New Guinea (Jones 1976) where cassowaries are people and people cassowaries, sickness, wherever else it might be imagined to be, is still inescapably here in the real reality where people are people. Every belief system allows for events believed not to be real: events imagined in other worlds, conjured up in fantasies, portrayed in plays, pretended in jokes, practiced in training, fabricated in telling lies.[7] Sickness is not exempt from these Goffmanesque transformations. One who is not "really" sick can pretend to be sick for the purpose of deception, play, theatrical performance, or physicians' training. The reality of a particular case of illness can be disputed. Some who think they are "really" sick are deemed by others to be imagining their ills; some who consider themselves really not to be sick at all are judged by others to be really very sick indeed. But all medical systems acknowledge that people really do get sick. They all acknowledge that there is a difference between thinking one is sick and really being sick. Compare sickness, in this regard, with "love" among those for whom "love" is real. In the belief system of a true lover, can one sincerely and wholeheartedly think one is in love without "really" being in love? Even things believed to be real vary in the firmness of their reality. The undeniable physical reality of sickness is one of its fundamental conceptual properties. Its reality is firm but, at the same time, peculiarly intangible. Sickness may be real, but coping with it seems often to require conceptual flights far beyond the levels of apparent reality.

Sickness is a happening. One "succumbs to," "catches," "gets," and "has" an illness; one does not "do" being ill unless one is acting, playing, or faking. Sickness is not an intentional act one performs, it is not a deed. In Heider's (1958: 167-68) somewhat awkward terminology, sickness is heteronomous, coming from outside oneself, rather than autonomous. There are, of course, belief systems within which one's autonomous acts, one's sins, or one's slights to the spirits, can cause illness. Cultures and individuals differ in their propensity to interpret illness and other misfortune as punishment for one's own misdeeds.[8] Considering the event of sickness itself, its construal as a happening, rather than a deed, is not as obvious and unproblematic as first appears. Sickness typically arises within one's body, often with no apparent external cause. It is an internal happening with a beginning, a course, and sometimes an end. Something is happening that involves a change of condition in the person, but this event is nowhere construed as an activity by that person. An ambiguity arises, however, in those systems, like our own, that allow for sicknesses that have behavioral properties or consequences. Consider someone who, in the midst of an epileptic seizure, does some property damage. In our conceptions of disease, both folk and professional, the behavior during the seizure is part of an illness. It is not something for which the patient can be held responsible. (Of course the fact that a condition like epilepsy is construed as happening to one does not prevent society from compounding the misfortune by placing a stigma on it.) If someone injures another person in what could be construed as an angry rage, the assailant can disclaim responsibility because of insanity, a sickness. In such cases an experiential property of sickness, its being a happening and not a deed, becomes a defining criterion of sickness. In the eyes of the law, if it can be somehow established that the assailant "knew what he was doing when he did it," then he was not sick; he committed an offense. A medical eye might, however, consider him sick in any case. In our society, the legal system, charged with diagnosing and treating autonomous acts, constantly runs into conflict along this front with the medical system. Drawing the

line between sickness, the unfortunate happening, and crime, the bad
deed, can be troublesome in other societies as well. Evans-Pritchard
(1937: 74-75), in his vivid account of Azande witchcraft, notes that
although witchcraft can account for almost any unfortunate happening,
it cannot excuse misdeeds: adultery, theft, disloyalty, and lies cannot be blamed on witches. A man who attempted to blame his having
lied to Evans-Pritchard on witchcraft was laughed at by his fellows.

Sickness is consequential. It matters. Other events matter
too; just about anything one experiences can, with a little imagination,
be construed as a significant happening to one. But sickness has
rather singular consequences. They are typically uncertain, but only
uncertain in how bad they will be. Occasions when some good comes
out of sickness are not unknown in human life; they are, however, rare
enough that people do not actively seek sickness, taking a risk of pain
for a gain of pleasure. Getting sick is not finding some "action."[9]

Sickness differs from some other kinds of consequential and
unpleasant happenings—involvement in a legal case for example—in
that it stays with one from situation to situation. It cannot be avoided
by switching tracks, by going from one's job to one's play, or even by
running away from it all on an adventure.[10] Sickness lends definition
to every moment of one's life. It threatens to encompass all other
events, derailing one from all other tracks, and ultimately from life
itself. Sickness, from the perspective of the afflicted, can, like war,
recession, and drought, be an event of very wide scope and impact.
Even a minor illness stands apart. It requires nothing beyond it, no
encompoassing event, to explain its interest. In this respect, an account of an illness is akin to a human interest story, what the French
call a fait-divers, a genre explicated by Roland Barthes (1972: 186):
"the fait-divers ... is total news ... no need to know anything about
the world in order to consume a fait-divers ..." And like the fait-
divers, sickness derives its interest, in part, from the challenge it
poses to our notions of causality.

Cause is critical, not only for sickness but for the interpretation of all experience. We construct our realities out of "things" and
"events." "Things" fill the space of one's world; "events" segment

the temporal stream of experience. The segments along this stream remain linked, and our language is rich in metaphors of the linkages: tracks, chains, strings, threads, and strands have all been seen as tying together the strips of eventfulness in our lives. Whatever the image of the linkages, their substance is causation. Events are coupled along their tracks as causes and consequences, every event the consequence of what precedes it and a cause of what follows. This is the "Law of Causality," mocked, as we have seen, by Bertrand Russell, but proclaimed by John Stuart Mill to be "the main pillar of inductive science ... the familiar truth, that invariability of succession is found by observation to obtain between every fact in nature and some other fact which has preceded it" (cited by Russell 1929: 185). Mill may not have captured a law of nature, but his depiction is familiar enough in the way we ordinarily account for things. We think of what is happening now as having consequences for the future and as being a consequence of what happened in the past.

But there is more to what is happening now. At any moment in time, things are likely to be happening on many fronts: He coughed and spilled his coffee when the interviewer crossed her legs; he thereby lost the thread of his conversation in a job interview which was crucial to him because jobs are hard to get during a recession; not only that, but it's raining outside so he can't play tennis afterwards; but he feels a cold coming on anyway: that must be why he coughed! Separate strands of causation converge on a given situation, some naturally, some by design, to cause what's happening. The trick in everyday life, as in history or in ethnography, is to sort out those strands, and discover those events, that have crucial significance for coping with the present situation and anticipating its outcomes. This is also the trick in etiological diagnosis, both in folk and scientific medicine.[11] A particular occurrence of illness, like any event, has multiple causes. The germ theory of disease has not simplified this model of causal complexity; it merely points to one very crucial link in the causal chain leading to some illnesses. But even diseases with known and treatable pathogens can be sensibly attributed to other causal events in the chain. When a person gets VD, the first cause that occurs to the victim is probably not the germ.

In folk medicine, with restricted access to the empirical causes of disease, the personal significance of a given case of illness dominates causal attribution. The question is: "Why me?" How is it answered?

Descriptions of folk medical systems almost always talk about both "natural" and "supernatural" explanations of illness. Some illnesses are accounted for in terms the investigator deems natural or ordinary, whereas others are attributed to supernatural or extraordinary causes. In spite of some controversy over the meaning of this distinction, and the desire of at least one investigator to rule out naturally caused illnesses from the domain "ethnomedicine as an ethnograph: category" (Glick 1967), the world-wide similarity of descriptions of folk medical systems in this regard is undeniable.[12]

The general rule appears to be: an illness is naturally caused unless there are special indications of supernatural intervention. Naturally caused illnesses are ordinary, "unmarked" (in the linguistic sense) occurrences. Ordinary occurrences are, in Goffman's (1974: 22) terms "undirected, unanimated, unguided." One way an occurrence otherwise ordinary becomes marked as special is when it can be seen as directed, animated, and guided. The event did not "just happen"; it was intended to happen by a motivated agent. The attribution of guidedness to an event can be critical for one's strategy for coping with it. If a coconut falls from a tree naturally (and I submit that all systems of belief in worlds where coconut trees occur allow for this to happen), one can avoid the consequences of being hit on the head by stepping out of the way. On the other hand, if someone is up in the tree throwing coconuts at you, simply stepping out of the way is no longer so effective, but, in compensation, new kinds of strategic possibilities, like pleading, persuading, or counterattacking open up. This type of distinction in causal attribution has been pointed out for various purposes by many commentators in a number of fields. One can note, for example, the literary critic Burke's (1945) distinction between motion and act, the sociologist Goffman's (1974) distinction between "natural and social frameworks," and the psychologist Heider's (1958: 100-109) distinction between "impersonal and personal causality." To an anthropologist, however, it would appear that there is another, at least partially independent, dimension to be teased out of these discussions, one that allows for the believed reality of extraordinary events, coconuts falling skyward or, worse yet, pursuing one across

the countryside (cf. Black 1976). There needs to be some "real"
place for the "supernatural" without it necessarily being considered
an aberration or transformation of frameworks for primary reality.
There are many belief systems, by no means restricted to "primitive"
societies, in which the supernatural is very real. In such a belief
system a supernatural event cannot be wished or believed away. It is
believed to really occur and real actions are based on this belief. The
supernatural of course is not obviously real; that's what makes it supernatural. What makes it real is when it is believed to cause events
that are obviously real. Real events have real causes in any belief
system. By this principle of causation, reality is extended beyond
immediate appearances.

Even though many ethnographers point out the difficulty of
distinguishing the natural from the supernatural in some other society
the way "we" do (i.e. in terms of attributed reality), there always
seems to be some kind of line to be drawn. Ethnographers seem generally able to sort out beliefs in the supernatural from other beliefs
in a way that makes some kind of internal sense. They are not just
imposing their own beliefs about reality on other people. Among
Philippine pagans I studied, "supernaturals" are "people" (along with
their pets and paraphernalia) who are not ordinarily visible to ordinary people. They really exist and cause a lot of trouble, including
sickness. But they are special, out of the ordinary, and have to be
handled in special ways, ways that make up a religious system (Frake
1964). Not only do many belief systems allow special kinds of extraordinary beings, but they also allow for ordinary beings and objects to
have extraordinary powers: this is the realm of magic, a realm everywhere distinguished from ordinary, natural technology.

When a person attributes an illness to the spirits, gods,
ghosts, witches, or sorcerers, he is attributing it to some agent, a
motivated being. If one is to attribute sickness to the motivated act
of some other being, then a degree of extraordinariness, of supernat-
uralness, is inevitable. Discounting obvious contagion, which is not
usually interpreted as a motivated act, there is no obvious, fully
apparent mechanism whereby an agent can cause another person to be
sick.[13] One must assume the affliction to be the work of ordinary
people using extraordinary means (sorcery) or of extraordinary agents,
the supernatural beings. There is a great difference in all societies

between being injured by someone in a direct confrontation and being
made sick by someone. Both situations may be equally real in a belief system, but they differ along the dimension that distinguishes ordinary appearances from extraordinary inferences. In the attribution
of causes to events, then, there are unmotivated ("natural") causes
and motivated causes, and there are ordinary causes and extraordinary
causes. The motivated causes of illness are inherently extraordinary.
The supernatural component in folk medicine is the consequence of
attributing some illnesses to the guided doings of motivated causal
agents. The problem has now become to understand why some, but
not all sicknesses, are believed to have motivated causes.

        Sickness, being a happening to one, is by that virtue alone
already a good candidate for suspicion of motivated cause. "The tendency to see ourselves as the focus of other people's actions" noted by
Heider (1958: 120) has as a corollary the tendency to see other people's
actions as likely causes of what happens to us.[14] Even seemingly inconsequential happenings are not exempt from this tendency. A Mayan
Indian from Highland Guatemala informs us: "When your eyes twitch
a lot, that is a sign that you are being talked about by people. But it
is not clear whether good words are being said about your or whether
you are being mocked. But this much is certain—your eyes will always
twitch when you are being talked about" (Butler and Fleming 1976).
(Note the reversal of the terms of the implication between the first and
last sentence. This characteristic twist of common-sense logic we
will encounter again.) Ponapeans (Ward 1976: 9) hold the spirits responsible for eye twitches. And, in our society, there are those among
us who are prone to attribute eye twitches and other minor misfunction-
ings of bodily machinery to a somewhat extraordinary motivated agent:
one's own unconscious. (This is to say nothing about the truth value
of psychiatric—or Mayan—attributions, but only that they make sense
as beliefs apart from their truth value.)

        The more consequential for us a happening appears, the more
appropriate seems a motivated cause. Bertrand Russell (1950: 151) has
noted this principle: "One of the odd effects of the importance which
each of us attaches to himself is that we tend to imagine our own good
or evil fortune to be the purpose of other people's actions." This tendency seems more pronounced when bad things happen to us. A reasonable amount of good fortune is only our fair share, but even a little

bit of bad luck may well be someone else's fault. We look somewhat more assiduously for objects deserving blame than for subjects due thanks. This paranoid streak in the principles of causal attribution, frequently remarked on by psychologists (Heider 1958: 121; Kelley 1973) is not limited to the man in the street accounting for his personal experience. Historians, contemplating happenings to the world, have, according to D. H. Fischer, a chronicler of "Historians' Fallacies," been guilty of explaining by blaming: "This pernicious practice is particularly common in attempts to explain disagreeable events, which are mostly contemporary events" (Fischer 1970: 182). Sickness is a happening with consequences, almost invariably rather unfortunate ones. That it arouses suspicion of motivated cause is therefore no surprise. What is needed to confirm these suspicions?

It is a commonplace observation that, in folk systems, the more serious the illness, the more likely it will be attributed to supernatural causes. There are, to be sure, qualifications to this generalization: sometimes serious illnesses are attributed to "natural" causes and sometimes extraordinary causation seems to be operating without a guiding agent. Another difficulty stems from complexities in the notion of "seriousness." An illness can be serious in several ways: diseases, in Fabrega's (1974: 146) alliterative description can be dangerous, disabilitating, discomforting, and discrediting.[15] Despite these qualifications, the relevance of seriousness to our problem seems unchallengeable. Seriousness is simply an augmentation of the properties that make any illness an event. The more serious the illness the more personal and the more unfortunate the experience, properties suggesting, as we have seen, motivated—and hence supernatural—causation.

Now, folk logic begins to work: if seriousness suggests motivated (and hence supernatural) causation, then any indicator or sign of seriousness (failure to respond to therapy, for example) is also a sign of supernatural interference; conversely, any sign of the supernatural is also a sign of seriousness. News of supernatural interference is bad news.

This news is relayed in a variety of ways, familiar even in our rational civilization.[16] There are the prodigies of experience,

the eerie noises, weird apparitions, and unaccountable behaviors.
These are occurrences remarkable in their own right, reportable
even out of any further context as eventful fillers in conversations
and newspapers, a stock category of the fait-divers. Interpreted in
a context related to illness, such occurrences acquire added significance. The strange, the unusual, the unexpected are signs of supernatural causation at work. The supernatural is strange. Strange
events are, therefore, signs of the supernatural.

Then there are occurrences, not particularly strange in form,
but unexpected in the timing of their appearance. Take "sudden" event
for example. The special signification of "sudden illness," familiar
to us, seems widespread in the world. It is commonly noted as a sign
of supernatural causation (see, for example, Harwood 1970: 49). For
the Cibecue Apache, sudden onset is "far and away the most definitive
feature of sorcerer's sickness and the one which is remarked upon
most frequently" (Basso 1970: 76). Since every event has conceptually
its moment of inception, what is it to say that an onset was "sudden"?

A sudden event is one which does not unfold from its precedent
in the manner of ordinary happenings. It appears "out of the blue."
This impression of frustrated causation results from a discrepancy in
magnitude or form that belies the presumed causal link between successive ordinary events: a loud noise when all was quiet, a bright light
when all was dark, a sharp pain when all was comfort. Ordinary
causes and consequences are presumed to be similar to each other:
heavy objects make loud noises (Kelley 1973: 121). Even historians
tend to assume, quite wrongly according to Fischer (1970: 177), that
big events have big causes and big consequences. It is assumed, for
example, that the defeat of the Spanish Armada, a big event in history,
must have had a fateful impact on the subsequent course of English and
Spanish history, even though, says Fischer, there is little real evidence for this conclusion. A minor causal discrepancy of this type
makes a good fait-divers: "An Englishman enlists in the Foreign
Legion—to avoid spending Christmas with his mother-in-law" (Barthes
1972: 190).[17]

Suddenness frustrates the expectation that successive events
on the same track will be appropriately linked as cause and consequenc
The converse frustration is coincidence: the appearance of a conse-

quential merging of events traveling along different tracks. If a coconut falls from a coconut tree that is nothing remarkable. If I should
sit under a coconut tree, were I fortunate enough to be in the habitat
of one, is again nothing remarkable. However, should a coconut fall
on my head while I am sitting under a coconut tree, that is a coincidence.[18] My bad luck. Or is it? Maybe anyone dumb enough to sit
under a coconut tree deserves to be hit on the head. Chance is a matter
of perspective. It emerges when otherwise ordinary occurrences have
quite significant outcomes. There is again a discrepancy between
cause and consequence. Something extraordinary must have acted to
pull the ordinarily separate causal strands together at that moment.
In our society these perplexities of chance are partially handled by the
notion of luck, which if not a supernatural force, has, at least, some
special properties. Because sickness and death are matters of such
personal concern, any remarkable coincident occurrence, even if not
particularly extraordinary in its own right, can be construed as an
extraordinary coincidence, a sign of the supernatural. Rain after
death is a classic example (cf. Levy 1973: 155). On Ponape alternating
fever and chills coincident with the rise and fall of the tides reveals
that the mangrove demon is at work (Ward 1976: 16).

   Repetition reinforces the sense of coincidence. A relatively
inconsequential occurrence, if it happens again and again, can signal
causal problems. "Repetition always commits us to imagining an unknown cause ... chance is supposed to vary events; if it repeats them,
it does so in order to signify something through them" (Barthes 1972:
191). In Tahiti (Levy 1973: 155) it signals the possibility of extraordinary causation: "a woman and her husband may accept her first two
miscarriages as natural occurrences and only after her third miscar-
riage begin to wonder if somebody is cursing her." Tahitians are not
alone in this kind of wonder.

   Any case of illness, even one not yet series, has many of
these symbolic properties of prodigy, suddenness, and coincidence.
The character of particular symptoms can seem prodigious, exhibiting strange resemblances to other things or behaving in aberrant ways.
Skin slimy like the mud of a mangrove swamp reveals to a Ponapean
that the mangrove demon may be responsible for his illness (Ward
1976). Ponapeans are also wary of symptoms that jump from place to
place as though fleeing therapy. "Bad sicknesses, like harmful spirits,

are elusive. They keep moving from one inconspicuous place, like
the inside of the ear or the nostrils or under the arms, to another"
(Ward 1976: 23). The onset of an illness, even if not dramatically
sudden, is typically unexpected. It is rarely the clear consequence
of preceding events. Any occurrence of illness seems, to the victim
at any rate, somewhat fortuitous, a matter, in our society, of bad
luck. When illness is not unexpected, as when there is an explanatory
ambient event—a plague, famine, or epidemic—individual cases of
even quite series illness may seem natural (cf. Jones 1976: 6). Of
course, the explanation of the ambient event, as a happening to one's
world, is a different matter. The symptoms of an illness can thus
have symbolic value apart from the direct assessment of their seriousness. The difference between a "symptom" and a "sign" (a distinction
commonly labeled in folk systems) is that a sign is pure symbol,
whereas a symptom has a reality of its own, quite independent of the
meanings attributed to it. Whatever a pain symbolizes, it also hurts.

The unusual, the sudden, and the fortuitous disappoint ordinary causal expectations, expectations that cause and consequence will
be both contiguous in time and space as well as similar in form and
magnitude. Being unexpected they can be taken as informative, as
having signification. They are signs. Like the pronouns of a language
they are deictic signs: they point to something whose identity must be
inferred by indexing them to some context. In the context of illness
they are likely signs of supernatural causation, and, because of that,
of motivated cause and of seriousness. The principles of folk causal
attribution that lead to this conclusion can be summarized as follows:

1. Motivated acts by others are notorious causes of one's own
misfortune.

2. Sickness is a misfortune; therefore, motivated acts are
possible causes of sickness.

3. The more of a misfortune a sickness is, i. e. the more
serious it is, the more likely a motivated cause is responsible; therefore, signs of seriousness point to motivated causes.

4. A motivated cause for an illness implies a supernatural
cause, an ordinary agent using extraordinary powers or an extraordin
ary agent.

5. Supernatural activity implies extraordinary occurrences; therefore, unusual things and unexpected events point to the supernatural.

6. The course and symptoms of an illness can be unusual and unexpected and therefore signs of the supernatural.

7. Signs of the supernatural point to motivated causes which imply seriousness.

Folk logic is fuzzy logic, with a hedge around every bend. But it has a rough implicative structure (cf. Hutchins 1974, 1978; D'Andrade 1971). If X points to Y (is a sign of Y), then Y (more or less) implies X. In the logic of the Mayan Indian cited previously, an eye twitch is a sign that people are talking about you (it can perhaps have other meanings as well), but people talking about you implies that your eyes will twitch. Unusual occurrences point to the supernatural, but, in a given case, they may turn out to be ordinary after all. The flying saucer was just a weather balloon. The eerie noise at night was the ethnographer's tape recorder squeaking. On the other hand, supernatural activity implies unusual happenings. A flying saucer cannot make an ordinary everyday appearance. A ghost cannot make an ordinary everyday noise.

These are principles underlying people's accounts of their experience to themselves and to others. They are ways of making sense of experience. They are not principles for reacting to primary experience, for processing sensory cues. They tell you, for example, what you must think and say about an event to warrant its being considered to have been "sudden." They do not tell you what are the stimuli out there in the world that lead you to sense "suddenness" at the moment of its occurrence. People react to each other's accounts and build conceptual worlds out of them as well as out of raw sensory data. In folk medicine, the symptoms and signs of illness are not simply experiential inputs to an automatic decision-making process that has a disease name, etiological determination, and therapeutic recommendation as an output. Diagnosis is a social performance, a verbal interpretation of an event. Symptoms and signs are verbally labeled concepts appealed to as criteria when formulating socially proposed interpretations of illness.[19] It is a common observation that final diagnosis may come after a therapeutic success or failure. The chain of events need not be: symptoms point to diagnosis points to therapy. It can be therapy implies diagnosis implies symptoms. If therapy is not dependent on diagnosis, why bother with diagnosis? People talk about illness in many contexts for many purposes other than therapeutic. An understanding of this talk as social behavior is a precondition for a full understanding of medical beliefs.

Therapy, finding ways to cure illness, remains, of course, the explicit goal of any medical system. The attribution of motivated causes to disease opens up the special ways of coping appropriate to motivated agents. One can supplicate, cajole, bribe, threaten, attack or otherwise attempt to influence the agents of disease. Religion provides ways of influencing the supernatural agents. Against human agents, sorcerers and witches, one can use counter magic or more direct, "natural" means familiar to the witches of Western historical tradition. The use of "medicines" in most folk systems, whatever their empirical efficacy in a given case, belongs to the sphere of magic rather than technology. It is motivated by the same symbolic principles of similarity and contiguity that underly the reading of the signs and symptoms of illness. Magic (and folk medicine) uses the symbolism of objects and of words to send rhetorical messages to the extraordinary power that makes it work (cf. Burke 1950: 40–42; Rosaldo 1975; Mahony 1976).

Focusing, as we have done, on the inexplicabilities that emerge at every turn when the principles of ordinary causation are applied to experience obscures the notable successes of common sense frameworks in human life. It is clear that ordinary events ordinarily do have ordinary causes. Persons who fail to follow common sense principles, who succumb to an all-embracing mysticism, do not start many fires, build very substantial houses, catch much game, grow very abundant crops, or sail very far from home shores. Modern science, pursuing the notion that ordinary events always have ordinary causes, and that all events are ultimately ordinary, has pushed the boundaries of apparent inexplicability outward toward the edges of the universe and inward toward—I'm tempted to say—the soul. An event formerly extraordinary, like an eclipse of the sun, is now seen as quite ordinary. Robbed of the signification of its extraordinariness an eclipse is no longer something that happens to us, something we must do something about. Pushing inward toward the self, modern medicine has successfully accounted for many diseases as natural phenomena, although it has problems with motivation as diseases get more "mental." But when we become sick, even with a very ordinary, very naturally caused disease, it, unlike an eclipse, remains a happening to us. Its significance to our life is not purely symbolic. It cannot be explained away. When we get sick, we are still left with the question, "Why me?" This is the causal perplexity questioned by common sense, the one to which folk systems give extraordinary answers ranging from the not-very-imaginative notion of bad luck to more creative and honestly supernatural agents and powers. In seeking to understand why the supernatural looms so large in folk medical beliefs throughout the world, we must remember that these belief systems seek an answer to a question which scientific medicine does not even ask.

NOTES

[1] The quotation is from Barthes' (1972: 188–89) intriguing study of the fait-divers, the human interest story used as a newspaper filler. Barthes' use of punctuation marks is, in itself, a model of inexplicability, forcing one to relax the rule of only quoting complete sentences.

[2] I was led once again (compare Frake 1961) to use medical beliefs as a vehicle for examining problems of meaning and interpretation by an invitation to discuss a paper by Roger Ward (Ward 1976) in a symposium he organized on Curing in Oceania at the meetings of the Association for Social Anthropology in Oceania, 1976. Although the arguments of my paper have drifted far from Oceanic shores, or any other ethnographic terra firma, the papers prepared for the symposium were a major source of ideas and information. I have also benefited from comments on an earlier draft by Jane Atkinson, Ray McDermott, Michele Rosaldo, and Harold Conklin.

[3] Advice given during lectures at Stanford University.

[4] Psychological and sociological interpretations abound. For the adaptation argument see Alland (1970).

[5] Thinking about "events," "situations," "settings," and "scenes" has been a long preoccupation of mine (Frake 1964a,b, 1969,

1975, 1977), one that has recently received much encouragement and intellectual nourishment from Raymond McDermott (1976) and Michael Agar (1973, 1974, 1975).

[6] The example is from Goffman (1963: 69).

[7] For a trip into these realms consult Goffman (1974).

[8] Heider (1958: 168-69), in another display of psychologists' jargon, speaks of "intropunitive" and "extrapunitive" persons.

[9] On "action" in this sense derivative of gambling, see Goffman (1967).

[10] The "track" metaphor is nicely employed by Lyman and Scott to discuss the elaborate Simmel's notion of "adventure."

[11] This point was extracted from an essay by R. G. Collingwood (1940: 296-397) on causation in the "practical" sciences, among which he includes scientific medicine.

[12] The distinction is repeatedly made in the papers prepared for the symposium mentioned in note 2. See also Lewis (1975). Two African examples that have come to my attention are Harwood (1970) and Warren (1975). My own ethnographic experience among Christian, Moslem, and pagan groups in the Philippines supports it.

[13] A possible exception would be provided by belief systems that allow for a patient's own inward motivation, his unconsciously wanting to be sick, to be a cause of illness. A hidden agent inside the self is, however, still a rather out-of-the-ordinary causal mechanism.

[14] I appeal here to some principles of what has come to be known in psychology as "causal attribution theory." The cross-cultural relevance of this theory has by no means been established. It has been challenged in one particular by Selby (1975).

[15] Discrediting, i.e. stigmatized, conditions are especially instructive to students of causal attribution (see Goffman 1963).

[16] A contemporary example of the supernatural at work (and of a fait-divers): The San Francisco Chronicle of February 3, 1976, reported that the Archbishop had called on local Catholics to pray for rain to end the severe drought plaguing California. In the early morning of February 5, two months of warm, dry winter weather "suddenly" came to an end: it snowed in San Francisco for the first time since 1887. The newspaper that day offered a different explanation: the snow was actually caused by the drought, which, despite appearances, was really still happening.

[17] It is a very common ethnographic observation that the higher the social standing of a patient, the more likely his affliction will be

considered serious and due to supernatural causes (e.g. Ward 1976,
Johannes 1976, Hamnett 1976). This is part of a more general phenomenon that social stature adds to the eventfulness of happenings to the
socially prominent. A trivial incident or minor ailment in the life of
a big man, chief, king, president, or movie star can be big news (cf.
Goffman 1963: 69). The magnitude of the event is increased to accommodate the rank of the person it affects.

[18] Compare Evans-Pritchard's (1937: 69-70) description of
the Azande upon whom a granary collapsed.

[19] On cues and criteria see Frake (1961).

REFERENCES

Agar. M. 1973. Ripping and running: a formal ethnography of urban
     heroin addicts. New York: Seminar Press.

_____. 1974. Talking about doing: lexicon and event. Language
     in Society 3. 83-89.

_____. 1975. Cognition and events. In M. Sanches and B. Blount,
     eds., Sociocultural dimensions of language use, pp. 41-56.
     New York: Academic Press.

Alland, A. 1970. Adaptation in cultural evolution: an approach to
     medical anthropology. New York: Columbia.

Barthes, R. 1972. Structure of the fait-divers. In R. Barthes,
     Critical essays. Translated by R. Howard, pp. 185-95.
     Evanston, Ill.: Northwestern University Press.

Basso, K. 1970. The Cibecue Apache. New York: Holt, Rinehart
     & Winston.

Black, P. 1976. Crime solving in Tobi. Paper presented at the
     meetings of the Association for Social Anthropology in
     Oceania, 1976.

Burke, K. 1945. A grammar of motives. New York: Prentice Hall.

_____. 1950. A rhetoric of motives. New York: Prentice Hall.

Butler, J., and I. Fleming. 1976. Tzutujil texts. Mayan Issue I,
     International Journal of American Linguistics Text Series.
     L. Furbee-Losee, ed. Chicago.

Collingwood, R. G. 1940. An essay on metaphysics. Oxford: Oxford
     University Press.

D'Andrade, R. 1976. A propositional analysis of U.S. American

beliefs about illness. In K. Basso and H. Selby, eds.,
Meaning in anthropology, pp. 155-80. Albuquerque: University of New Mexico Press.

Evans-Pritchard, E. E. 1937. Witchcraft, oracles, and magic among the Azande. Oxford: Clarendon Press.

Fabrega, H. 1974. Disease and social behavior: an interdisciplinary perspective. Cambridge: MIT Press.

Fischer, D. H. 1970. Historians' fallacies: toward a logic of historical thought. New York: Harper and Row.

Frake, C. O. 1961. The diagnosis of disease among the Subanun of Mindanao. American Anthropologist 63.113-32.

_____. 1964a. A structural description of Subanun "religious behavior." In W. Goodenough, ed., Explorations in cultural anthropology, pp. 111-29. New York: McGraw-Hill.

_____. 1964b. How to ask for a drink among the Subanun. American Anthropologist 66.6 (part 2).127-32.

_____. 1969. Struck by speech: the Yakan concept of litigation. In L. Nader, ed., Law in culture and society, pp. 147-67. Chicago: Aldine.

_____. 1975. How to enter a Yakan house. In M. Sanches and B. Blount, eds., Sociocultural dimensions of language use, pp. 25-40. New York: Academic Press.

_____. 1977. Plying frames can be dangerous: some reflections on methodology in cognitive anthropology. The Quarterly Newsletter of the Institute for Comparative Human Development, The Rockefeller University 1.3.1-7.

Glick, L. 1967. Medicine as an ethnographic category: the Gimi of the New Guinea Highlands. Ethnology 6.31-56.

Goffman, E. 1963. Stigma. Englewood Cliffs, N.J.: Prentice Hall.

_____. 1967. Where the action is. In Interaction ritual. Garden City, N.Y.: Doubleday.

_____. 1974. Frame analysis: an essay on the organization of experience. New York: Harper and Row.

Hamnett, M. 1976. Illness, diagnosis and curing in the Atamo Valley of Central Bougainville. Paper presented at the meetings of the Association for Social Anthropology in Oceania, 1976.

Harwood, A. 1970. Witchcraft, sorcery and social categories among the Safwa. London: Oxford University Press.

Heider, F. 1958. The psychology of interpersonal relations. New York: Wiley.

Hutchins, E. 1974. An analysis of interpretations of on-going behavior. Ms, Department of Anthropology, University of California, San Diego, 1974.

_____. 1978. Reasoning in discourse: an analysis of Trobriand Island land litigation. Ph.D. dissertation, University of California, San Diego.

Johannes, A. 1976. Many medicines in one: curing in a New Guinea Highlands society. Paper presented at the meetings of the Association for Social Anthropology in Oceania, 1976.

Jones, B. 1976. Faiwol attitudes toward curing and illness: origins and uses of variability. Paper presented at the meetings of the Association for Social Anthropology in Oceania, 1976.

Kelly, H. 1973. The processes of causal attribution. American Psychologist, February, pp. 107-28.

Levy, R. 1973. Tahitians: mind and experience in the Society Islands. Chicago: University of Chicago Press.

Lewis, G. 1975. Knowledge of illness in a Sepik society. London School of Economics Monographs on Social Anthropology no. 52. London: Athlone Press.

Linde, C., and W. Labov. 1975. Spatial networks as a site for the study of language and thought. Language 51. 924-39.

Lyman, S., and M. Scott. 1970. On the time track. In A sociology of the absurd, pp. 189-212. New York: Appleton, Century, Crofts.

Mahony, F. 1976. The innovation of medicines in Truk. Paper presented at the meetings of the Association for Social Anthropology in Oceania, 1976.

McDermott, R. 1976. Kids make sense: an ethnographic account of the interactional management of success and failure on one first-grade classroom. Ph.D. dissertation, Stanford University.

Rosaldo, M. 1975. It's all uphill: the creative metaphors of Ilongot magical spells. In M. Sanches and B. Blount, eds., Sociocultural dimensions of language use, pp. 177-204. New York: Academic Press.

Russel, B. 1929. Mysticism and logic. New York: Norton.

Selby, H. 1975. Semantics and causality in the study of deviance. In M. Sanches and B. Blount, eds., Sociocultural dimensions of language use, pp. 11-24. New York: Academic Press.

Ward, R. 1976. Ponapean diagnosis: the role of symptoms in the identification of illness on Ponape. Paper presented at the meetings of the Association for Social Anthropology in Oceania, 1976.
Warren, D. 1975. The role of emic analysis in medical anthropology. Anthropological Linguistics 17.117–26.

Part II.   The Subanun

6 | The Eastern Subanun of Mindanao

The literature on Subanun social organization dates from the seventeenth century, when these Mindanao pagans prompted Francisco Combés (1667: 31), a Spanish Jesuit, to write: "They are a people of little worth ... living in the hills with scant social life, like beasts, and placing their dwellings a league apart according to the whims of each. ' Actually, the Subanun live—not "like beasts" but like all human beings—in social groups. Though often informally organized and lacking obvious boundaries, these groups sustain a social life which, characterized by drinking, feasting, religious ceremonies, and almost constant litigation, is by no means scant. Nevertheless, a grain of truth underlies Combés's description. Small, non-continuous, two-generation family groups, living in dispersed households, maintain an unusual degree of corporate independence.

The present paper discusses the structure of the Subanun family and the kinship relations generated by its formation and dissolution. Other publications (Frake 1957a and 1957b) have dealt with the nature of wider social groups and the means by which a complex network of litigation flourishes within them without the benefit of formal political authority or the sanctioned use of force.

The Subanun, who number some 70,000, inhabit the interior of Zamboanga,[1] a mountainous peninsula, 17,673 square kilometers in area, connected to central Mindanao by a narrow neck of land. Here the majority derive their livelihood by alternately clearing, cultivating, and fallowing forested hillsides on which they grow rice and a variety of other grain, root, and tree crops. In recent years, population pressure and deforestation caused by the immigration of Christian Filipinos have forced the Subanun in a number of areas to supplement or replace swidden[2] farming by permanent-field agriculture.

Effectively isolated by geography and the activities of warlike Moslem neighbors, the Subanun have no knowledge of culturally or linguistically distinct mountain-dwelling pagans. To them, all mountain people are subanen ("upstream people"), who share a similar culture, social organization, and linguistic affiliation in contrast to known categories of outsiders who visit or inhabit the lowlands: the Moslem glenaun (Maranaw) and samal, the Christian bisaya' (Bisayan) and kasila' (Spanish mestizos), and the mercantile ginsik (Chinese). Relations with Subanun of the same or other groups are invariably devoid of warfare and class distinctions. External relations, on the other hand, have been marked by coercive exploitation and social inequality.

The peaceable and anarchic Subanun have long been prey to more strongly organized neighbors. Beginning before the Spanish conquest of the Philippines and continuing intermittently until the twentieth century, Moslems from Sulu and Lanao raided the Subanun for slaves, collected tribute, and established a system of forced trade.[3] In some coastal areas, to better enforce their control, they instated a hierarchy of titled Subanun officials (begalal) with the responsibility of collecting tribute and implementing trade. These individuals became the foci of indigenous political and judicial authority, deriving their power from their position as trade intermediaries and from the physical might of their backers. Moslem exploitation and hegemony in Zamboanga ceased with the American occupation. With the removal of the foundations of the incipient Sunanun political organization, the titled offices rapidly disappeared or lost their political significance.

In recent decades Christian settlers from the Bisayan islands to the north, encouraged by the weakening of Moslem power, by roadbuilding, and by the tractability of the native population, have invaded Zamboanga. Through markets, schools, tax collection, and land laws, Christian settlement has meant the gradual extension of a new political and economic system over the Subanun. While effective political control, heralded by the bestowal of the new titles of tininti (barrio lieutenant) and kunsyal (councilor), has been established only in the coastal and foothill areas of permanent cultivation, the threat of land appropriation, "tax" assessment, and police interference reaches the interior shifting cultivators.

Linguistically, Subanun constitutes a subgroup of the Central Philippine languages and embraces two closely related languages,

Eastern and Western Subanun. These are separated by a boundary across the low, narrow, middle portion of the peninsula, a division which was perhaps effected by Moslem penetration (Frake 1957c). The present study[4] concerns only the Eastern Subanun, who include some 55,000 people dispersed across the wider eastern sections of Zamboanga Peninsula.

The Eastern Subanun exhibit no overall formal organization or conscious unity; the social world of any one Subanun includes only a small fraction of the total population. Moreover, despite both dialect diversity and the restriction of individual social spheres, it is impossible to draw clearly defined linguistic or sociological boundaries between any adjacent groups. There is, rather, an overlapping network of small sociolinguistic communities, whose boundaries can be defined only from the point of view of each of the minimal discrete units of which Subanun society is built.

The distinction between discrete and non-discrete groups[5] is basic to Eastern Subanun social organization. The maximal social group—the total society from the point of view of one individual—is non-discrete. Of Subanun social groups, only the family, the household, and the settlement are discrete. The first two of these groups tend to be equivalent in membership and form the fundamental socioeconomic unit. A family's social relationships extend outward along ties of propinquity and bilateral kinship. Maximally they enconpass a politically unorganized circle of neighbors and kin whose membership overlaps with, but never precisely corresponds to, those of other families.

Whether cultivated by swidden farming or by permanent agriculture, areas of Subanun settlement always present much the same pattern: isolated small dwellings, each within its own fields, usually on a prominence overlooking the crops. What nucleation there is derives from the practice of cultivating adjacent fields in order to reduce the perimeter exposed to faunal enemies. In areas of shifting cultivation, settlements can be better defined as clusters of adjacent or nearly adjacent swiddens than as clusters of households. A Subanun locates, and periodically relocates, his dwelling according to agricultural requirements and, if anything, endeavors to place his house as far from any neighboring dwelling as is consistent with these requirements.

The value placed on household isolation is explicit. When I showed
an informant photographs of compact house clusters among other shifting cultivators, his response, typically legalistic, was: "Bah, if I
were there, I would fine them. Are they so suspicious of each other
that they must live where they can always watch one another?"

The settlement is an unnamed, discrete local group generally
comprising from three to a dozen dispersed households. Its boundaries, though not always geographically apparent, can at any one time
easily be defined with reference to the quantity and quality of social
activities among its members (Frake 1957b). Over time, however,
the settlement exhibits little stability or continuity. The unity of its
component families is a temporary product of current agricultural
opportunities, impermanent kinship obligations, and fluid social ties.

The Subanun house—a rectangular, thatched pile dwelling—
has among its physical aspects three characteristics of sociological
importance. First, it is small. Floor space averages about twelve
square meters and rarely exceeds twenty. This small size reflects
single family occupancy, but it has the consequence of limiting the
number of persons that can assemble together. With the exception of
a few religious ceremonies, all Subanun social functions take place
indoors in a dwelling house; there are no outdoor areas or other buildings for such purposes. Although an all-night drinking party, a legal
case, a wedding, or a religious ceremony may pack people until there
is literally standing room only, attendance at social gatherings can
exceed forty or fifty persons only with difficulty. I have never seen
as many as one hundred Subanun in one place at one time. Their social
life takes place entirely within small groups.

Second, a Subanun house has only one room and one hearth.
Household space is defined functionally—the sleeping area, the living
area, the cooking area—and finds architectural expression only in
slightly different floor levels. Within the household there can be little
privacy in working, cooking, eating, or conversation. Darkness alone
brings the privacy necessary for licit and illicit sexual activity. (With
regard to the latter, the granaries, the only non-dwelling structures
in a Subanun settlement, sometimes acquire a sociological function.)

Third, a Subanun house is a temporary construction. A new
house is usually built within the annual grain swidden every other

year, or at most every third year, as old swiddens are fallowed.
Longer occupancy, even if feasible agriculturally, cannot contend
with increasing vermin infestation and disintegrating thatch. A house,
therefore, has no value as permanent real estate, nor, since there
are no tenure rights to land per se, does an unoccupied house site.

Typically a house is occupied by a single nuclear or polygynous family, the minimal discrete social group of Subanun society and
the maximal corporate unit. A full family comprises a man and his
wife or wives, with or without real or adopted unmarried offspring.
Dissolution of a full family through death or divorce produces one or
more partial families, each consisting of a surviving or divorced
spouse with or without unmarried offspring. Completely orphaned
children are absorbed by adoption into existing families. Partial families, especially those consisting of a single individual, often join with
a full family to form a single household, but by doing so they do not
lose their socioeconomic independence. Compound households, comprising more than one full family, are rare, and are invariable temporary (and disliked) expedients to facilitate access to new swiddens.

Whether nuclear or polygynous, full or partial, a Subanun
family (seŋglaŋan) is strictly limited to two generations: parents and
unmarried offspring. It is not a descent group with continuity beyond
the life span of its founders. Its lateral extension by polygyny, occurring in less than 10 percent of recorded families, increases the family's life expectancy by adding female members to the spouse set, but
in no way alters its basic character. A family of any type exhibits a
series of characteristics, each distinguishing it from all other Subanun
social groups:

1. Its formation, through marriage, and its dissolution, through death
   or divorce, require legal action.
2. Its members always live together in a single house, sharing a common hearth and a common, unpartitioned living space.
3. It has joint title to all property brought into, created by, or inherited by its members.
4. It has collective legal responsibility.
5. It always jointly cultivates a single annual swidden and/or plowed
   field. (Male adolescent offspring may, in addition, cultivate individual swiddens for several years prior to their marriage.)

6. It is entirely responsible for its own economic support through its own resources.

Taken together, these characteristics give the family a unique corporate nature. Every Subanun acquires membership in one such corporate family (his family of orientation) through birth or adoption, and normally enters into the formation of a new similar unit (his family of procreation) through marriage. Not only does marriage establish a new corporate unit; it terminates in perpetuity the membership of both partners in their families of orientation. Once married, a Subanun, to enjoy the rights of membership in a full family, must remain married—though not necessarily to the same person—throughout his life.

The formation of independent family units is consequently a continual process in Subanun society. The establishment of a new family of procreation through marriage requires the concluding of a legal contract between the families of orientation of the prospective spouses. This contract, guaranteed by the payment of a substantial bride-price, defines the interest of the two sponsoring families in the sponsored family.

Any two families may sponsor a new family by a marriage between their respective offspring, providing only that no member of the parental generation of one sponsoring family is an offspring in the other. Incest taboos exclude marriage with siblings and parents' siblings—persons who have shared membership in one's own or one's parent's family of orientation. This rule does not exclude first-cousin marriage; indeed, this is quite common, even though it violates verbally stated ideals and requires payment of a token fine. The behaviorally manifest preference for cousin marriage reflect's Murdock's (1949: 318-20) "positive gradients of propinquity and kinship" in the absence of correspondingly strong negative gradients, as well as the fact that marriage with a close neighbor and/or kinsman facilitates negotiation of the marital contract and obviates difficulties in the choice of postmarital residence. Furthermore, because of the corporate independence of families, even when closely akin, a marriage between cousins unites fundamentally distinct groups by the ties of joint sponsorship of a new corporate unit.

On the other hand, no social, economic, or political advantages are to be gained by marital alliances between wider social groups —kindreds and settlements. These groups are consequently agamous, i. e. irrelevant in the choice of marital partners.

The complex legal negotiations preliminary to marriage often begin before the prospective couple has reached puberty. The acceptance by the girl's family of a token from that of the boy signals willingness to enter into negotiations and establishes a relationship of bina' ("engagement") between the families. It then becomes a legal offense for either party to open negotiations with a different family without formally breaking the engagement by legal action, for which there must be sufficient grounds. Go-betweens conduct all negotiations, draw up the final agreement, and serve as witnesses to the terms of the unwritten contract in the event of subsequent dispute. To qualify as a go-between a man cannot be a member of either sponsoring family, but he must be a close kinsman of the family he is representing. Above all, he must be skilled in legal procedure, for marital alliances emerge only from litigious combat.

When the couple are ready for marriage and the groom's family has raised an acceptable down payment on the bride-price, the wedding can take place. During the ceremony the bride-price must be calculated in terms of traditional, non-exchangeable units of value (kumpaw), also used in reckoning fines, that are assigned to each of the items composing it (see Frake 1957a). These units of value are in turn artibrarily represented by kernels of maize laid out in patterned groups and rows, the kernels in each of the traditionally named groups having different, and again purely arbitrary, values. The complex procedure of laying out the pattern which properly represents the total value of the bride-price, and then of removing kernels from appropriate rows as items in the down payment are paid, is marked at every step by prolonged debate and often takes most of the night to complete. Upon receipt of the down payment, the bride's family must distribute a large portion of it to kinsmen who have contributed to the wedding expenses, to the attending legal authorities and go-betweens, and to others who, by figuring significantly in the girl's life history, have established a claim to a share in her bride-price.

Following the maize-kernel computations the participants must agree on the details of payment of the future installments on the bride-price by the new family and on the duration of bride-service. The latter obligation, usually lasting three or four years, functions as security on the unpaid portion of the bride-price. A couple cannot ordinarily leave bride-service until these payments have been completed. It is possible, through clever legal argument and an impressive, or even total, payment on the bride-price, to eliminate bride-service altogether, but this rarely occurs except in cases of secondary or polygynous marriages. In primary marriages the total bride-price, including down payment and later installments, generally has a cash value ranging from 50 to 100 Philippine pesos, an amount several times the annual cash income of an average family.

The newly married couple sets up a household of their own as soon as feasible. Since both partners have married out of their natal families to form a new and independent corporate unit, marriage is neolocal in terms of corporate-group affiliation. In terms of the geographical location of their initial residence, the only requirement is that it be sufficiently close to the household and fields of the girl's family of orientation to make bride-service possible, so that in this sense initial residence is matrilocal. Bride-service constitutes a demand-right held by the girl's family of orientation entitling it to periodic agricultural labor from the family it sponsored. The latter family, however, from the moment it is instituted by marriage, is an independent economic unit responsible for its own support through the cultivation of its own fields. Its obligation to contribute a certain amount of labor to another family is simply a corporate liability and in no way infringes on its fundamental independence.

After fulfillment of its bride-service obligations a family can make its periodic residence changes without necessary regard for the location of the woman's family of orientation. Nevertheless, couples normally continue to live near the parents of one spouse or the other, often alternating between the two. Ultimately, especially after the dissolution of their parents' families, residence becomes in every sense neolocal. Unlike a corporation in the Western legal sense, a Subanun family does not have continuous existence irrespective of that of its members. It resembles a partnership in that its continuity as an economic unit depends upon the existence of a legal bond (marriage) between a man and one or more women. It may augment its personnel by procreating new members but is deprived of these members as soon as they marry. Termination of the relationship between marital partners dissolves the family corporation and requires settlement of its estate. The non-recognition of property rights in land by the Subanun shifting cultivators simplifies the division of property (Frake 1956). An estate consists principally of movable property such as Chinese jars, gongs, jewelry, and currency; of perishable goods such as stored grain and planted crops; and of intangible assets such as credits and outstanding legal claims. Rules of estate settlement are simple in principle but complex in details of application to specific cases. The dissolution of a Subanun family involves litigation often as intricate as that which attended its formation.

In cases of divorce the problem is twofold: to settle any obligations the broken family may have to its sponsoring families and to divide the remaining estate between the two resulting partial families. Sponsoring families are in part responsible for underpaid and overpaid portions of the bride-price. The complexities enter when attempting to determine in a given case the respective rights of each of the four families involved (the two sponsors and the two divorced partial families). These rights depend primarily upon the establishment of legal responsibility for the failure of the marriage.

Procedures following the death of a spouse are somewhat simpler, for the question of responsibility does not arise. Malevolent supernaturals cause most deaths, and these beings enjoy immunity from legal prosecution.

Rights to the estate of a family terminated by the death of a parental member follow from the basic principle of inheritance, according to which the ultimate title rests with the offspring of that family, among whom the estate is divided regardless of sex or relative age. Problems arise over the allotment of specific items, over the rights of offspring who were members of their family of orientation at the time of a parent's death as opposed to the rights of offspring who had already married out, and over the rights of the surviving spouse and his (or her) subsequent offspring after he marries again. The resolution of these problems in particular cases depends upon a variety of factors related to the life histories of the individuals concerned, to the kinds of property at stake, and—not the least important—to the respective legal skills of the opposing claimants.

The principles of estate settlement, despite their litigation-engendering complexities, clearly point up a fundamental fact of Subanun social organization: a full family broken by death or divorce ceases to exist as a corporate group. Partial families are not surviving members of a full family corporation; they are new corporations. A partial family can become a full family in only one way: by the remarriage of a surviving spouse, which, in turn, establishes a new and different corporate unit.

Being independent corporate entities, partial families, whether or not they establish independent households, are responsible for their own support by the only means open to any Subanun family, namely, agriculture. This is as true for an elderly widow as for a young divorcee. In order to clear and cultivate its annual grain swidden, a partial family, especially when lacking an adult male member, must ordinarily recruit additional labor. This it can do by drawing upon kinship obligations such as that of bride-service, by providing an equivalent amount of labor in exchange, by offering a feast, or by paying wages in crops or cash. However, a family cannot long depend upon labor recruitment without seriously depleting its resources. The insistence on the independence of partial families makes their lot a hard one and puts a premium on remarriage.

Several factors facilitate secondary marriage. Foremost among these is the institution of levirate and sororate marriage, whereby a sponsoring family has the legal obligation to provide a new spouse from its membership as a replacement if this is at all possible. A second is polygyny, which enables a married man to absorb a widow and her children into his existing family unit. A third is the relative legal simplicity of secondary marriage for a woman, especially one whose parents are deceased, since in such cases the bride-price is minimal and bride-service is not ordinary required.

Subanun definitions of family and marriage assure that the population will at all times be divided into a maximum number of independent full-family units—social groups which are not only large enough

to be economically self-sufficient but which can also procreate the
personnel to produce new families. By way of summarizing Subanun
family organization, these definitive factors can be listed as follows:

1. A family, full or partial, is an independent corporate unit.
2. A family is strictly limited to two generations.
3. Once married, a person can never rejoin his family of orientation.
4. A new family is bound by an intricate legal contract to two sponsoring families.
5. Every full family must eventually dissolve into one or more partial
   families.
6. A partial family can resolve its subsistence difficulties only by
   becoming a full family through the remarriage of its parental member.
7. Remarriage is facilitated by levirate and sororate obligations, by
   polygyny, and by simplified legal procedure.

The continual process of family formation by sponsorship
engenders a set of important relationships among the parental members
of the sponsoring and sponsored families. These fundamental relationships receive distinctive linguistic designation in the basic kinship terminology. Any discussion of Subanun kinship terminology, however,
must begin by delimiting the particular linguistic material involved.

In the Eastern Subanun language there is a vast corpus of
words and phrases, often with overlapping referents, which have kinship meaning. The traditional dichotomy between terms of reference
and terms of address does not suffice to segregate this terminology
into meaningful contrastive sets. There are, for example, at least
sixteen alternative single-word designations applicable in reference
to any cousin. In addition, there are a large number of possible multi-
verbal constructions specifying attributes such as sex or describing
the relationship more precisely in terms of other relationships. All
this is apart from the fact that a Subanun Ego must also make choices
among the several ways he may be related to many of his kinsmen.

The Subanun are not unique in possessing co-existing sets of
relationship terms. A similar situation prevails in other Philippine
languages, in English, in German, and in Javanese.[6] It is doubtless
common elsewhere, but reliance on the genealogical method alone to

elicit terms will not document it. Kinship terms must be recorded in
use in a variety of cultural situations. It is no accident that existing
descriptions of multiple alternatives in kinship designation have come
from investigators who are native speakers (e.g. Schneider and Homans,
Koentjaraningrat) or unusually fluent speakers of the languages concerned.

Our primary concern here is with terms that function to define
kinship relations, in contrast to terms used to name individuals as subjects of discourse in address or reference. The latter terms in Subanun are morphologically and syntactically distinct. The choice of alternatives among them reflects social distance much as does our own
alternative use of the proper nouns "Joe," "Uncle Joe," or "Uncle"
in reference or address to a kinsman designated by the common noun
"my uncle" (Schneider and Homans 1955). Terms used as names, here
called nominals, do not designate classes of kin; they merely identify
single individuals. Designative terms, on the other hand, denote an
individual as a member of a class of kinsmen whose distinctive features
are signified by the term (Lounsbury 1956: 167-68).

A Subanun chooses among alternative designative terms according to the degree of specification required in a particular cultural context. Some contexts require only a distinction between kin and non-kin;
others, such precise distinctions as that between mother's brother's
elder daughter and mother's brother's younger daughter. At different
levels of contrast the Subanun kinship system exhibits different fundamental distinctions. At one level cousin terminology is of the Hawaiian
type; at another, of the Eskimo type. At one level siblings-in-law are
differentiated by sex; at another, by the sequence of affinal and collateral
links; at still another level, appearing only in special types of discourse,
they are not differentiated at all.

Although the kinds of distinctions that the Subanun are capable
of making at various levels in their hierarchy of kinship taxonomy is
a subject of considerable interest, we are at present concerned with
the maximal, obligatory distinctions that they must make in response
to the query: mekendun 'amu run ni X? ("How are you related to X?").
If we change our query to meguseba 'amu run ni X? ("Are you a consanguineal of X?"), or to kandun mekpated 'amu rua' ni X? ("How are
you a sibling-cousin of X?"), we will obtain responses at different

levels of specification. Obligatory responses to the query "How are you related to X?" yield a set of single-word terms which designate sixteen mutually exclusive classes of kinsmen at a single level of contrast. These classes are the basic kinship categories. Eliminating dialect synonyms and terms reserved for drinking songs and other special types of discourse, we are left with a corpus of sixteen distinct basic kinship terms. These terms are listed and defined at the end of the paper.

The criteria by which the sixteen basic kinship categories are differentiated have significant cultural correlates in the processes of family formation. The importance of marriage, the institution through which new families are formed, is reflected in the kinship terminology by the observance of the criterion of affinity throughout the system. This criterion segregates all kin in Ego's generation who are connected to Ego by one or more marriage links, as well as kinsmen in different generations who are connected to Ego by at least one marriage link in the first descending generation. A consistent analysis of Subanun kinship criteria requires this special definition of affinity, for the Subanun classify parent's sibling's spouse with parent's sibling and spouse's sibling's child with sibling's child. They differentiate these consanguineals from such affinal categories as spouse's parent's sibling and sibling's child's spouse.

The kinship terminology further segregates the pivotal, i.e. parental, members of each of the five families with which an individual normally relates during his lifetime in the process of family formation and sponsorship. These families are listed below, the term designating each kin type being indicated in parentheses:

1. Ego's family of orientation, in which his father (gama') and mother (gina') are the pivotal members.
2. Ego's family of procreation, in which he and his spouse (sawa) are the pivotal members.
3. Ego's spouse's family of orientation, in which Ego's spouse's parents (penugaŋan) are the pivotal members.
4. Ego's child's family of procreation, in which Ego's child (bata') and Ego's child's spouse (minugaŋan) are the pivotal members.
5. Ego's child's spouse's family of orientation, in which Ego's child's spouse's parents (bela'i) are the pivotal members.

These are the families which Ego forms by marriage (2), which sponsor his marriage (1 and 3), which Ego sponsors (4), and which act as co-sponsors with Ego (5).

The five pairs of pivotal kinsmen fall into three generations: Ego's, the first ascending, and the first descending generations. The basic kinship terminology distinguishes these three generations throughout the system and lumps all consanguineals in other generations into one category (gapu') signifying "consanguineal kin more than one generation removed." Affinal kinship is not extended beyond the first ascending and descending generations.

These five kin pairs, finally, are all connected to Ego by lineal, affinal, or a combination of lineal and affinal links. Unlike other basic kinship categories, all of which include collateral kin, the designata of the terms for these categories are not infinitely extendable; the terms can denote only these kin types and no others. We shall label as lineal categories those classes of kin with finite designata, and define a lineal as any kinsman not connected to Ego by any collateral links. Thus defined, the distinction between lineals and collaterals pertains only in the three crucial generations: Ego's and the two generations adjacent to his.

The three basic criteria of Subanun kinship classification—affinity, generation, and lineality—intersect, in short, in such a manner as to distinguish the five pivotal pairs of kinsmen from each other and as a group (lineals) from all other kin (collaterals). Among consanguineals, all kin not included in the five pivotal pairs are segregated only by generation and, in the first ascending generation, by sex. Degree of collaterality is nowhere recognized in basic terminology beyond the distinguishing of lineals (zero-degree collaterals) from collaterals (see Lounsbury 1956: 168). The "uncle" and "aunt" terms (kia', dara') extend to all collaterals in the first ascending generation; the "sibling-cousin" term (pated) to all collaterals in Ego's generation; and the "nephew-niece" term (manak) to all collaterals of the first descending generation.

That a society which attaches such marked importance to the independence of nuclear families should fail to distinguish siblings from cousins in basic terminology may seem paradoxical, since siblings but not cousins share family membership with Ego. However, both Ego and his siglings ultimately marry out of their common family of orientation, establishing independent families of their own, and it is only the parental members of a family, upon whom its existence depends, who receive distinctive kinship designation. Siblings become parental members of independent families collateral to Ego's, and Ego's patterned relationships with families founded by siblings is not significantly different from those with families founded by cousins. In situation where a greater degree of specification is required, e.g. in designating marriageable kin, a special derivative term, gagunapu', may be empooyed to distinguish those consanguineals of Ego's generation who are not siblings.

Among affinals, complex types of linkage with Ego must be distinguished from simple types in both lineal and collateral sets. A complex lineal affinal is connected to Ego by two lineal links, one down and one up in this order. A complex collateral affinal is connected to Ego by two affinal links and one indefinitely extendable collateral link. Observance of this criterion in Ego's generation segregates child's spouse's parents from spouse and spouse's sibling's or cousin's spouse from spouse's sibling or cousin. Complex collateral affinals are further distinguished by the criterion of whether the relationhip is between males or not between males, the latter covering cases where Ego, or the relative, or both are female. In these categories only male speakers differentiate sex of relative, and the terminology remains reciprocal.

Figure 1 diagrams the intersection of all criteria to form the basic kinship categories. The consanguineal categories can be extended indefinitely in both vertical and lateral directions to embrace all persons with whom Ego can or cares to trace genealogical ties. The affinal categories are infinitely extendable along collateral links, but cannot be extended, in designative nomenclature, by the addition of further affinal links. Affinals not included in the basic categories can be designated only by special derivative or descriptive terms, which are not part of the basic terminology.

Pivotal kin stand out not only in the linguistic designation of basic categories but also in the behavioral correlates of kinship classification. Patterned kinship behavior among the Subanun falls along a continuum from intimacy to formality or reserve. Varying possibilities

Generation and complexity		Consanguineal			Affinal		
		Collateral		Lineal		Lineal	Collateral
		Female	Male	Female	Male		Between males	No betw mal
+2, +3, etc.		gapu'						
+1		dara'	kia	gina'	gama'	penugaŋan	kayug	
0	Simple	pated		EGO		sawa	bati'	gipa,
	Complex					bela'i	bilas	
-1		manak		bata'		minugaŋan	kayug	
-2, -3, etc.		gapu'						

Fig. 1. Subanun basic kinship categories

in the use of nominal kinship terms to name individuals, which are themselves aspects of kinship behavior (Murdock 1949: 97) permit a fivefold division of this continuum. Distinctive behavior patterns characterize each division. In the table below, these behavior patterns are roughly identified in English, the included kin are noted for each pattern, and the definitive nominal usage in reference or address is indicated by means of the following symbols: N—personal name, nickname, or reciprocal nickname; K—nominal kinship term (these terms are distinct from the designative terms discussed above); O—no nominal usage possible (personal names cannot be mentioned).

Within the relationships of informality and mutual respect, Subanun kinsmen can express a wide latitude of social distance by means of alternative kinship terms and types of nicknames, alone or in combination with personal names. Non-kin can be brought into the framework of these relationships and named by a kinship term appropriate to an existing or desired social relationship. On the other hand the extreme relationships of intimacy, obedience, and reserve are more circumscribed in permissible behavior and in nominal usage.

Scale of Patterned Kinship Behavior

Patterned behavior	Included kin	Nominal usage
Intimacy	Spouse, child	N
Informality	Collateral consanguineals	K, N
Mutual respect	Collateral affinals	K $\pm$ N
Obedience	Mother, father	K
Reserve	Parent-in-law, child-in-law	O

These patterns prevail only between lineals and include all the pivotal
kin pairs except child's spouse's parents (who are usually treated with
mutual respect and are named with one of the terms applied to collateral affinals). The appearance of lineals at both extremes of the scale
of patterned kinship behavior provides further illustration of the distinctive importance of these kin in Ego's life history.

Subanun kinship terminology and behavior reflect the fundamental significance of the relationships generated by the establishment
of new families. There are, of course, many other kinds of relationships linking independent families, for example, those fostered by
economic, religious, festive, and legal activities. Nevertheless,
despite this network of formal and infmal social ties among families,
there have emerged no large, stable, discrete sociopolitical units.
The Subanun family remains, like that of the Iban, largely a "sovereign
nation" (Freeman 1958: 8).[7] But unlike the Iban bilek or the Gilbertese
oo (Goodenough 1955), the Subanun family is not a descent group. Its
corporate unity endures only as long as does the marriage tie of its
founders. The continuity of Subanun society must be sought in the continuous process of corporate group formation and dissolution rather
than in the permanency of the groups themselves.

The kinship terms listed below are the basic designative terms
of the Gulu Disakan dialect of the Eastern Subanun language. Other
dialects exhibit different forms at several points, but the system is
much the same throughout the Eastern Subanun area. The category
kayug, however, is absent in southern dialects. Several synonyms of
dialectical origin may be common in any one region, e.g. gyaya' for

dara' and giras for bilas in the Gulu Disakan region. It might be noted
here that the writer has found no evidence of the bifurcate collateral
terminology reported by Christie (1909: 116) and discussed by Kroeber
(1919: 79) in any dialect of Eastern or Western Subanun for which he
has recorded the kinship terminology.

List of Kinship Terms

1. gapu': grandparents; ascendants of grandparents; siblings, cousin
   and siblings' (and cousins') spouses of the foregoing; grandchildren
   grandchildren of siblings and cousins and of spouse's siblings and
   cousins; descendants of the foregoing. Distinctive criteria: consanguineal; more than one generation removed.

2. gama': father. Distinctive criteria: consanguineal; first ascending generation; lineal; male.

3. gina': mother. Distinctive criteria: consanguineal; first ascendir
   generation; lineal; female.

4. kia': parents' brothers and male cousins; husbands of parents'
   sisters and female cousins. Distinctive criteria: consanguineal;
   first ascending generation; collateral; male.

5. dara': parents' sisters and female cousins; wives of parents'
   brothers and male cousins. Distinctive criteria: consanguineal;
   first ascending generation; collateral; female.

6. pated: siblings; cousins (with indefinite lateral extension). Distinctive criteria: consanguineal; Ego's generation.

7. bata': sons and daughters. Distinctive criteria: consanguineal;
   first descending generation; lineal.

8. manak: children of siblings and cousins; children of spouse's siblings and cousins. Distinctive criteria: consanguineal; first
   descending generation; collateral.

9. sawa: spouse (husband or wife). Distinctive criteria: affinal;
Ego's generation; lineal; simple.

10. bela'i: child's spouse's parents. Distinctive criteria: affinal;
Ego's generation; lineal; complex.

11. bati': wife's brothers and male cousins; husbands of sisters and
female cousins (male speaking). Distinctive criteria: affinal;
Ego's generation; collateral; simple; between men.

12. gipag: wife's sisters and female cousins; wives of brothers and
male cousins (male speaking); husband's siblings and cousins;
spouses of siblings and cousins (female speaking). Distinctive
criteria: affinal; Ego's generation; collateral; simple; not between
men. -

13. bilas: spouses of spouse's siblings and cousins. Distinctive criteria: affinal; Ego's generation; collateral; complex.

14. penugaŋan: spouse's parents. Distinctive criteria: affinal; first
ascending generation; lineal.

15. minugaŋan: spouses of sons and daughters. Distinctive criteria:
affinal; first descending generation; lineal.

16. kayug: wife's parents' brothers and male cousins; wife's parents'
sisters' (and female cousins') husbands; siblings' (and cousins')
spouses' fathers (male speaking); siblings' (and cousins') spouses'
parents' brothers, male cousins, and sisters' (and male cousins)
husbands (male speaking); siblings' (and cousins') daughters' husbands (male speaking); wife's siblings' (and cousins') daughters'
husbands; children's spouses' brothers and male cousins (male
speaking); siblings' (and cousins') children's spouses' brothers
and male cousins (male speaking); wife's siblings' (and cousins')
children's spouses' brothers and male cousins. Distinctive criteria: affinal; one generation removed; collateral; between men.

NOTES

[1] As a geographical designation, Zamboanga refers to the
area included in the political units of Misamis Occidental Province,
Zamboanga del Norte Province, Zamboanga del Sur Province, and
Zamboanga City.

[2] This term is now established in the literature (see Conklin
1957: 1). In most areas, Subanun agriculture is of the type which
Conklin calls "integral swidden farming" (Frake 1955).

[3] See Christie 1909: 17-32; Combés 1667; Finley and Churchill
1912: 8-15; Forrest 1779: 327.

[4] Based on field work among the Subanun in 1953-54 and 1957-
58 financed by grants from the United States Government (under the
Fulbright Act) and the Yale University Southeast Asia Studies Program
The data, especially all linguistic forms cited, pertain specifically to
a group of about 500 Eastern Subanun inhabiting the area drained by
the upper Disakan, Muyu, and Duhinob (duinid) rivers in north-central
Zamboanga del Norte, but surveys made in other areas indicate that
the analysis presented herewith is generally applicable to the Eastern
Subanun as a whole.

[5] Discrete social groups are those that divide a population in
such a way that if individual A belongs to the same group as B, and B
belongs to the same group as C, then A and C belong to the same
group. Discrete groups are mutually exclusive; every individual belongs to one and only one group of the same kind. Lineages, army
platoons, and Hindu castes are examples of discrete groups. Non-
discrete groups, in contrast, divide a population in such a way that
one cannot predict common membership of A and C in a group from
the fact that A and B belong to one group and that B and C belong to
one group. Friendship groups are usually non-discrete; that Joe and
Bill are friends, and that Bill and Tom are friends, does not imply
that Joe and Tom are friends. Other examples of non-discrete groups
include bilateral kindreds and suburban neighborhoods.

[6] Conklin 1951; Schneider ahd Homans 1955; Naroll 1958;
Koentjaraningrat 1957.

[7] It should be noted that the family exhibits independence in
many spheres not discussed here, e.g. in trade with lowlanders
(Frake 1957b) and in attending to life-crisis events.

REFERENCES

Christie, E. B. 1909. The Subanuns of Sindangan Bay. Philippine
Bureau of Science Division of Ethnology Publications 6.1-121.
Combés, F. 1667. Historia de las islas de Mindanao, Iolo. y sus
adyacentes. Madrid. New edition, Madrid, 1897.
Conklin, H. C. 1951. Co-existing sets of relationship terms among
the Tanay Tagalog. Unpublished ms.
_____. 1957. Hanunóo agriculture. Food and Agricultural Organ-
ization of the United Nations, Forestry Development Papers
12.1-209. Rome.
Finley, J. P., and W. Churchill. 1913. The Subanu. Carnegie Institution of Washington Publications 184.1-236.
Forrest, T. 1779. A voyage to New Guinea. London.
Frake, C. O. 1955. Social organization and shifting cultivation
among the Sindangan Subanun. Unpublished dissertation,
Yale University.
_____. 1956. Malayo-Polynesian land tenure. American Anthro-
pologist 58.170-73.
_____. 1957a. Litigation in Lipay. Proceedings of the Ninth
Pacific Science Congress (in press). Bangkok.
_____. 1957b. Sindangan social groups. Philippine Sociological
Review 5.ii.2-11.
_____. 2957c. The Subanun of Zamboanga: a linguistic survey.
Proceedings of the Ninth Pacific Science Congress (in press).
Bangkok.
Freeman, J. D. 1958. The family system of the Iban of Borneo.
Cambridge Papers in Social Anthropology 1.15-52.
Goodenough, W. H. 1955. A problem in Malayo-Polynesian social
organization. American Anthropologist 57.71-83.
Koentjaraningrat, R. M. 1957. A preliminary description of the
Javanese kinship system. New Haven.
Kroeber, A. L. 1919. Kinship in the Philippines. Anthropological
Papers of the American Museum of Natural History 19.69-84.
Murdock, G. P. 1949. Social structure. New York.
Naroll, R. 1958. German kinship terms. American Anthropologist
60.750-55.
Schneider, D. M., and G. C. Homans. 1955. Kinship terminology
and the American kinship system. American Anthropologist
57.1194-1208.

7 | The Diagnosis of Disease among the Subanun of Mindanao

Although my original field work among the Eastern Subanun, a pagan people of the southern Philippines, was focused on a study of social structure, I found it exceedingly difficult to participate in ordin-ary conversations, or even elicit information within the setting of such conversations, without having mastered the use of terminologies in several fields, notably folk botany and folk medicine, in which I initially had only marginal interest. Effective use of Subanun botanical and medical terminologies required more knowledge of verbal behavior than linguists typically include in their conception of a structural description. To generate utterances which were grammatical (Chomsky 1957: 13-17) but not necessarily meaningful or congruent (Joos 1958 did not suffice. Yet descriptive linguistics provides no methods for deriving rules that generate statements which are semantically as well as grammatically acceptable. Having acquired only an unsystematic and intuitive "feel" for the use of certain portions of the Subanun lexi-con during a first field study, I attempted during a second study a more rigorous search for meanings. This investigation became a major focus of my field work. Presented here is a partial analysis of one of the less numerous terminologies: 186 'disease names.' (Single quotation marks enclose glosses, English labels which substitute for, but do not define, Subanun terms.)[1]

The Subanun

Some 50,000 Eastern Subanun inhabit the eastern portion of Zamboanga Peninsula, a 130-mile-long extension of the island of Mindanao in the Philippines. Most of this population practices swidden farming in the mountainous interior of the peninsula, leaving the coasts to Christian immigrants of recent decades from the Bisayan Islands to the north. Prior to this century the coasts were controlled, and sporadically occupied, by Philippine Moslems, who established an exploitative hegemony over the pagan Subanun in certain locales (Christie 1909; Frake 1957b).

In terms of segmentation and stratification, Subanun society displays remarkable simplicity. Each nuclear family is the focus of a partially unique and variable network of social ties with kin and neighbors which constitutes, for that family, the "total society." This maximal, non-discrete, sphere of social relationships has no corporate organization and is not segmented into lineages, age-sets, secret societies, territorial districts, political factions, or the like. Despite this simplicity of their social structure, the Subanun carry on constant and elaborate interfamily social activities: litigation, offerings, feasts—all well lubricated with ample quantities of rice wine. Warfare is lacking (Frake 1961).

All Subanun are full-time farmers. Special statuses are few in number, filled by achievement rather than ascription, restricted in domain, and limited in economic rewards. The status of legal authority has been discussed elsewhere (Frake 1957a). In the sphere of making decisions about disease, differences in individual skill and knowledge receive recognition, but there is no formal status of diagnostician or even, by Subanun conception, of curer. Everyone is his own 'herbalist' (memulun). There are religious specialists, 'mediums' (belian), whose job it is to maintain communications with the very important supernatural constituents of the Subanun universe. Mediums hold curing ceremonies, but the gods effect the cure. They make possible verbal communication with the supernaturals, but again the information received comes from the gods. The medium is but a channel for the divine message.

A consideration of disease etiology, together with etiologically derived therapy, would require extended discussion of Subanun relations with the supernatural world. In limiting ourselves to diagnosis, on the other hand, we can largely ignore information derived from very noisy, supernaturally produced signals.

Disease Concepts

"Am I sick?" "What kind of disease do I have?" "What are my chances?" "What caused this disease?" "Why did it happen to me (of all people)?" Illness evokes questions such as these among patients the world over. Every culture provides a set of significant questions, potential answers, and procedures for arriving at answers. The cultural answers to these questions are concepts of disease. The information necessary to arrive at a specific answer and eliminate others is the meaning of a disease concept.

The Subanun patient, no matter how minor his illness, rarely depends upon introspection to answer these questions. He solicits the readily proffered judgment and advice of kin, neighbors, friends, specialists, deities, and ethnographers. Sickness comprises the third most frequent topic of casual conversation (after litigation and folk botany) among Subanun of my acquaintance, and it furnishes the overwhelmingly predominant subject of formal interviews with the supernaturals.

Because disease is not only suffered and treated, but also talked about, disease concepts are verbally labeled and readily communicable. Their continual exposure to discussions of sickness facilitates the learning of disease concepts by all Subanun. Subanun medical lore and medical jargon are not esoteric subjects; even a child can distinguish buni from buyayag—two fungous skin infections not, to my knowledge, differentiated by Western medical science—and state the reasons for his decision.

This corpus of continually emitted and readily elicitable verbal behavior about disease provides our evidence for the existence and meaning of culturally defined disease concepts. We begin with actual disease cases—instances of 'being sick' (miglaru) by Subanun identification. We note the kinds of questions the Subanun ask about these cases, we record the alternative (or contrasting) replies to each kind of question, and then we seek to differentiate the factors by which a Subanun decides one reply, rather than an alternative, applies in a particular situation.

Among the questions evoked by a disease case, there invariably appears one of a set of utterances which demands a 'disease name' (ŋalan mesait en) in response. Answering a question with a 'disease name' is diagnosis. Subanun diagnosis is the procedure of judging similarities and differences among instances of 'being sick, ' placing new instances into culturally defined and linguistically labeled categories. Diagnostic decisions pertain to the selection of 'medicinal' (kebuluŋan) therapy, to prognosis, and to the assumption of an appropriate sick role by the patient. They do not answer, nor depend upon, the crucial etiological questions that guide the search for 'ritual' (kanu) therapy in severe and refractory cases. The Subanun thus discriminate among the various constellations of disease symptoms and react differentially to them. They diagnose kinds of disease.

Disease Names

The fundamental unit of Subanun diagnosis is the diagnostic category (or "disease") labeled by a 'disease name.' Whereas an illness is a single instance of 'being sick, ' a diagnostic category is a conceptual entity which classifies particular illnesses, symptomatic or pathogenic components of illness, or stages of illness. The course of an illness through time and its symptomatic components at any one time do not always fit into a single diagnostic category. Consequently, a single illness may successively or simultaneously require designation by several disease names.

Although not all illnesses can be diagnosed by a single disease name, every disease name can diagnose a single illness. Disease names thus differ from designations of kinds of symptoms, such as 'itch' (matel), or kinds of pathogenic agents, such as 'plant floss' (glaŋis), which do not function as diagnostic labels for illnesses.

The question "What kind of illness is that?" (dita? gleruun ai run ma iin) will always elicit a diagnostic description. Actually, however, a Subanun rarely states this question explicitly; rather he implies it when making an assertion such as "I feel sick" (what do you think is wrong with me?); "You look sick" (what is the matter with you?); "I hear he's sick" (do you know what he's got?). When

accompanied by the proper intonation and inserted particles to express
worried concern, such utterances invariably stimulate diagnostic discussions resulting in a consensual linguistic description of a particular illness.

If none of the linguistic components of a description of an illness can by itself describe a disease case, then the description as a
whole constitutes a disease name, labeling a single diagnostic category. Thus the description mesait gulu 'headache' labels a single
diagnostic category, for neither mesait 'pain' nor gulu 'head' can alon
diagnose an illness. On the other hand, the description mesait gulu
bu? mesait tian 'headache and stomach ache' constitutes two diagnostic categories because each component can itself serve as a description of an illness. A single disease name is a minimal utterance that
can answer the query "What kind of illness is that?"

At the most specific level of contrast (see below), we have
recorded 186 human disease names (apart from referential synonyms),
and the productivity of Subanun disease terminology permits the formation of an indefinite number of additional names. For example, we
never recorded mesait kulenkay 'little-finger pain' as a disease name,
but should a Subanun find occasion to communicate such a concept he
could unambiguously do so by constructing this label.

Standard descriptive phrases of the productive (polylexemic)
type, such as mesait tian 'stomach ache' and menebag gatay 'swollen
liver,' label a number of common ailments. A few other disease
names, which one might call "suggestive" rather than "descriptive,"
have constituents not productive in the formation of new disease names
for example, the derivative penabud 'splotchy itch' < sabud 'to scatter
as chicken feed.' There remain 132 diagnostic categories which possess unique, single-word labels. The Subanun must consequently rote
learn unique and distinctive labels for the vast majority of his disease
a situation paralleled even more markedly in the botanical lexicon of
well over one thousand items. The fact that all Subanun do, in fact,
learn to use such a copious vocabulary of disease and plant terms with
great facility reflects the prominent place of these terminologies in
daily conversation.

Levels of Contrast

In a given diagnostic situation, a Subanun must select one disease name out of a set of contrasting alternatives as appropriately categorizing a given set of symptoms. Before considering his criteria of selection, we must determine which disease categories, in fact, contrast with each other. Two disease names contrast if only one can correctly diagnose a particular set of symptoms. (We consider later the question of disagreement about "correctness.") A particular illness may require the diagnoses of more than one set of symptoms for complete description, as with the case of 'being sick' with both a 'headache' and a 'stomach ache.' In such cases the linguistic construction with 'and' (bu?) makes it clear that the illness comprises a conjunction of two contrasting diagnostic categories. With reference to the set of symptoms of pains in the head, only one of the contrasting responses is applicable. Any difficulties caused by conjunctive descriptions of illnesses can be obviated by taking evidence for contrast only from illnesses described by a single disease name.

When the same set of symptoms elicits different single-disease-name responses, and informants consider each response to be correct, two things may be responsible. The disease names may be referential synonyms; i.e. the categories they designate are mutually inclusive or equivalent. This happens when, for example, the terms are dialect variants or variants appropriate to different kinds of discourse, such as casual as opposed to formal speech. The second possibility, and the one that concerns us here, is that one category totally includes another; it is superordinate and operates at a less specific level of contrast.

An example from English illustrates the meaning of levels of contrast. If we confront English-speaking informants with a dog, say a poodle, and collect designations applicable to it, we would eventually have a corpus of words such as poodle, dog, animal, and (from the zoologically sophisticated) canine, mammal, vertebrate. Since all of these words correctly designate the same object, they do not contrast at the same level. Neither are they referential synonyms, for whereas all poodles are dogs, the converse is not true. The category "dog" totally includes the category "poodle." A poodle is a kind of dog, a dog a kind of mammal, a mammal a kind of vertebrate, and so on. Arranging classes by inclusion produces a hierarchy of levels, each ascending level being less specific and including more than its predecessor.

Now suppose, still pointing to a poodle, we ask our (zoologically unsophisticated) informants the following questions:

1. "Is it a plant?"
2. "Is it a cat?"
3. "Is it a collie?"

The responses are, respectively:

1. "No, it's an animal."
2. "No, it's a dog."
3. "No, it's a poodle."

Animal thus contrasts with plant, dog with cat, and poodle with collie.

ANIMAL—contrasts with—PLANT

DOG—contrasts with—CAT (dog and cat are kinds of animals)

POODLE—contrasts with—COLLIE (poodle and collie are kinds of dog)

We could, of course, elicit many more contrasts at each level, and, working with zoologists or dog lovers as informants, we could isolate additional levels.

A taxonomic hierarchy comprises different sets of contrasting categories at successive levels, the categories at any one level being included in a category at the next higher level. Taxonomies divide phenomena into two dimensions: a horizontal one of discrimination (poodle, collie, terrier) and a vertical one of generalization (poodle, dog, animal).

The importance of recognizing levels of contrast in Subanun disease nomenclature first became apparent when, early in the field work, I had an infectious swelling on my leg. I asked all visitors for

the name of my ailment and received a variety of different answers
(all single disease names) from different people or even from the
same people on different occasions. Subanun disease naming seemed
to be an inconsistent and unpredictable jumble. Further interrogation,
together with closer attention to the sociolinguistic contexts of responses, soon made it clear that all respondents were right; they were just
talking at different levels of contrast. Some—especially those who
wished to avoid a detailed medical discussion of my ills in favor of
another subject—were simply telling me I had a 'skin disease' (nuka)
and not another kind of external disease. Othere were informing me
that I had an 'inflammation' (meŋebag) and not some other 'skin disease.' Still others —habitual taxonomic hair-splitters and those who
had therapeutic recommendations in mind—were diagnosing the case
as 'inflamed quasi bite' (pagid) and not some other kind of 'inflammation.'

Figure 1 diagrams the taxonomic structure of a portion of the
twenty-nine specific 'skin disease' (nuka) categories. Superordinate
categories stand above their subordinates. A given category contrasts
with another category at the level at which the two share an upper horizontal boundary not crossed by a vertical boundary. Any case, for
example, diagnosed as telemaw glai 'shallow distal ulcer' can also be
labeled telemaw 'distal ulcer,' beldut 'sore,' or nuka 'skin disease'
depending on the contrastive context. If, pointing to a 'shallow distal
ulcer,' one asks:

1. Is it a telemaw glibun ('deep distal ulcer')?
2. Is it a baga? ('proximal ulcer')?
3. Is it a meŋebag ('inflammation')?
4. Is it a samad ('wound')?

The predictable responses are, respectively:

1. No, it's a telemaw glai ('shallow distal ulcer').
2. No, it's a telemaw ('distal ulcer').
3. No, it's a beldut ('sore').
4. No, it's a nuka ('skin disease').

The clearest examples of different levels of contrast appear
when a disease category subdivides into "varieties." Systemic con-

samad 'wound'	nuka 'skin disease'												
	menebag 'inflammation'				beldut 'sore'						buni 'ringworm'		
					telemaw 'distal ulcer'		baga? 'proximal ulcer'						
pugu 'rash'	nuka 'eruption'	pagid 'inflamed quasi bite'	bekukan 'ulcerated inflammation'	menebag 'inflamed wound'	telemaw glai 'shallow distal ulcer'	telemaw glibun 'deep distal ulcer'	baga? 'shallow proximal ulcer'	begwak 'deep proximal ulcer'	beldut 'simple sore'	selimbunut 'spreading sore'	buyayag 'exposed ringworm'	buni 'hidden ringworm'	bugais 'spreading itch'

Fig. 1. Levels of contrast in 'skin disease' terminology

ditions producing discolored urine, for example, known generally as glegbay, have 'red' (glegbay gempula) and 'white' (glegbay gemputi?) subcategories. The 'distal ulcer' telemaw subdivides into telemaw glai 'male (i.e. shallow) ulcer' and telemaw glibun 'female (i.e. deep ulcer.' Although in these examples, subordinate levels of contrast are indicated by attaching attributes to superordinate disease names, such linguistic constructions are not necessarily evidence of inclusion Thus beldut pesui 'sty,' literally 'chick sore,' is not a kind of beldut 'sore' but a kind of 'eye disease' (mesait mata). It is the way linguistic labels are applied to phenomena and not the linguistic structure of those labels that points to levels of contrast.

As a matter of fact, when we systematically investigate the contrasts of each Subanun disease term, we find a number of cases in which the same linguistic form appears at different levels of contrast. The term nuka 'skin disease,' for example, not only denotes a general category of ailments which includes conditions like baga? 'ulcer,' but it also denotes a specific kind of skin condition, a mild 'eruption' that contrasts with baga? (see Figure 1). In all such cases, if the context (especially the eliciting utterance) does not make the level of contrast clear, respondents can indicate the more specific of two levels by means of optional particles; e.g. tantu nuka 'real nuka,' i.e. 'eruption,' not any 'skin disease.'

The use of the same linguistic form at different levels of contrast, while a source of confusion until one attends to the total context in which a term is used, should not surprise us. It is common enough in English. The word man, for example, designates at one level a category contrasting with non-human organisms. At a more specific level, man designates a subcategory of human organisms contrasting with woman. Subordinate to this we find the contrast: man (adult male) —boy. Man can even appear at a still more specific level to designate a kind of adult male human, as in Kipling's "... you'll be a man, my son."

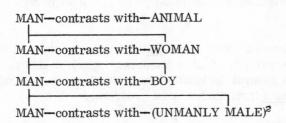

MAN—contrasts with—ANIMAL

MAN—contrasts with—WOMAN

MAN—contrasts with—BOY

MAN—contrasts with—(UNMANLY MALE)?

This use of single forms at several levels of contrast seems particularly characteristic of Subanun disease terminology. It appears elsewhere as well, in botanical nomenclature and kinship terminology for instance, but not so extensively. The reasons for its use in disease terminology become, in part, explicable when we consider the use of disease names to designate sequential stages of illness.

The changing and unpredictable course of disease symptoms considerably complicates diagnosis. Of course other phenomena also change. A plant, passing from seedling to mature tree, changes radically in appearance. But a seedling of one kind invariably produces a mature plant of the same kind. A papaya seedling never grows into a mango tree. Consequently, the members of a plant category can be identified at any stage of growth, and terminological distinctions of growth stages do not affect classifications of kinds of plants. Given an illness at a particular stage of development, on the other hand, its symptoms may proceed along a variety of different courses or it may heal altogether. Just as one illness sometimes requires several disease names for complete description at any one time, so its course over time may pass through several distinct diagnostic categories.

Every disease name designates a potential terminal stage: a stage of 'being sick' immediately preceding 'cure' (or 'recuperation') or 'death.' But some disease stages, potentially terminal, may also be prodromal stages of other terminal diagnostic categories. This situation occurs especially among the skin diseases. Each sequential stage leading to an ulcer or an itchy skin disease is, in itself, a potential terminal stage designated by a disease name. A case of nuka 'eruption,' for example, sometimes heals without complication; at other times it eventually develops into one of 23 more serious diseases Consequently, nuka not only designates a terminal disease category but also designates a stage of development in a variety of other diseases.

Figure 2 shows that nuka is the pivotal stage in the development of the majority of 'skin diseases.' And it is this term that also serves as a general designation for 'skin diseases,' including some for which nuka 'eruption' is not a prodrome.

The term nuka thus has three uses:

1. As a general designation for 'skin disease,' applicable to any skin disease at any stage of development;
2. To designate a prior stage of some, but not all, 'skin diseases';
3. To label a terminal diagnostic category, 'eruption,' which contrasts with other 'skin disease' categories.

The reader will find further examples of multiple semantic uses of single linguistic forms by comparing Figures 1 and 2.

Subanun disease terminology well illustrates the proviso, often stated but rarely followed through in semantic analysis, that the meaning of a linguistic form is a function of the total situation, linguis-

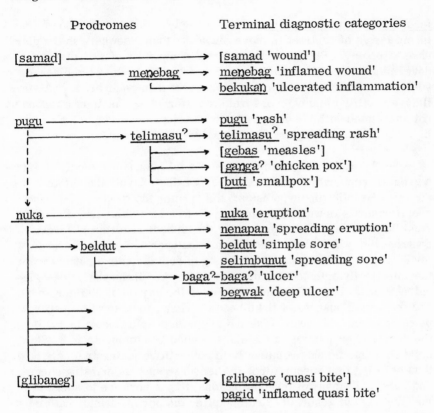

Fig. 2. Skin disease stages. Only a few of the diseases arising from
nuka 'eruption' are shown. Diseases enclosed in brackets are not
classifiable as nuka 'skin disease.'

tic and non-linguistic, in which the form is used. Essentially it is a
matter of determining with what a term contrasts in a particular situation. When someone says, "This is an x," what is he saying it is
not? (cf. Kelly 1955: 59-64).

Figures 1 and 2 reveal a partial relation between levels of
contrast and stages of development in 'skin disease' terminology.
Among 'skin diseases,' where the course of development through dif-

ferent diagnostic categories is most complex, the segregation of different levels of contrast is more elaborate than elsewhere in the disease taxonomy. But the terminological complexity of skin disease development does not suffice to explain why this area of the disease vocabulary exhibits more levels of contrast than other areas. A similar variability of number of levels in different segments of a taxonomy, not correlated with the designation of developmental stages, also occurs in botanical and zoological nomenclature.

To explain why some areas of a folk taxonomy subdivide into a greater number of superordinate-subordinate levels than others, we advance the following hypothesis: the greater the number of distinct social contexts in which information about a particular phenomenon must be communicated, the greater the number of different levels of contrast into which that phenomenon is categorized. Skin diseases, for example, enter into a wide variety of social contexts, apart from therapeutically oriented discussions. They can influence bride-price calculations. Here, the concern is over the degree of disfigurement and the contagiousness of the disease. They can be used to justify, perhaps to one's spouse, a failure to perform an expected task. Here the disabling properties of the disease must be communicated. Skin disease terms figure prominently in competitive joking and maligning, thus entering into special kinds of discourse such as drinking songs and verse. In many of these situations it is imperative to speak at just the level of generality that specifies the pertinent information but leaves other, possibly embarrassing, information ambiguous.

The same hypothesis should hold cross-culturally. If the botanical taxonomy of tribe A has more levels of contrast than that of tribe B, it means that the members of tribe A communicate botanical information in a wider variety of sociocultural settings. It does not mean that people in tribe A have greater powers of "abstract thinking." As a matter of fact it says nothing about general differences in cognition, for when it comes to fish, tribe B may reveal the greater number of levels of contrast.

Folk taxonomies are cultural phenomena. Their structural variation within and between cultures must be explained by the cultural uses to which a taxonomy is put, and not by appeal to differences in the cognitive powers of individual minds (cf. Brown 1958: 284-85).

Diagnostic Criteria

A 'disease name,' it will be recalled, is a minimal, congruent (i. e. meaningful) answer to the question "What kind of illness is that? (dita? gleruun ai run ma iin)." Alternatively, it is a congruent insertion in the frame "The name of (his) disease is _____. (ŋalan en ig mesait en _____)." Since different illnesses, that is, different instances of 'being sick' (miglaru), may elicit the same disease-name response, a disease name labels a class of illnesses: a diagnostic category.

Given a set of contrasting disease names, the problem remains of determining the rules which govern the assigning of one name rather than another in a particular diagnostic situation. Rules of use may be analytic, perceptual, or explicit in derivation.

Analytic derivation of meanings ideally yields distinctive features: necessary and sufficient conditions by which an investigator can determine whether a newly encountered instance is or is not a member of a particular category. The procedure requires an independent, etic (Pike 1954: 8) way of coding recorded instances of a category. Examples are the "phone types" of linguistics and the "kin types" of kinship analysis (Lounsbury 1956: 191-92). The investigator classifies his data into types of his own formulation, then compares "types" as though they were instances of a concept. From information already coded in the definitions of his "types," he derives the necessary and sufficient conditions of class membership. Thus, by comparing the kin types of English "uncle" (FaBr, MoBr, FaSiHu, etc.) with the kin types in every other English kin category, the analyst finds that by scoring "uncle" for features along four dimensions of contrast (affinity,[3] collaterality, generation, and sex) he can state succinctly how "uncles" differ from every other category of kinsmen. The definition of "uncle" as "non-affinal, first-degree collateral, ascending generation male" suffices to enable an investigator to predict whether any new kin type he encounters (such as FaMoSiHu) is or is not an uncle. This is not, however, the same thing as a definition which states how people in the society, in fact, categorize persons as "uncles" (Wallace and Atkins 1960: 75-79). (When analytically derived features are probabilistically, rather than necessarily and sufficiently, associated with category membership, then we may speak of correlates rather than of distinctive features. A correlate of the uncle-nephew relation is that uncles are usually, but not necessarily, older than their nephews.)

    To arrive at rules of use one can also direct attention to the actual stimulus discriminations made by informants when categorizing. What perceptual information enables one to distinguish an oak tree from a maple tree, a cold from the flu? Perceptual attributes relevant to categorization, whether distinctive or probabilistic, are cues. Discovering cues in ethnographic settings requires as yet largely unformulated procedures of perceptual testing that do not replace the culturally relevant stimuli with artificial laboratory stimuli (cf. Conklin 1955: 342).

    Finally, one can simply ask his informants about meanings: "What is an uncle?" "How do you know he is an uncle and not a father?" Such procedures yield the culture's explicit definitions or criteria of categories (cf. Bruner's 1956: 30 "defining attributes" and Wittgenstein's 1958: 24-25 use of "criteria" and "symptoms," the former being distinctive, the latter probabilistic).

    These different procedures for determining rules of use are not equally applicable to every system of contrasting categories. Distinctive feature analysis becomes impractical without an economical, minimally redundant, and highly specific etic coding device. Explicit criteria may be lacking or highly inconsistent where category discriminations and decisions do not require verbal description. In some cases, consistent criteria may be present, yet provide an unsatisfactory description of behavior: compare the inutility of seeking informants' explanations in certain tasks of formal linguistic analysis. Yet there are categories—like those pertaining to supernatural phenomena—which are known only through verbal descriptions by informants. The difference between a 'deity' (diwata) and a 'goblin' (menemad) can only be what my informants tell me it is.

    Our choice of procedures for arriving at meanings of disease names is, in part, a function of the kind of category such names label, and, in part, of the kind of field data we succeeded in obtaining about diagnostic behavior.

Distinctive-feature analysis is ruled out on both counts. The
preliminary denotative definitions would require a listing of illnesses
assigned to each disease category in recorded diagnoses. The only
meaningful etic units available for such a list are the diagnostic categories of Western medicine. Practical and methodological problems
prevent their use. We had neither facilities nor personnel to make
competent Western diagnoses of all disease cases we observed. Yet,
as useful as such information would be for many other purposes, it
would, in fact, prove of little help in defining Subanun diagnostic categories. For one thing, too few illnesses actually occurred during our
stay in the field to sample adequately a sufficient proportion of Subanun
diagnostic categories. Moreover, even if one could match each Subanun diagnostic category with a series of Western diagnoses, the latter
would still provide very deficient etic types. We cannot assume, as
we can when working with phone types or kin types, that every Western
diagnostic category will be totally included by some Subanun category.
Every case diagnosed by Western criteria as tuberculosis will not receive the same Subanun diagnosis. Furthermore, a Subanun category
such as peglekebuun 'chronic cough,' which sometimes matches with
tuberculosis, will not always do so. The criteria and cues of the two
diagnostic systems are too disparate for one-to-one or one-to-many
matching. The problems presented to the analyst by this overlapping
of categories in the two systems are compounded by the superabundance
of information encoded in a Western diagnostic category. Knowing only
that Subanun disease X partially matched Western diagnostic categories a, b, c, and that Subanun disease Y partially matched Western categories d and e, one could not easily extract from medical knowledge
about a, b, c, d, and e distinctive features defining the contrast between X and Y. For all of these reasons, distinctive-feature analysis
from lists of matched native and scientific names is not feasible for
folk taxonomies of disease nor, for that matter, of plants, animals,
and most other natural phenomena as well.

Inadequacies of our data largely prevent confident definition
of Subanun diagnostic categories by distinctive stimulus attributes, or
cues, of illnesses. The discovery of what cue discriminations informants are making when contrasting one disease with another is exceedingly difficult. Many apparently pertinent cues, such as the ones that
enable a Subanun patient to distinguish 'headache' (mesait gulu) from
'migraine' (tampiak) are known only by verbal descriptions. A disease

"entity" such as 'headache' is not something that can be pointed to,
nor can exemplars of diseases ordinarily be brought together for visual
comparison and contrast as can, say, two plants. Moreover, situation-
al features other than stimulus attributes of the illness bear on the
final diagnostic decision. The same degree of pain, if objectively measured, could probably lead to a diagnosis of either 'headache' or 'migraine' depending on current social or ecological role demands on the
patient. Nevertheless, very few diagnostic decisions are made by the
Subanun without some apparent appeal to stimulus properties of illness;
and in the majority of diagnoses these are the overriding considerations.

It is difficult, then, to define Subanun diagnostic categories in
terms of analytic or perceptual attributes of their denotata. On the
other hand, these very difficulties facilitate recognition of diagnostic
criteria: explicit defining attributes of disease categories. Since one
cannot point to a disease entity and say "That's a such and such, " as
one can with a plant specimen, and since no one individual ever personally experiences but a fraction of the total number of diseases he
can, in fact, differentiate, the Subanun themselves must learn to diagnose diseases through verbal description of their significant attributes.
It is thus relatively easy for a Subanun to describe precisely what
makes one disease different from another. He can tell us, for example
that the ulcer begwak produces a marked cavity, unlike the ulcer baga?.
He can describe the difference in appearance between glepap 'plaque
itch' and penabud 'splotchy itch, ' the difference in locale between the
'ringworms' buni and buyayag, the difference in pathogenesis between
menebag, an 'inflamed wound, ' and beldut, a spontaneous 'sore.' This
is not to say that the evaluation of the cues of a particular illness as
exemplars of diagnostic criteria is always easy or consistent. Informants operating with identical diagnostic concepts may disagree about
the application of these concepts in a particular case, but they rarely
disagree in their verbal definitions of the concepts themselves.

The procedures for eliciting and analyzing diagnostic criteria
parallel those used to determine the system of nomenclature: we collect contrasting answers to the questions the Subanun ask when diagnosing disease. By asking informants to describe differences between
diseases, by asking why particular illnesses are diagnosed as such
and such and not something else, by following discussions among the
Subanun themselves when diagnosing cases, and by noting corrections

made of our own diagnostic efforts, we can isolate a limited number
of diagnostic questions and criterial answers.

A classification of Subanun diagnostic criteria follows from
(1) the questions which elicit them and (2) the status of the answers as
diagnostic labels.

    1. By eliciting question
        1.1. Pathogenic criteria
        1.2. Prodromal criteria
        1.3. Symptomatic criteria
        1.4. Etiological criteria
    2. By status of the answer as a diagnostic label
        2.1. Elementary criteria
        2.2. Complex criteria

    1.1. Pathogenic criteria are diagnostically significant respon-
ses to questions of 'pathogenesis' (meksamet), which is different from
'etiology' (melabet). 'Pathogenesis' refers to the agent or mechanism
that produces or aggravates an illness, 'etiology' to the circumstances
that lead a particular patient to contract an illness. Thirty-four elementary diagnostic categories require pathogenic information for diagnosis. Examples are 'wound' (samad), 'burn' (pasu?), 'intestinal
worm' (bulilan), 'skin worm' (tayeb), 'pinworm' (glelugay), 'exposure
sickness' (pasemu⁴). In such cases, where the identification of a pathogen is criterial to diagnosis, the association between the pathogen
and the illness is relatively obvious both to the investigator and to his
informants.

    In addition, the Subanun posit the existence of many pathogens
—such as 'plant floss' (glanis), 'microscopic mites' (kamu), 'intrusive
objects' (meneled), 'symbolic acts' (pelii), 'stress' (pegendekan),
'soul loss' (panaw i gimuud)—which are not diagnostically criterial.
These non-criterial pathogens, whose presence generally must be
determined independently of diagnosis, provide clues in the search
for etiological circumstances and serve as guides to prophylactic measures. But standard, named pathogens, whether criterial or not, have
a limited range of pertinence. In the cognitive decisions occasioned
by an illness, pathogenic mechanisms are significant only when they
are necessary appurtenances to diagnosis or to etiological explanations.

Otherwise they are of little interest. Like Western physicians, the
Subanun do not know the pathogenic agents of many of their diseases,
but, unlike the former, the Subanun consider this lack of knowledge to
be of trivial rather than of crucial therapeutic significance. Consequently a large number of Subanun diseases lack standard pathogenic
explanations, and many disease cases go by without any effort (except
by the ethnographer) to elicit them from consultants or supernaturals.

1.2. Prodromal criteria are diagnostically significant responses to questions of the origin or 'prodrome' (puunan en) of a given illness, the 'prodrome' always referring to a prior and diagnostically
distinct condition. A derivative disease is one whose diagnosis depends
on its having a specified prodrome. When referring to a derivative
disease, a query about its prodrome must be answered by another disease name, previously applicable to the illness. A spontaneous disease, in contrast, is one for which the response to a query about pro-
dromes can be 'there is no prodrome' (nda? ig puunan en).

Figure 2 shows a number of illnesses whose diagnoses depend
on their having passed through specific other stages. One canot have
begwak 'deep ulcer' unless one has previously, as part of the same
'illness,' had nuka 'eruption,' beldut 'sore,' and baga? 'ulcer,' in
that order. 'Eruption' (nuka), on the other hand, need have no prodrome, though it sometimes begins as 'rash' (pugu). The latter disease is always spontaneous.

For any derivative disease, a given prodrome is a necessary
but not a sufficient diagnostic criterion. If the evidence of other criteria overwhelmingly points to a contrary diagnosis, one must conclude—since the criteriality of the prodrome cannot be discounted—
that the previous diagnosis, or current information about it, is erroneous. Thus an informant insisted that an inflammation on my leg was
an inflamed insect bite (pagid) rather than an inflamed wound (tantu
meŋebag), even though I had told him I thought it originated as a 'minor
cut.' I simply, according to him, had not noticed the prodromal bite.
In such cases the existence of the prodrome is deduced from its criteriality to a diagnosis actually arrived at on other grounds. Our data
would have been much improved had we earlier recognized the importance of these ex post facto classificatory decisions as evidence of
criteriality.

1. 3. Symptomatic criteria are diagnostically significant responses to a variety of questions about the attributes of an illness
currently perceptible to patient or observer. These are the most
frequent, wide-ranging, and complex of diagnostic criteria. Our data
are not, in fact, complete enough to list, or even to enumerate, all
the questions, with all their contrasting responses, necessary to define in explicit Subanun terms the symptomatic differences among all
disease categories. Moreover, we can present here, in analyzed
form, only a small proportion of the data we do have.

To exemplify symptomatic criteria we shall discuss several
major questions that occur repeatedly in the diagnosis of a variety of
illnesses; then we shall illustrate how these and other criterial contrasts intersect to define a segment of skin disease terminology.

Specifications of locale along several dimensions provide
fundamental criteria of Subanun diagnosis, closely relating to selection of appropriate therapeutic measures, to prognostic judgment,
and to the evaluation of the disabling potential of an illness. First of
all, disease symptoms can be located along a dimension of depth or
penetration with two basic contrasts: 'external' (dibabaw) and 'internal' (dialem), depending on the presence or absence of visible lesions
on the surface of the body. An external disease may penetrate to
produce internal symptoms as well as external lesions, in which case
the disease has 'sunk' (milegdaŋ). Rarely, a disease may penetrate
to the other side of the body producing 'balancing' (mitimpaŋ) or
'pierced' (milapus) lesions. Penetration is prognostic of seriousness;
the therapy of a number of skin diseases aims at preventing 'sinking.'

Those diseases which may be pinpointed anatomically (in
Subanun terms, of course) are localized diseases. Should an initially
localized condition begin to spread to adjacent areas within the same
penetration level, then it will often fall into a new and distinct disease
category. The distinction between circumscribed and spreading conditions pertains especially to external lesions. If a 'sore' (beldut)
becomes multilesional (misarak), it is no longer beldut, but selim-
bunut 'spreading sore.' Other diseases for which spreading is an
important diagnostic criterion are 'spreading rash' (telimasuʔ),
'spreading eruption' (nenapan), 'yaws' (buketaw), and 'spreading itch'
(bugais). The Subanun describe an external condition that covers all

or most of the body surface as mipugus or miluup, the latter term
also designating a completely dibbled rice field.

Degree of penetration and spreading correlate closely with
prognostic severity, hence their diagnostic importance. Distinctions
of specific locales seem to reflect in part the disabling potential of a
disease. Thus, lesions on the hands and feet often receive different
designations from similar lesions elsewhere on the body; compare
baga? 'proximal ulcer' with telemaw 'distal ulcer.' Among itchy skin
diseases which seldom cause severe discomfort, distinctions of locale
correspond with unsightliness. Thus the Subanun, who regard these
diseases as extremely disfiguring, distinguish lesions hidden by cloth-
ing from those visible on a clothed body: compare buni 'hidden ringworm' with buyayag 'exposed ringworm.'

Specifications of interior locales usually refer to the area
below an external reference point: the 'head,' 'chest,' xiphoid,' 'side,'
'waist,' 'abdomen,' and so on. The only internal organs commonly
named as disease locales are the 'liver' and the 'spleen.' The liver
in Subanun anatomical conceptions is somewhat akin to the heart in
popular Western notions. (We recorded no Subanun diseases attributed
to the heart.) The choice of the spleen as a disease locale seems to
represent an instance of Subanun medical acumen. The term for spleen
nalip (identified during dissections of pigs), names a disease characterized by externally visible or palpable swelling attributed to this
organ. The Subanun regard nalip as a complication of actual or latent
malaria (taig). In Western medicine, an enlarged spleen (splenomegaly)
may indicate malaria infection (Shattuck 1951: 50).

Most peoples probably single out disorders of sensation as
one of the most pertinent characteristics of diseases: witness our own
stock query, "How are you feeling?" The Subanun ask, "Does it hurt?"
(mesait ma). The contrasting replies to this question are, first, an
affirmative, "Yes, it hurts"; second, a denial of pain followed by a
specification of a contrasting, non-painful, but still abnormal sensation, "No, it doesn't hurt; it itches"; and, third, a blanket negation
implying no abnormal sensation. Thus the Subanun labels a number
of contrasting types of sensation and uses them to characterize and
differentiate diseases.

The contrast between 'pain' (<u>mesait</u> or <u>megeel</u>) and 'itch' or 'irritation' (<u>matel</u>) has special relevance to skin lesions. 'Sores' 'hurt,' whereas scaly lesions 'itch.' But should a sore-like lesion both 'itch' and at the same time multiply and spread, a distinctive and serious disease is indicated: <u>buketaw</u> 'yaws.' The type of sensation also indicates possible pathogenic agents. Pain usually follows some kind of trauma so if the patient has suffered no obvious injury, the supernaturals have very likely inflicted an invisible wound. Itchiness signals the presence of an irritating agent, often <u>glaṇis</u> 'plant floss.'

Once a condition has been labeled 'painful' in contrast to other possibilities, the kind of pain can be specified at a subordinate level of contrast. However, the Subanun make such specifications more in contexts of complaining about discomfort than in diagnosing. Consequently the terms descriptive of pain are often chosen for their rhetorical rather than denotative value. Such terms resemble English metaphors: 'burning,' 'piercing,' 'splitting,' 'throbbing.'

There are, of course, many other sensations criterial to diagnosis and a long list of diagnostic questions referring to appearances and to bodily functions. Rather than attempting to discuss each of these, it will be of greater methodological advantage to illustrate how a series of questions with their contrasting answers defines one small segment of the disease terminology. Figure 3 diagrams the criterial definitions of the types of 'sores' (<u>beldut</u>) distinguished by the Subanun (cf. Figure 1). The 'sores' contrast with 'inflammations' (<u>meṇebag</u>) in having the prodrome <u>nuka</u> 'eruption.' 'Inflammations' and sores,' on the other hand, fall together in contrast to many other skin diseases in being 'painful' (<u>mesait</u>) rather than 'itchy' (<u>matel</u>). Answers to questions of spread, severity, distality (hands and feet vs. rest of body), and depth differentiate all the sores.

Depth, and especially severity, are not sharply defined by distinctive cues. In the case of 'sores,' size, persistence, and a variety of specific symptoms may point to severity: suppuration (<u>dun ig mata nen</u>), opening (<u>miterak</u>), hot sensation (<u>minit</u>), throbbing pain (<u>kendutendut</u>), intermittent burning pain (<u>metik</u>). Although not explicitly stated, judgment of severity is, in fact, partially a function of social-role contingencies. Do the patient and his consultants wish to emphasize the former's crippling disability, which prevents him from dis-

Levels of terminological contrast	beldut 'sore'					
	telemaw 'distal ulcer'		baga? 'proximal ulcer'			
	telemaw glai 'shallow distal ulcer'	telemaw glibun 'deep distal ulcer'	baga? 'shallow proximal ulcer'	begwak 'deep proximal ulcer'	beldut 'simple sore'	selimbunut 'multiple sore'
depth	sh	dp	sh	dp		
distality	distal		proximal			
severity	severe				mild	
spread	single					mult.
Diagnostic questions	Range of contrasting answers					

Fig. 3. Criterial contrasts differentiating the 'sores'

charging an expected obligation? Or do they wish to communicate that the patient's lesion is not serious enough to interfere with his duties? Diagnosis is not an automatic response to pathological stimuli; it is a social activity whose results hinge in part on role-playing strategies.

     1.4. Etiological criteria are diagnostically significant responses to questions of 'etiology'; how did the patient 'encounter' (melabet) his illness? These questions ask "Why did it happen to me?" rather than "What causes this kind of disease?" Diagnostic knowledge of the kind of disease does not give knowledge of 'etiology' in this sense. Confident determination of etiological circumstances requires com-

munication by divination or seance with the supernaturals. Since this
kind of communication tends to be costly, patients reserve etiological
searching for cases when ordinary 'medicinal' (kebuluŋan) treatments
predicated on diagnosis have not met with success. Etiological determination generally enables the patient to undertake propitiatory rituals
(kanu) with therapeutic value. But some etiological circumstances,
notably those involving human agency, cannot be counteracted by pro-
pitiations to supernaturals. These cases require treatment with spec-
ially acquired 'medicines' such as 'charms' (pegbeliŋen), 'amulets'
(buluŋ penapu), 'potions' (gaplas), and 'antidotes' (tekuli ?). When illnesses have a medicinally treatable etiology, the disease is then named
for the etiological circumstance regardless of previous symptomatic
diagnosis. There are seven such diseases, only two of which were
recorded as diagnoses during my two years in the field: mibuyag
'bewitched' and pigbuluŋan 'poisoned.'

In view of other descriptions of primitive medicine, the surprising fact about Subanun diagnosis is that in naming all but seven of
the 186 human disease categories, diagnostic questions refer directly
to the empirical evidence of the disease itself and its history. The
exceptional cases result from these few etiological circumstances
whose determination by divination or seance necessitates renaming
the illness they caused. Otherwise the results of etiological determin-
ations do not affect previously determined empirical diagnoses. A
deity may have to inform a Subanun how and why he got sick, but the
symptoms themselves normally provide the information to name the
disease, and by naming it, the Subanun is well on the road to prognosis
and preliminary therapy.

2.1. Elementary criteria are those whose linguistic expression is not a disease name. 'Pain (mesait) is an elementary criterion
because mesait, by itself, cannot function as a disease name.

2.2. Complex criteria are themselves diagnostic categories
labeled by a disease name. 'Malaria' (taig), for example, is diagnosed
by the presence of the disease 'fever' (panas) plus the elementary criterion of 'periodic chills' (seleŋaun). The disease 'fever' (panas) is,
in turn, diagnosed by the presence of the disease 'malaise' (mesait
glawas) plus the elementary criterion of 'feeling feverish' (mpanas).
Earlier we noted that some illnesses require a simultaneous conjunc-

tive description by more than one disease name, e.g. 'stomach ache and headache.' A few conjunctive combinations diagnose distinct disease categories. The diseases 'stomach ache' (mesait tian), 'difficult breathing' (bektus), and 'chest pains' (mesait gegdeb) function as complex criteria in the diagnosis of ba?us, a systemic disease for which we have devised no satisfactory gloss.

The Significance of Diagnosis

The diagnostic criteria distinguishing one Subanun disease from another, in their explicit verbal formulation by informants, define conceptually distinct, mutually exclusive categories at each level of contrast. Informants rarely disagree in their verbal descriptions of what makes one disease different from another. This does not mean, however, that they are equally consistent in their naming of actual disease cases. Two informants may agree that the ulcers baga? and begwak differ in degree of penetration, yet disagree on whether a particular ulcer they are examining exhibits sufficient depth to exemplify begwak. The "real" world of disease presents a continuum of symptomatic variation which does not always fit neatly into conceptual pigeon holes. Consequently the diagnosis of a particular condition may evoke considerable debate: one reason a patient normally solicits diagnostic advice from a variety of people. But the debate does not concern the definition of a diagnostic category, for that is clear and well known; it concerns the exemplariness of a particular set of symptoms to the definition (cf. Goodenough 1956: 215).

Conceptually the disease world, like the plant world, exhaustively divides into a set of mutually exclusive categories. Ideally every illness either fits into one category or is describable as a conjunction of several categories. Subanun may debate, or not know, the placement of a particular case, but to their minds that reflects a deficiency in their individual knowledge, not a deficiency in the classificatory system. As long as he accepts it as part of his habitat and not 'foreign,' a Subanun, when confronted with an illness, a plant, or an animal, may say he does not know the name. He will never say there is no name. The conceptual exhaustiveness of the Subanun classification of natural phenomena contrasts with the reported situation among many other peoples.

Diagnosis—the decision of what 'name' to apply to an instance of 'being sick'—is a pivotal cognitive step in the selection of culturally appropriate responses to illness by the Subanun. It bears directly on the selection of ordinary, botanically derived, medicinal remedies from 724 recorded alternatives. The results of this selection, in turn, influence efforts to reach prognostic and etiological decisions, which, in their turn, govern the possible therapeutic need for a variant of one of 61 basic, named types of propitiatory offerings. All of these decisions and resulting actions can have far-reaching social and economic consequences.

In this paper we have presented some methodological devices which we feel are effective in delimiting the basis for decisions underlying terminological systems. Unfortunately, while in the field we did not reach even the methodological sophistication of this article. Consequently, our data have proved deficient at a number of critical points.

NOTES

[1] Field work among the Subanun, conducted in 1953–54 and 1957–58, was supported by grants from the U.S. Government, Yale Southeast Asia Studies Program, and Smith, Kline, and French Co. The bulk of the data upon which this analysis is based were obtained in 1957–58 in the Gulu Disakan and Lipay regions northeast of Sindangan Bay in the interior of Zamboanga del Norte Province. All linguistic forms cited are from the Eastern Subanun dialect of this region. The frequent use of the first person plural in this article is not a rhetorical device but reflects the indispensable participation of my wife, Carolyn M. Frake, in the collection of field data. My handling of this material has profited from lengthy discussions with Harold Conklin and Volney Stefflre. Dell Hymes and Clyde Kluckhohn made helpful criticisms of an earlier draft of this paper.

[2] There is no standard lexeme labeling the category that contrasts with man in the sense of manly male. The most likely polylexemic designation is probably "not a real man."

[3] English kinship classification requires a special definition of affinity to contrast "in-laws" with other kin, some of whom (like FaSiHu) are connected to Ego by a marriage link but are categorized with consanguineals (like FaBr). This definition provides that kin of

different generations connected by a marriage link qualify as affinals
only if the marriage link is in the lower generation.
⁴ Latin Americanists should recognize this term (see Redfield
and Redfield 1940: 65). Disease names adopted from Spanish pasmo
or pasma are widespread in the Philippines. This was the only Subanu
disease name of obvious Spanish origin that we recorded.

REFERENCES

Brown, R. 1958. Words and things. Glencoe, Ill.: The Free Press.
Bruner, J. S., J. J. Goodnow, and G. A. Austin. 1956. A study of
    thinking. New York: Wiley.
Chomsky, N. 1957. Syntactic structures. The Hague: Mouton.
Christie, E. B. 1909. The Subanun of Sindangan Bay. Manila:
    Bureau of Science, Division of Ethnology Publications 6.
Conklin, H. C. 1955. Hanunóo color categories. Southwestern
    Journal of Anthropology 11. 339–44.
Frake, C. O. 1957a. Litigation in Lipay: a study in Subanun law.
    Bangkok: Proceedings of the Ninth Pacific Science Congress
    (in press).
_____. 1957b. The Subanun of Zamboanga: a linguistic survey.
    Bangkok: Proceedings of the Ninth Pacific Science Congress
    (in press).
_____. 1961. Family and kinship among the Eastern Subanun. In
    G. P. Murdock, ed., Social structure in Southeast Asia (in
    press).
Goodenough, W. G. 1956. Componential analysis and the study of
    meaning. Language 32.195–216.
Joos, M. 1958. Semology: a linguistic theory of meaning. Studies
    in Linguistics 13.53–70.
Kelly, G. 1955. The psychology of personal constructs, vol. 1.
    New York: Norton.
Lounsbury, F. G. 1956. A semantic analysis of the Pawnee kinship
    usage. Language 32.158–94.
Pike, K. L. 1954. Language in relation to a unified theory of the
    structure of human behavior. Part I, Preliminary edition.
    Glendale: Summer Institute of Linguistics.
Redfield, R., and M. P. Redfield. 1940. Disease and its treatment

in Dzitas, Yucatan. Contributions to American Anthropology and History 32, Carnegie Institution of Washington, publication 523.

Shattuck, G. C. 1951. Diseases of the tropics. New York: Appleton-Century-Crofts.

Wallace, A., and J. Atkins. 1960. The meaning of kinship terms. American Anthropologist 62. 58–80.

Wittgenstein, L. 1958. Blue and brown books. New York: Harper.

8 | Litigation in Lipay: A Study in Subanun Law

The literature of Philippine ethnography, incomplete as it is, provides in the works of Barton (1919, 1930, 1935, 1949) some of the classic treatments of primitive law. The interest attracted by Barton monographs has resulted not only from their merits as ethnographic accounts, but also from their significance to comparative studies of legal systems. The peoples of northern Luzon described by Barton display, on the one hand, an intense preoccupation with litigation, and on the other, a very weak development of the formal judicial and political institutions usually associated with the application and enforcemen of law. Elsewhere among many of the pagan peoples of the Philippines these same tendencies appear, but it would be difficult to find a people more litigious and at the same time more lacking in formal legal institutions and roles than the Subanun of Lipay and adjacent regions in the interior of northern Zamboanga.

This paper describes how a system of legal or quasi-legal activities functions in Lipay: who makes legal decisions, how they are made, and the way they are enforced.[1] Whether these activities correspond at all points with what has been isolated as legal behavior in other cultures may be moot, but that they pertain to the general problem of leadership and social control in informally organized groups is certain.

Lipay is a geographical region comprising about twenty-five square kilometers of mountainous topography in the northern interior of the Province of Zamboanga del Norte on the island of Mindanao. Within this area a population of 220 pagans grouped in five settlements supports itself by shifting cultivation. This population forms a sociological unit of personal acquaintances who interact frequently. How-

ever, no boundaries of language, political allegiance, or cultural
uniqueness separate them from adjacent regions. Indeed they share
a common language, culture, and social organization with 55,000
Eastern Subanun scattered in dispersed settlement throughout throughout the wider eastern portion of Zamboanga Peninsula.[2] But this cultural homogeneity is not reflected by any sort of political organization,
embracing either the Eastern Subanun as a whole or subdivisions of
them.

Subanun society is one in which there are few formal ties
linking minimal social units into larger aggregates. Each nuclear or
polygynous family, living in an isolated household within its own annual
clearing, forms a highly independent unit. Its social relationships,
unmarred by warfare, extend outward along ties of proximity and bilateral kinship. They encompass a politically unorganized circle of
neighbors and kin whose membership overlaps with, but never precisely corresponds to, those of other families.

Beyond the family, the only discrete social group of Subanun
society is the settlement, a local group of about three to twelve dispersed households whose members in a particular year are cultivating
adjacent or nearly adjacent swiddens. Close kinship ties link all or a
majority of settlement mates, but different settlements at different
times exhibit highly varied kinship structures. The independence of
established nuclear families, local agamy, and a succession of matrilocal, bilocal, and neolocal residence patterns serve to assure the
heterogeneity of settlement kinship structure. The same factors prevent the integration of the settlement as a stable corporate group.
Instead it is an informal, politically unorganized grouping of close
neighbors who, at a particular time, are sharing in enough activities
so that interactions among them are both more frequent and of a different order than interactions with outsiders.

Around any particular settlement there is a roughly defined
zone of individuals who maintain face-to-face social relationships.
This maximal local group, or region, normally includes some 200-
500 persons. Bilateral kinship ties cut across these local group affiliations and extend beyond them. The kinship system defines the types
of relationships that may pertain between individuals and also furnishes
a basis for social group affiliation. But the groupings of bilateral kin

around a particular ego in Subanun society have little in common with
the discrete divisions of a population made possible by unilinear kin
groups or even with the functionally important bilateral kin groups of
the Ifugao and other sedentary agriculturists of northern Luzon. The
boundaries of a Subanun kindred must be defined with reference to a
particular ego, and its functions are limited to activities centering on
ego. The kindred does not act collectively vis-à-vis equivalent group

The anarchic and peaceable Subanun have long been prey for
more strongly organized neighbors. It is through these contacts with
outsiders that political authority has impinged on Subanun life. Beginning before the Spanish conquest and continuing intermittently until the
twentieth century, Moslems from Sulu and Lanao raided the Subanun
for slaves, collected tribute, and established a system of coerced
trade. In some coastal areas, to better enforce their control, they
instated a hierarchy of titled Subanun officials with the responsibility
of collecting tribute and implementing trade. These individuals became the foci of indigenous political and judicial authority, deriving
their power from their position as trade intermediaries and from the
physical might of their backers. The ultimate punishment they could
wield was to turn over a subject to the Moslems as a slave. After the
American occupation, Moslem exploitation and hegemony in northern
Zamboanga ceased. With the removal of the foundations of the incipient Subanun political organization, the titled political offices rapidly
disappeared or lost their significance.

In recent decades Christian settlers from the Bisayas, encou
aged by weakened Moslem power, road building, and a tractable native
population, have invaded northern Zamboanga. Through the media of
markets, tax collection, schools, and land laws, Christian settlement
has meant the gradual extension of a new political system over the
Subanun. Effective political control, heralded by the bestowal of the
new titles tininti and kunsyal, has been established only in the coastal
and foothill areas of permanent cultivation but the threat of land appro
priation, "tax" collection, and police interference reaches the interior
shifting cultivators. In cases of offenses against lowlanders or of a
rare case of homicide among themselves, most Subanun groups can
expect police intervention. Nevertheless, litigation in interior region
such as Lipay—which never deals with anything on the scale of homicide—goes on largely unhampered by the shadow of political authority.

Sixty-four legal cases involving Lipay residents between July 1953 and June 1954 provide the basic data for this study. During an eight-month period I personally witnessed the proceedings of forty-two of these cases, an average of more than one case a week among 220 persons. Of the total case record, only one, a theft against a lowlander, resulted in police interference. There was only one clear case of theft against a fellow Subanun, and that remained unsettled. Only two cases dealt explicitly with sexual offenses, although violations of stated sexual mores were common occurrence. There were no cases of homicide or serious assault. The remainder of Lipay litigation dealt with person affronts (22 cases), minor breaches of custom (13 cases), inner-family quarrels (9 cases), breaches of ordinary contract (7 cases), breaches of marital contract (5 cases), disputes over inheritance (5 cases). Except, perhaps, for the large number of inner-family quarrels in Lipay, a similar distribution of case types appears in data collected in neighboring regions and from material culled from informants' memories of the past.

The volume and nature of Lipay litigation present two basic problems: first, how does the legal system operate in the absence of formal authority and of the sanctioned use of physical coercion; and, second, why the need for so much legal activity in a society where theft, homicide, and other major categories of crime are practically unknown? Consideration of these two questions draws our attention not to abstract "laws" but to the process of litigation itself and to the role of the person who effects legal decisions.

During the period of observation, one or more of seven men decided the ultimate disposition of all legal cases in Lipay. One of these men effected decisions only in minor disputes within his settlement. Five others practised on a region-wide basis, while the seventh, a resident of a nearby region, was active in Subanun litigation from Lipay to the coast. As a group these men were noteworthy neither for their wealth nor for their age. None held any titled social position or possessed means of calling upon physical force to sanction his decisions. None derived sufficient income from litigation to exempt him from the full round of subsistence activities engaged in by all Subanun. These men, distinguishable only by the fact that they repeatedly made effective legal decisions, we shall call "legal authorities."

Any adult male who can exercise sufficient verbal skill to make and uphold a legal decision is, by virtue of that fact, a legal authority. The status is not a formally defined jural position with explicit rules of ascription, but is achieved through the gradual and informal recognition of a person's ability in legal argument. His ancestors, his relationship to the supernatural, his wealth, and his physical prowess have no direct bearing on the achievement of the status. The successful performance of a legal role does, however, depend on at least two non-legal skills: the ability to sing a type of competitive drinking song and the ability to "hold one's liquor." Singing and drinking are part of any formal trial. The competent legal authority must remain in the forefront of these activities if he is to present his case effectively. Musical and, especially, bibulous talent come easily to most Subanun, but only a few individuals have the forensic proficiency to uphold a legal decision. Yet among these skilled few, prowess in manipulating interpersonal relations by legal persuasion is sought as consciously and with the same passionate interest as is military prowess in many other societies.

The behavior of the legal authorities and other participants in Lipay litigation always relates to the assessment and distribution of payments in a special unit of value known as the kumpaw.[3] We consider such behavior equivalent to legal activity because it always involves (or anticipates) a jural decision, concerning who is to be assessed how much, for what reason, and how the payment is to be distributed. These decisions are based on past precedent and in turn become precedents for future decisions. They thus fulfill the criteria set forth by Pospisil (1956) to define the sphere of law. The kumpaw payment is an acknowledgment of the "legality" of the decision.

Specific kinds of property have independent and unalterable kumpaw values. Twenty centavos in Philippine currency has the value of one kumpaw. Each of the many types of imported Chinese jars has its distinctive kumpaw value, as do brass betel ingredient containers, brass gongs, knives, and trade cloth. Agricultural products and home manufactures such as pottery, baskets, and implements have no kumpaw value, though they may be exchanged in economic transaction for kumpaw property. The kumpaw itself, however, is not a unit of economic exchange. Six kumpaw worth of currency (1.20) cannot be exchanged for a six-kumpaw jar. The latter may bring twenty pesos or

more in ordinary economic transactions. An amount expressed in
kumpaw is therefore meaningless until the kinds of property required
to meet the payment are specified. This specification is a crucial
part of a legal decision.

Kumpaw payments have two basic functions in the legal system: in some situations they represent fines imposed for offenses;
in others (principally marital negotiations) they are transactions
which formalize and guarantee a legal contract. We shall limit ourselves here to legal activity that concerns the imposition of fines in
order to avoid the special complexities of marital negotiations. The
latter, however, share the distinctive characteristics of all Lipay
legal activity.

There are three ways in which the distribution of kumpaw
payments as fines can occur: (1) in anticipation of a legal decision,
(2) by legal decision but without formal trial, and (3) by legal decision
in a formal trial.

Certain types of improper behavior can be legalized beforehand by paying a fine to the potential offended party, thus anticipating
a legal decision and averting further legal action. Such fines are the
geklek fine for marrying a cousin, the tulak fine for escaping levirate
or sororate obligations, and the delaray fine for marrying a younger
sister of an unmarried girl.

Fines imposed by legal decision but without formal trial are
known as dalan pitulu', "way of instruction." They are always small
and can be imposed only for minor breaches of custom. The defendent
can challenge the decision and precipitate a formal trial.[4] Women
suffer most frequently from dalan pitulu', for they less often have the
skill or motivation to contest the verdict.

The majority of fines in Lipay are imposed only after prolonged formal litigation. Such litigation arises when someone regis-
ters a public complaint that another person has committed a fineable
offense. The complainant may be a plaintiff in a dispute (palaw) or he
may be a legal authority eager to uphold "the law" (betad)—and to collect fines.

Cases initiated by a plaintiff usually arise from personal affronts or from a failure to fulfill contractual obligations. The former category comprises offenses such as slandering, malicious gossip, false accusations, insults, and, rarely, bodily assault in the form of a drunken pinch or slap. In the latter group belong failure to pay debts, to perform agreed services, and to abide by property or marriage contracts.

These disputes are considered affairs between individuals and do not involve opposing social group alliances. A person may proceed against any individual outside his nuclear family, from his married son to a stranger in another region, providing he can find someone willing to attempt a settlement. He must proceed with caution, however. A favorite device of legal authorities in arbitrating disputes is to eliminate the plaintiff by demonstrating that he too is at fault, thereby collecting fines from both parties. Legal authorities try cases and render decisions but do not act as representatives of either party. They are under no obligation to support the cause of settlement mates or kin. Bias on the part of legal authorities—itself a common cause of litigation—is usually attributed to bribery rather than to personal or social loyalties.[5]

The presence or absence of a plaintiff in a case depends more on circumstance than upon the nature of the offense. An improper suggestion to a member of the opposite sex, if resented, could lead to plaintiff-initiated litigation. Or, if not resented but overheard by a legal authority, it could be construed as an offense against public morals. In the latter case, the legal authority could either treat the recipient of the remark as a victim deserving financial retribution, or he could attempt a real coup by fining both parties, the girl on the grounds that she did not resent the remark as a proper girl should.

Cases lacking a plaintiff commonly arise during festivities when a legal authority interprets an act of some participant as finable and attempts to argue a conviction. Since the offense is usually a mere facetious remark or an unintentional slight of etiquette, the real threat to society is inconsequential. But these cases provide opportunities for a legal authority to test his skill against his rivals by demonstrating the serious legal implications of an apparently innocuous act. However, a false accusation is itself a finable offense, so that an

outmatched legal expert may soon find the roles of defendant and
prosecutor reversed.

The formal trial (bisala) of a legal case is a festive occasion
requiring, as do all festivities, the assemblage of a large group of
people, provisions for a feast, and ample quantities of drink. Since
few Subanun would pass up the delights of rice wine, feast food, and
social merrymaking, even at the risk of being the victim in ensuing
litigation, the summoning of participants to a trial rarely meets
opposition. Indeed, it is undoubtedly the prospect of feasting as much
as the possibility of winning fines that leads to the instigation of many
a trial. Once the festivities are underway, those who "know how to
talk" discuss the case over a jar of wine, from time to time interro-
gating the plaintiff,defendant, and witnesses. Anyone may participate
in the discussion by suggesting pertinent evidence, commenting on the
validity of the arguments, or by himself attempting to assume the role
of a legal authority. A settlement (gusay) is reached when someone
successfully convinces the others of the legitimacy of his analysis of
the merits of the complaint (bubutan) versus the defense (da'awa) and
the appropriateness of the proposed fine (sala' or gukuman). Included
in the decision may be a dandi', a formal warning that a more severe
penalty will be invoked if the offense is repeated.

The fine goes to the person who effected the decision. He in
turn divides it among any successful plaintiffs and among all those
who participated in settling the case, including himself. Often the
opposing litigants are subjected to a daga' ceremony whereby chicken
blood is wiped on their hands to signal the end of animosity.

The distribution of the fine and the performance of daga' need
not end the matter however. It frequently happens that a superior
legal debater not present at the trial hears of the case (perhaps from
a disgruntled participant) and calls a retrial, fining, if successful, the
persons who effected the erroneous first decision. In particularly
complex litigation this process can continue until every legal authority
in the area has entered the contest. For this reason there is rarely
a "closed case" in the mental files of a Subanun litigator.

Anyone who refused to comply with the decision of a Lipay
legal authority would suffer no threat of being confined, beaten, or

executed. Yet compliance is invariable. No one attempts to evade
paying a fine levied against him—unless it is by further litigation.
Although they are neither formalized nor explicit, the social control
mechanisms embodied in the Subanun legal system are effective.

Some students of primitive law maintain that the diagnostic
characteristic of law is the way it is enforced. According to Hoebel
(1954), for example, a law is a social norm sanctioned by the application of socially recognized physical force "in threat or in fact."
There are no such norms within the Subanun social system; physical
force has no sanctioned place in relationships among Subanun adults.
Sanctioned physical force is felt only through contacts with Christian
lowlanders. But occasions for its use are rare and when used, force
applied by lowland officials derives its sanctions not from Subanun
society but from the external Filipino political system.[6] If sanctioned
physical force is accepted as the essential criterion of law, then there
is no true law in Subanun society. From this viewpoint, the Subanun
are devotees of lawless litigation.

Physical force, however, represents only one type of sanction a social group can apply. There are other sanctions, available
especially to primary groups of intimate acquaintances, which are
much more reliable, and probably much more threatening, than phyi-
cal force. One's position in a social group—one's social status—is
held only at the sufferance of the group. Compliance with the norms
of the group is the price of continued participation as a member. The
force of this social control mechanism in particular groups varies in
direct proportion to the importance of status in that group to its members (La Pierre 1954). To the Subanun, status in the primary group
that demands compliance with legal decisions is all-important, for it
is the maximal social group to which he belongs. For him it is society
His social relationships with other Subanun are almost exclusively
primary relationships with neighbors and kin. Loss of status in this
group is paramount to loss of all societal support.

Subanun legal activity is a way of mustering the social control mechanisms of the primary group against a particular offense.
A legal authority is a person who has the skill to convince the group
that an offense has indeed occurred and can make a decision concerning the disposition of the case which the group will accept not only as

applicable to this particular case but also as a precedent for future
cases. Any norm enforced in this way, by litigation, is a legal norm,
a law (Pospisil 1956). Potentially, any rule of custom can become a
law if there is occasion to make it the subject of litigation. But no
rule, no matter how much it sounds like a "law" on the lips of an informant, is of significance in legal activity, as here defined, unless
it is at some time the basis of an actual legal decision.

Litigation in Lipay, however, cannot be fully understood if
we regard it only as a means of maintaining social control. A large
share, if not the majority, of legal cases deal with offenses so minor
that only the fertile imagination of a Subanun legal authority can magnify them into a serious threat to some person or to society in general. But the innocuousness of Subanun law-breaking by no means dulls
their passion for litigation. A festivity without litigation is almost as
unthinkable as one without drink. If no subject for prosecution immediately presents itself, sooner or later, as the brew relaxes tongues
and actions, someone will make a slip.

In some respects a Lipay trial is more comparable to an
American poker game than to our legal proceedings. It is a contest
of skill, in this case of verbal skill, accompanied by social merrymaking, in which the loser pays a forfeit. He pays for much the same
reason we pay a poker debt: so he can play the game again. Even if
he does not have the legal authority's ability to deal a verbalized "hand,"
he can participate as a defendant, plaintiff, kibitzer, singer, and
drinker. No one is left out of the range of activities associated with
litigation.

Litigation nevertheless has far greater significance in Lipay
than this poker game analogy implies. For it is more than recreation.
Litigation, together with the rights and duties it generates, so per-
vades Lipay life that one could not consistently refuse to pay fines and
remain a functioning member of society. Along with drinking, feasting, and ceremonializing, litigation provides patterned means of interaction linking the independent nuclear families of Lipay into a social
unit, even though there are no formal group ties of comparable extent.
The importance of litigation as a social activity makes understandable
its prevalence among the peaceful and, by our standards, "law-abiding"
residents of Lipay.

NOTES

[1] All ethnographic data presented in this paper pertain to the period 1953-54 when the writer did field work among the Subanun supported by a U.S. Government Fulbright Grant and a grant from the Yale University Southeast Asia Studies Program. Historical data are from Combés (1667), Forrest (1779), and Christie (1909). Further field work among the Subanun by the writer is currently in progress.

[2] The Western Subanun, occupying the southwestern extension of Zamboanga Peninsula, speak a language distinct from, but very closely related to, that of the Eastern Subanun.

[3] The kumpaw was originally a unit of exchange, equivalent to one fathom of trade cloth, used for calculating the value of Moslem trade goods.

[4] The alternatives are similar to those faced by an American soldier when offered a choice between company punishment (Article 15) and court martial. One alternative offers the certainty of light punishment, the other the chance of acquittal but the risk of much heavier punishment.

[5] The sociological significance of the Lipay legal system thus differs from that of the Ifugao, where members of a kindred have collective legal responsibility and never proceed against one another, and from that of the Tagbanuwa, where jural status is validated by descent and legal authorities are described as the "jural guardians of the kindred" (Fox 1954).

[6] Even in terms of that system its "legitimacy" is often questionable.

REFERENCES

Barton, R. F. 1919. Ifugao law. University of California Publications in American Archaeology and Ethnology 15.1-186.

_____. 1930. The half way sun: life among the headhunters of the Philippines. New York.

_____. 1935. Philippine pagans: the autobiographies of three Ifugaos. London.

_____. 1949. The Kalingas: their institutions and custom law. Chicago.

Christie, E. B. 1909. The Subanuns of Sindangan Bay. Bureau of
    Science, Division of Ethnology Publications, 6. Manila.
Combés, Francisco. 1667. Historia de Las Islas de Mindanao, Iolo,
    y sus Adyacentes—Progressos de la Religion y Armas Catol-
    icas. Madrid.
Forrest, T. 1779. A voyage to New Guinea. London.
Fox, R. B. 1954. Religion and society among the Tagbanuwa of
    Palawan Island, Philippines. Unpublished Ph.D. disserta-
    tion, University of Chicago.
Hoebel, E. A. 1954. The law of primitive man. Cambridge.
La Pierre, R. T. 1954. A theory of social control. New York.
Pospisil, L. J. 1956. The nature of law. Transactions of the New
    York Academy of Sciences 18.746-55.

9 | A Structural Description of Subanun "Religious Behavior"

The purpose of this paper is not to present anything approach ing a complete description of Subanun "religion" but rather to raise the question of what kind of statement would constitute an adequate ethnographic description of an aspect of a culture.[1] This is not, I think, a trivial question to ask. A theory of how to describe cultural behavior implies a theory of culture. Ethnography, the science of cultural description, can potentially fill a role as critical to our general theoretical understanding of the nature of culture as has modern descriptive linguistics toward our understanding of the nature of language.

A description of a culture, an ethnography, is produced from an ethnographic record of the events of a society within a given period of time, the "events of a society" including, of course, informants' responses to the ethnographer, his queries, tests, and apparatus. Ethnographic technique, ignored in this paper, is the task of devising means for producing an adequately ample record of events. Ethnographic theory is the task of devising criteria for evaluating ethnographies. These three aspects of the ethnographic task are interdependent. The adequacy of the record and the validity of the methodology cannot be determined unless the data are subjected to analysis and the results tested against the criteria of the theory during the course of field investigation. The production of an ethnography should imply a task more challenging than "writing up one's notes."

When an ethnographer first enters a strange society, each encountered event is new, unanticipated, improbable, and, hence, highly informative in the communication-theory sense. As he learns the culture of the society, more and more of what happens becomes familiar and anticipatable. The ethnographer can plan his own activities on the basis of these anticipations. The more he learns of a culture, the more his anticipations match those of his informants. Similarly for a person born in a society, as he learns his culture, the events of his life become more probable, becoming parts of familiar scenes which he and his fellows plan for, stage, and play their roles in. To describe a culture, then, is not to recount the events of a society but to specify what one must know to make those events maximally probable. The problem is not to state what someone did but to specify the conditions under which it is culturally appropriate to anticipate that he, or persons occupying his role, will render an equivalent performance. This conception of a cultural description implies that an ethnography should be a theory of cultural behavior in a particular society, the adequacy of which is to be evaluated by the ability of a stranger to the culture (who may be the ethnographer) to use the ethnography's statements as instructions for approrpriately anticipating the scenes of the society. I say "appropriately anticipate" rather than "predict" because a failure of an ethnographic statement to predict correctly does not necessarily imply descriptive inadequacy as long as the members of the described society are as surprised by the failure as is the ethnographer. The test of descriptive adequacy must always refer to informants' interpretations of events, not simply to the occurrence of events.

With this criterion of descriptive adequacy in mind, the formulation of an ethnographic statement would seem to include at least the following tasks: (1) discovering the major categories of events or scenes of the culture; (2) defining scenes so that observed interactions, acts, objects, and places can be assigned to their proper scenes as roles, routines, paraphernalia, and settings; (3) stating the distribution of scenes with respect to one another, that is, providing instructions for anticipating or planning for scenes. These three methodological problems will be discussed with reference to a portion of the Subanun record, a record which is inadequate at several points because much of this analysis was completed only after I had left the field.

The Subanun are a pagan people practicing swidden agriculture in the mountainous interior of Zamboanga Peninsula on the island of Mindanao in the Philippines. The data of this paper pertain only to the Eastern Subanun of the Gulu Disakan and Lipay regions northeast of Sindangan Bay in the interior of Zamboanga del Norte Province, studied in the field in 1953-54 and 1957-58. In terms of segmentation and stratification, Subanun society displays remarkable simplicity. Each nuclear family is the focus of a partially unique and variable network of social ties with kin and neighbors which constitutes, for that family, the "total society." This maximal, non-discrete sphere of social relationships has no corporate organization and is not segmented into lineages, age-sets, secret societies, territorial districts, political factions, or the like. Despite this simplicity of their social structure, the Subanun carry on constant and elaborate interfamily social activities—litigation, offerings, feasts—all well lubricated with ample quantities of rice wine. Warfare is lacking (Frake 1957, 1960; Christie 1909).

The Identification of "Religous Behavior"

One of the most frequent and regularly recurrent events in the Subanun record is eating. Most, but not all, Subanun events which we would consider instances of "eating" as a category of activity fall into an easily distinguishable Subanun scene, a 'meal.'[2] To qualify as a 'meal' a scene must include at least one actor, the 'eater,' and a 'cooked starchy-staple food.' A meal characteristically marks a clear interruption of other activity, requiring the performers to squat before a setting of food on the floor or ground; it is scheduled at least once daily; it requires prior planning and preparation; and, although one actor is sufficient, it is generally staged as a social performance.

In the typical recorded meal, those participating in the role 'joint eaters' belong to a single nuclear family, the side dish is a non-meat food, the staple may be a root crop or a cereal, and no 'rice wine' (gasi)[3] is served. These are ordinary meals. If one of the features of an ordinary meal changes, the others change as well. Meals with multifamily joint eaters, meat side dish, cereal staple, and 'rice wine' are festive meals or, simply, feasts.

Festive meals occur at irregular intervals and must be occasioned; i.e. there must be a legitimizing event which serves as a reason for the feast. It is always appropriate to ask in Subanun, "What is the reason for this feast?" To ask, "What is the reason for this meal?" would sound somewhat odd in uncontrived contexts. Festive meals

substitute for ordinary ones. A meal is scheduled at least once daily.
If there is a legitimizing occasion and the necessary components are
procurable, a festive meal is staged; otherwise an ordinary meal is
staged. A central part of Subanun planning involves anticipating festive
occasions so that the necessary components for staging a feast be procurable whenever a legitimizing event occurs. The occurrence of one
of the components, as an event, can itself be a reason for a feast, requiring the mustering of the other essential components. If a wild pig
(meat side-dish component) is caught in a trap, its consumption requires
a feast. If guests congregate (multifamily-performance component),
they must be feasted. The festive meal itself occurs in a context of a
wide range of other activities: competitive drinking, displays of verbal
art, singing, dancing. All activities occurring from the arrival to the
departure of participants in a feast together constitute a <u>festivity</u>.

During some festivities occur episodes which themselves
seem to be feasts, but of a rather special sort. The festive provisions
are set up on distinctive paraphernalia and the 'eaters,' though sometimes audible, are not visible to the ethnographer nor, by report, to
the ordinary Subanun. Feasts of this sort whereby 'mortals' feed the
various categories of 'non-visible' or 'supernatural' inhabitants of the
Subanun universe, the Subanun call <u>kanu,</u> here glossed as 'offerings.'
During the course of a festivity, one to several offerings may be performed. A festivity during which offerings occur is a <u>ceremony</u>. A
ceremony may be <u>simple</u> or <u>complex</u> depending on whether one or more
than one offering is held. This contrast between simple and complex
ceremonies is not matched by a lexical distinction in Subanun, but is
necessary in order to describe the denota of names for types of offerings and ceremonies. Ceremonies are named for one constituent offering. Thus <u>beklug</u> denotes a particular kind of offering or a ceremony
in which the <u>beklug</u> offering is one of many constituents. If a Subanun
offering name is given as "instructions to perform," one must know
from context whether the referent is an offering or a ceremony and, if
a ceremony, whether it is simple or complex. The term <u>kanu</u> may
likewise, depending on context, refer to an offering or to a ceremony.

A ceremony, then, is one kind of festivity. Other kinds are
'litigation,' 'labor-recruiting feasts,' 'game-sharing feasts,' 'meat-
division feasts,' and 'hospitality feasts.' Several kinds of festivities
may be jointly held. If for some reason it is necessary to provide a

feast, it is often economic to discharge as many festive functions as possible during its course. Thus a legal case and an offering may occur during a festivity originally staged as a hospitality feast.

To the naive observer an offering may seem like a minor episode in a festive event. But when one considers how offerings and ceremonies vary in paraphernalia, social participation, routines, planning, and programming, and when one considers the range of events which are relevant to staging ceremonies, it becomes clear that the behavioral complex centering on offerings penetrates deeply into many crucial areas of Subanun life. The programming and staging of ceremonies forms a major segment of Subanun cultural activity comparable in scope and content to the traditional ethnographic category of "religion." This comparability suggests (but does not require) the term religious behavior as a label for this activity, and it suggests Subanun religion as a label for what is described by an ethnographic statement which accounts for this behavior. But the only criterion of whether a particular act is an instance of religious behavior is its relevance to the programming and performing of 'offerings.' The ethnographic (in contrast to the ethnological) issue is not whether instances of religious behavior so defined conform to any particular cross-cultural notion of "what religion is," but whether they do in fact comprise a meaningful descriptive category of Subanun cultural activity and, if so, how is this category to be described.

The Performance of an 'Offering'

The first step in describing Subanun religious behavior is to describe the performance of offerings themselves in terms of discovered categories of constituent locales, objects, performers, and acts. Only a brief outline of the constituent structure of offerings as performances can be presented here.

Settings. There are no special buildings, rooms, or outdoor areas reserved for staging offerings. Offerings may be held inside nuclear family residences, in house yards, in fields, in forests, or on stream banks, the specific locale depending on the type of offering as well as on sociological, ecological, and meteorological conditions.

Provisions. A festive meal must be provided for both mortal and supernatural participants. A feast for supernaturals requires special components: the staple must be of rice, eggs are added to the required meat side dish, the proffered wine (or fermented mash) must be of rice and be ritually prepared, the proffered betel quids must be prepared with domesticated betel-pepper leaf and areca palm nuts (mortals often use substitute ingredients). Some categories of supernaturals take their food raw, others in a cooked state. These provisions are first offered to the invited supernaturals on an altar, then removed and consumed, generally as part of a larger feast, by humans. (The supernaturals conveniently consume only the 'intangible essence,' seŋaw, of food and drink.) The kind and quantity of provisions within these constituent categories vary with type of offering, with the kind of event occasioning the offering, with the whims of individual supernaturals, and with particular bargains struck beforehand between mortal host and supernatural guest. From an economic standpoint the side dish, requiring sacrifice of valuable livestock, is the most significant feature of an offering. The market value of pigs and chickens slaughtered for the offering and accompanying feast provides a direct index of the occasion's importance.

Paraphernalia. Humans settle for a banana leaf on the floor, but the supernaturals demand elaborate devices from which to partake of their meals. The Subanun construct at least thirty types of altars, varying in number of platforms, method of construction, materials employed, means of support or suspension, decoration, and size. Sometimes the type of altar is determined by the deity being propitiated. Thus the 'raw-food-eating gods' (kemuŋluq) always eat from a platformless seleŋsaŋan, but a personal 'guardian god' (tipun) generally prefers a bibalay altar, the defining attributes of which are rectangular shape, no sides, stick floor, and parallel legs. More often the type of altar or altars is specific to a particular kind of offering or ritual occasion, and a variety of supernaturals will in turn eat from it during the ceremony. Some more elaborate offerings require special equipment other than altars: various kinds of barriers to inhibit the movements of malevolent supernaturals, folded cloths to capture lost souls, miniature wooden replicas of weapons, model rafts and canoes, decorative and rustling leaves. With few exceptions all of this equipment is constructed anew (usually in a rather slipshod fashion) for each offering and then discarded. Since human drinking and feasting cannot pro-

ceed until the offering is completed, the few Subanun who are prone
to spend time lavishing care on the construction of ritual paraphernalia
become the butt of criticism from their more secular-minded fellows.
Every offering also requires a resonant porcelain bowl (struck rhyth-
mically to announce the occasion to the supernatural guests) and incense (the fumes of which augment the aroma of the offering as a lure).

Participants. The participants in an offering all belong to
the category of 'persons' (getaw), those 'living things' (tubuqan) with
whom one can establish communicatory relations. A dichotomous
dimension of reported conscious visibility divides 'persons' into two
subcategories with fundamentally distinct roles in offerings. 'Persons'
reported to be consciously visible to the ordinary Subanun are 'mortals'
(kilawan). 'Persons' whom the ordinary Subanun are reportedly unable
to see consciously are 'supernaturals' (kanaq kilawan). Only the exceptional perceptual powers of certain prominent 'mediums' can reportedly record a conscious visual image of the 'supernaturals.'
Others may 'see' a supernatural without being aware of it—a possible
cause of illness if the unconscious image is particularly terrifying.
The non-empirical nature of Subanun 'supernaturals' refers only to the
visual sense; these beings are (reportedly) able to make an impression
on one's auditory and tactile senses.

The English word 'supernatural' thus serves as a label for
the Subanun category of 'persons' reportedly not consciously visible
to the ordinary Subanun. There are, of course, in the verbally revealed Subanun universe many creatures ('persons' and 'non-persons')
which the ethnographer feels confident he will never see and which
many informants admit they have never seen (but only because they
have never encountered them, except perhaps in the dark). Some of
these "natural" (i. e. visible) but rarely encountered phenomena play
an important role in Subanun life, but they do not appear at offerings
and hence are not relevant to the present discussion. Only by attending to Subanun criteria can we assign the bow-and-arrow wound-
inflicting menubuq pygmies to the category 'supernatural' and the body-
dismembering menayaw marauders to the category 'mortal.' Neither
class appears to the ethnographer to have any empirically substantiat-
able members in the Subanun habitat at the present time, though they
both may once have had. Yet to discuss both categories together as
aspects of Subanun religion because they are both "supernatural"

according to the ethnographer's notions would seriously distort the structure of Subanun culture.

At the most general level of terminological contrast the Subanun classify 'supernaturals' as 'souls' (gimuud), 'spirits' (mitubuq), 'demons' (getau–telunan), and 'gods' (diwata) (cf. Table 1). Two semantic dimensions suffice to define these four categories in terms of necessary and sufficient contrasts in verbal descriptions:

1. Inherent connection with mortals
   1.1. Inherently connected with a living mortal
   1.2. Once inherently connected with a mortal now dead but still remembered by at least one living mortal
   1.3. Not inherently connected to a living or remembered mortal
2. Habitat connection with mortals
   2.1. Regularly residing with mortals in 'this world' (glumban)
   2.2. Not regularly residing in 'this world'

Using the numbering of the outline above, the four categories are definable as follows:

   'Souls'   : 1.1
   'Spirits' : 1.2
   'Demons' : 1.3 2.1
   'Gods'   : 1.3 2.2

'Souls' play a role in offerings through attempts to use offerings to recapture, for the sake of their owner's health, lost souls lured away by fragrant blossoms, attractive supernaturals, and the offerings of sorcerers. ('Souls,' a kind of 'supernatural,' must be distinguished from gina 'life stuff,' associated with consciousness, cognition, and emotion but not a 'person' who attends offerings.)

After death the soul survives to become a 'spirit,' a bodiless soul who wanders about 'this world' until sent on a tour of sacred places and other worlds by a series of offerings performed on his behalf by his survivors. Becoming eventually forgotten in the sky world, he then acquires the necessary attributes of a 'god' (cf. definitions

Table 1. Categories of Participants in Subanun 'Offerings'

'persons' <u>getaw</u>:

*1.   'supernaturals' <u>kanaq kilawan</u>
1.1.   'souls' <u>gimuud</u>
1.2.   'spirits' <u>mitubuq</u>
1.3.   'demons' <u>getau-telunan</u>
1.3.1.   'ogres' <u>menemad</u>
1.3.2.   'goblins' <u>memenwa</u>
1.3.3.   'pygmies' <u>menubuq</u>
1.4.   'gods' <u>diwata</u>
1.4.1.   'sky gods' <u>getau-laŋit</u>
1.4.2.   'raw-food-eating gods' <u>kemuŋluq</u>, <u>meŋilaw</u>
1.4.2.1.   'sunset gods' <u>getau-sindepan</u>
1.4.2.2.   'sea gods' <u>getau-dagat</u>
1.4.2.3.   'ocean gods' <u>getau-laud</u>
1.4.3.   'sunrise gods' <u>getau-sebaŋan</u>, <u>tumiag</u>
1.4.4.   'underworld gods' <u>getau-bayaq</u>
2.   'mortals' <u>kilawan</u>
*2.1.   'functionaries' <u>sug mikanu dun</u>
2.1.1.   non-professional functionaries
2.1.2.   'professional functionaries' <u>belian</u>
2.1.2.1.   'invocators' <u>bataq belian</u>
2.1.2.2.   'mediums' <u>gulaŋ belian</u>
2.1.2.2.1.   'shamans' <u>guleligan</u>
2.1.2.2.2.   'interviewers' <u>meninduay</u>
2.2.   'assistants' <u>gimpaŋ</u>
*2.3.   'beneficiaries' <u>sug pikanuan dun</u>
2.4.   'audience' <u>sug suminaup dun</u>

---

* Marks categories which must be represented at any offering.

above). It is the spirits of the recent dead—close kin whom he remember-bers personally and toward whom he still has ritual obligations—that concern a Subanun. When he dies, others will remember him, and those he remembered will be forgotten. Ties between spirits and mortals are reformulated in successive generations rather than continuing through time as an ancestor cult—just as the corporate social

groups of Subanun society, the nuclear families, do not survive
through successive generations as descent groups but are constantly
dissolving and reforming (Frake 1960).

Remembered spirits are important to the Subanun because
they are the closest friends a mortal has among the supernaturals.
They willingly attend seances for sentimental reunions with their loved
ones (though even they demand an offering of food and drink). At
seances they typically act as intermediaries between mortals and less
friendly supernaturals, often filling a role not unlike that of a legal
authority in arbitrating a dispute between plaintiff (the offended supernatural) and defendant (the mortal offender and victim of the plaintiff's
wrath). Spirits respond to emotional appeal "for oldtimes' sake" and
consequently tend to be less greedy in their demands than other supernaturals. They can be troublesome, however, if their mortal kin
shirk their ritual obligations. Also they may become so afflicted with
the prevalent Subanun sentiment of 'loneliness' (bugaq) that they desire
to transform a mortal loved one to spirit status, a transformation few
mortals are willing to undergo, no matter how fond they were of the
departed. Several informants have voiced a suspicion, founded on
their remembrance of the deceased, that the spirit in such cases is
not always as sentimental as he pretends; he has merely discovered
a neat wedge for extorting food and drink from his survivors.

'Demons,' while not usually so viciously malevolent as the
'raw-food-eating gods,' are dangerous because they live so close at
hand. Any chance encounter with them is likely to result in illness,
and the disturbance of many of their habitats caused by swidden activities requires regular propitiation.

Of greatest importance among the 'gods' are the various types
of 'raw-food eaters' (see Table 1) who periodically ascend the streams
of Subanun country to inflict severe illness and epidemics and through
their 'pets,' the rats and locusts, cause agricultural disasters. Their
annual 'new year's' propitiation at strategic river confluences provides
a common ritual interest for all settlements whose drainages converge
upon a single convenient blocking place.

Other 'gods,' especially the 'sky gods,' are generally much
less malevolent if not actually friendly. Perversely, they do not par-

ticipate nearly so regularly in human affairs, although some exert
important control over rice growth. During the course of an illness-
studded life, most adult male Subanun acquire a personal 'guardian
supernatural' (tipun), frequently a 'sky god, ' who must receive annual
propitiation at harvest time for the sake of the health of the man's
family and rice.

'Gods' and 'demons' come in large numbers of varieties distinguished by habitat specifications, appearance, malevolence, diet,
altar preferences, natural phenomena under their provenience, and
so on. The verbal expositions of this pantheon vary greatly from informant to informant and from region to region. To present any one
of these systems in all of its detail as "the Subanun pantheon" would
do violence to cultural reality. The striking feature of Subanun theol-
ogy is that, at any but the most general levels (see Table 1), it is not
a consistent body of cherished lore at the tip of everyone's tongue.
Beyond the generalizations given here, Subanun 'supernaturals' are,
with some exceptions, diffuse in their functions. Almost any supernatural can cause almost any ailment or interfere in almost any activity. Consequently an elaborate and precise taxonomy of supernaturals
correlated with their functional roles need not be shared by all participants in the performance of an offering. Individuals and groups can
differ considerably in their theological speculations with little consequence for the practical conduct of religious behavior.

Direct observation and Subanun descriptions of role performances both make it clear that a 'mortal' participant in an offering
occupies at least one of the following roles: 'functionary, ' 'assistant, '
'beneficiary, ' or 'audience' (see Table 1).

The 'functionary' has the task of extending the invitation to
the supernatural guests once the offering has been prepared. He in-
vokes the supernaturals by incantation, bowl striking, and incense
burning. The functionary, furthermore, assumes the responsibility
of supervising all proceedings connected with the offering to ensure
their proper performance. Every adult male household head has fre-
qnent occasion to serve as functionary for simple household ceremonies. Women rarely assume this role in fact, except during one type
of agricultural offering, but are not proscribed from it by custom.
A person must always act as his own functionary in offerings to his
personal 'guardian god' (tipun).

The complexity of Subanun religious techniques, however, demands specialized knowledge of functionaries for all but the simplest offerings. A 'professional functionary' (belian) is an acknowledged specialist in religious techniques who regularly acts as a functionary for offerings involving beneficiaries outside his own household. If a 'professional functionary' has one or more supernatural 'familiars' (bilaq) and can thereby conduct seances, he is a 'medium' (gulaŋ belian, or simply belian if context makes the level of contrast clear); otherwise he is an 'invocator' (bataq belian, literally, "a little bit of a professional functionary"). There are two kinds of 'mediums': 'shamans' (guleligan), who are 'possessed' (tenaqan) by their familiars, and 'interviewers' (meninduay), who carry on conversations with the supernatural guests as the latter partake of the offering.

Of the special statuses which a Subanun can achieve, that of 'medium' is the most formalized in method of recruitment and in social acknowledgment. It can never, however, replace a Subanun's full-time occupational role of farming. There are two routes, open to any adult man or woman, for becoming a medium: by 'training' (pigubasan) and by 'revelation' (gemaw). All mediums of my acquaintance selected the former route, involuntarily, when the supernaturals imposed the role upon them as the price of recovery from an illness. In this manner the gods recruit new members to the profession which is so essential to their well-being. A person so selected assists a qualified medium and acts as an 'invocator' until the gods inform him that he is ready to assume a medium's role himself. A medium of the other type (gemaw) allegedly receives his training direct from the gods and needs no apprenticeship.

The Subanun expects a good medium to exhibit certain peculiarities of 'habitual behavior' (kebetaŋ). His personality should emphasize to a fault the Subanun virtues of a quiet, passive, rather phlegmatic approach to interpersonal relationships with the consequence that he becomes, by Subanun evaluation, somewhat impractical in daily affairs. These traits of the personality type called melemen are the polar opposites of the forceful aggressiveness (gembeluq) required of a legal authority (Frake 1957). Hence the same person cannot easily occupy both the role of mediator with the supernaturals and the role of mediating among human disputants. Furthermore, by Subanun standards, the personality expected of a medium is more commendable, if less entertaining, than that of the extroverted legal authority.

Almost every settlement has someone who can assume the role of 'invocator' for certain ceremonies, but, in the area of my field work, over half of the settlements lacked resident mediums. Mediums must therefore extend their services beyond their own settlements on a community-wide or even a region-wide basis, depending on their reputation. The travel required takes sufficient time from the medium's agricultural and technological tasks at home to counterbalance what material rewards his profession brings—a problem paralleling that of prominent legal authorities. Probably the most important material reward for mediums is the opportunity they have to attend a large number of feasts and drinking parties without any obligation to reciprocate. In addition, when called upon to perform special ceremonies for the cure of illness, they collect a small fee. They receive no fee for communal ceremonies in which they themselve are beneficiaries.

The other roles assumed by participants at an offering are functions of the particular social context; they are not permanent attributes of a person's status in the society at large. 'Assistants' are any persons who, under the functionary's supervision, prepare and set up food and material equipment for the offering. They are recruited for the occasion from apprentice mediums, personnel of the beneficiary's household, the beneficiary himself, or simply from people "who like to do that sort of thing." The 'beneficiary' is the person or persons for whose benefit the offering is being given. The beneficiary may be one person, a household, a settlement, or even an entire region, depending on the purpose of the offering. The responsibility of providing a locale for the ceremony, of securing the necessary provisions, and of recruiting assistants falls to the beneficiaries. Any person or family intending to assume the role of beneficiary must make a contribution to the offering.

The 'audience' comprises all persons who are present because of the offering but who have no special role in its actual performance. It may include uninvited people who "happened to drop by" (in unexpressed anticipation of a feast), but it is largely composed of people with a special interest in the beneficiary. Major ceremonies of illness and death provide the only formalized occasions which bring large numbers of a person's dispersed kindred together as participants in a single event. Scheduled agricultural and prophylactic ceremonies, on

the other hand, recruit audience and group beneficiaries along lines
of local group affiliation. Except during seances, the majority of the
audience and even beneficiaries, when these are in large number, generally show very little interest in the proceedings of the offering proper; that is the task of the functionary and his assistants. A Subanun
offering is a technique for accomplishing a practical purpose. It is
not an obvious source of inspiration or a forceful expression of ultimate values to an awe-stricken congregation. There are, of course,
sources of inspiration and forceful expressions of values in Subanun
life, but they are more likely to be communicated during secular
gatherings around rice-wine jars after the offering is completed.
Seances, however, rival legal disputes as foci of lively interest:
they provide all persons present with an opportunity to interrogate,
beg, cajole, bargain, and debate with the supernaturals themselves.

Routines. To complete a description of the constituent structure of offerings there should be an analysis of the actions or routines
followed in the performance. Such a description, however, would require a much more detailed discussion of offerings in all their varieties than is possible here. Consequently I merely list below the categories under which such a description of routines would be organized:

1. Preliminary staging talk
2. Assembly of participants
3. Preparing of provisions and paraphernalia
4. Setting up of offering
5. invocation
6. Seance, if any
7. Removing provisions
(Routines 4-7 repeated for each offering of the ceremony)
8. Festivities (routines of festive eating, drinking, singing, etc.)
9. Dispersal of participants
10. Postperformance critique

The Distribution of 'Ceremonies'

If we assume that the foregoing description adequately accounts for the identification and performance of offerings within ceremonial contexts, the problem remains of formulating a statement

which accounts for the scheduling of ceremonies in relation to other scenes of the culture. A distributional analysis seeks to answer the question: what does the occurrence of a given event imply to the knower of the culture about the occurrences of other possible events in the system? A statement of the distribution of ceremonies will specify what features of a Subanun's experience are relevant to the staging of a religious performance of a given kind at a given time.

Formulating a statement of the distribution of religious scenes requires examination of the ethnographic record for observed and reported events which, by the criteria already formulated, are instances (or "tokens") of this scene. Next we list the other scenes regularly occurring before and after religious scenes. To judge the extent to which the occurrence of one scene implies another, the record of observed sequences must be checked against the record of informants' statements about anticipated sequences and of their interpretations of actual sequences in terms of these anticipations. This list of scenes provides a distributional frame for the set of events labeled 'religious scenes' or 'ceremonies.' The diagram A| |B, where A is the set of scenes regularly anticipated before ceremonies and B the set regularly anticipated after ceremonies, represents the frame. Such a distributional frame specifies the necessary conditions for anticipating the occurrence of a ceremony. Note that these conditions depend not only on the actual occurrence of an anticipated event, but also on plans made for producing or coping with future events. The model of distributional structure is a two-sided, before-and-after frame, such as that required in linguistic description, and not a Markov chain in which the probability of an event is a sole function of the outcome of the preceding event. In acting as well as in speaking persons have an image of the pattern to be completed and make plans accordingly (cf. Miller et al. 1960).

Description of a frame requires a statement of (1) the probability of the events that comprise the frame, (2) the alternative scenes, other than ceremonies, that can be anticipated to occur in the same frame, (3) the alternative kinds of ceremonies that can be anticipated to occur given the occurrence of a ceremony.

The significance of ceremonies in Subanun life relates strikingly to the probability of events which, in terms of legitimate cultural

expectations, imply ceremonies. Among the most probable events of
Subanun life are those that make up the scenes of the annual agricultural
cycle: swidden slashing, felling, burning, planting, protecting, and
harvesting. The annual staging of each of these scenes in this order
by each family is an essential feature of the Subanun ecological adaptation. These scenes and their constituents provide a frame for scheduling about nine annual complex ceremonies, the exact number varying
locally. Each of these ceremonies is of a specific named kind with
prescribed settings, kinds of provisions, paraphernalia, routines, and
social participation. These ceremonies are scheduled ceremonies.
Their distribution has the following characteristics:

1. The scenes of the distributive frames are highly probable.
2. Each frame calls for a specified kind of ceremony.
3. There are no anticipatable alternatives to any of these
   ceremonies.

Thus the annual occurrence of a given kind of scheduled ceremony is highly probable, and learning that a given scheduled ceremony
has indeed occurred is not very informative (it is not "news") to the
person who knows the culture. The occurrence of a scheduled ceremony is, in effect, a structural marker of the anticipatable sequence
of scenes in Subanun culture. It signals that events are unfolding as
scheduled. [Compare the linguistic frames marked in the following
English utterance: "I want| |go| |Hawaii. " The person who knows
English can legitimately anticipate only one form, to, in the first slot;
whereas in the second slot a number of alternatives can be anticipated:
to, through, by, near, away from, etc. The actual occurrence of a
given form in the second slot is less probable and much more informative about the non-linguistic world than the occurrence of a form in the
first slot which can inform us only whether or not the utterance is
correctly constructed (cf. Ziff 1960: 41-42.]

To the Subanun, the occurrence of a scheduled ceremony not
only signals the expected unfolding of events, but is is also necessary
if future anticipations of probable events are to be fulfilled. The failure of one of the scenes of the agricultural cycle to occur as anticipated
is a sign of a major crisis—an unanticipatable occurrence with far-
reaching consequences for future anticipations. If harvesting does not
follow swidden planting and protecting, then a crisis—drought, locusts,

crop disease, human sickness—has occurred. The anticipated structural sequence of scenes has been broken. Correspondingly, to the Subanun, the failure properly to stage the correct ceremony on schedule can only lead to crisis. Unanticipated crises are caused by the supernaturals when their anticipations of regular feasts are not met. The explicit rationale for performing scheduled offerings is to prevent the occurrence of crises, to ensure the proper unfolding of events.

The performance of scheduled ceremonies is necessary to prevent crises, but, as is obvious to any Subanun, it is by no means sufficient to do so. Serious crises do occur. The distributive frames of many ceremonies are composed of unscheduled events that disrupt the ordinary routine of activities. Since their scheduling in relation to other scenes cannot, with great probability, be planned in advance, ceremonies occupying such frames are unscheduled ceremonies. Their distribution has the following characteristics:

1. The events which comprise the distributive frame are relatively improbable in the sense that other events could more legitimately have been expected at that time instead.
2. In a given frame there are often alternative courses of action to staging a religious scene.
3. Given the staging of a religious scene, a variety of types of ceremonies can occur in many of these frames.

Thus, knowing Subanun culture, one cannot predict when the conditions for an unscheduled ceremony will occur, and given the occurrence of such conditions, one cannot directly predict if a ceremony or an alternative scene will be staged, and given the staging of a ceremony, one cannot directly predict what kind of ceremony will be held. In a typical unscheduled situation there are a number of alternative courses of action—a range of doubt over what to anticipate. When a particular course of action is selected from these alternatives, the decision is highly informative—it is news—even to one who knows the culture.

The occurrence of illness exemplifies an unscheduled frame. Oversimplifying somewhat (by ignoring disease stages and states of 'relapse' and 'recuperation'), the anticipated outcomes of an illness are continued sickness, cure, or death, giving the frame:

| sickness | diagnosis | continued sickness
cure
death |

All English terms comprising the frame are labels for categories of events as identified by the Subanun. The alternatives anticipatable are:

1. No formal therapy
2. 'Medication' (one or more of about 800 alternatives)
3. 'Religious' therapy
    3.1. Consulting the supernaturals
    3.2. 'Ritual contract'
    3.3. Performance of a 'contracted offering'
        3.3.1-61 +. (List of alternative types of offerings)

The initial choice is made in relation to the anticipatable outcome, or prognosis, predicated by diagnosis, and subsequent choices are made in relation to the results of previous choices (Frake 1961). 'Medication' (kebuluŋan), relying on the special power inherent in certain, generally botanical, substances, comprises a set of techniques conceptually distinct both from reliance on 'skills' (kependayan) and from appeals to the supernaturals through offerings. These three contrasting techniques are applicable to a wide range of endeavors apart from illness: agriculture, technology, social control, love-making, etc.

Because of the greater expense and more elaborate planning required, religious therapy for illness is resorted to only if medication fails or its failure is immediately obvious from prognosis. If religious therapy does occur, it is informative of the seriousness of the case. The particular kind of ceremony required, if any, cannot be determined from diagnosis, but only by consulting the supernaturals through divination or seance.

Once a patient has learned he must perform a specific kind of ceremony and has ritually acknowledged his intention to do so, he has acquired a binalaq, a term appropriately glossed as 'ritual debt,' for a Subanun's procrastination and legalistic evasion with binalaq obligations closely parallels his handling of ordinary 'debts' (gutaŋ) with his fellow mortals. The 'ritual acknowledgment' (penebiin) of a

binalaq, which generally follows considerable haggling with the supernaturals, can be labeled 'ritual contract.' It is sound policy to contract to pay one's ritual debt after one is cured. In this way one is
assured that the supernaturals will abide by their side of the agreement. The Subanun knows that even the most generous offering does
not always cure his afflictions, and that, if he pays his ritual debts
while he is sick, the supernaturals may keep him sick in the hope of
extorting more and more from him.

   But in this contest between mortal and supernatural, the former shows no more conscientiousness in fulfilling his obligations than
the latter. Once he is cured, the Subanun patient becomes very reluctant to expend his resources on the supernaturals. Yet most Subanun
have had enough experience with relapses of sickness to be somewhat
wary of neglecting their ritual obligations without making an effort to
do it legitimately by obtaining an extension of the contract through
assiduous divination or through pleading with the supernaturals during
a seance. Obtaining an extension often means an increase in the offering as interest, but despite past experience, the Subanun frequently
hopes that with enough extensions his supernatural creditors will eventually forget about the debt and not inflict illness on him again in an
effort to recover it. These hopes are generally in vain. The supernaturals hound their debtors with the same diligence as mortal creditors. Sooner or later, the Subanun who has neglected a ritual debt
becomes ill. Then he remembers his outstanding obligations, which
are likely to be numerous, and, if indications from seances and divination are affirmative, he may actually perform the contracted offering
But he may also acquire a new obligation pertinent to his new illness
and penalizing him for the long delay in paying the debt for the old.
With the new obligation, depending on the course of the illness, he
may go through the same delaying tactics until he is once again afflicted. Because of these tactics of debt evasion, in many a crisis ceremony of disease the beneficiary is indeed sick but not with the illness
that originally incurred the obligation to perform that ceremony.
(There are, of course, many complexities and deviations from this
simplified description that cannot be dealt with here.)

Summary

In contrasting religious scenes with alternative and complementary kinds of cultural activity, it becomes clear that the entire behavior complex of which 'offerings' are the ultimate constituents serves the Subanun essentially as a technique, a way of getting things done. To build a house, to grow crops, to cure disease, or to make love, a Subanun may rely on his own 'skills' (kepandayan), resort to the 'medicinal' properties of certain substances (kebuluŋan), or call upon the supernaturals for assistance (kanu). Religion, generally the most expensive and complex of these techniques, belongs especially to the context of crises or potential crises—unanticipatable events with severe consequences and uncertain outcomes. The regular performance of scheduled ceremonies is designed to prevent crises. Unscheduled ceremonies are staged to cope with crises and put events back on their proper course.

The rationale for religion (i. e. 'offering'-focused behavior) as a technique lies in the belief that one can accomplish an end by inducing others to act in his behalf. This principle, valid enough in social relationships, the Subanun extend by peopling the universe with unseen beings who have the power to inflict and thereby cure illness. These beings, the 'supernaturals,' are terminologically a species of 'persons' (getaw), and they can be influenced by methods resembling those proved effective in social relationships among mortals: offering food and drink, verbal appeals, attention to paraphernalia. A unique network of relationships, canalized by ritual obligations incurred through illness and the threat of illness, links each Subanun with the supernatural inhabitants of the universe, just as his network of social ties is patterned by secular obligations. The supernaturals sanction their demands with their power over health, whereas one's mortal fellows generally employ subtler sanctions of public opinion. In both cases the sanctions prove effective: social relationships are maintained, the supernaturals are fed, and the Subanun patient, if not cured, is perhaps consoled.

These characterizations of Subanun religion are summaries of the distributional properties of a structural segment of Subanun cultural activity with respect to contrasting and complementary activities. They are not, in intention at any rate, simply intuitive impressions of "the meaning of religion in Subanun life" unrelatable to operations performed on ethnographic data. As an adequate ethnographic statement the present paper is deficient in detail and rigor. It merely suggests some of the methodological features of such a statement.

NOTES

[1] A shorter version of this paper was read at the Tenth Pacific Science Congress, Honolulu, 1961. The notions of ethnographic method presented here owe much to Bruner (1957), Conklin (1962), Garfinkle (1961), Goodenough (1957), Miller et al. (1960), Pike (1954), Barker and Wright (1955), and Goffman (1958).

[2] English terms appropriated as labels for descriptive categories are marked by single quotes or italics, the former indicating glosses, i.e. English terms which substitute for, but do not define, Subanun expressions. Frequently used glosses and labels appear unmarked after initial mentioning, but they always carry only whatever meaning has been assigned to them in this paper. The fact that a descriptive category is not given a gloss here does not mean that the Subanun cannot or do not talk about that category and its members. Evidence from Subanun discussions of scenes as well as from verbal and non-verbal performances within scenes was used in isolating all descriptive categories. But frequently the problem of how the Subanun talk about something is more complex than simply a question of "whether they have a word for it." For example, a variety of Subanun expressions may be used to point to an event as being a feast in contra to an ordinary meal. Any reference to the provision of 'rice wine' (gasi) will suffice, as will a specification of a kind of festivity, such as 'labor-recruiting feast' (pesilut), during which the 'meal' is consumed.

[3] Gasi is a rice-yeast-fermented beverage made of a rice, manioc, maize, and/or Job's-tears mash. It contrasts in linguistic labeling, drinking technique, and social function with palm toddy (tuba) and sugar-cane wine (sebug).

REFERENCES

Barker, R. G., and H. F. Wright. 1955. Midwest and its children:
    the psychological ecology of an American town. New York:
    Harper & Row.
Bruner, J. S. 1957. Going beyond the information given. In Contem-
    porary approaches to cognition: a symposium held at the
    University of Colorado. Cambridge: Harvard, pp. 41-70.
Christie, E. B. 1909. The Subanuns of Sindangan Bay. Manilla:
    Bureau of Science, Division of Ethnology, Publication 6.
Conklin, H. C. 1962. Lexicographical treatment of folk taxonomies.
    In Fred W. Householder and Sol Saporta, eds., Problems in
    lexicography. Bloomington: Indiana Research Center in
    Anthropology, Folklore, and Linguistics, Publication 21.
Frake, C. O. 1957. Litigation in Lipay: a study in Subanun law.
    Proceedings of the Ninth Pacific Science Congress, Bangkok.
    (In press.)
_____. 1960. The Eastern Subanun of Mindanao. In G. P. Mur-
    dock, ed., Social structure in Southeast Asia. Viking Fund
    Publications in Anthropology, 29, Wenner-Gren Foundation
    for Anthropological Research, Inc., pp. 61-64.
_____. 1961. The diagnosis of disease among the Subanun of Min-
    danao. American Anthropologist 63.113-32.
Garfinkle, Harold. 1961. Reflections on the clinical method in psychi-
    atry from the viewpoint of ethnomethodology. Paper presented
    at a conference on ethnoscience, Stanford University, 1961.
Goffman, Erving. 1958. The presentation of self in everyday life.
    University of Edinburgh Social Science Research Centre,
    Monograph 2.
Goodenough, W. H. 1957. Cultural anthropology and linguistics. In
    Paul L. Garvin, ed., Report of the Seventh Annual Round
    Table Meeting on Linguistics and Language Study. George-
    town University, Monograph Series on Languages and Lin-
    guistics 9, pp. 167-73.
Miller, G. A., Eugene Galanter, and K. H. Pribram. 1960. Plans
    and the structure of behavior. New York: Holt.
Pike, K. L. 1954. Language in relation to a unified theory of the
    structure of human behavior, part I, preliminary ed. Glen-
    dale: Summer Institute of Linguistics.
Ziff, Paul. 1960. Semantic analysis. Ithaca, N.Y.: Cornell.

10 | How to Ask for a Drink in Subanun

Ward Goodenough (1957) has proposed that a description of a culture—an ethnography—should properly specify what it is that a stranger to a society would have to know in order appropriately to perform any role in any scene staged by the society. If an ethnographer of Subanun culture were to take this notion seriously, one of the most crucial sets of instructions to provide would be that specifying how to ask for a drink. Anyone who cannot perform this operation successfully will be automatically excluded from the stage upon which some of the most dramatic scenes of Subanun life are performed.[1]

To ask appropriately for a drink among the Subanun it is not enough to know how to construct a grammatical utterance in Subanun translatable in English as a request for a drink. Rendering such an utterance might elicit praise for one's fluency in Subanun, but it probably would not get one a drink. To speak appropriately it is not enough to speak grammatically or even sensibly (in fact some speech settings may require the uttering of nonsense as is the case with the semantic reversal type of speech play common in the Philippines. See Conklin 1959). Our stranger requires more than a grammar and a lexicon; he needs what Hymes (1962) has called an ethnography of speaking: a specification of what kinds of things to say in what message forms to what kinds of people in what kinds of situations. Of course an ethnography of speaking cannot provide rules specifying exactly what message to select in a given situation. If messages were perfectly predictable from a knowledge of the culture, there would be little point in saying anything. But when a person selects a message, he does so from a set of appropriate alternatives. The task of an ethnographer of speaking is to specify what the appropriate alternatives are in a given situation and what the consequences are of selecting one alternative over another.

Drinking defined. Of the various substances which the Subanun consider 'drinkable,' we are here concerned only with a subset
called gasi, a rice-yeast fermented beverage made of a rice, manioc,
maize, and/or Job's-tears mash. Gasi, glossed in this paper as 'beer,'
contrasts in linguistic labeling, drinking technique, and social context
with all other Subanun beverages (tebaq 'toddy,' sebug 'wine,' binu,
'liquor,' sabaw 'juice-broth,' tubig 'water').

The context of drinking. Focused social gatherings (Goffman
1961) among the Subanun fall into two sharply contrasted sets: festive
gatherings or 'festivities' and non-festive or informal gatherings
(Frake 1964b). The diagnostic feature of a festivity is the consumption
of a festive meal as a necessary incident in the encounter. A 'meal'
among the Subanun necessarily comprises a serving of a cooked
starchy-staple food, the 'main dish,' and ordinarily also includes a
'side dish' of vegetables, fish, or meat. A festive meal, or 'feast,'
is a meal with a meat side dish. A 'festivity' comprises all socially
relevant events occurring between the arrival and dispersal of participants in a feast. Apart from a feast, the necessary features of a
festivity are (1) an occasioning event, (2) multifamily participation,
and (3) beer. The drinking of beer, unlike the consumption of any
other beverage, occurs only during a festivity and must occur as part
of any festivity. It occupies a crucial position as a focus of formal
social gatherings.

Drinking technique. 'Beer,' uniquely among Subanun drinks,
is drunk with bamboo straws inserted to the bottom of a Chinese jar
containing the fermented mash. Just prior to drinking, the jar is
filled to the rim with water. Except in certain types of game drinking,
one person drinks at a time, after which another person replenishes
the water from an agreed-upon 'measure.' As one sucks on the straw,
the water disappears down through the mash where it picks up a surprising amount of alcohol and an indescribable taste. After initial
rounds of tasting, drinking etiquette requires one to gauge his consumption so that when a full measure of water is added, the water
level rises exactly even with the jar rim.

The drinking encounter. Each beer jar provided for a festivity
becomes the focus of a gathering of persons who take turns drinking. A
turn is a single period of continuous drinking by one person. Each

Table 1. Subanun Drinking Talk

Encounter stages	Discourse stages	Focus of speech acts	Function
1. Tasting	1. Invitation-permission	Role expression	Assignment of role distances and authority relations to participants
2. Competitive drinking	2. Jar talk	Role expression and context definition	Allocation of encounter resources (turns at drinking and talking)
	3. Discussion 3.1. Gossip 3.2. Deliberation	Topic	Exchange of informatio disputation, arbitratio deciding issues on basi of cogent argument
3. Game drinking	4. Display of verbal art	Stylistic	Establishment of eupho ia. Deciding issues or basis of skill in use of special styles of discourse (singing, verse

Segments of a drinking encounter: Segments of drinking talk:
1. A turn (continuous drinking   1. An utterance (continuous speech
   by one person)   by one person)
2. A round (a set of related   2. An exchange (a set of related
   turns)   utterances)
3. Encounter stage (a set of   3. Discourse stage (a set of relate
   related rounds)   exchanges)

change of drinkers marks a new turn. A circuit of turns through the
gathering is a _round_. As drinking progresses, rounds change in char
acter with regard to the number and length of constituent turns and to
variations in drinking techniques. Differences in these features amor
successive sets of rounds mark three distinct stages of the drinking
encounter: tasting, competitive drinking, and game drinking (Table 1)

The first round is devoted to _tasting,_ each person taking a
brief turn with little regard to formal measurement of consumption.

Successive turns become longer and the number of turns per round
fewer, thus cutting out some of the participants in the encounter.
These individuals go to other jars if available or withdraw from drinking during this stage of competitive drinking. Measurement is an important aspect of competitive rounds, participants keeping a mental
record of each other's consumption. Within a round, successive
drinkers must equal the consumption of the drinker who initiated the
round. In later rounds, as the brew becomes weaker, the measure
tends to be raised. Continued competitive drinking may assume an
altered character signaled by accompanying music, dancing, and singing. The scope of the gathering may enlarge and turns become shorter.
Special types of drinking games occur: 'chugalug' (saŋgayuq) and dual-
drinking by opposite-sexed partners under the cover of a blanket.
These rounds form a stage of game drinking.

   Drinking talk. The Subanun expression for drinking talk,
taluq bwat dig beksuk 'talk from the straw,' suggests an image of the
drinking straw as a channel not only of the drink but also of drinking
talk. The two activities, drinking and talking, are closely interrelated in that how one talks bears on how much one drinks, and the converse is, quite obviously, also true. Except for 'religious offerings,'
which must precede drinking, whatever business is to be transacted
during a festivity occurs during drinking encounters. Consequently
drinking talk is a major medium of interfamily communication. Especially for an adult male, one's role in the society at large, insofar as it
is subject to manipulation, depends to a considerable extent on one's
verbal performance during drinking encounters.

   Subanun society contains no absolute, society-wide status
positions or offices which automatically entitle their holder to deference from and authority over others. The closest approximation to
such a formal office is the status of religious specialist or 'medium'
who is deferred to in religious matters but who has no special voice
in affairs outside his domain (Frake 1964b). Assumption of decision-
making roles in legal, economic, and ecological domains depends not
on acquisition of an office but on continuing demonstration of one's
ability to make decisions within the context of social encounters. This
ability in turn depends on the amount of deference one can evoke from
other participants in the encounter. Although relevant, no external
status attributes of sex, age, or wealth are sufficient to guarantee

such deference; it must be elicited through one's skill in the use of
speech. Apart from age, sex, and reputation from performances in
previous encounters, the most salient external attributes brought to
an encounter by a participant are his relational roles based on kinshi
neighborhood, and friendship with specific other participants. Becau
of consanguineal endogamy and residential mobility, the relationship
ties between an ego and any given alter are likely to be multiple and
complex, giving wide latitude for manipulation of roles within particular encounters. Moreover, most kinship roles permit a range of
interpretation depending upon other features of the relationship such
as friendship and residential proximity.

The strategy of drinking talk is to manipulate the assignmen
of role relations among participants so that, within the limits of one'
external status attributes, one can maximize his share of encounter
resources (drink and talk), thereby having an opportunity to assume
an esteem-attracting and authority-wielding role. Variations in the
kinds of messages sent during periods devoted to different aspects of
this strategic plan mark four distinct discourse stages within the dri
ing talk of the encounter: invitation-permission, jar talk, discussion
and display of verbal art (Table 1). The constituents of a discourse
stage are exchanges: sets of utterances with a common topic focus.
(Boundaries of exchanges in American speech are often marked by
such expressions as "Not to change the subject, but ... " or "By the
way, that reminds me ... ") The constituents of exchanges are utterances: stretches of continuous speech by one person.

1. Invitation-permission. The Subanun designate the discour
of the initial tasting round as 'asking permission.' The provider of t
jar initiates the tasting round by inviting someone to drink, thereby
signaling that this person is the one to whom he and those closest to
him in the encounter owe the greatest initial deference on the basis o
external status attributes. The invited drinker squats before the jar
and asks permission to drink of the other participants. He has two
variables to manipulate: the order in which he addresses the other
participants and the terms of address he employs. Apart from the
latter variable, message form remains relatively constant: naa, A,
sep pa u 'Well, A, I will be drinking.' (A represents a term of address.) Role relations with persons who are not lineal consanguineal
or lineal affinal kin (Mo, F, Ch, Sp, SpPr, ChSp, ChSpPr) permit a

variety of forms of address each with different implications for social
distance with respect to ego (Frake 1960). The drinker's final opportunity to express role relations comes when he finishes tasting and
invites another (ordinarily the person who invited him) to drink.

2. Jar talk. As competitive drinking begins, asking permission is reduced in scope and importance, and there is an increase in
messages sent during drinking itself. The topic focus of these exchanges is the drink being consumed. The drinker responds to queries about the taste and strength of the beer, explanations are advanced
for its virtues and defects, and the performance of drinkers is evaluated. During this stage the topic of messages is predictable. The
informative aspect of the messages is the quantity and quality of verbal
responses a drinker can elicit. This information signals the amount
of drinking and talking time the gathering will allot him. Those who
receive little encouragement drop out, and the encounter is reduced
generally to less than half a dozen persons, who can thereby intensify
their interaction with each other and with the beer straw.

3. Discussion. As the size and role-structure of the gathering become defined, discourse changes in topic to removed referents,
usually beginning with relatively trivial gossip, proceeding to more
important subjects of current interest, and, finally, in many cases
arriving at litigation. Since there are no juro-political offices in
Subanun society, a legal case is not only a contest between litigants,
but also one between persons attempting to assume a role of legal
authority by settling the case. Success in effecting legal decisions
depends on achieving a commanding role in the encounter and on de-
bating effectively from that position. Since there are no sanctions of
force legally applicable to back up a decision, the payment of a fine
in compliance with a decision is final testimony to the prowess in
verbal combat of the person who made the decision.

4. Display of verbal art. If drinking continues long enough,
the focus of messages shifts from their topics to play with message
forms themselves, following stylized patterns of song and verse composition. Songs and verses are composed on the spot to carry on discussions in an operetta-like setting. Even unsettled litigation may be
continued in this manner, the basis for decision being shifted from
cogent argument to verbal artistry. The most prestigious kinds of

drinking songs require the mastery of an esoteric vocabulary by mea of which each line is repeated with a semantically equivalent but formally different line. Game drinking is a frequent accompaniment to these displays of verbal art. Together they help assure that the fest vity will end with good feelings among all participants, a goal which i explicitly stated by the Subanun. Participants who have displayed marked hostility toward each other during the course of drinking talk may be singled out for special ritual treatment designed to restore good feelings.

The Subanun drinking encounter thus provides a structured setting within which one's social relationships beyond his everyday associates can be extended, defined, and manipulated through the use of speech. The cultural patterning of drinking talk lays out an order scheme of role play through the use of terms of address, through dis cussion and argument, and through display of verbal art. The most skilled in "talking from the straw" are the de facto leaders of the society. In instructing our stranger to Subanun society how to ask for a drink, we have at the same time instructed him how to get ahead socially.

NOTE

[1] The Subanun are pagan swidden agriculturists occupying the mountainous interior of Zamboanga Peninsula on the island of Mindan in the Philippines. This paper refers to the Eastern Subanun of Zam boanga del Norte Province. Descriptions of Subanun social structure festive activities, and some aspects of gasi manufacture are given in Frake 1960, 1963, 1964a, and 1964b. The ethnographic methodology o this paper is that described in Frake 1964b. Single quotation marks enclose English substitutes for (but not translations of) Subanun expressions.

REFERENCES

Conklin, Harold C. 1959. Linguistic play in its cultural setting. Language 35.631-36.
Frake, Charles O. 1960. The Eastern Subanun of Mindanao. In

George P. Murdock, ed., Social structure in Southeast Asia.
Viking Publications in Anthropology 29, pp. 51-64.
Frake, Charles O. 1963. Litigation in Lipay: a study in Subanun
law. Proceedings of the Ninth Pacific Science Congress,
1957, vol. 3. Bangkok.
_____. 1964a. Notes on queries in ethnography. American Anthro-
pologist 66.3.132-45, Part 2.
_____. 1964b. A structural description of Subanun "religious
behavior." In Ward G. Goodenough, ed., Explorations in
cultural anthropology: essays in honor of George Peter
Murdock. New York: McGraw Hill.
Goffman, Erving. 1961. Encounters: two studies in the sociology of
interaction. Indianapolis: Bobbs-Merrill.
Goodenough, Ward G. 1957. Cultural anthropology and linguistics.
In Paul L. Garvin, ed., Report of the Seventh Annual Round
Table Meeting on Linguistics and Language Study. Georgetown University Monograph Series on Language and Linguistics 9.167-73.
Hymes, Dell H. 1962. The ethnography of speaking. In T. Gladwin
and W. C. Sturtevant, eds., Anthropology and human behavior. Washington, D.C.: Anthropological Society of Washington, pp. 15-53.

Part III.   The Yakan

11 | Struck by Speech: The Yakan Concept of Litigation

> Tiyaq ku tawwaq bissāh
> Here I am struck by speech
>
> —Remark of an accused in a trial

The Yakan legal system is manifest almost exclusively through one kind of behavior: talk. Consequently the ethnographer's record of observations of litigation is largely a linguistic record, and the legal system is a code for talking, a linguistic code. In this paper we focus initially on a small part of this talk, that representing the concept of litigation. We subsequently attempt to illustrate how a definition of this concept guides a description of the legal system and, finally, points the way toward meaningful comparisons with legal systems of other cultures.

The Yakan are Philippine Moslems inhabiting the island of Basilan located off the southern tip of Zamboanga Peninsula, a western extension of the island of Mindanao.[1] Southwest of Basilan stretches the Sulu archipelago, a chain of small islands extending some 200 miles to within a few miles of the northeast coast of Borneo. Some 60,000 Yakan share Basilan's 1,282 square kilometers with Christian Filipinos concentrated along the north coast and with Tausug and Samal Moslems living mostly in coastal villages all around the island.[2] The Yakan are close linguistic kin of the seafaring Samal but, unlike them, practice an exclusively land-oriented economy: diversified grain, root, and tree-crop agriculture on plowed fields and swiddens, commercial copra production, and cattle raising. Supplementary economic activities include plantation labor, distribution of cigarettes smuggled from

Borneo by their Moslem brothers, and banditry. These economic
activities bring the Yakan into close contact with the Philippine economy, political system, and army. Having been given this much infor
mation, the anthropological reader has probably already classed the
Yakan as "peasants, " which is appropriate as long as the concept doe
not bring to mind a downtrodden, economically exploited, culturally
deprived people submerged by the weight of some "great tradition. "

Houses, mosques, and graveyards dot the Yakan countryside
rarely revealing any obvious patterns of spatial clustering. Each,
however, represents the focus of a pattern of social alignment. Hous
are occupied by nuclear families, independent units of production and
consumption. The family is the unit of membership in a parish, a re
ligious and political unit under the titular leadership of a mosque
priest (qimam). Parishes are alliances of independent families; affil
iation is by choice, not by residence or kinship ties. Parishes comprise only several dozen families, and any family has a network of
social relations with kin and neighbors extending beyond the parish.
Ancestors, buried in conspicuously decorated graves, define network
of cognatic kinship ties among the living. Although these networks ar
unsegmented by discrete, corporate groups of any kind, the Yakan tal
about groupings of kin in ways that would do credit to a social anthropologist. Note, for example, the contrast between paŋkat baqirah
"the unrestricted, non-unilineal descent group defined by an ancestor
(female) named Baira" and qusba baqirah "the kindred centered arour
an ego named Baira. " Like the legal expressions we are about to dis
cuss, this talk about social groups must be understood to be a part of
social behavior as well as a description of it.

Defining Litigation

A description of a culture derives from an ethnographer's
observations of the stream of activities performed by the people he
is studying. As a first step toward producing an ethnographic statement, the investigator must segment and classify the events of this
behavior stream so that he can say, for example, of two successive
events that they are repetitions of the "same" activity. If the ethnographer claims his people do X three times a week, verification of his
statement requires not simply counting occurrences of X, but also

assessing the criteria for distinguishing X from all the other things people do during the week and for deciding that all the different events construed as instances of X in fact represent the "same" activity. Information about what is the "same" and what is "different" can only come from the interpretations of events made by the people being studied.

Within the stream of behavior observable in Yakan society, there are some events that are difficult to characterize initially except as "a group of people talking together." There seems to be no focus of activity other than talk—no distinctive settings, apparel, or paraphernalia. We might postulate that all such events are manifestations of the same category of cultural activities, that all are repetitions of the same scene. At a very general level we could justify this decision. All these activities can be labeled magbissāh 'talking to each other' in response to a query such as magqine siyeh 'what are they doing?'[3] But, as the English glosses indicate, this categorization is not particularly informative, especially to an observer of the scene. To discover a more refined categorization we must attend to the way the Yakan talk about talking.

Yakan, like English, provides a large number of linguistic expressions for talking about a great variety of aspects of speech behavior. Of these, we sort out for consideration the following set of semantically related expressions, all possible responses to the query "What are they doing?" (Only the variable portion of the response is shown.[4] Some of these forms, especially hukum, have different, but related meanings in different contexts. Etymological information is given for later discussion.) (1) mitiŋ (from English) 'discussion'; (2) qisuŋ 'conference'; (3) mawpakkat (from Arabic) 'negotiation'; (4) hukum (from Arabic) 'litigation.'

The structure of inclusion and contrast relations manifest in the use of these terms to denote events is shown in Figure 1. Let A, B, C, D represent situations that can be labeled mitiŋ, qisun, mawpakkat, and hukum, respectively. Then it is the case that mitiŋ can label the set of situations ABCD, qisun the set of situations BCD, mawpakkat the set CD, whereas hukum can label only D. Thus these expressions form an ordered series, the situations labelable by a given term including all those labelable by each succeeding term.

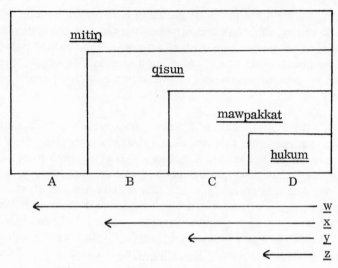

A, B, C, D: situations represented
w, x, y, z: features of meaning

Figure 1. Semantic structure

However, it is also the case that mitiŋ can be used to contrast situation A with each of the other situations (A not B, C, or D) as in the
exchange magqisuŋ qenteq siyeh 'they seem to be conferring.' Duma-
qin, magmitiŋ hadja qiyan 'no, they're just discussing.' The form
hadja 'just, merely' specifies that mitiŋ is to be construed in its minimal sense, but its use is not obligatory to convey this sense. Similar
ly, qisun, mawpakkat, and hukum can be used to contrast B, C, D,
respectively, with each of the other situations. We have, then, a case
of the use of the same form at different levels of contrast, a situation
common in semantic representation (Frake 1961), and one that has
caused some controversy over interpretation (Bright and Bright 1965:
258).

In the use of the same expression at different levels of contrast, there is in Yakan a distinction between those cases, such as the
present example, in which use at the less inclusive level is specifiable

by a de-emphatic particle (for example, hadja 'just, merely') and those
in which it is specifiable by an emphatic particle (such as teqed 'very,
true, real'). Contrast magmitiŋ hadja qiyan 'they're just discussing'
(and not 'conferring,' 'negotiating,' and the like) with magpoŋtinaqi teqed
qiyan 'they're real siblings' (and not 'half-siblings,' 'cousins,' and so
on). The use of the same term at different levels of contrast results,
in the former case, from a specification of the basic general sense of
an expression. In the latter case it results from an extension of the
basic specific sense of an expression. Cases of specification, such
as the present example, can be interpreted as manifestations of "marking," a phenomenon widespread in linguistic representation in phonology and morphology as well as in semantics (Jakobson 1957, Greenberg 1966).

    Semantic marking means that given two expressions, A and
B, sharing some feature of meaning $\underline{x}$ but differing with respect to
some feature $\underline{y}$ and in that sense contrasting, the difference is not

    term A represents the meaning: $\underline{x}$ $\underline{y}$
    term B represents the meaning: $\underline{x}$ $\underline{\bar{y}}$

but rather

    term A represents the meaning: $\underline{x}$
    term B represents the meaning: $\underline{x}$ $\underline{y}$

The use of term B necessarily implies feature $\underline{y}$, but the use of term
A does not necessarily say anything about the presence or absence of
$\underline{y}$. Term B is marked for $\underline{y}$. In our series each term is marked for
a feature (or features) not necessarily implied by its predecessor:

    mitiŋ 'discussion': $\underline{w}$
    qisun 'conference': $\underline{w}$ $\underline{x}$
    mawpakkat 'negotiation': $\underline{w}$ $\underline{x}$ $\underline{y}$
    hukum 'litigation': $\underline{w}$ $\underline{x}$ $\underline{y}$ $\underline{z}$

The next task is to characterize the features of meaning represented
above as $\underline{w}$, $\underline{x}$, $\underline{y}$, $\underline{z}$; w being what the set has in common and $\underline{x}$, $\underline{y}$, $\underline{z}$
being successive increments to this common meaning.

At the outset we should be clear about just what linguistic
and cognitive operations of our informants we are trying to account
for. It is not simply a case of determining the perceptual cues for
distinguishing one object from another. If a Yakan sees some people
engaged in mutual speech behavior (that categorization he can make
perceptually) and wants to know what they are doing, he will in all
probability ask them. In this case the object of categorization, a
group of people engaged in some activity, is aware of what it is doing.
This awareness is, in itself, an attribute—a necessary one—of the
category. Just as in classifying a plant one might apply a test of taste
or smell to determine a criterial property, in classifying these speech
events one applies a test of eliciting a linguistic response from the per
formers of the activity. It is impossible for people engaged in 'litigation' or in 'conference' not to be aware of what they are doing and not
to be able to communicate their awareness. For people engaged, say,
in 'litigation' to be able to state that they are 'litigating' is a necessary
condition for the activity to be 'litigation,' but it is not a sufficient con
dition. They might be lying or, more probably in Yakan life, they
might be joking. Being funny is a prominent goal of Yakan speech behavior, and semantic incongruity is a standard way of adding humor to
speech—but the effect is dependent on the hearer's ability to recognize
the incongruity. What we are trying to formulate, then, are the conditions under which it is congruous, neither humorous nor deceitful, to
state that one is engaged in 'litigation.' These conditions are the semantic features of the concepts in question. Our evidence for semantic features does not come from informants' statements about the linguistic representations of these concepts (though such explicit definitions of terms are often useful guides for preliminary formulations),
but from informants' interpretations of the situations that the concepts
represent. Our aim is not to give an elegant formulation of minimal
contrastive features, but a statement that reflects the various dimensions of speech behavior revealed in the use and interpretation of
these expressions.

Let us consider first the features common to the whole set,
those that distinguish all events construable as mitiŋ 'discussion' from
other things Yakan do. This set of events includes the events labeled
by the other expressions. Then we will consider what each successive
term adds to these common features. Four dimensions of speech behavior appear to be involved in contrasting 'discussion' with other
activities.

1. Focus. The focus of 'discussion' is on the topic of messages. There is a subject of discussion. Excluded are speech events in which the focus is on message form: storytelling, riddling, exchanging verses, joking, prayer (which, being in Arabic, has no semantic content for the Yakan).

2. Purpose. The purpose of the gathering is to talk. Excluded are activities in which the intent to accomplish something other than talking is responsible for the gathering of participants.

3. Roles. Speaking time is distributed among the participants. Each role in the scene, whatever its other characteristics, is both a speaking and a listening role. Excluded are monologues, in which speaking time is monopolized by one person.[5]

4. Integrity. Integrity refers to the extent to which the activity is construed as an integral unit as opposed to being a part of some other activity. A 'discussion' must have sufficient integrity not to be construable as incident to or accompanying some other activity. A 'discussion' can occur within the context of another kind of event, but only as a recognizably bounded interruption, as when participants disengage from some other activity to talk something over. (This dimension will sound less fuzzy when we consider its relevance to the contrast between 'litigation' and other kinds of 'discussion.')

The expression mitiŋ 'discussion' necessarily implies only these features. Each of the succeeding expressions in the series adds some necessary implications along one or more of these dimensions (Table 1):

qisun 'conference'

1. Focus. The subject of discussion is an issue, some topic that presents a problem to be decided: when to plant rice, when to go on a trip, what price to pay in a transaction.

2. Purpose. A 'conference' has an expected outcome, a decision about the issue. Participants meet in order to reach a decision, and, if a decision is made, the conference is concluded.

3. Roles. No added implications.

Table 1. Semantic Features

	Topic	Purpose	Role structure	Integrity
'discussion'	subject	talk	undifferentiated	minimal
'conference'	issue	decision	undifferentiated	minimal
'negotiation'	disagreement	settlement	opposing sides	moderate
'litigation'	dispute	ruling	court	maximal

4. Integrity. No added implications.

mawpakkat 'negotiation'

1. Focus. The issue in 'negotiation' is a disagreement, a topic over which participants have conflicting interests.

2. Purpose. The decision is a settlement, a legally binding resolution of the disagreement.

3. Roles. Participants are divided into two protagonistic sides. Witnesses may be present.

4. Integrity. No clear added implications. Although _mawpak-kat_ is more likely to refer to an integral event than _qisun,_ and _qisun_ than _mitiŋ,_ these are not necessary implications.

hukum 'litigation'

1. Focus. The disagreement is a dispute, a disagreement that arises from a charge that an offense has been committed. A dispute can also be handled by negotiation, but the topic of litigation is necessarily a dispute. A dispute handled by litigation is a case.

2. Purpose. The settlement takes the form of a legal ruling based on precedent and having special sanctions.

3. Roles. In addition to protagonists and optional witnesses, 'litigation' requires a court, a set of neutral judges who control the proceedings and attempt to effect a ruling.

4. Integrity. 'Litigation' is always an integral activity. If it is interrupted by a different kind of activity—eating, for example—there is a new instance of litigation, a different court session. 'Discussion,' 'conference,' and 'negotiation,' in their minimal senses, can occur as parts of 'litigation,' but 'litigation' cannot occur as a part of these other activities.

Each expression in our series except the terminal one has a maximal and minimal sense, depending on whether the speaker intends to include or exclude the meanings marked by succeeding expressions. 'Mere discussion' (mitiŋ hadja), the minimal sense of mitiŋ, implies the features listed as common to the whole set, but the topic is simply a subject to discuss, not an issue to be decided, a disagreement to be settled, or a case to be ruled on. The purpose is to talk, but there is no expected outcome that terminates the event, no decision to be reached, no settlement to be negotiated, no ruling to be handed down. Role structure is undifferentiated and integrity minimal, although it is still greater than that implied by magbissāh 'talking to each other.' A mitiŋ in its minimal sense more closely resembles an American "bull session" than what we would call a "meeting."

'Mere conference' applies to situations in which the issue is not a dispute, the decision not a settlement, and role structure remains undifferentiated. 'Mere negotiation' applies to situations in which, though the disagreement may be a dispute, the intended outcome is a settlement that is not a legal ruling and that is reached without the aid of judges.

The flexibility of reference afforded by this semantic structure, the ability to be ambiguous about whether a general or specific sense is intended, reflects the fact that not only are these expressions used to talk about speech behavior, but their use is also a part of the behavior they describe. A Yakan uses terms like mawpakkat and hukum not simply to give serious answers to probes for information, but also to further his own objectives in speech situations by advancing a particular—perhaps ostensibly incongruous—interpretation of an event and by representing this conceptualization linguistically in an effective way. He can, for example, call for a 'conference' without immediately committing himself to an interpretation of the divisiveness of the issue; he can call for a 'discussion' without implying that there is an issue at stake.

For these reasons, stylistic features of expressions—selections among alternative linguistic representations of a given conceptual distinction—figure importantly in their use and affect their semantic properties. In our set, mawpakkat is considered more learned than the other terms, all of which are ordinary, everyday words. Although the word is widely known, it occurs most often during 'litigation' when 'negotiations' are being talked about. In other contexts the notion of 'mere negotiation' is more likely to be referred to as qisun, using 'conference' in its general sense. It is probably a consequence of this stylistic difference that the semantic contrast between mawpakkat and qisun seems less sharply drawn than that between the other pairs of expressions. In direct questioning about the meaning of these terms, many informants have stated offhand that mawpakkat and qisun have the same meaning. No one has said that of hukum and any other term in the set. The same informants will still agree that if, for example, several guests at a festivity get together to decide when to leave, this is a case of qisun but not of mawpakkat. The two expressions are not synonymous but the difference between them is somewhat harder to uncover than is the difference between the other terms. The concept of "negotiation" can also be represented by expressions referring to the distinctive aspects of the event, for example: pagsulutan 'agreement, settlement'—not including legal rulings (hukuman); qalegdah (from Spanish) 'to settle a dispute by any means'; janjiqan (from Malay) 'negotiated contractual promise.'

Any citation of Yakan legal terms illustrates another property of these expressions—that is, the large percentage of forms that are loan words from the languages of both of the "great traditions" impinging on the Yakan: Arabic and Malay of the Malaysian-Moslem tradition, English and Spanish of the Filipino-Western tradition.[6] These loans have been acquired through contact with intermediary languages (Tausug and Zamboangueño), and their prevalence is not a reflection of a crushing impact of either Moslem or Western legal concepts upon Yakan law, but of the stylistic coups a speaker of Yakan scores by displaying a knowledge of foreign words. This process apparently has a long history. Many loans, such as hukum (from Arabic), are now completely assimilated and are not now recognized as foreign. The term mitin, currently much more popular than alternative designations of 'discussion,' seems to be on the verge of losing its loan-word aura. English loans used in current litigation include: wantid, holdap, kidnap

wadan ('warrant'), supenah, pospon, pendiŋ, qokeh ('approval'), and
qistodok ('strategy,' from "stroke").

Describing Litigation

Our formulation states that litigation is a kind of topic-focused
mutual speech behavior, the distinctive attributes of which pertain to
the content and role structure of talking. An observer of Yakan litigation would have difficulty finding any other element that sets it apart
from other activities. There are no distinctive settings, no courtrooms
in which litigation takes place. A site for a trial should be neutral and
should require no one to play a host role—a role that requires the offering of food. A typical result of these considerations is convocation on
the porch of the house of one of the judges (in Yakan terms, "on" the
house but not "within" it). But a wide variety of other activities takes
place here as well. There are no distinctive paraphernalia associated
with litigation: no law books, no gavel, no judges' bench, no witness
stand. There is no provisioning of participants. They may smoke and
chew betel, but the rules for soliciting and proferring smoking and
chewing makings are the same as for other informal gatherings. There
is no distinctive dress associated with litigation—no judges' robes—and
participants do not dress up to go to court as they do to go to ceremonies. If one were to make distinction in Yakan activities between festive and non-festive, formal and informal, litigation would clearly fall
on the non-festive, informal side. As speech-focused activity, litigation is outside the domain of ceremonies, feasts, technological tasks,
and other object-focused activities. We must therefore organize a
description of litigation along those dimensions of speech behavior
found to be significant.

Cases

The topic of litigation is a 'case' (pākalaq, from Malay from
Sanskrit), a 'dispute' brought to court. A 'dispute' arises when an
identified party is 'charged' with an 'offense' and the accused counters
the charge. To make a charge is to publicly proclaim a particular
interpretation of an act. To counter a charge is to advance another
interpretation. Clearly the key descriptive problem is to state the
roles for interpreting an act as an offense. Equally clear is that these

rules cannot be perfectly consistent in their formulation or straightforward in their application. There must be room for argument if
there is to be litigation.

Offenses. 'Offenses' (salaq) are a subset of 'wrongs' (duseh)
—those wrongs against persons that can lead to a dispute. There are
also wrongs against God (tuhan), such as desecrating a Koran; wrongs
against this-world supernaturals (saytan, from Arabic), such as cutting down a tree they inhabit; and wrongs against ancestors (kapapuqan)
now in the other world (qahilat, from Arabic), such as selling an heir-
loom. But these beings need not rely on courts to seek redress.

The Yakan employ a large number of linguistic expressions
for talking about different kinds of offenses along a variety of semantic dimensions dealing with the nature and consequences of acts as
well as with the social relationships between offender and victim. The
saliency of dimensions with respect to one another can vary in different portions of the domain. For example, physical assault with intent
to kill (bonoq) and sexual assault (hilap, from Arabic, and many other
expressions) are terminologically distinguished unless the offense is
also a wrong against God, as is the case if victim and offender are
primary kin or primary affines. There is one term, sumbaq, to cover
these grievous sins against both man and God. One might say that the
contrast "sex versus killing" is neutralized when an expression is
marked for "interference by God." (It might be noted that sexual relations are often designated euphemistically or facetiously by metaphors based on expressions for killing or fighting. "To make a killing" in Yakan does not refer to business success.) We will state here
only a few general inferences about the nature of the concept of 'offense
which have been drawn from Yakan talk about particular kinds of
offenses.

At the most general level, for an act to be interpretable as
an offense it must be a threat to a dapuq relationship. The term dapuq
occurs together with a possessive attribute in response to the same
query that elicits kinship terms and other relationship expressions.
Unlike kinship relations, however, a person may be dapuq of an object
as well as of another person. Being someone's or something's dapuq
implies having an economic interest in him (it) and a responsibility
for him (it). The notion includes, but is broader than, that of owner-

ship. To be a <u>dapuq</u> of a person in no way implies that the person is
one's slave. One is <u>dapuq</u> to his children, his legal wards, his spouse,
and himself. To be a <u>dapuq</u> of an object does not necessarily imply
that one has rights of use, possession, or sale, but only that one has
a legitimate interest in its use or disposal. A water source, for example, has its <u>dapuq</u> (<u>dapuq boheq</u>)—those who use it and who would
suffer economic loss if it were destroyed—but it has no owner. The
<u>dapuq</u> of a mosque (<u>dapuq laŋgal</u>) is not its owner—there is such a
person—but the entire congregation. The <u>dapuq</u> of an inheritance
(<u>dapuq pusakaq</u>) is a potential heir. Any threat to a <u>dapuq</u> relationship
can be interpreted as an economic threat, a threat whose gravity is
expressible in pesos and centavos. All offenses, including murder,
can be compensated for by money. The purpose of Yakan litigation is
not to mete out punishment, but to award compensation for injury.

There are two ways in which an act can be an offense. First,
it can challenge a person's status as a <u>dapuq</u>, usually in the form of a
claim that some other person is properly the <u>dapuq</u> of a given object
or person. Second, an act can damage an object or person in such a
way as to reduce its economic value to its <u>dapuq</u> (including, in the case
of persons, the victim himself). Since a given object or person is
likely to have more than one <u>dapuq</u>, an offense generally produces several plaintiffs. A sexual assault, for example, is an offense against
the victim (<u>dapuq badannen</u>, '<u>dapuq</u> of one's body'), her parents (<u>dapuq
qanakin</u>, '<u>dapuq</u> of the child'), and if she is married, her husband (<u>da-
puq qandahin</u>, '<u>dapuq</u> of the wife').

<u>Charges</u>. It is up to a victim of an offense to make a charge
(<u>tuntut</u>); all Yakan law is civil law. He must, furthermore, determine
the identify of the offender and assume responsibility for the identification. Offenses in which victim and offender do not meet face to face
or in which the victim does not survive are difficult to prosecute. Even
though theft, ambush shootings, and murder are among the more common—and certainly the most complained about—offenses in Yakan life,
they rarely reach the courts. It is largely sex and, to a lesser extent,
fights and property disputes that keep court agenda full.

An initial charge can be made in the form of a complaint (<u>dik-
lamuh</u>, from Spanish) to a court or even by directly confronting the
accused. More often an accuser will utilize gossip channels to make

his charge known to the accused. In this way he can feel out the response of his opponent before being irrevocably committed. A way out is left open through denying the truth or serious intent of the gossip. One of the dangers of Yakan life is limorok (literally, 'slip through'): 'inadvertently instigating a dispute by incautious gossip in the presence of someone who is likely to relay the accusation to the accused.'

There are three strategies available for countering a charge:

1. One can deny the validity of the accuser's definition of the offense in question, disputing the meaning of a concept. Does, for example, the notion of sexual offense include all acts in which a male makes unnecessary physical contact with a female not his spouse, or only those acts in which a male has sexual designs on the woman?

2. One can deny that the act in question has the properties to qualify it as an instance of an offense, disputing what really happened. For example, granted any physical contact as described above is an offense, did any such contact actually occur in the particular instance?

3. One can deny responsibility for the act because (a) someone else committed it; (b) the accused was provoked by the accuser; (c) the accused was incited by some third party (a much stronger excuse for wrongdoing among the Yakan than among ourselves); (d) the act was unintentional.

To deny a charge is at the same time to make a charge against one's accuser, for a false charge is in itself an offense: it threatens the economic interests of the accused. The set of arguments propounded by one side in a dispute to counter the charges of the other is their daqawah (from Arabic) or "case" in the sense of "the defense rests its case."

Disputes. Once a charge has been made and countered, a dispute exists. Disputants may simply decide to live with the dispute, they may attempt to dispose of each other, or they may seek a settlement. If they decide on the last course of action, they may either 'negotiate' or 'litigate.' In 'negotiation' two opposing parties meet to settle a disagreement by mutual agreement. The disagreement need

not be a dispute (that is, the outcome of a charge). Negotiating a contract, property settlements, marriage (which involves all of the preceding) are cases to point. Negotiations are often sufficient to handle
minor disputes and are necessary for major disputes difficult to place
under the jurisdiction of any Yakan court. An agreement is specific
to the negotiating parties and need not derive from legal precedents;
the breaking of an agreement, however, is an offense and can result
in a dispute taken to court. Marriages are made by negotiation but
dissolved by litigation. To settle a dispute by litigation requires that
it be reported to a court, at which point the dispute becomes a legal
case. The party that considers itself offended against should report
first, but often by the time a case reaches court, there is such a complex of charges and countercharges that any distinction between plaintiff and defendant becomes obscure.

Courts

What distinguishes litigation from other methods of settling
disputes is the presence of a court (saraq, from Arabic)—a set of persons, performing the role of judge, who are ostensibly neutral on the
issue and whose task it is to formulate a settlement. The Yakan court
has few of the tangible manifestations of its Western counterpart: professional judges holding an office, courthouses, explicit and continuous
schedules, and well-defined jurisdictions. On the other hand, a set of
judges is not recruited ad hoc to try each case that appears. Particular sets of judges meet more than once and may try more than one
case in a single session. Furthermore, there is a fundamental difference between a single case appearing again in a subsequent session of
the same court—a continuation of a single trial—and a case appearing
again in a different court—a retrial of the same case. One may also
report to a court when the court is not in session—to file a charge, for
example, or to seek asylum. The crucial problems in a description
of Yakan courts are those of legal authority and of jurisdiction. How
are persons recruited to the role of judge? How are cases assigned to
particular courts?

Judges. To act as a judge, a person must be a parish leader
with the ability and knowledge to perform the role and with sufficient
political power at the jurisdictional level of the court to make his voice
effective. Parish leadership is not a political office with formal rules

of recruitment, but a position achieved by accumulating influence and prestige by a variety of means: religious learning, economic success, military prowess, forensic ability, acquisition of a title, pilgrimage to Mecca, election to a local office in the Philippine political system (councilor or barrio captain), or simply growing older. (The most common expression for a leader is bahiq 'elder.') Typically, parish leadership is vested in a small group of close kinsmen, each specializing in one or more of these routes to power. One man may be the priest and litigator, another the entrepreneur, another the fighter. Larger political groupings are informal and unstable alliance of parishes. To exert leadership at this wider level, one must also be a leader at the parish level. One does not rise to higher positions; one merely extends the range of his influence. An exceptional position is that of titular tribal chief (datuq) of all the Yakan, a hereditary office now held by the Westernized son of a Christian Filipino escaped convict, who, during the latter part of the Spanish regime, fled to Basilan. There he assumed political leadership over the Yakan and achieve formal recognition of his position by both the Spaniards and the Sultan of Sulu.

Jurisdiction. The jurisdiction of a court is a function of the social distance between the judges who comprise it and the disputants before it. This distance, in turn, is a response to the need to preserve neutrality with respect to the cases brought before it. The rule for assignment of a case to a court is to maintain minimal social distance between court and protagonists consistent with preserving neutrality. This rule has the effect that the greater the social distance between protagonists and the more serious the case, the higher the jurisdiction of the court that can try the case. If both protagonists belong to the same parish, then one or more of their own parish leaders may be found who, by kinship and other dimensions of social affiliation, are equidistant from both sides. If, however, the protagonists belong to different parishes, the court must comprise representatives of both parishes. The seriousness of a case is measured by the number of active supporters recruited by each disputant. As the number of active supporters surrounding each disputant increases—that is, as each party of protagonists grows larger—the further afield one must go to find judges who are not involved on one side or another. Because of these considerations, there is a certain ad hoc nature to the formation of

courts as adjustments are made to handle particular cases. Nevertheless, three basic jurisdictional levels can be distinguished: parish, community, and tribal.

The tribal court, composed of leaders appointed by the tribal
chief, meets in the yard of the chief's Western-style house in the town
of Lamitan. Although in theory it is a sort of supreme court for all
the Yakan, handling cases local courts have failed to settle, in practice its jurisdiction and its composition are geographically limited to
the side of the island where the court meets. Parish courts are generally formed ad hoc to try relatively trivial disputes—fights among
young men, for example—among parish members. Occasionally a
parish trial will be conducted with the absolute minimum personnel:
two disputants and one judge. The bulk of litigation occurs at what
might be called the community level. In most areas there are regular
court sessions about once a week. Adjustments are made in these
courts to handle particular cases. Any court intermediate between a
regular community court and the tribal court is an ad hoc formation
to handle a special case. Before reaching the tribal level, however,
there is a limit beyond which jurisdiction cannot be stretched, where
judges who are neutral and at the same time sufficiently close socially
to act together cannot be found. Disputes at this level may be referred
to the tribal court or to government courts, or a settlement by negotiation may be attempted. Frequently, however, disputants resort to
violence at this point.

Other roles. Added to the basic role structure of litigation—
a court and two opposing sides—there is a further differentiation of
roles within each part of protagonists: (a) the principal, the one primarily involved in the original dispute, the person who, as the Yakan
say, was 'struck' by speech (tawwaq bissāh) or who 'collided' with
litigation (lumaŋgal si hukum); (b) his guardian, the one who assumes
responsibility for accepting or rejecting a ruling and complying with
it. The guardian may be the principal himself, a parent or parental
surrogate, or a spouse; (c) senior and peer supporters.

The Yakan speak about this role structure in the language of
kinship, using an ideal model in which the principal is a child, the
court his elders, the guardian his parent, and his supporters his sen-

ior and peer kin. A final role is that of witnesses, who may be called
by either side or by the court.

Rulings

The intended outcome of litigation is a ruling (hukuman) on a
case handed down by the court. The crucial fact shaping Yakan legal
rulings is that the court has no powers of coercion to force compliance
with a ruling. It must resort to persuasion. What distinguishes a
ruling from an agreement arrived at by negotiation consists largely
of the elaborate verbal trappings that go along with a ruling and lend
it a sacrosanct aura. The ideology expressed in talking about rulings
during the process of proclaiming them should not be taken as an expression of the manner in which rulings are actually derived, but as
part of the behavior of making a ruling in the most effective way. The
basic principle for actually arriving at successful rulings seems to be
the same as those for agreements, namely to give each side somewhat
less than full satisfaction but something better than the worst they
might expect—in other words, to effect a compromise. The basic objective of both litigation and netotiation is to eliminate a dispute, to
reestablish normal social relations between the disputants. It is not
to do justice whatever the cost.

A ruling may call for one or more of three acts: payment of
a fine (multah, from Spanish; qātaq, from Malay from Sanskrit), listening to an admonition (nasihat, from Arabic; pituwah, from Arabic;
tōqan) from the court, and performing a prayer (duwaqah, from Arabic) of reconciliation. A fine, in turn, has one or more of three components: a compensation for the offense, an amount serving to "wipe
away" any sin against God associated with the offense (which the court
collects), and a payment to the court, the baytalmāl (from Arabic
'treasury'). Fines are calculated in ten-peso units (laksaq) and paid
in Philippine currency (₱1 = $.25). In proposing a ruling, the court
must explain in detail how the amount was arrived at, relating it to
traditional fines for the offense and to the particular exigencies of the
case at hand. In one case involving two youths who had been in a fight,
one side claimed damages for bodily injury and presented a medical
bill for the amount of ₱180.25 from a Christian Filipino physician.
The court suggested a fine of ₱100 to the injured party, explaining its
decision as follows:

P120 for paying the medical bill (principle: never give full
      satisfaction).

-50 in recognition of the countercharge of collusion between
      the plaintiff and the physician. The court was careful
      to state that it did not necessarily believe the counter-
      charge, but since there were no witnesses, account
      must be taken of the possibility.

+50 for the offense against the plaintiff.

-20 for the plaintiff's responsibility in instigating the fight.

P100

If an admonition is part of the ruling, it is given in the form
of a lecture by the court to both sides at the end of the trial. It is
designed to make both parties feel their share of responsibility for the
dispute, to smooth ruffled feelings, and to warn of the grave consequences of repeating the offense. Admonitions are especially common
in rulings over marital disputes and fights among youths.

If a prayer of reconciliation is called for, it is performed at
a later time in the form of a different scene, a religious ceremony.
Its performance involves expenses, instructions for the payment of
which is an important aspect of the ruling. The prayer unites the former disputants in a divinely sanctioned ritual-sibling tie. A call for
prayer is especially common in cases of violence.

Upon suggesting a ruling, the court argues for compliance,
not only by carefully justifying the form of the decision, but also by
pointing out the dire consequences of refusal to comply. God and the
ancestors may mete out sickness upon the offender and his kin. Oppon-
ents may resort to violence against the offender and his kin. The
offender's kin, under threat from these sanctioning agents, may withdraw support or even disown the offender. Judges threaten to wash
their hands of the case and withdraw political support, and finally the
case may be referred to Philippine government legal system with its
expensive lawyers and prisons. Figure 2 diagrams these sanctioning
forces converging on an offender.

If the litigants agree to the ruling, those who are called upon
to hand over money almost never pay in full on demand, this being a

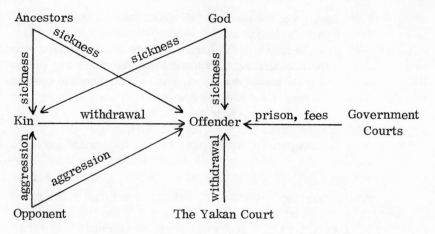

Figure 2.   Sanctions and sanctioning agents

rule in all monetary transactions. They ask for _tanguh_, a deferment
of part of the payment until a specified later date. As might be expected, failure to pay _tanguh_ when due is itself a major cause of disputes.

If a court fails to formulate an acceptable ruling, the litigants
may attempt to take the case to another Yakan court, seek redress in
a government court, or drop attempts to settle the dispute by litigation
Another alternative is to turn the decision over to God. In a religious
ceremony each disputant swears (_sapah_) on the Koran to the validity of
his arguments in the case. God decides who is right and announces
his decision by inflicting fatal illness (_kasapahan_) upon the person who
swore a false oath or upon his kin. Swearing is a serious matter,
rarely resorted to in fact. The threat of it, however, figures prominently in legal debate. One can protect himself from false charges by
challenging his opponent to participate in a swearing ritual. In several
recorded cases young men saved themselves from conviction on charges of sexual assault by this tactic. The fact that God may punish not
only the offender but also his kin may seem capricious to Western
moralists; yet it greatly increases the effectiveness of the punishment
Support of one's kin is crucial in a dispute, but they will be extremely
reluctant to carry this support to the point of swearing unless they are
firmly convinced of their kinsmen's innocence. Furthermore, if the

disputants are in any way related to each other, as they often are, this relationship tie must be dissolved before swearing. Consanguineal kinship ties can be formally broken in a religious ceremony. The term for the ritual payments required to disown a kinsman is tallak, from the Arabic word for the formula spoken by a husband to divorce his wife (Yakan divorce is not that simple).

Procedures and Schedules

Our formulation of the concept of litigation states that litigation is an integral activity never performed as part of another scene. It is a maximal unit of planning and scheduling. The description of the manifestations of this aspect of the concept requires a statement of the constituent structure of the scene—the sequence of parts that make up the whole—and of the scheduling of litigation with respect to other scenes in the society.

Procedures. Unlike mere negotiation or conference, litigation is conducted according to definite procedural rules. Although these rules are much looser than those of Western courts, they are, by Yakan standards, fairly strict and explicit. During proceedings judges frequently make reference to the following general rules governing the conduct of court sessions.

1. Speaking time is a free good available in unlimited quantity to any person present as long as what he says is relevant to the case.
2. A speaker has the right to finish before being interrupted.
3. Judges have the right to call on a person to speak, but one may speak without being called upon.[7]
4. Litigants should address all their arguments to the court.
5. Overt expression of anger, and especially any violence, must be avoided. Allowance should be made for the necessity, in litigation, for people to say unkind things about one another. Disputants must be allowed to accuse, judges to admonish.
6. Each party of protagonists, as well as the judges, has the right to confer in private whenever necessary.
7. A continuous period of time should be allotted to each case during a single court session.

Although there is some variation by type of case, the usual sequence of events is as follows:

1. Presentation of the case by the person to whom it was reported.

2. Taking testimony from each side and from witnesses.

3. Arguments from each side presented together (one side does not present its complete case and then defer to the other side).

4. Private conference of the judges.

5. Presentation of a ruling.

6. Further argument (optional but inevitable).

7. Private conference of each side (optional).

8. Expression of acceptance or refusal by each side.

9. Final decision for disposition of case.

10. Payment of fines, listening to court's admonition (if required).

11. Ritual handshaking (salam, from Arabic) with the judges signaling the termination of a trial session.

Steps 2 and 3 often occur simultaneously; steps 4-8 may be repeated several times.

Schedules. Fixed timing is not an attribute of litigation, as it is, say, of some calendrical religious ceremonies and agricultural activities. Court sessions are fitted into vacancies left by the schedules of other scenes. As a matter of convenience, community courts generally have regular scheduled meetings (Friday afternoon after mosque service is a favorite time), but these are easily accommodated if schedules conflict. The tribal court meets two afternoons a week. Court sessions must be scheduled between meals, with allowance made for participants to return home to eat. The five daily prayers of Islam, performed in most localities only by a few religiously inclined individuals, cause no problem. If someone wants to say a prayer, he can always go off and do so.

Comparisons

In this section we make a few summary comparisons with another Philippine legal system. The purpose is not to offer an explanation of these differences, but to demonstrate that the ethnographic approach argued for here, rather than hampering cross-cultural comparison as some critics seem to fear, provides a basis for determin-

ing which units are comparable and points up significant dimensions
of comparison.

The Eastern Subanun are pagan swidden agriculturists inhabiting the interior of Zamboanga Peninsula on the island of Mindanao.[8]
The Yakan and Subanun are not in direct contact, but they speak related
languages and, along with other central Malaysian peoples, share
many basic technological and social-organizational features. Subanun
communities are much smaller and more scattered, although the basic
principles of settlement pattern are the same: nuclear family household dispersed in individual fields. The difference is that the Yakan
practice continual exploitation of privately owned fields and groves.
Both groups have long been subject first to Moslem, then to Christian
cultural influence, political authority, and economic exploitation. The
Yakan accommodated where necessary and resisted where possible.
They became Moslems, they participate in Philippine politics; and
they market copra. At the same time they have retained a marked
cultural distinctiveness and some freedom to run their own affairs
and, above all, their land. The Subanun, on the other hand, retreated
or succumbed entirely. They have remained pagan and retained temporary economic and political independence at the price of increased
isolation and loss of land. Perhaps not unrelated to this difference in
adaptation to external pressures is a marked difference in the behavior
of the two peoples today: the Subanun drink, whereas the Yakan fight.

There is among the Subanun a set of activities that, in contrast
to other Subanun activities, can be defined in much the same terms as
Yakan litigation: an integral speech event concerned with settling disputes by means of a ruling formulated by neutral judges. A brief description of litigation in one Subanun community appears elsewhere
(Frake 1963). Here we will restrict ourselves to a few comparisons
along the dimensions of topic, outcome, role structure, and integrity.

Topic

Subanun legal cases arise in much the same way as Yakan
ones, except that they need not be initiated by a plaintiff. A judge can
try someone for an offense even if no complaint has been made. It
seems ridiculous, however, to call this criminal law, since the offenses in question are generally slanderous or flirtatious remarks made

by an incautious drinker, often not at all resented by the victim.
Otherwise the definitions of particular kinds of offenses are similar.
(A major difference is that the Yakan consider sexual relations with
an affine as incestuous, whereas the Subanun practice levirate and
sororate marriage and sororal polygyny.) There are great differenc₁
however, in the kinds of offenses that occur (violence is almost unknown among the Subanun) and the types of cases that reach court.
Adultery, for example, fills the agenda of Yakan courts, whereas it
is rarely the overt basis of a Subanun legal case. This fact is not a
comment on Subanun virtue but one on the weakness of Subanun legal
sanctions.

Outcome

        The rulings of a Subanun court, like those of the Yakan, gen-
erally demand financial compensation (but fines are calculated in unit
of twenty centavos rather than of ten pesos) and may call for admonitions and rituals of reconciliation. But not only does the Subanun
court have no legal sanctions of force to back up a decision, there is
also little realistic threat of illegal force it can bring to bear. The
Subanun offender may fear a certain amount of social censure—a real
enough sanction, to be sure—but he need not fear a shotgun blast inte₁
rupting his evening meal, the outcome of more than one Yakan disput₁
The Subanun also lack an Almighty God to mete out justice when litiga
tion fails. For this reason, "A large share, if not the majority, of
legal cases deal with offenses so minor that only the fertile imagination of a Subanun legal authority can magnify them into a serious thre₁
to some person or to society in general" (Frake 1963: 221). Yakan
courts, too, cannot cope with the full range of offenses committed,
but the Yakan, by absolute standards, commit much more serious
crimes. A Parkinsonian cynic viewing Yakan and Subanun life and lav
might conclude that the severity of crime increases with the ability of
a legal system to cope with it.

Role Structure

        Subanun courts are always formed ad hoc to try a particular
case. There are no court schedules or regular meeting places. The
role of judge is open to any adult male with the ability to formulate
successful decisions, and performance in the role is largely a route

to community leadership, rather than a result of it. Unlike the Yakan, where a parish priest is generally a political leader as well, Subanun roles of legal and religious authority are quite distinct and typically filled by separate individuals. Subanun litigation less often musters bodies of kin in support of disputants, partly because there is usually less of common interest at stake,and kin do not share collective responsibility under mortal and divine sanctioning agents.

Integrity

The striking difference between Subanun and Yakan litigation, and one that does not derive from differences in socioeconomic complexity in any obvious way, is the place of the activity in the overall structure of cultural scenes. Subanun activities are sharply divisible into festive and non-festive scenes, the former always involving feasting and drinking (Frake 1964b). Subanun litigation is festive behavior, performed as part of a larger scene and accompanied by eating, drinking, and merrymaking. In this respect it is the same kind of behavior as the performance of religious offerings; the two activities, in fact, often occur together as parts of the same festivity. Subanun litigation, then, is less of an integral unit of performance and scheduling than is the comparable Yakan activity. Subanun legal arguments, as they develop in the course of drinking, exhibit more obvious attention to message form. Litigants and judges employ esoteric legal language, often arranged into verse and sung to the tune of drinking songs (Frake 1964a). Thus, whereas the Yakan try relatively serious cases in scenes of informal discussion, the Subanun devote themselves to trivial disputes in scenes of formal festivities. This difference is crucial to any functional interpretations of litigation in the two societies. Participation in litigation has different meanings and different consequences in the two societies because of it.

NOTES

[1] Field work among the Yakan in 1962, 1963-64, and 1965-66 was supported by a United States Public Health Service Grant under the National Institute of Mental Health and by an auxiliary research award from the Social Science Research Council. The statements in this paper are at a level of generality applicable to the Basilan Yakan

as a whole and represent knowledge that any adult Yakan could be expected to have. Yakan expressions are represented by a linguisticall motivated orthography, but certain canons of traditional phonemic an ysis are ignored ("a," for example, represents both /a/ and /e/ whe this contrast is neutralized). This practice enables dialect differenc to be accounted for by special rules applicable to a uniform orthograp /q/ is a glottal catch, /e/ a mid-front vowel, /j/ a voiced, palatal affricative. The ethnographic record upon which this description is based includes the investigator's observations of court sessions, tran criptions of forty-three tape-recorded trial sessions at all jurisdictio levels, and informants' interpretations of the content of these observa tions and texts. In addition, by living in Yakan households during the entire field period, the investigator was continually exposed to conve sations related to litigation. Special acknowledgment is due to Samue Pajarito and Reuben Muzarin for assistance in recording and transcri ing court sessions and to Hadji Umar of Giyung for many long discus sions about Yakan law.

[2] There are also Yakan speakers on Sakol, Malanipa, and Tumalutab islands just east of Zamboanga City. These communities are beyond the scope of this paper.

[3] Single quotes enclose English glosses. These are to be assigned the meaning given to the Yakan expressions for which they substitute.

[4] In response to magqine (< N 'active' + pag 'mutuality' + qine 'what'), 'What is the mutual activity or relationship?' the forms cited, all unanalyzable morphemes, replace qine 'what': magqine siyeh 'What are they doing?', magqisun 'conferring with each other.' Note also: magqine siyeh 'How are they related to each other?', magpoŋtinaqih 'as siblings.'

[5] The mutuality of the behavior is represented by the prefix pag in the sequence N + pag > mag. See note 4.

[6] The source of etymological information on Malay and Arabi loans is Wilkinson (1932). Yakan expressions are marked as Malay loans only when there are phonological grounds for distinguishing loans from inherited cognates.

[7] The question of someone's refusing to testify never seems to arise.

[8] Reference is to the Eastern Subanun of the Lipay area of Zamboanga del Norte, studied in the field in 1953-54 and 1957-58.

REFERENCES

Bright, J. O., and W. Bright. 1965. Semantic structures in northwestern California and the Sapir-Whorf Hypothesis. American Anthropologist 67.5.2.249-58.
Frake, C. O. 1961. The diagnosis of disease among the Subanun of
Mindanao. American Anthropologist 63.113-32.
_____. 1963. Litigation in Lipay: a study in Subanun law. Pro-
ceedings of the Ninth Pacific Science Congress, 1957. Vol.
3. Bangkok.
_____. 1964a. How to ask for a drink in Subanun. American
Anthropologist 66.127-32, Part 2.
_____. 1964b. A structural description of Subanun "religious
behavior." In Ward G. Goodenough, ed., Explorations in
cultural anthropology: essays in honor of George Peter
Murdock. New York: McGraw-Hill.
Greenberg, J. H. 1966. Language universals. In T. Sebeok, ed.,
Current trends in linguistics, vol. 3. The Hague: Mouton.
Jakobson, R. 1957. Shifters, verbal categories and the Russian
verb. Cambridge: Harvard University, Russian Language
Project.
Wilkinson, R. J. 1932. A Malay-English dictionary (romanized).
Mytilene, Greece.

12 | Kin and Supporters among the Yakan

By virtue of its lack of unilineal descent groups, Yakan society qualifies for the stock anthropological pigeonhole labeled "cognatic." In spite of the shift in anthropological terminology from "bilateral" to "cognatic" and much recent discussion of such things as kindreds and non-unilineal descent groups, the notion of "cognatic society" still implies nothing more than the absence of unilineal descent. Cognatic societies are the unaccounted-for residue of social anthropological theory, a theory that seems to view social structure as a set of nested boxes that exhaustively partitions a population into social groups. A description of social structure states the numbers and arrangements of boxes, the rules for assigning people to their proper box, and the social functions of each kind of box. The beauty of unilineal descent is that it provides a way of sorting a population into a discrete, enumerable set of boxes on the basis of kinship. However, when one examines the kinship organization of so-called cognatic societies, it is generally hard to find very many boxes. Membership in boxes overlaps, and it is often not very clear when one has a real box or some kind of pseudo-box—witness the argument over whether a kindred is "really" a social group. When described in these terms, the social structure of a "cognatic" society, such as the Iban, seems very simple when compared with a "unilineal" society such as the Tallensi. Yet, among the Iban, groups of people engage in social activities fully as complex as those of the Tallensi. An adequate description of Iban social structure, one that accounted for the full range of their social behavior, would surely equal one for the Tallensi in complexity.

The analysis of Yakan social groupings presented here derives from an effort to describe cultural behavior in terms of rules for performing significant categories of activities or "scenes" (Frake 1964, 1969). Scenes have schedules, settings, paraphernalia, roles. And they have actors. Actors are recruited to play roles in scenes on the basis of social attributes they possess. A category of actors qualifying for a particular role is a social unit. It is part of the economy of cultural organization that the same social unit may play different roles in a variety of scenes. Some social units consist of more than one person jointly performing a role. Such units may have an organization and identity apart from particular scenes. They may have control over paraphernalia and resources pertinent to a number of scenes. They may, in other words, qualify for one or more of the various definitions of "social group" that have been proposed. The ethnographic task is to discern what significant categories of actors in fact emerge in the performance of the scenes of a given society and to specify their properties. It is not to decide in advance what a social group "really" is and then to look for something in the society that qualifies. The present discussion takes the analysis of a particular Yakan scene, the performance of 'litigation,' as given (see Frake 1969) and proceeds to examine the recruitment of actors to one role in that scene, that of 'supporter' of a disputant.

Support Groups

The minimal role differentiation for the performance of litigation consists of a set of 'judges' and two sets of 'protagonists.' The focal role within each set of protagonists is that of 'disputant,' the person who allegedly committed an offense or was offended against. Except in very trivial disputes, each disputant is the focus of a set of supporters. In theory a disputant draws his support from his circle of consanguineal kin, the obligation to give support being inversely proportional to the genealogical distance from the disputant. This rule derives from the often enunciated tenet of Yakan ideology that consanguineal kin are obligated to support one another and that a set of consanguineal kin, a kindred if you will, is dabebbeg 'one unit of support.' It can be shown that the Yakan in fact apply this rule as a guide to social behavior, yet when we look at the constituency of actual support groups in particular legal cases, we find that the outcome of the application of this rule is by no means straightforward. Typically not all one's kin out to some prescribed genealogical range are included;

closer kin may ally themselves with one's opponent, and non-kin are frequently included. This outcome is the product of applying a simple rule to the complex realities of Yakan social life.

In the first place the Yakan's social world is not sharply divided into kin and non-kin, nor is the infinitely expandable circle of kin neatly partitioned by lesser circles of genealogical distance. The Yakan make judgments about the relative closeness of kinsmen not only on the basis of the number of connecting links, but also on the degree to which linking kinsmen are known and the degree to which one has a close social relationship with the kinsman. A kinsman's status with respect to closeness can change through time. Persons previously considered non-kin may, after diligent application of the Yakan version of the genealogical method, become kin, and kin may move outside one's social field to be forgotten. As a Yakan epigram expresses it: baŋ takíteh qusbah; baŋ gay takíteh tîman lúdaq. 'When in view, a kinsman; Out of sight, discarded trash.' An added complication to calculating kinship distance derives from frequent consanguineal intermarriage, sometimes across generations, that produces multiple paths of kinship linkage between individuals. 'Affines' (pam- ikit), it should be pointed out, are sharply excluded both from the cat gories of 'kin' (qusbah) and 'non-kin' (qàqa seddíih). For one thing, affines cannot be married. There is no levirate, sororate, or soror polygyny.

Then there is the inevitable problem whenever networks of overlapping ego-focused relations (whether kinship relations or not) form the basis for social alignments: there may be some individuals equally closely related to each of two, perhaps unrelated, egos. Although this situation complicates a disputant's recruitment of support ers, it helps assure that in any dispute there will be someone who is neutral and yet has ties of solidarity with the disputants. The recruit ment of persons to fill the role of 'judge' is, in fact, dependent on thi kind of situation.

A more serious obstacle to the recruitment of a support gro according to kinship ideology is the bitter fact that close kin so often turn out to be on the other side in a dispute. Like Radcliffe-Brown, the Yakan are staunch advocates of the principle of sibling solidarity, but there is a complementary force, which the Yakan, at least, recog nize, of sibling dissolidarity. There are all kinds of reasons why Yakan close kin get into disputes with one another—women, for example—but it is mainly on the rock of property rights that the ship of sibling solidarity founders. In the nested-box model of society, we have a picture whereby two closely related small boxes may fight, but, if one small box gets into an argument with a box in another nest, the two small boxes unite to form a larger box. Larger boxes unite to form still larger boxes until finally the entire society is united in opposition to some other society. The Nuer may behave this way but not the Yakan. What happens among Yakan kinsmen parallels what happened among the Balkan states before World War II. In the Balkans at that time there were a lot of little states that sometimes fought one another. Also they were sometimes threatened by big states like Germany and Russia. Did the little states combine to form a big state in opposition to this threat? No, the states nearest to Germany allied themselves with Russia and the states nearest to Russia allied themselves with Germany.

Figure 1a portrays a model of a Yakan descent line founded by ancestor G. Any two persons occupying positions at terminal nodes in this model could easily come into conflict, A and B, for example, over rights stemming from E; B and C over rights stemming from G. In a sibling-solidarity model of alliances, even though A and B may fight, should either come into conflict with C, then A and B should unite against C and D. This can happen among the Yakan providing there is no serious conflict between A and B. Otherwise the resulting alliances are more likely to pit A and C against B and D. In other words, if C opposes B, A can be expected to join with the enemy of his opponent rather than to suppress his conflict with B in the interest of sibling solidarity. Thus the resulting support groups of each disputant include their most distant rather than their closest kin. Figure 1b, a model of three interrelated descent lines, illustrates how non-kin can be drawn into support groups. Each terminal node in this model has a unique kindred. The kindred of K, for example, includes J and L but excludes M, with whom K shares no common ancestor. If K gets into a dispute with M, he can expect, according to kinship ideology, to receive support from J, whereas L should, in theory, be neutral. Suppose, however, that, because of property disputes, each adjacent pair is in conflict with each other. The resulting alliances may well

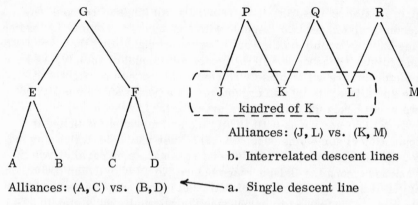

Alliances: (A, C) vs. (B, D)   ← a. Single descent line

Figure 1. The principle of sibling dissolidarity

pit J and L against K and M, each support group being made up of non-kin. [1]

Sibling dissolidarity can lead to affinal solidarity, thereby drawing a disputant's spouse's kin into his support group. If a man and his brother, for example, are involved in a property dispute, the man can expect support from his wife's kin, who have a vested interest in the economic success of their daughter's (or sister's) family. Furthermore, unless they are disputing with each other, spouses, being a focus of a single economic unit, have a common interest in a dispute involving one of them, as well as a moral obligation to support one another. Failure to render such support is, itself, a cause of marital conflict, which can lead to costly disputes between husband's and wife's kin. To join an affine's support group, even when there is no tangible common interest, publicly asserts the absence of such conflict in a given case.

Considerations such as these result in support groups with a quite varied composition; nevertheless, in essence, they remain kinship groups. It is kinsmen who have an a priori obligation to be supporters. Kin become non-supporters only because of special contingencies. An effective support group must retain some close kin as a

solid core of that group. It is seemingly impossible to muster a
reliable support group with no reliance on kin ties. Persons without
consanguineal kin ties in their community, such as spouses, teachers,
or visitors from distant areas or different ethnic groups, are in a
very precarious position if they become involved in local disputes.
When talking about the recruitment of support groups in a particular
case, the Yakan not only use the terminology of kinship but also make
constant reference to kinship ideology. This ideology provides a
basis for rationalizing one's own and criticizing one's opponent's
alliances. It is bolstered by the fact that God takes the principle of
sibling solidarity very seriously. So if, for example, an accused
swears a false oath on the Koran, divine retribution can fall on any of
his kin. Consequently a disputant's kin, whether supporters or not,
have a stake in any case that reaches the point of swearing. When
disputants are related to each other, the consanguineal kin tie must
be ritually dissolved in a formal ceremony of "kinship divorce" before
swearing can take place. There are other occasions when kin ties,
even parental ties, are formally renounced. When this is done, it
guarantees that the disowned kinsman will never be a member of the
disowner's support group. Conversely, consanguineal ties can be
ritually established, a common reconciliation of blood feuds. Ritually
created kin are inescapably bound to be members of each other's support groups. The solidarity of divinely created siblings cannot be
denied. Thus there are limits beyond which kinship ideology cannot
be stretched without formally altering the composition of one's kindred.

Thus far we have been describing the principles for recruiting actors to fill one role in one kind of scene. When we turn to other
scenes, we find the same principles, hence the same sets of actors
reappearing. In any conflict situation, whether handled by litigation,
direct negotiation between disputants, or violence, support groups
emerge. A person does not recruit supporters ad hoc in each situation calling for this role but relies on a common core of supporters
throughout his life—subject to expansion and contraction and occasionally to fission when a former supporter becomes an opponent. One of
the strategies of Yakan life is to attract as large and stable a support
group as possible. Support groups also fill roles other than furnish-
ing allies in situations of conflict. In weddings, which are an elaborate formalization—almost a parody—of legal trials, the bride and

groom must each have their supporters even though the outcome is
predictable and matters of dispute (notably the bride price) have been
settled by negotiation beforehand. The ceremony of graduation from
Moslem religious training is another occasion for a support group to
display itself despite the absence of an opposed group. Supporters
also provide a pool of friends and associates for a variety of informa
occasions. Because of these associations, supporters are likely
through time to become linked by a number of ties of social obligation
additional to those that lead to their initial alliance.

Parishes

The support-group structure of Yakan society, like the kinsh
structure upon which it is based, is an ego-focused, diffuse, and ove
lapping network of social alignments. The nested-box image of socia
structure forces one to consider this kind of arrangement as a problem. This image errs, I think, in overemphasizing discreteness of
groups as a prerequisite to structure—networks exhibit structure as
well as sets. Nevertheless network structure does cause problems
for certain kinds of social functioning, and it is undoubtedly a poor
foundation for large-scale political integration. Kinship relations,
being non-transitive, cannot provide a basis for discrete social group
unless there is a restriction placed on the qualifying foci of relations
Unilineal reckoning represents perhaps the neatest way of restricting
ancestral foci in descent groups, but there are others (see Goodenou
1955). The Daughters of the American Revolution is an example of a
discrete, non-unilineal descent group based on a set of peculiarly
restricted ancestors. With respect to ego-focused kindreds, most di
cussion has centered on restrictions on their range: out to second
cousins, third cousins, etc. But an arbitrary restriction on the rang
of an ego-focused kindred will not suffice to make it a discrete divisic
of a population. Discreteness can be achieved only by restricting the
egos who qualify as foci. The Yakan population does, in fact, sort
into a set of discrete boxes (although not nested ones) based on such a
restriction on the ego-foci of support groups.

The network of individual support group alignments becomes
the basis for affiliation in discrete social groups in the following way:

1. There is a restricted set of individuals who, by virtue of being able to provide a mosque and a priest for a congregation, hold the status of 'leader.'

2. A leader is the focus not only of his own individual support group, but also of a 'parish,' whose membership is a subset of his support group.

3. Every Yakan must publicly affiliate with one and only one parish, selecting a parish whose leader is (or is willing to become) a member of his support group.

All members of a single parish are thus included in their parish leader's support group, but the support groups of individual parish members are not necessarily co-extensive. No one's support group is necessarily limited to the confines of one parish.

Parish leadership may be shared by several close allies (whose support groups are nearly co-extensive), but generally one person emerges as the economic and political focus of the group. The number of parish leaders is restricted by the requirement that every parish must have a priest, a status requiring extensive and costly training. The parish leader may himself be priest or he may enlist a close ally to fill the role. A leader must also command the economic resources and political skills to attract and hold a following. In theory it is necessary, and in practice useful, to validate leadership status through descent from previous leaders.

There are no formal kinship or territorial requirements for parish affiliation. It is in principle a matter of free and mutable choice, a freedom which is, however, constrained by the following factors:

1. The unit of choice is not the individual but the nuclear family. Husband, wife, and dependent children must belong to the same parish. (Co-wives, who among the Yakan maintain separate households, need not belong to the same parish.) After marriage a couple must agree on a common parish affiliation just as they must agree on a common place of residence. Insofar as the support group of a young married person, who may not yet have built up a distinctive set of allies

and enemies, is co-extensive with that of a parent, there is a high
probability that a couple's initial choice of parish affiliation will be
that of either the husband's or wife's parents. There is neither nor-
mative preference nor statistical tendency for either patri- or matri-
affiliation.

2. One seeks a parish whose leader is a strong supporter of
oneself and in which the majority of members belong to one's own
support group. One avoids parishes whose membership includes enemies. The last consideration leaves some persons in parishes that
are unusually distant genealogically and/or spatially.

3. The parish mosque should be within convenient walking
distance. A radius of one mile from the mosque will generally include
all parish households. It will, however, include other households as
well.

Unlike the individual support group or the kindred, the parish
has a locus as well as a focus. Every parish has one mosque which,
together with the leader's house (almost invariably located next to the
mosque), provides the setting for parish-wide activities. But although
it has a spatial locus, the parish has no territory. It does not divide
the landscape into discrete geographical units. One can change parish affiliation without changing residence.

Functionally, the Yakan parish is most conspicuous as an
organization of actors to perform religious scenes. Its most prominent edifice, the mosque, furnishes a stage for such performances, and
its most visible social identity, the priest, acts as director. In theory
parish organization should include positions of curer, midwife, morti-
cian, and specialist in agricultural ritual, but actually these practi-
tioners tend to attract a circle of clientele independent of parish affiliation, as do diviners and mediums. The religious activities of the
parish center on prayer services, of minor importance in most areas,
and on the performance of an annual cycle of religious ceremonies.
These ceremonies are scheduled according to the Moslem lunar calen-
dar and thus are not correlated with the annual seasonal cycle. Sea-
sonally scheduled agricultural rituals, together with crisis rituals of
sickness, are largely divorced from formal religious organization, a

situation in marked contrast to that prevailing among Philippine pagans. It is by freeing ceremonial life from the ecological cycle and by assigning performance of these ceremonies to what is in essence a political unit that Islam has, I think, had its most profound impact on Philippine society. Islamic influences on the content of both religious and legal concepts and practices seem superficial by comparison. Yakan religious ceremonies become political rites manifesting the solidarity of a leader's support group. Religion and politics bolster each other in that to be a Moslem one must belong to a parish. To be a nominal Moslem but to have no mosque (like the boat-dwelling Samal) is to be a social outcast. On the other hand, one cannot be a parish member without being a Moslem. A Yakan who succumbs to the attractions of Christianity forfeits his right to a full social life within his society.

In spite of its religious functions and ideology, the parish is at heart a political unit. People select a parish for political advantage, not because it has an impressive mosque or an inspiring priest. When priest and leader are different individuals, the focus of affiliation is the leader's, not the priest's, support group. Apart from formalizing, and thereby assuring, a basis of support for both leader and parish member in their conflicts with outsiders, parish leadership provides the basis for filling judiciary roles in litigation. A plaintiff in a case normally takes his complaint to his parish leader, that is, to the member of his support group who has leadership status. If both disputants are members of the leader's support group, as parish-mates will be, then the leader will attempt to effect a settlement himself. The leader is, of course, anxious to avoid conflict within his support group. If disputants come from different parishes, then the case must be tried by a set of judges comprising the parish leaders of each disputant, together with one or more leaders from other parishes to help assure neutrality.

Parish organization, by providing discrete, minimal political units, and parish functioning, which requires the cooperation of leaders of different parishes in litigation, would seem to lay a foundation for wider political organization on the same principles. If a restricted set of parish leaders achieved sufficient political strength to incorporate other leaders into their support groups, they could become foci of formalized regional political units. Eventually one could have a hierarchy of such units, parish, district, region, state—a set of

nested boxes, in other words. The Yakan, however, have not gone
very far in this direction. There are alliances of parishes, but the
overall distribution of allies and enemies again reveals a balkanized
pattern. A given parish's bitterest opponent is likely to be the parish
that has most recently segmented from it and hence is nearest to it in
spatial and genealogical distance. Some leaders have extended their
support groups to include leaders of other parishes, but the result is
nothing more than extra-large and powerful individual support groups
which are as diffuse and overlapping as any support group. One difficulty with building a hierarchy of political units upon a parish base is
that although parishes divide the Yakan population into discrete units,
they do not discretely divide the Yakan territory. Perhaps it is also
relevant that Islam has priests but no bishops; thus there is no religious
rationale for the organization of parishes into wider discrete units.

The most notable manifestation of Yakan political integration
came not through building up from parish foundations but was imposed
from the top. Late in the Spanish period a Christian Filipino fleeing
from a Spanish prison in Zámboanga established himself on Basilan,
gathered a gang of followers, and after building up a legend of fantastic
military prowess, managed somehow to number all the Yakan as his
supporters. He identified as a Yakan, became a Moslem, and was
acknowledged as supreme chief (datuq) of the tribe. His legal court
and that of his successor, who died in 1931, became a sort of supreme
court for all the Yakan. It was here that cases which could not be settled locally, such as disputes between two prominent leaders, were
tried. Part of the basis of the chief's power was that he was the intermediary between the Yakan and Spanish (later American) authority.
There still is a formally recognized chief, the son of the first chief,
and a tribal court, but they are vestiges of a former era. Today Yakan
leaders participate individually in the Philippine political system, a
system which, rather than bringing new stability and integration, has
augmented conflict by adding new dimensions of factionalism and alternative routes to power. The Moslem neighbors of the Yakan, some of
whom, like the Tausug, had an impressive political apparatus of
which the Yakan were one time a marginal part, have been reduced to
a similar state of near anarchy above the level of the support groups
of local leaders. These Moslem brothers are—by the principle of sibling dissolidarity—the Yakan's bitterest enemies, but intertribal warfare, like intratribal feuding, has been balkanized into small bands

fighting each other and making alliances according to their perceived
political interests without necessary regard for ethnic affiliations.
Since the imposition of martial law by the Philippine government in
1972, a further dimension has been added to these conflicts, a brutal
confrontation between Moslem insurgency and Christian military government that overshadows previous ethnic and factional divisions.
The Yakan, their homeland a major battleground in the ensuing war,
have not fared well.

NOTE

[1] Compare the analysis of alliances and oppositions in a unilineal society by Barth (1959).

REFERENCES

Barth, F. 1959. Segmentary opposition and the theory of games: a
        study of Pathan organization. Journal of the Royal Anthropo-
        logical Institute 89.1.5-21.
Frake, C. O. 1964. A structural description of Subanun "religious
        behavior." In Ward G. Goodenough, ed., Explorations in
        cultural anthropology: essays in honor of George Peter Mur-
        dock. New York: McGraw-Hill.
————. 1969. Struck by speech: the Yakan concept of litigation.
        In L. Nader, ed., Law in culture and society. Chicago:
        Aldine.
Goodenough, Ward G. 1955. A problem in Malayo-Polynesian social
        organization. American Anthropologist 57.71-83.

13 | How to Enter a Yakan House

Even if Poor-Boy was asked to come up to the porch, he
wouldn't come up. Finally he came up to the top of the ladder. For two days the Sultan's daughter kept telling him to
come inside. Even her parents told him. For two days Poor-
Boy was there at the top of the ladder. Finally he ventured
onto the porch. After three more days he approached as far
as the floor beam at the doorway. For three days he was
there. Even when he was given clothes he couldn't wear them.
Even when he was given money he wouldn't take it. After four
days he finally went inside from the doorway floor beam.
Then, because he was already there inside, he and the Sultan'
daughter were able to get married. But after they had been
married a long time, he still hadn't slept with his wife. He
had not yet entered the room of the Sultan's daughter.

—excerpt from a Yakan story

The Yakan construe Poor-Boy's plight as humorous because
he is acting out a parody of cultural expectations governing the occupancy of a physical setting for a social encounter. These expectations
derive from a cultural code that defines distinctive settings in and
around a house, the sequence whereby one moves through settings, and
the signals for initiating and terminating moves. To one who knows
the code, variations in performances signal something about the social
occasion at hand. A record of actual performances, matched with informants' interpretations of performances as appropriate, awkward,
gracious, hostile, self-conscious, ridiculous, insincere, etc., provides evidence for the existence and character of the code. Our purpose is neither to describe what has happened nor to predict what will

happen, but to set forth what one needs to know in order to make sense
of what does happen. To the extent that we succeed, our statement is
a description of that portion of Yakan culture of which these behaviors
are an artifact.

The domain of behavior being considered is special in several ways. One way in which it is special for the anthropologist is that
it is not at all special for the people being studied. Entering a house
is commonplace, everyday activity. It is high-frequency behavior,
and it is also incidental behavior. It is not planned and performed
for its own sake but occurs as an incident within some encompassing
event. When a Yakan is queried about his plans for tomorrow, he is
not likely to reply: "Well, the first thing I'm going to do is go out and
enter a house." Another special feature of this behavior is that its
domain is defined by the spatial boundaries within which it occurs. We
are concerned with the various behaviors that occur in a given setting,
rather than taking a given kind of behavior and considering, as one of
its attributes, the various settings in which it occurs. Finally, the
performances involved are largely verbal.[1] The topic, then, is an
example of high-frequency, incidental speech behavior entailed in the
occupancy of a behavior setting.

The Yakan are Philippine Moslems inhabiting the island of
Basilan, which lies just off the southwestern point of Mindanao at the
northeastern end of the Sulu Archipelago.[2] They are strictly land-
oriented agriculturists, in contrast to the sea-oriented Moslems, the
Samal, who inhabit coastal villages around the island. The northern
portion of Basilan is occupied by Filipino Christians. The Yakan live
in dispersed neighborhoods of nuclear family dwellings organized into
small, local political units based on Mosque affiliation. Warfare
among these political units, as well as against Christians and other
Moslem groups (notably the Tausug), is endemic. The weaponry includes not only locally made spears, swords, and shotguns but also
the latest in U.S. military small arms—a fact not without relevance to
the construction of a Yakan house.

The Yakan house (lumaq) is a rectangular, ridge-roofed,
single-room dwelling raised on piles some two to three meters off the
ground. A cooking shed of similar structure but smaller dimensions
is attached by a platform to either end of the house. Floor space var-

ies from about 30 to 100 m^2. Floors and walls are thickly planked.
The floor has a hole or two drilled in it for betel expectoration, and
the end wall opposite the cooking shed has a window opening, either
very small or securely sealable. The steeply pitched, concave-sided
roof is thatched. The main room has two doorways, one connecting to
the platform leading to the cooking shed, the other, located midway
along one side, leading to a roofed porch running the length of the
house. Ladders or notched poles connect both porch and cooking shed
platform to the ground. Individual houses are dispersed in fields and
groves and are never attached to other structures. There is no physically demarcated house yard. Houses vary in construction details:
a few have bamboo rather than planked walls; a regrettably increasing
number substitute a hotter, less aesthetically pleasing, more expensive
but more prestigeful galvanized-iron roof for the traditional thatch; and
an occasional house lacks a porch—the only variation relevant to the
present discussion.[3] (Sultans' daughters may have private rooms, but
there are no sultans to be found in the Yakan habitat.[4]) In spite of
these variations, any Yakan dwelling is easily distinguishable from the
homes of other ethnic groups, either Christian or Moslem, on Basilan.

Yakan dwellings are also easily distinguishable from other
structures built by the Yakan: field huts, graves, and mosques. Field
huts are simply temporary work shelters built in fields that are some
distance from the owner's residence. Graves are ditched mounds
topped with a carved and painted boatlike structure and clustered with
other graves in groves of ritual trees. Mosques are similar in size
and structure to dwellings, except that the porch is at one end, which
is unwalled. At the other end is a projecting semicircular apse.
Houses, mosques, and graves all differ in orientation. The long walls
of a house are alighed along the east-west axis, with the wall opposite
the doorway—known as the 'head wall' (kokan lumaq)—facing 'up-slope'
(padiataq).[5] "up-slope" is a conventional directional axis at right angles to the east-west axis but oriented northward in southern Basilan
and southward in northern Basilan. Mosques are oriented with their
long walls aligned with the Meccan axis (kiblat) so that the apse faces
Mecca. In Basilan the Meccan axis points WNW. Graves are oriented
along the 'Meccan axis of the dead' (kiblat mamateyin), at right angles
to the Meccan axis proper, so that a body lying on its right side is
facing Mecca (Figure 1).

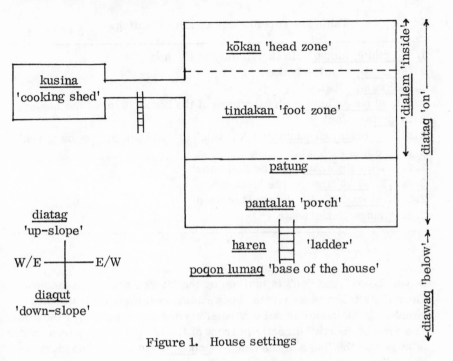

Figure 1.   House settings

Field huts, graves, and mosques all have specialized social
functions, whereas the limited variety of physical locales afforded by
a Yakan house must serve as settings for a wide variety of social
events. The Yakan conceptually organize the space within and around
a house into an arrangement of discrete settings (Figure 1).[6] These
settings are labeled hierarchically (Table 1). In locating people, objects, and events with respect to a house, one can select a level of
contrast according to the degree of specificity required. Saying that
someone or something is 'at a house' (si lumaq) can denote any setting
closer than 'in the vicinity of a house' (si bihing lumaq). Using 'on'
(diataq) a house denotes any setting above 'below' (diawaq). There is
no physical demarcation of the outer limits of "in the vicinity," nor
of the boundary between "vicinity" and "below." "Vicinity" is any
position within sight and calling range of a house. "Below" is any position on the ground below (but not "underneath") the house within normal
conversation range with someone "on" the house. The boundary be-

Table 1. Terminology of House Settings

---

1. <u>si bihing lumaq</u> 'in the vicinity of the house'
2. <u>si lumaq</u> 'at the house'
2.1. <u>diawaq</u> 'below'
2.1.1. <u>si poqon lumaq</u> 'at the base of the house' (foot of the ladder)
2.2. <u>diataq</u> 'on'
2.2.1. <u>si bukut, si pantalan</u> 'outside' (= "in back"), 'on the porch'
2.2.2. <u>dialem</u> 'inside'
2.2.2.1. <u>si tindakan</u> 'at the foot zone'
2.2.2.2. <u>si kōkan</u> 'at the head zone'
2.2.3. <u>si kusina</u> 'in the cooking shed'
2.3. <u>silung</u> 'underneath'

---

tween "below" and "on" is marked by the kitchen and porch ladders.
Since the kitchen is a private "back room" reserved for household
members, its ladder is not a normal access to the house for outsiders.
The area of "below" directly in front of the bottom of the porch ladder
is known as the 'base of the house' (<u>poqon lumaq</u>). The boundary between "outside" (on the porch) and "inside" (the main room) is marked
by a 'floor beam' (<u>patung</u>) that runs along the base of the wall fronting
the porch and appears at the doorway slightly raised above the floor.
Poor-Boy exemplifies a common use of the <u>patung</u> as a sitting place
neither clearly inside nor outside. The top of the ladder provides a
similar niche neither clearly below nor on. At night, or when no householders are at home, these access points are removed. Ladders are
raised and doorways barred shut. 'Inside' (<u>dialem</u>) is further divided
into 'head zone' (<u>kōkan</u>) and 'foot zone' (<u>tindakan</u>, literally 'kicking
zone'), the "head zone" being the portion of floor space adjacent to the
head wall opposite the doorway. The head zone is the sleeping area
for household members. During the day, when sleeping mats are
rolled up, it is simply bare floor, physically undistinguishable, but
conceptually quite distinct, from the adjoining "foot zone" floor space.
The head wall, not the entrance wall, defines the "front" of the house
facing "up-slope." From the perspective of a person inside the house,
someone on the porch is 'in back' (<u>si bukut</u>). This means that one
enters a Yakan house through what is conceptually the back door,
there being no entrance in front.

The physical arrangement of household settings, together with the hierarchical structure of their terminology, reflect the sequence of positions through which an outsider must pass in gaining entrance to a house. One can characterize a social encounter between householder and outsider by the degree of penetration of household settings achieved by the outsider, penetration being measured by the number of moves across setting boundaries required to reach a given position. Thus, to achieve maximal penetration to the head zone requires the following moves:

1. from "vicinity" to "at"
2. from "below" to "on"
3. from "on" to "inside"
4. from "foot zone" to "head zone"

The accomplishment of these moves requires displays of proper etiquette (addat) by both the householder and the outsider. (Terms for describing these routines, together with some examples of specific formulas, are listed in the Appendix.) Proper etiquette requires the householder to 'render attention' (asip) to the outsider; the outsider, in turn, should 'display respect' (moqo mātabat). The householder issues 'invitations' (pellun) to advance to the next setting —each move has its unique invitation—and proffers provisions requisite to social engagements in each setting: tobacco or betel quids on the porch, snacks or a meal inside. The outsider's display of respect requires that he never withdraw from a setting without asking 'permission to leave' (baqid) and receiving this permission from the householder, usually in the form of a drawled aweq 'OK,' an expression that is a hallmark of the Yakan.

Grammatically, invitations appear as active imperatives, requiring the use of a second-person pronoun optionally accompanied by a term of address. The use of a term of address, selected on the basis of age, sex, kinship, and title, enables marking of status relationships and expression of special affect, but, since this use is optional and pronoun selection is indifferent to status, invitations can be issued in a status-unmarked form.[7] It is not the form of the invitation so much as the context of its issuance that carries social meaning.

Gross categories of household entrance events can be sorted out according to the number of verbal engagements that occur in

occupying their ultimate setting. First, by manner of entrance, we
can easily distinguish two classes of people: class one, those who can
legally enter a house, penetrating to any setting without pause and
without saying a word; and class two, those who cannot proceed beyond
the setting "below" without a verbal invitation from a member of class
one. Class one consists of all the residents of the household; class
two consists of all other persons. This contrast between interaction
among those who have legal free access to a setting and interaction
and those who do not pertains to all behavior settings. Any Yakan behavior setting—house, mosque, field, water hole, trail—is public to
the social group whose members have legal free-access rights, and
private to all others.[8] An outsider cannot enter a setting private to
him without an invitation from an insider. A violation of this rule will
be interpreted not simply as humorous, discourteous, or stupid but
as downright illegal. The offender has violated a proprietory relationship and is subject to legal penalties, if not to on-the-spot elimination.
The concern of this study is with how an outsider enters a private setting; the patterns of informal interaction among householders will be
ignored.

The second major cut we can make sorts not people but kinds
of occasions. There are events that enable outsiders, after receipt
of a distinctive greeting reserved for such occasions, to immediately
approach the house, climb the stairs, and enter without pauses or further verbal exchanges along the way. These events all share the property of having been scheduled in advance. We will set them aside for
later consideration.

In order to uncover the meaning of household entrance, we
focus initially on cases involving the unscheduled arrival of one or
more outsiders, situations of uncertainty in which the acts of householder and outsider become informative signals of the other party's
intentions as well as strategic devices to further one's own intensions.
This uncertainty, together with the fact that neither party can uniquely
determine the outcome, gives household entrance a gamelike character. There are two players: householder and outsider. The game
goes through a fixed sequence of plays corresponding to the sequence
of household settings. At each stage of play except the last, one of
three outcomes is possible: terminate, hold, or advance. In the last

stage advance is not a possible outcome. The outcome of a play is
the product of the respective moves by each player.

The initiation of play is up to the outsider; it is he who has
the option of appearing on the scene or not. As he comes to the "vicinity" of the house, he can adopt one of two strategies: 'making a pass'
(palabey) or 'approaching' (pasōng). In making a pass, the outsider
simply walks on by a regular trail. The rule in this situation is that
if any householder is visible, then permission to pass must be called
out. If no householder is visible, no interaction will take place. A
householder, upon receiving a call for permission to pass, has the
option of immediately granting it by yelling back aweq 'OK,' thereby
terminating interaction, or he can pose a "customary question" (see
Appendix). A "customary question," in this context, is subject to
interpretation performatively either as a 'greeting' (sagina) or as a
real question inviting further interaction. An exchange of greetings,
whereby interaction is initiated by a customary question (e.g. Where
are you headed for?) and terminated by a customary response (e.g.
Over there yonder someplace), is an interaction sequence appropriate
to encounters taking place in a setting, such as in town or on a trail,
to which both parties have legal free access. In a hosted encounter,
where one participant is an outsider, such an exchange is not appropriate. The outsider is accountable for justifying his presence on the
scene. Provided that the trail is a public setting for the passer-by, a
construal by both participants of the question-response exchange as a
simple greeting exchange terminating further interaction is possible.
Of course, further interaction after a greeting can occur. The desire
for continuance is signaled by the nature and elaborateness of questions
and responses, in effect, the mutual construing of grammatical inter-
rogatives as performative questions. Further signals for continuance
include requests for betel and tobacco and, I am sure, non-verbal ges-
tures and posturings that have escaped my observation. Unlike a trail
encounter, however, the passing-by scene is conducted not at normal
conversation range but at calling range. Furthermore, one participant
is in a setting private to him. For continued interaction to take place,
the outsider must approach the house (which at this point, having adopted the "making a pass" strategy, he can do only upon invitation), or
the householder must go out to the trail (in most circumstances a
rather rude signal that no invitation to enter the house will be forthcoming). In either case the householder has control over the continu-

ance of interaction. If the outsider accepts an invitation to come to
the house, he approaches to "below" and house-entrance play begins.

   If the outsider initially elects the option of approaching, he
can enter "below" as far as the base of the ladder (poqon lumaq) and
stand there. This move is functionally equivalent to a knock on the
front door in our society. It is a "summons" (cf. Schegloff 1968), albei
an inaudible one. It is incumbent on the householder to 'notice' (batik)
the outsider standing there. He must answer the summons. Failure
to notice is a serious breach of etiquette as well as an unusual lapse
of security. The householder reveals that he has noticed by posing a
"customary question, " but in this case not as a greeting. A summons
presupposes that the summoner has a topic of conversation to pose.
A response to a summons, in the form of a question, is an invitation
to the summoner to present something to talk about, something to justify his presence in a private setting. Change, or lack of change, in the
householder's physical position is an important element of this summon
response sequence. The householder has the option of changing his pos
tion to one closer to that of the outsider. If he is inside, he may move
to the porch. If he is on the porch, he may join the outsider below.
The most unmarked position for the householder to assume initially is
on the porch. This spot allows comfortable conversation with the outsider below while not ruling out the possibility of either early termination or prompt advance of the outsider to share the porch. For the
householder to join the outsider below signals rather strongly that he
wishes the engagement to advance no further. For the householder to
remain inside, where conversation with someone below is somewhat
difficult, is, depending on whether or not an invitation is forthcoming,
a strong signal of either desired advance or desired termination. The
householder cannot, in any case, withdraw to a setting further removed
from the outsider before the encounter terminates.

   Once play has been engaged, the interplay of moves by householder and outsider determines further progress through the sequence.
Although the inventory of verbal routines seems rich, in fact there is
a severe restriction on the kinds of moves available to each party. A
householder can only invite; he cannot ask a guest to leave. An outsider can only ask permission to leave; he cannot invite himself further
into the setting. These rules, though they sound familiar to us, are
not so obvious as they seem. In Yakan social encounters where neither

Outsider

House- holder	Ask permission	Don't ask permission
Invite	HOLD	ADVANCE
Don't invite	TERMINATE	HOLD

Figure 2. Matrix of invitation-permission outcomes

party has exclusive rights of free access to the setting, the rules are
quite different. For example, if two people meet and engage in conversation on a public trail, it is perfectly polite for one party to terminate the interaction by saying: "You go now." Similarly, in public
settings one party can freely request tobacco or betel from the other,
behavior that would be a violation of etiquette by an outsider in a private setting. The rules for making moves in house entrance give the
householder explicit control over who can come into each of the settings under his control, and give the outsider control over termination
of the event. The householder can prevent advance by not signaling
invitation; the outsider can prevent termination by not signaling permission to leave. Once a signal has been sent, the other party can
accede to it, or he can make a countermove returning play to its original state. These possibilities can be represented by a gamelike
matrix (Figure 2).

If both parties do the same thing, either both move or both
not move, play holds in the same setting. If householder moves and
outsider does not, play advances to the next setting. If outsider moves
and householder does not, play terminates.

The gamelike performances I have been describing occur
when the rules of house entrance are applied in encounters whose
course and outcome are initially uncertain. Household entrance loses
its gamelike character when guests arrive for a scheduled event. In
such cases a 'prior invitation' (pasan) has been issued. The issuance
of an 'invitation' (pellun) to advance upon arrival is predictable and

uninformative. Householders greet approaching guests with a call of 'approach' (pasōng), a blanket invitation to move up to the setting appropriate to the occasion. "Conferences," "negotiations," and "litigation" are generally held on the porch (Frake 1969). The householder is providing a setting but is not really a host. Religious rites, shamanistic seances, life-cycle celebrations, and weddings are held inside.[9] The householder is a host and must provide food for his guests. Rituals are held at the "head zone," with functionaries entitled to a position there throughout the duration of the gathering. The unscheduled arrival of a very high-status person heralds a special event calling for immediate blanket invitation and procuring of the provisions to make a formal scene. At the opposite extreme of formality are the daily routines of householders themselves, who may freely pass through settings without ritual. Thus, the etiquette of household entrance is simplest at the two extremes of the formality scale of events, precisely the cases in which there is minimal ambiguity about what is going on. It is in the ambiguous cases, in which house entrance etiquette becomes a way of defining the formality of the occasion, and not simply a reflection of predetermined formality, that moves become complex and their outcomes informative.

There is one occasion, however, when the Yakan make fun of their code of house entrance, staging an elaborate parody of the whole procedure. The occasion is the event of "fetching the bride," which takes place on the first night of the three-day wedding ceremony. The bride must be taken by the groom's party from a house where she is secluded to the house where the wedding ceremony will be performed. At the approach of the groom's party, the bride's party is jammed onto the porch, forming a tight barricade at the top of the ladder. The groom's party is interrogated at length in a parody of the routine of "customary questions." They are required to put on singing, dancing, and oratorical performances before finally being allowed up to the porch. There, mock accusations are hurled at the groom's party. Trials are held and fines extracted before the groom's party is allowed inside, where snacks are served while mock arguments continue over the bride price (an issue settled, in fact, long before), the qualifications of witnesses, the whereabouts of allegedly key representatives of the groom, and so on. Finally, as dawn approaches, members of the groom's party are allowed to go to the "head zone" and fetch the bride from under a canopy. Permission to leave each setting is not granted until token fees are paid to the bride's party. The bride, despite being tightly veiled, hangs onto doorway and porch posts until the groom's party pays up. Poor-Boy's performance, then, was only an exaggeration of what every groom goes through—a parody of a parody.

House entrance rules have restrictions in scope: they are not for kids and they are not for sex. Children do not have authority to invite outsiders in, but as outsiders they can enter freely without formality—a fact that makes them useful as message and gossip carriers (cf. Hotchkiss 1967). If householder and outsider are of opposite sex, sexually mature, and without other companions on the scene, household entrance is a new game with a new set of rules, including legal rules that proscribe, but by no means prevent, the issuance of an invitation to enter.

One other special contingency deserves mention. Some houses lack porches, thereby eliminating a behavior setting from the sequence. Such houses, generally small and bamboo-walled, are restricted to a few relatively poor people, often widowed or divorced women heading partial-family households. Lack of a porch condemns one to a somewhat marginal position socially, since there are a wide variety of informal events that one cannot host. When a visitor arrives, he must be invited in right away if a sustained social encounter is to take place. The only house that did not have a porch in the community where I spent most of my time belonged to a young divorcee who did not participate much in social affairs but was allegedly very hospitable to male visitors.

Any set of rules for social behavior also has its "unless" clauses that may be invoked at times of unpredicted crises. The inclement weather unless clause permits a traveler caught in the rain to seek shelter (pasaindung) underneath a house, calling up an announcement of his presence. He can generally expect to be invited up. This is the only situation in which 'underneath' (silung) a house becomes a setting for outsider-householder interaction. The refugee unless clause covers eloping couples, people fleeing from enemies, and people forced to evacuate their homes because of hostilities or some natural disaster such as fire. It also covers a large class of people, called in Yakan wantid, sought by Philippine authorities. In emergencies all such people can expect entrance into houses of friends, kin, and allies without worrying about the niceties of etiquette. Sometimes when rules have been broken on the grounds of emergency, there is room for argument over whether the emergency was serious enough to justify the violation. A divorce case arose when a woman, caught out at night in a sudden rainstorm, took shelter in the house of her husband brother who was alone at the time. The husband claimed that his brother should have broken the rule of granting shelter in times of inclement weather rather than breaking the rule of not spending the night with someone else's wife.

The everyday behavior of Yakan house-entering routines bear on at least three general problems in the understanding of social encounters: the analysis of speech acts in actual performative contexts; the use of these verbal performances to situate events both physically in space and conceptually along a dimension of formality; and the relation between actual performances and the "rules" for their interpretat

Yakan invitation-permission routines represent a genre of speech act sequences concerned with the progress and termination of social encounters. Summons-response sequences and greeting exchanges are other genres concerned with the initiation of encounters and the mutual recognition of participants. The illocutionary force (Searle 1969) of a given utterance is a product of the outcome of a sequence of utterances and non-verbal signals exchanged between two parties. It cannot be determined from an analysis, no matter how deeply pursued, of the structure of an isolated utterance. It cannot be matched with the grammatical form of an utterance. What is grammatically an interrog tive may be used performatively as a summons response, a greeting, a request, or, on occasion, to ask a question (Hymes 1971). Similar kinds of speech acts seem to appear everywhere, but their diversity and complexity are such that a complete inventory and description of performative genres can be achieved only by careful ethnographic description of speech behavior. The research method of current theoretical linguistics—conjuring up examples from inside the theoretician's head—is not sufficient. The anthropologist's distinction between "term of reference " and "terms of address" represents a naive and incorrect typology of speech acts. What is "address"? A greeting? A summon A tag? The use of a proper noun in any speech act?

Rather than removing events from their temporal and spatial context and grouping them under functional rubrics such as economic, religious, or legal, we have here been experimenting with a sorting of events by the setting they occupy, in this case a house. Unlike our own culture, in which we have special settings for many kinds of events —classrooms for classes, churches for religious rites, law courts for litigation, concert halls for music—among the Yakan a single structure, the house, provides a setting for a great variety of social occasions. But a house, even a one-roomed Yakan house, is not just space. It is a structured sequence of settings where social events are differentiated not only by the position in which they occur but also by the positions the actors have moved through to get there and the manner in which they have made those moves. There is first of all a contrast between "insiders," those who have legal free access to the setting, and "outsiders." Social events involving only insiders proceed differently from those in which some participants are outsiders. For one thing, an outsider cannot enter a setting without an invitation from an insider. Any interaction in which all participants are outsiders is thereby illegal. These rules apply to all Yakan behavior settings: mosques, cemeteries, fields, etc., as well as houses.

A second, and independent, dimension of social events displayed by house-entering behavior is that of "formality." We can say, for example, that Yakan litigation, which takes place on a porch, thereby requiring only one move to reach and involving no feasting, is a less formal activity than a ceremony of graduation from Koranic school, which takes place inside and involves rites at the "head zone" and provision of festive food by the host. Formality is a cultural marking of social events as special, a phenomenon akin to what is called marking in linguistic theory (see Greenberg 1966). A marked category is signaled by adding something to an unmarked category. In language it may be voicing, nasalization, an affix, or a component of meaning. Social events are marked in our society by things like neckties, refined speech, fancy food, and explicit rules of etiquette. Social events in a Yakan house are marked by, among other things, the degree of penetration required for an outsider to reach their setting. Marked social events, like marked linguistic forms, occur less frequently than corresponding unmarked categories. In language, marking often neutralizes contrasts appearing within the unmarked category: fewer nasal vowels than oral vowels, fewer case distinctions in the plural than in the singular, etc. Similarly marked social occasions often allow abeyance of social distinctions relevant elsewhere.

Formality is a dimension of social events in all cultures, but there are differences not only in the number of differentiations of degree of formality but also in the way different kinds of events are positioned on this scale. Among the Yakan, house-entering behavior reveals three degrees of formality, corresponding to porch, "foot zone" and "head zone" of the house.[10] Litigation falls into the least formal category. Among the Subanun, a Philippine pagan group, the formality scale is binary; events either are formal, requiring festive food and drink, or they are not. Subanun litigation is a formal event. Subanun houses, it is interesting to note, lack porches. One is either inside or below (Frake 1964, 1969).

This study purports to describe a code for interpreting the speech acts (including non-verbal moves) involved in occupying the behavior settings of a house. The code can be considered as the "competence" a person must have to play the game of entering a Yakan house. Actual performances, however, are not automatically "generated" by this competence. Participants make use of it to send and read messages whereby they construct—give an interpretable structure to—a particular social encounter. The shared expectations of participants derived from this competence provides a background against which special meanings —hostility, affection, humor—can be marked. The expression of humor especially, is highly valued and ever present among the Yakan. Even their rites, as we have seen, often portray, not symbolic representations of underlying metaphysical oppositions, but jokes on themselves. The Yakan play with, bend, and break their codes for fun. House entrance etiquette is no exception. Teen-age girls will approach a friend's house and yell out, "Hey, start cooking; we're here!" a gross violation of the "rules" that, in another context, could cause deep trouble. The problem is that a rule violation signaling humor in one situation may signal hostility in another. One must bend the rules with care for expression of hostility, ridicule, or scorn can be very dangerous. Violence, as well as humor, is a fact of Yakan life. One must be constantly on guard. Not even the most formal scheduled event can be depended on to unfold according to the rules. One party of guests, upon approaching the site of a major celebration, was greeted with a shower of spears causing several deaths, an incident in a long, bloody

feud. The rules of house-entering etiquette presented here will not
enable you to predict when you might be greeted with a spear instead of
a speech act, but they will tell you that if you are, you, like the victims
in the incident just described, have a right to be surprised.

APPENDIX

Yakan Terminology and Formulas of House-entering Etiquette

addat   custom, appropriate behavior; habitual or typical behavior.
pagaddatan   behaving appropriately toward someone; showing respect.
mātabat   respect.
moqo mātabat   display respect.
asip   attending to a guest, rendering a guest his due according to addat.
batik   noticing, verbally responding to a summons, the obligation of a
   householder to verbally acknowledge the approach to "below" (a summons) of an outsider. A typical formula is kaqu hep yuq 'So it's you
   there! (an assertion that is invariably correct), followed by a greeting.
sagina   a verbal greeting (a non-verbal greeting is salam). Yakan
   greetings are, grammatically, always questions. The proper use of
   greetings and greeting responses is addat magtilewin 'questioning custom.' Typical greeting formulas, grammatical questions to which
   terms of address may be added, are the following:

   amban kew   'Where are you coming from?'
   tungan kew   'Where are you going?' (not appropriately asked
      of someone who has approached to "below").
   sine saweqnun   'Who's your companion?' (most appropriately
      posed as a greeting to someone who is alone).
   ine binoqonu lu   'What are you carrying there?' (most appro-
      priately asked of someone who is carrying something the
      identity of which is obvious, a string of fish, for example—
      otherwise the utterance would be subject to construal per-
      formatively as a real question).

pellun   on-the-spot invitation to advance in a household setting. An
   invitation issued beforehand to come to some later event is pasan.
   Typical invitation (pellun) formulas, grammatical active imperatives
   to which terms of address can be added, are the following:

pesōng be kaqam   'Approach you-all!' (a blanket invitation
to immediately proceed to the appropriate setting for a
scheduled event. Used only when a pasan has been issued
beforehand).
pitu be kew   'come' (to below).
manaqik be kew   'climb up' (to the porch).
parialem be kew   'enter' (to inside).

segeq   to persist in a pellun in spite of outsider's requests for permission to leave.
ohatan   to hold a guest, dissuade him from leaving by persistent invitations to advance, to eat, to confer, etc.
baqid   asking permission to leave or pass through a setting with respect to which the speaker is an outsider. Typical formulas, grammatically active declarative sentences, are the following:

moleq ne ku   'I'm leaving now.'
hap lumaq ne ku   'I'm going home now.'
palanjal ne kami   'We're continuing on' (said when the encounter has not proceeded beyond "below").
pitu du kami   'We'll be on our way' (said when the encounter
has not proceeded beyond "vicinity").
tiaq kami palabey ēq   'We'll just pass by, huh' (permission
to pass by).

ngaweq   the granting of permission. Typical formulas are the following:

aweq   'OK.'
anduquq   'a pity' (formal or jocular).
gaq kaqam legga   'You weren't treated badly?' (jocular).

NOTES

[1] That is to say, my observations have been restricted largely
to the verbal aspects of house-entering performances. A large amount
of non-verbal signaling, which has escaped my attention, undoubtedly
takes place. The present account suffers accordingly. For a study of
non-verbal greeting performances in American society, see Kendon
and Ferber (1973).

[2] Field work among the Yakan was conducted in 1962, 1963–64, and 1965–66 under a grant from the National Institute of Mental Health. Subsequent brief visits were made through 1972. During the course of this work, I was a member of two Yakan households in different areas of Basilan. I have performed as both an insider and an outsider in house-entering events. Yakan critiques of my performances, often awkward or unintentionally humorous, have made me painfully aware of the problematic nature of everyday behavior.

[3] The porch of some houses lacks a roof, which extends the domain of the "inclement weather unless clause" (to be discussed) and thereby restricts the range of events likely to be held on the porch.

[4] Since the time of field work, the titular 'chief' (datuq) of the Yakan (who is of Christian descent) has proclaimed himself a sultan (sūtan). He lives in a largely Christian market town in a Western-style house that, to be sure, has private rooms.

[5] An acceptable alternative arrangement, occasionally employed, is to have the head wall facing west.

[6] There are two alternative locations of the ladder. The one shown in Figure 1 was selected for diagrammatic convenience. It is actually somewhat more common to locate the ladder at the end of the porch away from the cooking shed. This positioning of the ladder allows more space between the entrance to "on" and the entrance to "inside," a more comfortable arrangement for large parties of outsiders, since they can fill space on the porch niche without moving away from the access point to "inside."

[7] Yakan address term usage is similar to that of their close linguistic kin, the Balangingi Samal, as described by Geoghegan (1969).

[8] Frake (1969) describes a relationship of 'legitimate interest' (dapuq) that can pertain between an individual and an object or another individual. "Legal free access" is the dapuq relation applied to a behavior setting. The dapuq lumaq 'householders' are those with legal free access to a house.

[9] At very large gatherings guests may be fed outside and many participants may remain outside most or all the time. All, however, have been officially invited in and may enter the house freely.

[10] A complete analysis of formality contrasts among Yakan events would, of course, require consideration of events held in other settings. In mosques, for example, formal events are held whose participants all have legal free access to the setting.

REFERENCES

Frake, Charles O. 1964. How to ask for a drink in Subanun. Amer-
ican Anthropologist 66.127-32.
_____. 1969. Struck by speech: the Yakan concept of litigation.
In L. Nader, ed., Law in culture and society, pp. 147-67.
Chicago: Aldine.
Geoghegan, William. 1969. The use of marking rules in semantic
systems. Working Paper 26, Language-Behavior Research
Laboratory, Berkeley, Calif.
Greenberg, Joseph. 1966. Language universals. In T. A. Sebeok,
ed., Current trends in linguistics. Vol. III, Theoretical
foundations, pp. 61-112. The Hague: Mouton.
Hotchkiss, John. 1967. Children and conduct in a Ladino community
of Chiapas, Mexico. American Anthropologist 69.711-18.
Hymes, Dell. 1971. Sociolinguistics and the ethnography of speaking.
In E. Ardener, ed., Social anthropology and language. ASA
Monograph 10. New York: Tavistock.
Kendon, Adam, and Andrew Ferber. 1973. A description of some
human greetings. In R. P. Michael and J. H. Crook, Com-
parative ecology and behavior of primates. London: Academ
Press.
Schegloff, Emanuel A. 1968. Sequencing in conversation openings.
American Anthropologist 70.1075-95.
Searle, John R. 1969. Speech acts: an essay in the philosophy of
language. New York: Cambridge University Press.

14 | Languages in Yakan Culture

Contemporary sociolinguistic research has repeatedly revealed the critical importance to linguistic and sociological theory of taking seriously the great variability of linguistic repertoires exhibited by many speech communities. But linguistic diversity can be a social resource even in speech communities whose members themselves display rather limited repertoires of language use. Languages are more than codes for use. They are also cultural objects for thought. By local standards the speech community of the Yakan of Basilan Island, the Philippines, is relatively homogeneous; yet a variety of languages, some rarely spoken or heard locally, play complex roles in the displays of cultural knowledge that comprise Yakan social life.

In Basilan, the Yakan speech community, Yakan society, and the population sharing Yakan culture are largely coterminous. In the eyes of Yakan and non-Yakan alike, to speak Yakan as a native speaker is to be a Yakan. The language is the appropriate medium of all conversation among Yakan. It is possible to be a member of Yakan society and know only Yakan (though one must at least know of other languages). Such a person, however, is cut off from all but an audience role in religious scenes, from leadership roles, and from writing as a channel of communication. It is also the case that very few non-Yakan speak Yakan; yet the Yakan have important interconnections with other speech communities on political, military, educational, religious, and economic fronts. The functioning of the society and the continuance of the cultural tradition require that some members of Yakan society learn, or at least acquaint themselves with, other linguistic codes. Seven languages other than Yakan are of significance as cognitive objects in Yakan culture and also, in some cases, as media of communication with members of other societies: Samal,

Tausug, Zamboangueño, Malay, Tagalog, Arabic, and English. The
Yakan are in direct contact with communities of native speakers of
only the first three of these languages.

Distribution of Local Languages

On Basilan Island, speakers of Yakan occupy a coastal belt
of foothills and mountain slopes extending from the northeast and
around the south coast to the west side of the island. The interior of
the island is an uninhabited lumber company preserve. Except in
plantation labor camps and in some communities on the frontiers of
Yakan occupation, Yakan communities are distinct from communities
of speakers of other languages. One does not find, on Basilan, Yakan
communities which include a substantial portion of native speakers of
some other language.

Samal, locally sama, is a chain of dialects spoken by the populations of the smaller islands and atolls and of the littoral zones of
larger islands from North Borneo throughout the Sulu archipelago to
Basilan and the southern coasts of Zamboanga Peninsula (Pallesen
1977). The boat-dwelling peoples of Sulu, generally called Bajao in the
literature (a term also applied to land-dwelling Borneo Samal), speak
a dialect of Samal and are regarded locally as outcast Samal (sama
luwaqan), not as a distinct cultural or linguistic group.

Native speakers of Tausug are concentrated on the island of
Jolo, which they consider to be their homeland, but communities composed largely of, or at least dominated by, native Tausug speakers can
be found throughout the Sulu-Basilan-Zamboanga area (Pallesen 1977).
Outside of Jolo, Tausug are usually associated with littoral settlements.
They have, however, attempted some inland agricultural settlement on
the west coast of Basilan.

Zamboangueño speakers occupy much the same ecological
niche as the Yakan: coastal (but not littoral) zones of hills and slopes.
Zamboangueño settlement extends along the southern tip of Zamboanga
Peninsula and the northern coast of Basilan Island. Zamboanga City
proper, as well as the larger towns in the area, are populated not only
by Zamboangueños, but also by other Christian Filipinos (especially

Cebuano Bisayans), Chinese, and some Americans and Europeans.
The native languages of these latter groups are, however, of little
relevance in the Yakan language-contact situation.

Although there are scattered individuals in the area who speak
Tagalog, English, and even Arabic as their native language, there are
no communities for which any of these languages, or Malay, is the
native tongue, and few Yakan have an opportunity to hear these languages spoken by native speakers. Malay, Tagalog, Arabic, and English, nevertheless, play a significant role in Yakan culture.

The following tabulation presents an estimate, based on 1960
Philippine census figures, of the number of native speakers of the
four principal languages spoken on Basilan. It is not possible accur-
ately to distinguish Samal from Tausug speakers in the census data.
The majority in the Samal-Tausug categories of this tabulation are
Samal.

Basilan Island proper:	
Zamboangueño	40,000
Yakan	55,000
Samal and Tausug	26,000
Offshore islands:	
Samal and Tausug	29,000

Genetic Affiliations

Yakan, Samal, Tausug, Tagalog, and Malay affiliate geneti-
cally with the Western or Hespernesian branch of Austronesian languages, a branch that includes all Philippine languages and all but a
few of the Austronesian languages spoken in Southeast Asia outside of
Formosa. Yakan belongs to the Samalan group of closely related languages and dialects which embraces all the indigenous vernaculars of
the Sulu archipelago except Tausug. Although there is a distinct language boundary between Samal and Yakan, and all Yakan dialects share
a number of distinct linguistic features that set them apart from all
Samal dialects, for historical purposes at least, Yakan and Samal can
almost be considered dialects of the same language. Tausug and Tagalog are the southernmost and northernmost representatives of the

Central Philippine subgroup, which includes the languages of the Bisayan Islands and many Mindanao languages. Malay stands slightly apart and is about equidistant from both Samal and Central Philippine subgroups.

Zamboangueño is a dialect of Philippine Creole Spanish, spoken also in Cavite on Manila Bay. Its lexicon is about 75 percent of Spanish origin, the remainder being derived from Central Philippine languages, primarily Tagalog and Hiligaynon (Frake 1971). Its grammatical structure is more similar to other Creoles in the world than to either Spanish or Philippine languages. However one wishes to interpret the genetic affiliations of a creole language, Zamboangueño is clearly not Austronesian. Thus it, together with English and Arabic form the set of unrelated languages in the Yakan contact situation. A classification of these languages by categories of geographic and genetic distance with respect to Yakan is presented in the tabulation below

	Contact	Non-contact
Closely related	Samal	
Related	Tausug	Tagalog, Malay
Unrelated	Zamboangueño	Arabic, English

Roles of Other Languages in Yakan Culture

Samal. The Yakan are in direct contact with Samal communities along the coast and on the offshore islands of Basilan. Thus situated, the Yakan and Samal occupy complementary ecological niches and are mutually interdependent. Yakan have occasion to interact with Samal when they go to markets in Samal communities to buy fish, when they sell agricultural products, rattan, timber, and dugout hulls to the Samal, when they hire Samal boats for coastwise travel, when Samal and Yakan participate in each other's festivals, religious worship, and litigation, when Yakan act as agents or retailers for Samal smuggled goods, and also, as sometimes happens, when Yakan and Samal intermarry. These are on the whole friendly relations between non-competing peers.

A major factor in Yakan-Samal language contact is the very close linguistic relationships between the two languages. It is relatively easy for a speaker of one to gain receptive control of the other and only slightly more difficult for him to acquire productive control. The two languages are mutually unintelligible largely because the common particles and question words are different and there are some critical phonological and morphological differences. Once these are learned, and the patterns of sound correspondences grasped, receptive control, at least, is very easy.

The two languages are also similar in what might be called their sociolinguistic status in Sulu-Moslem society. Neither language is widely spoken by non-native speakers as an auxiliary language. In interacting with outsiders (other than Samal or Yakan), neither the Samal nor the Yakan can expect the other to know their language. Neither language is written; neither is a vehicle for transmitting religious lore, technical knowledge, or legal decrees to other groups. One difference, however, is the much greater geographical dispersal of Samal speakers as opposed to the concentration of Yakan on Basilan. Whereas all Yakan can be expected to have some exposure to Samal, only those Samal living in Basilan or vicinity can be expected to have any knowledge of Yakan.

The close linguistic and sociolinguistic relationship of Samal and Yakan makes possible a variety of adjustments in intercommunication. The linguistic resolution of a given interaction situation will depend on the extent to which the respective participants are familiar with each other's language, on whether the interaction takes place in a Samal or a Yakan setting, and on the numbers of participants speaking each language. The kinds of speech situations with distinctive resolutions can be labeled as one-one, one-many, many-many, and one-many-many:

One-one: One or several speakers of each language not significantly involved with a larger group in a distinctively Yakan or Samal setting. Either language or both will be used depending on the productive and receptive competencies of each speaker.

One-many: One or several speakers of one language among many speakers of the other and/or involved in a cultural scene of the other. The language of the majority will be used. Those who do not control it will be largely cut off from group interaction.

Many-many: Two sizable and approximately equal-sized groups in joint interaction, as at a festivity. Each party will speak its own language and utilize only receptive control of the other.

One-many-many: Two groups in interaction being addressed or interrogated by a single speaker. The single speaker will address each group in its language and both groups as a unit in his language. He will, in turn, be addressed in the language of the person speaking to him. For example in a legal case involving Samal and Yakan with, let us say, a Yakan legal authority, the legal authority will address Samal witnesses in Samal, Yakan witnesses in Yakan, and he will give his summation and decision in Yakan. Participants will address the court in their own language. An exception to this outcome occurs in some formal Samal settings where a Samal speaker, even when addressing an exclusively Samal audience, may use Tausug. A Yakan speaker in a corresponding situation will never do so—a reflection of Yakan attitudes about Tausug discussed below.

The resolution of Yakan-Samal language-contact situations is thus intermediate between that typically occurring when speakers of two dialects of the same language interact and that typically occurring when speakers of two clearly distinct languages interact. In the former case, as say with British and American English, each speaker speaks his own dialect. In the latter case, as say with English and Russian, the speakers select a single common language in which to communicate. In the Yakan-Samal situation either resolution may occur. What does not occur is the use of an intermediate jargon or pidgin which is not clearly Yakan or Samal. Another possibility, the use of Tausug, the Sulu Moslem lingua franca widely known by both Samal and Yakan, rarely occurs when Samal and Yakan interact with each other.

Tausug. The Tausug people, whose homeland is the island of Jolo, have long enjoyed cultural, and frequently social and political ascendency throughout the Sulu archipelago. Their language serves as the lingua franca of Sulu Moslems and as the literary vehicle of Sulu Moslem culture. The Yakan are on the peripheries of Tausug hegemony. Although they recognize the Sultanate of Sulu as the highest political office among Sulu Moslems, they accord it no authority over them and resist by force attempts by Tausug to further extend their settlements and political authority on Basilan. The Yakan have little good to say of the Tausug as people. To the Yakan they are all treacherous bandits. I have never known a Yakan to pretend to an outsider that he was a Tausug or to address an audience of fellow Yakan in Tausug—both acts being commonly observed among Samal. Nevertheless, the Yakan recognize the "cultural" superiority of the Tausug. In the Yakan view, this superiority is not the result of any virtue on the part of the Tausug. It is the result of their having been fortunate enough to have received the Moslem tradition first. They are therefore more knowledgeable about it and possess a language written in the script of the Koran (a script, however, which the Yakan insist on calling sulat yakan 'Yakan writing' even though it is not used to record Yakan speech).

The Tausug language is important to the Yakan in the following contexts:

1. Writing. Throughout the Sulu-Basilan-Zamboanga area, Tausug is the only local language regularly written. The Arabic alphabet is used under conventions apparently modeled more on Koranic Arabic than on Malay orthography. The Malay letter representing /ŋ/ (a three-dot 'ain) is used, but unlike Malay, Tausug writing always employs vowel marks (as does the Koran) and uses existing Arabic letters (ghain and fa) to represent /g/ and /p/ rather than the Malay modifications of kaf and fa. Tausug also uses the geminate consonant sign which has no place in Malay orthography. The Yakan, and probably most Sulu Moslems, learn Arabic writing in Koranic schools and simply transfer this knowledge to the writing of Tausug. There are no dictionaries, spelling books, or large bodies of written literature to effect standardization of Tausug spelling. Consequently, especially with the surplus of consonant signs in the Arabic alphabet, spellings can be bewilderingly varied (Cameron 1917, Lewis 1954).

The Yakan are exposed to a small amount of published material, generally mimeographed, in Tausug religious tracts, calendars, election materials—posters, leaflets, and sample ballots. There are some Tausug signs around Basilan: government notices and prohibitions posted in markets and towns, Moslem restaurant signs in towns, and the invariable "No Bladed Weapons Allowed" sign posted at plantation gates. The Yakan write Tausug to send messages to each other,

to make copies of religious tracts and Tausug religious songs, to
keep records, for example, of the order of arrival of guests at a
festivity (which determines eating order), and, as an alternative to
Roman orthography, to write in names of candidates when voting in
government elections. No use is made of Tausug or any other writing
system, to record Yakan legal proceedings, decisions, and codes.
None of these functions of literacy is essential to being a Yakan, but
the ability to read and write, as well as speak, Tausug is important
to any Yakan who aspires to a leadership role in religious or political
spheres. Probably less than one-tenth of the adult Yakan population
is literate in Tausug.

2. Religious education. Tausug is frequently the medium of
instruction in Koranic schools among the Yakan. A number of such
schools have been set up by Magindanao religious teachers from Cota
bato Province. As carriers of the Islamic tradition, the Magindanao
rival the Tausug in prestige among the Yakan and have the advantage
of not being political enemies. Yakan-Tausug distrust is too great to
permit Tausug religious teachers in most Yakan communities. The
Yakan would suspect the Tausug of using such a prestigious position
as a lever for political and economic advantage, and the Tausug would
fear extermination at the slightest pretext. Both fears would, in most
cases, be entirely realistic. The Moslem educational field is consequently left open to the Magindanao who come from a land too far away
to constitute a threat. However, since Yakan and Magindanao do not
speak each other's languages, they use Tausug for intercommunication
In Magindanao-taught schools among the Yakan, therefore, one finds
native speakers of one language (Magindanao) teaching native speakers
of a second language (Yakan) a third language (Arabic) using a fourth
language (Tausug) as a medium of instruction.

3. Songs. Two types of 'songs' (luguq) important in Yakan
culture have Tausug lyrics: the saqil (< Malay shaer < Arabic shi'r)
on religious subjects such as Mohammed's ascent to heaven and the
padaŋsabil (< Malay peraŋ sabil 'Holy War') relating exploits of
famous fighters such as the notorious Tausug bandit Kamlun. Both
song types are currently popular as entertainment and the saqil has,
as well, a prescribed place in wedding ceremonies. These songs,
as well as Arabic religious songs, which are a part of Yakan cultural
scenes, are known as luguq yakan 'Yakan songs,' whatever the language of the lyrics.

4. Cross-cultural contacts. Since a Tausug could not be expected to demean himself by learning Samal or Yakan, a Yakan must be prepared to use Tausug in verbal interaction with Tausug individuals. The only alternatives would be Zamboangueño or English, the two other local lingua francas, if both participants happened to know one of these languages. Yakan interaction with Tausug occurs largely on economic and military fronts. Yakan purchase Tausug jewelry, are occasionally involved in Tausug rum-smuggling operations, and sometimes confer with Tausug leaders in attempts to negotiate a cease-fire in some local outbreak of hostilities. In towns and markets there are numerous occasions for casual contacts with Tausug. There are also occasions to use Tausug with non-Tausug. Police and local government officials sometimes speak Tausug but rarely any Yakan. Political candidates may have their speeches (delivered in Zamboangueño or English) translated into Tausug if there is a Moslem audience. A Yakan who participates in Samal activities is likely to be exposed to more Tausug than within his own society. There are often Tausug resident in Samal communities and the Samal sometimes use Tausug as a prestigious vehicle for formal orations and narrations.

The Yakan learn Tausug informally in the contexts just described. Since the contacts are less frequent and the linguistic differences greater, knowledge of Tausug by Yakan is less common than of Samal. The majority of Yakan have some acquaintance with the language but probably not more than one-fourth of the adult male population speak it well.

Because of its role as a vehicle of religious lore, the fact that it is written, and the social and political position of its speakers, the Tausug language has high prestige among the Yakan, the highest of any local language. Its prestige, however, is constrained by two factors: the Yakan enmity toward the Tausug people and the recognition that the language's role in the Moslem world is rather confined. From Meccan pilgrims' accounts of Singapore, from smugglers' accounts of Borneo, from accounts of Cotabato and Lanao, the Yakan have learned that Tausug, in spite of its local utility, does not, in fact, carry one very far. And in the handing down of the Moslem tradition from its Arabic source, there is a language yet closer to that source (and also to the source of smuggled goods) than Tausug—namely Malay.

Malay. The Malay language is a conceptual object in Yakan culture, not a code of communication. The Yakan have no contact with native speakers of the language nor are they likely to participate in any situations in which Malay is spoken. North Borneo is the northeastern limit of the use of Malay as a lingua franca. Only those Tausug and Samal who travel or reside there have direct contact with the language. Yakan knowledge of the language is by heresay, and I have yet to meet a Yakan who speaks more than a few phrases of the language. Yet interest in Malay is keen and the prestige accorded someone who can give Malay words for things or who can read Malay introductions to Arabic religious books printed in Singapore is great. One Samal shaman is famous throughout southern Basilan because he speaks to his spirit familiars in Malay. When the ethnographer was introduced to new people by old Yakan friends, frequently the best thing the latter could think of to say about him was that he could speak and write Malay (fortunately the limited extent of this knowledge was never put to a severe test).

This remarkable prestige of a remote language results first of all from its conceptual position between Arabic and Tausug as the conveyor of the Moslem tradition into Sulu. The Yakan conception of the flow of Islam into Sulu is historically accurate, a fact impressed on the outside investigator (though not recognized by the Yakan) by the large number of Malay loan words pertaining to religion shared by Yakan, Samal, and Tausug. The term for daily worship in these languages, for example, is not Arabic but Malay (sambahayaŋ < Malay sembahyaŋ).

The homeland of the Malay, Singapore (siŋapurah) to the Yakan, is renowned not only as a religious center, but also as the source of such items as gambir (whose botanical source is not known to the Yakan), highly valued textiles, Arabic religious books including the Koran, medicines, and Moslem radio broadcasts now becoming familiar through the ubiquitous transistor radio. The Malay homeland is also known as the domain of legendary creatures: the tiger, the elephant, and (inaccurately) the bird of paradise. Malay, spoken in North Borneo, is also the language of the source of smuggled goods, an association with economic power.

Adding to the prestige of Malay is the fact that it is written, and usually printed (rather than mimeographed) in Arabic orthography.

The Yakan encounter printed Malay in the introductions to locally
purchased Korans (naturally a very prestigious setting), and on medicine and perfume bottle labels (the Malay perfume "Ayer Mata Duyung,"
'Sea Cow's Tears,' is a stock smuggling item). Although the Yakan
generally encounter written Malay in Arabic rather than Roman orthography, a knowledge of Tausug orthographic conventions does not enable
one to read, even in the minimal sense of producing noises, unvoweled
Malay script. The ability to read Malay is a sign of special learning.

   Arabic. Arabic is the language of communication with God,
a communication focused on the proper transmission of signals in the
proper contexts with minimal concern for the semantic content of individual messages. There is a finite set of messages recorded in sacred
books, of which the Koran is basic. There is no production of novel
messages. Thus the task faced by a Yakan with Arabic is not the
mastery of a productive linguistic code, but, maximally, the ability
to produce oral signals from their graphic representations, to repro-
duce graphic sign sequences, and to commit a substantial portion of
the finite set of messages to memory. He must also learn the appropriate context for producing the fixed, rote-learned messages, these
contexts being in fact the meaning of the messages to the Yakan. If
one asks a Yakan, even an expert in religious lore, what bismillah
(< bi-smi llahi 'in the name of God') means, he will say: "That's
what one says before eating, what one writes at the beginning of a
letter, how one begins certain prayers, etc." In the context calling
for oral production of Arabic, the language is always chanted in a
prescribed manner so that emphasis is on intonation contours rather
than on the accurate production of segmental phonemes. The proper
rendition of Arabic messages requires the mastery of a few new phone
types—one should at least make his Arabic sound different than Yakan
—but even the most skilled make wholesale reductions in Arabic phonology. There are a large number of Arabic loan words in Yakan, a
subset of these being recognized by the Yakan as Arabic. To use such
Arabic words in Yakan conversation, especially if one can pronounce
them "Arabic-style" (e.g. to say qarbaqah instead of qalabaqah 'Wednes-
day') is a way of displaying one's erudition.

   Yakan children and youths of both sexes study Arabic in Moslem schools (madrasatih) taught by Yakan specialists (guruh) or, in
some localities by qualified Moslem teachers (qustad) from Cotabato.

Given the linguistic problem, already referred to, of the latter schools
(Magindanao teaching Yakan Arabic in Tausug), it is perhaps fortunate
that full mastery of Arabic as a linguistic code is not the aim of instruc
tion. Moslem schools are in competition with public schools, whose
objective in the eyes of the Yakan is to teach English. Probably about
half the Yakan population receives some formal instruction in Moslem
schools. More girls than boys are currently in attendance, apparently
because of the desire to give boys an exposure to English, a more
practical language for current economic and political life. An elaborate ceremony, akin to a wedding ceremony in costuming and provisioning, celebrates a youth's completion of a Moslem education (Wulff
1963).

Zamboangueño. Zamboangueño is the language through which
the Yakan confront the Filipino-Western cultural tradition and the Philippine governmental system. It is a native language to some 100,000
Christians in southern Zamboanga and northern Basilan. Within this
area it is used as a lingua franca among Christians of differing linguistic backgrounds, and also between Moslem and Christian. Thus, like
Tausug, Zamboangueño has auxiliary language status in a restricted
area, but, unlike Tausug, it is not regularly written and almost never
printed. There are no books, magazines, newspapers, signs, government notices, or election materials written in Zamboangueño. It must
be the only language in the Philippines with more than a handful of
speakers in which portions of the New Testament have not been published by Protestant missionary groups. Even Yakan is ahead of Zamboangueño in this respect.

For the Yakan, Zamboangueño is a language of political and
economic relations with the external, non-Moslem world. It is important to Yakan leaders who must interact with Christian officials and
police, to those who carry on business transactions in towns and especially in Isabella or Zamboanga, to plantation workers who must interact with Christian foremen, to students in town schools who must
interact with the Christian students. Because of its utility as an entree
to the Western world, a certain amount of prestige attaches to Zamboangueño, a prestige, however, mitigated by three factors: its useful-
ness as an auxiliary language is geographically very restricted, it is
not written, and it is spoken by bisayaq (literally 'slaves') 'Filipino
Christians,' who are held in a certain amount of contempt and distrust
by most Yakan.

In view of the long contact between Zamboangueño and Yakan, manifest by a striking lexical and phonological influence of Zamboangueño on Yakan, the number of Yakan who speak Zamboangueño seems relatively small. I know many Yakan who have worked on plantations, who travel frequently to towns, or who have attended elementary school with Zamboangueño children, yet who cannot carry on a conversation in Zamboangueño. Those who learn Zamboangueño are those who have special roles in Christian culture: students, political leaders, traders.

Tagalog. Tagalog, the official national language of the Philippines (under the name "Pilipino"), is a relatively new arrival on the Yakan linguistic scene. Like Malay it is as yet of importance largely as a conceptual object: a link between English at the source of the Western tradition and Zamboangueño. The association of Tagalog with Manila assures it of prestige. The place name manilaq is well known to the Yakan as designating the seat of government authority, the site of the "highest" prison, and a local near the source of the Western tradition. Older Yakan have, in fact, sometimes confused Manila with America as the homeland of English speech and the Western tradition.

Tagalog is taught as a subject (with English as the medium of instruction) in all Philippine schools. It is the language of Philippine-produced movies shown throughout the islands, and, although it rarely appears on signs, in government documents, or newspapers, it is the language of very popular and widely distributed pulp magazines and comics. Through these influences, it is gaining utility as an auxiliary language in Christian areas of Zamboanga and Basilan, areas outside the realm of Cebuano, the lingua franca for most of the rest of Mindanao. Except for some exposure of children in schools, few Yakan participate in any situations where Tagalog is used. The only adult Yakan likely to know Tagalog are those who have served sentences in the national prison near Manila.

English. Thanks to its being a medium of instruction in public schools, English is widely spoken in the Philippines. In spite of the official promotion of Tagalog as the national language, English is still the only nation-wide lingua franca. It is the language of government and courts, of all major newspapers, of signs, of most radio programs. The ability to speak and read English is synonymous with

education. Although the Yakan are outside the mainstream of Filipino
society and have a competing notion and linguistic criterion of being
educated (Moslem lore and Arabic), the desire to learn English is
almost universal among younger Yakan, and it is being increasingly
recognized by the older generation. To the Yakan, English has a number of unique attributes which bear upon its position in their culture.

First, like Arabic, it is a language to be learned by formal
instruction in schools, and the purpose of schools is to impart this
knowledge. It is only in the last few decades that public elementary
schools have been established throughout Basilan. Today a school
teaching the lower elementary grades is within reach of the majority
of Yakan children. Higher elementary education is still out of reach
of many, and for high school education (necessary for any useful command of English), one must travel to one of the towns: Isabela, Malu-
so, Lamitan, or Zamboanga. There is also an American missionary
school near Lamitan that dates from prewar days. This school is
justly considered much superior for learning English than local public
elementary schools, but it also very forceably attempts to indoctrinate
pupils in its fundamentalist version of Christian practice, requiring,
for example, church attendance on Sunday and providing on Friday,
the Moslem sabbath, a day of recreational activities designed to draw
children away from Moslem worship in their home communities.
Probably because of the anti-Moslem and anti-Yakan attitude of this
mission, there is considerable antagonism toward schooling among
older Yakan in eastern Basilan. The Moslem and Filipino-Western
traditions are seen as more fully in conflict here than elsewhere in
Basilan where religion is not so prominently an issue in learning
English.

Except for a few products of the mission school who have
gone on to high school or even college, very few Yakan have much
command of written and especially of spoken English, even those who
have completed elementary education. Since those who continue
school long enough to learn English rarely have the time or motivation
to study Arabic, knowledge of the two languages and the two orthogra-
phies is largely mutually exclusive. A young Yakan today bent on
achieving a prestigious position in society has essentially two choices:
to follow the road of English and the Western tradition or of Arabic
and the Moslem tradition. The latter route has the advantage that it

leads to a fully Yakan role within the society, whereas the former leads to roles within or in relation to Filipino-Western society: teacher, government worker, politician. As yet the authority positions in Yakan society are dominated by the Moslem traditionalists, but the importance of English as the language of government, especially in the written form of land titles, tax notices, receipts, court summons, warrants, gives the younger, secular-oriented Yakan who knows at least written English a wedge into political and economic roles of importance.

Conceptually English, spoken by the milikanuh 'Americans, Europeans (other than Spaniards),' is the language of the source of the Western tradition, the technological superiority of which even the most staunch Moslem traditionalist, as eager as any Yakan for wealth and comfort, readily admits. Consequently, in spite of the conflicts with the Moslem tradition, English is accorded a prestige rivaled only by Arabic.

Summary

The following appear to be some of the significant differentia of the roles of the various languages in Yakan culture.

The "Great Tradition" to which they belong. The roles of these languages can first be differentiated by their function as vehicles of one of the two "great traditions," Sulu-Moslem and Filipino-Western, that impinge on Yakan culture. Arabic, Malay, Tausug, Samal, and Yakan itself are vehicles of the Sulu-Moslem tradition. The Yakan identify each of these languages as media for communicating Islamic lore and consider this lore to have a proper place within their own culture. English, Tagalog, and Zamboangueño are vehicles of the Filipino-Western tradition, an alien tradition to the Yakan but also an appealing one in certain, largely material, respects.

Function as a vehicle of a great tradition. Within each great tradition, one language is looked upon as representing the source of the tradition: Arabic, spoken by God, in the one case; English, spoken by Americans, in the other. The sources of these traditions, makka 'Mecca' and milikah 'America,' are, in both cases, remote from the Yakan homeland. Although the Yakan have access to written material

in the source languages, reception and interpretation of the tradition
depend on their being transmitted in stages through other languages.
(This is especially true for the Moslem tradition since the reading of
Arabic by the Yakan is a purely phonological exercise.) The transmitter languages are Malay and Tausug for the Moslem tradition and
Tagalog and Zamboangueño for the Western tradition. Samal and
Yakan are part of the Sulu-Moslem tradition but have receiver roles
only. They are not vehicles for communicating that tradition to other
speech communities. A minor anomaly in this picture is that the
Moslem tradition is also transmitted to the Yakan by native speakers
of Magindanao but by means of Tausug.

Contact distance. Contact distance refers to the directness
of contact with native speakers of a given language. Non-contact languages are those with whose native speakers the Yakan have little or
no face-to-face contact, namely Arabic, English, Malay, and Tagalog.
Direct access to these languages is mostly limited to written material
and to formalized contact with non-native speakers such as school
teachers. The remaining languages, Tausug, Samal, and Zamboangueño, are contact languages.

The dimension of contact distance intersects the category of
transmitter languages yielding non-contact transmitters (Malay and
Tagalog) and contact transmitters (Tausug and Zamboangueño) for
each tradition. The non-contact transmitters are linking languages
connecting (by Yakan conception) the source languages and the contact
transmitter languages of each tradition. Thus, ignoring the receiver
languages, the remaining six languages are divided by the dimension
of tradition affiliation and this division is cross-cut by a three-way
contrast (source, link, and contact transmitter) produced by the intersection of distance and role dimensions. Since the Yakan associate
each language with a locale, this pattern maps onto a geographical
model (see Table 1).

Mode of acquisition. Arabic, English, and Tagalog are studied by formal instruction in schools. Knowledge of the other languages
is acquired informally by contact with native speakers or in the case
of Malay by hearsay.

Writing. Arabic, Malay, Tausug, English, and Tagalog are
written, the first three in Arabic script, the last two in Roman orthog-

Table 1. Tradition: Language and Locale

	Tradition: language		Tradition: locale	
	Moslem	Western	Moslem	Western
Source	Arabic	English	Mecca	America
Link	Malay	Tagalog	Singapore	Manila
Contact	Tausug	Zamboangueño	Jolo	Zamboanga

raphy. The study of Arabic and English is conceived as learning to write and read. To learn only spoken Arabic or English is virtually inconceivable to the Yakan. The fact that Tausug is the only contact language that is written greatly augments its prestige.

Auxiliary language status. Tausug, Zamboangueño, English, and Tagalog are all used as auxiliary languages in the Zamboanga-Basilan area (the use of Zamboangueño does not extend to Jolo), each with a somewhat specialized role. For the Yakan, Tausug is needed to communicate with other Moslems (except Samal), Zamboangueño to communicate with Christians, and English to understand and respond to formal oral and written communications from Filipino authorities. Tagalog is as yet of little importance as a lingua franca to the Yakan, its local use being largely restricted to communication among middle- and upper-class, well-traveled and well-educated Christian Filipinos.

Prestige. A further attribute of these languages is the relative prestige they lend to a Yakan who displays a knowledge of them. The ranking of the languages in terms of relative prestige is quite clear. Arabic and English have by far the greatest prestige. Although individual Yakan may differ in their relative evaluation of the two languages, no one would place any other language above them. Malay and Tagalog rank next, though—since few Yakan have any real ability in these languages—their prestige is of a rather abstract kind, expressed by comments about the languages themselves rather than about Yakan who know the languages. Next comes Tausug, then Zamboangueno. Knowledge of Samal is a utilitarian matter that confers no significant prestige. These relative rankings appear to be primarily a function of the closeness of a language to the source of its tradition,

Table 2. Languages in Yakan Culture

Languages		Characteristics				
Sulu-Moslem tradition	Filipino-Western tradition	Contact distance	Role as tradition vehicle	Instruction	Writing	Prestige
ARABIC qarab	ENGLISH qiŋlis	non-contact	source	formal	written	great
	TAGALOG tagalug					substan-tial
MALAY malayuh			trans-mitter			
TAUSUG sūk						
	ZAMBOANGUEÑO bisayaq	contact		informal	not written	some
SAMAL samah			receiver			
YAKAN yakan		native				none

Moslem or Western. This function produces the basic ranking of Arabic and English above Malay and Tagalog, and the latter pair above Tausug and Zamboangueño. The ranking of Tausug over Zamboangueño can be attributed to the association of Tausug with the Moslem rather than the Christian tradition, to the fact that it is written, and to the existence of a language, Samal, of lesser prestige within its tradition. The advantages accruing to Arabic over English by being associated with the Moslem tradition are offset by the much greater utility of English as an auxiliary language.

Apart from the prestige accorded other languages, there is a separate matter of pride in one's own language manifest by such behavior as its exclusive use in all contexts, formal and informal, within the society, a speaker's willingness to identify himself as a native speaker of his language to outsiders, perceptions of prestige accorded one's language by outsiders, evaluative comparisons of one's own language with others, the emphasis placed on differential skills in speech by native speakers, and, perhaps, the resistance to using loan words as substitutes for existing terms. Using these criteria I would judge the Yakan to have more pride in their language than the Samal, the Tausug more than the Yakan. Zamboangueños seem hardly willing to grant their tongue the status of a language at all.

The roles of these eight languages in Yakan culture is displayed in Table 2. The Yakan names for the languages appear below the English terms.

REFERENCES

Bureau of Census and Statistics, Philippines. 1962. Census of the
    Philippines, 1960. Vol. 1. Manila.
Cameron, C. R. 1917. Sulu writing. Zamboanga: The Sulu Press.
Frake, C. O. 1971. Lexical origins and semantic structure in Phil-
    ippine Creole Spanish. In Dell Hymes, ed., Pidginization
    and creolization of languages. Cambridge: Cambridge
    University Press.

Lewis, M. B. 1954. A handbook of Malay script. London: Mac-
     millan.
Pallesen, A. K. 1977. Culture contact and language convergence.
     Ph. D. dissertation, University of California, Berkeley.
Wulff, I. 1963. The Yakan graduation ceremony. Folk 5. 325-32.

Part IV.   Zamboanga and Sulu

15 | Lexical Origins and Semantic Structure in Philippine Creole Spanish

History of Philippine Creole Spanish

    The linguistic consequences of Hispanicization in the New World and in Southeast Asia differed markedly.[1] In the Philippines, in spite of rapid Spanish conquest, almost total conversion to Christianity, and over three hundred years of occupation, the Spanish language failed to establish itself. Spanish replaced no indigenous Philippine language, and its role as an auxiliary language was sufficiently tenuous that it was quickly supplanted by English after the American occupation. Today, apart from the many Spanish loan words in Philippine languages and a few speakers of Spanish in the upper echelons of society, the linguistic legacy of Spain in the Philippines is limited to the existence of several communities that speak a Spanish creole language as their mother tongue. Philippine Creole Spanish is not simply a Philippine language with unusually heavy Spanish lexical influence, nor is it Spanish with a large number of Philippine loan words. It is a distinct language, easily distinguishable from both its Romance and its Austronesian progenitors. As implied by the name I have given it,[2] Philippine Creole Spanish shares enough in common with the classic creoles of the Caribbean that no one, whatever his position in the various controversies on the subject, would, I think, challenge its assignment to the category 'creole language.'

    Philippine Creole Spanish (PCS) known in the Philippines as Chabacano, is spoken as the native language of over 10,000 people in several communities along the south shore of Manila Bay and by over 100,000 people in Zamboanga City and Basilan Island in the southern Philippines.[3] In the latter region, an area of great linguistic and ethnic diversity, it is also an important auxiliary language. The

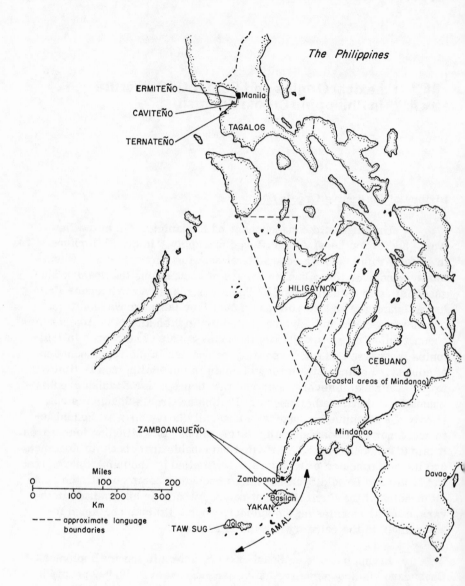

Philippine Creole Spanish dialects and relevant Philippine languages

speech of Zamboanga (Zamboangueño, Zm) represents a distinct dialect of PCS opposed to the dialects of Manila Bay Creole (MBC) spoken
in Ternate (Ternateño, Tr), Cavite City (Caviteño, Cv), and formerly
in the Manila district of Ermita (Ermiteño).[4] Speakers of MBC dialects can be found in a number of other towns in Cavite Province and
once inhabited the fortress island of Corregidor at the entrance to
Manila Bay (B&R 36.237)[5] (see map). These locations suggest something about the origin of PCS. Zamboanga, from the beginning of the
seventeenth century to the end of the nineteenth, was a Spanish military base in the heart of hostile Moslem territory. Cavite was a major
naval base and shipyard; Ternate and Corregidor guarded the entrance
to Manila Bay against Moslem raiders (de la Costa 1961: 475; B&R 36.
237). Although I have found no direct evidence in the Spanish literature, it seems reasonable to assume that Spanish military and naval
units in the Philippines, known to have been composed of men speaking diverse Philippine languages and officered by Spaniards, used a
Spanish-based pidgin for communication. Such a military pidgin
could then have been creolized as the native language of certain permanent garrison communities.

Also suggestive is the name of the Philippine town of Ternate,
and here we have both historical documentation and local Ternateño
tradition to go on.[6] There is an island named Ternate in the Moluccas
which in the sixteenth and seventeenth centuries was the focus of Portuguese, Spanish, and Dutch conflict for control of the spice trade.
In 1606 the Spanish captured Ternate from the Dutch, who had recently
taken it from the Portuguese but evacuated it, as well as their garrison in Zamboanga, in 1663 in order to concentrate forces in Manila
against a threatened attack by the Chinese warlord Ch'eng-kung (Kox-
inga). From Ternate the Spanish took with them a group of local
Christians, the product of Jesuit missions in the Moluccas and northern Celebes, and allowed them to settle in a community, which they
named Ternate, near the Tagalog town of Maragondon on Manila Bay.
These people, known as Márdikas,[7] frequently served in Spanish military forces and were responsible for guarding the entrance to Manila
Bay. Soon after their arrival they are reported to have spoken their
"own language," Tagalog, and Spanish (B&R 24.41; 36.237). Eventually
they came to speak PCS as their native tongue. Whether they invented
it themselves, adopted a Philippine Spanish military pidgin, or relexi-
fied a Portuguese pidgin brought from the Moluccas is not known. The

Spanish reoccupied Zamboanga in 1718. I have not yet found any record
or tradition of native creole-speaking Márdikas participating in the
resettlement of Zamboanga and thereby being responsible for the establishment of a dialect of PCS there. Zamboangueño may represent an
independent creolization of the same pidgin. The similarities between
Zm and MBC, however, are such to make historically independent
derivation from Spanish unlikely. I have yet to find any texts, descriptions, or even explicit reference to Zamboangueño in Spanish sources
other than statements such as Montero y Vidal's (1888: 37): 'Los nat-
urales de Zamboanga hablan todos, aunque imperfectamente, español.'

Problems

The kinds of problems raised by a consideration of the Philippine element in the Zamboangueño lexicon are illustrated by the PCS
pronouns displayed in Table 1.

First note that the plural pronouns differ in each of the dialects of PCS. The Cv and Tr forms all clearly derive from Spanish
although they differ from the corresponding Spanish forms. The Zm
plural pronouns are identical to those of several Central Philippine
languages. The attributive forms of these plurals (?ámon, ?áton,
?ínyo, ?íla) are also of Philippine derivation. The first question,
then, is: (1) 'Does Zm differ consistently from the other dialects of
PCS in the direction of greater penetration of Philippine-derived
forms?' The second question is: (2) 'If the Philippine element in Zm

Table 1. PCS Pronouns: Full Nominative Stylistically
Unmarked Forms

	Singular		Plural	
			MBC	
Person	PCS	Zm	Cv	Tr
1	yó	kamí	nisós	motro
1 + 2		kitá		
2	tú	kamó	busós	tedi
3	?éle	silá	ilós	lotro

Table 2. Zm Second Person Pronouns:
Stylistic Alternatives

		Singular	Plural
respect	+	?usté	?ustédes
			bosótros
	0	tú	
			kamó
	–	?ebós	

is unique to that dialect, then from what language or languages does
it derive?' The latter question cannot be answered from the data
present in Table 1, but it is answerable and the answer is somewhat
surprising. It will reveal that, not only is Zm no longer in contact
with Spanish, it also is not in effective contact with its major Philippine sources. There is consequently no difficulty in delimiting Zm
from other linguistic codes used in the area—there is no Jamaica-like
continuum from creole to standard language (cf. Cassidy and Le Page
1961)—and one can consider separately the contact situation which gave
rise to the language and the contact situation which is influencing it
now.

Thirdly consider the distribution of Philippine-derived pronouns within this semantic domain. The set of personal pronouns in
Zm, as in most languages, shares distinctive semantic, syntactic,
and morphological properties, and its members appear with high frequency. It certainly cannot be considered a peripheral part of the
lexicon. Yet the set is split right down the middle between forms of
Spanish and of Philippine derivation. We all know, of course, that
'languages don't mix,' but this must be one of the closest existing
approximations to that impossible state. The third question, then, is:
(3) 'Is this a random mixture or is it interpretable according to some
kind of pattern? If so, is this pattern one that corresponds to traditional theories of lexical influence of one language upon another?'
Such questions are not so easily raised with other creole languages.
The prominence and clear identifiability of the Philippine element, not
only in Zm lexicon, but also in syntax, morphology, and phonology,

contrast sharply with the situation of Caribbean creoles where the
nature and extent of African substratum influence, if any, is a subject
of considerable controversy. Actually there are two aspects to this
question. One concerns the distribution of Philippine forms across
semantic domains, across the topics of speech if you will. The other
concerns the distribution of Philippine forms across speech events,
the selection of expressions at a level of formality appropriate to the
situation. In pronouns the latter consideration is relevant to the selection of second person forms, members also of the domain of terms of
address (see Table 2). (Note the discrepancy in respect usage between
the singular and plural pronouns and the participation of a single Philippine form in the latter set.)

Finally, note the semantic structure of the domain of pronouns in Zm. The differentiation between the inclusive and exclusive
first person plural and the lack of sex or gender distinctions in the
third person correspond to Philippine rather than Spanish pronominal
semantics. On the other hand, the differentiation of second person
pronouns by the degree of respect they accord the addressee is more
complex than that of any Philippine language I know of, and it does not
quite correspond to Spanish usage. Comparisons of the semantic
structure of given domains in Zm with corresponding domains in
Spanish and in the relevant Philippine languages provide a nice test
case of language-culture interrelations. Speakers of Zm share a
basically common culture with other Christian Filipino groups and
with them belong to the same larger sociopolitical system. Yet unlike other Christian Filipinos, they do not speak one of a closely
related group of Austronesian languages. To the extent that the semantic structure of a language mirrors culture, one would expect the semantics of Zm and other PCS dialects to resemble that of Philippine
languages rather than that of Spanish. This is something that cannot
be tested with Caribbean creoles since their speakers no longer participate in the same culture and society as their West African ancestors.

Data relevant to each of these questions will now be presented.

Data

Comparisons Between Zm and MBC

The two variants of PCS share enough distinctive differences from regular Spanish or regular Philippine usage that they must be considered historically related dialects of the same language. There is evidence that the Spanish-derived element in PCS underwent some revision in Zm. Where Spanish-derived forms in Zm differ from those in MBC, the Zm forms generally more closely correspond to the shape of the form in modern Spanish. But the most conspicuous difference between the two dialects is the much larger number of Philippine-derived forms in Zm and the deeper penetration of these forms into core grammatical and semantic sets. About 20 percent of the total vocabulary of Zm collected thus far (1,000 out of 5,000 words) and 10 percent of the 200 words Swadesh list are of Philippine origin. Philippine forms occur among the high-frequency adverbial enclitics, conjunctions, negatives, and pronouns. The productive derivational affixes of Zm are almost all of Philippine origin. Although comparable data for MBC are not yet available, the much lesser impact of Philippine languages on these dialects is readily apparent from casual inspection of texts.

One cannot explain the more prominent Philippine element in Zm by postulating that Zm has suffered much more intensive language contact in situ with Philippine languages. If anything the reverse is the case. MBC speech communities are, and presumably always have been, tiny islands in a Tagalog-speaking sea. Probably almost all of its speakers are bilingual and use Tagalog daily.[8] Zamboangueño, on the other hand, is the dominant language of the Christian population of Southwestern Mindanao and of Basilan Island. Its local competition is divided among a half-dozen other Philippine languages. But, more significant, it is not the languages with which Zm is in contact locally that are responsible for its Philippine element.

Provenience of Philippine-derived Forms in Zm

Before the intrusion of the Spanish, the Zamboanga-Basilan area was occupied by speakers of Samalan languages, a clearly distinct subgroup of Philippine languages. The early Christian community in Zamboanga, prior to its evacuation in 1663, included Samal-speaking converts (de la Costa 1961: 445, 451). The development and spread of Zamboangueño Creole in the area, which probably began after the reoccupation of Zamboanga in 1718, took place in the midst of a Samalan-speaking area. Zamboangueños remain in close contact with, and in many communities in almost symbiotic economic relations with, Samalan speakers. Yet Samalan languages have had little discernible influence on Zm.[9] It is readily apparent from inspection that the Philippine element in Zm is drawn from one or more language of the Central Philippine (or 'Tagalic') subgroup of Philippine language a group including Tagalog, the 'Bisayan' languages of the Central Philippines, and Tausug, the language of Joló and an auxiliary language for Moslems throughout the southwestern Philippines. Of these Central Philippine languages, Zm is in contact with Tausug, a competing auxiliary language in Christian-Moslem interaction, with Cebuano Bisayan the dominant language of Christian areas throughout most of the rest of Mindanao as well as the native language of the majority of recent immigrants to the Zamboanga area, and with Tagalog, which through school instruction, movies and popular magazines, is gaining utility as an auxiliary language among Christians. This role of Tagalog in the area is a recent one and does not involve extensive contact with native speakers of the language. Until the twentieth century, Zamboangueños were not in direct contact with any Central Philippine language other than Tausug .[10] Since then the major new contact has been with Cebuano Bisayan.

Determination of the specific Central Philippine languages responsible for the Philippine element in Zamboangueño is obscured by the lexical similarities among the relevant languages. Nevertheless, a determination on linguistic grounds is possible. By plotting the occurrence of Zm forms among Central Philippine languages, one can formulate a minimal set of Philippine languages necessary to account for the Philippine-derived portion of the Zm lexicon. This procedure has been completed only for about three hundred of the about one thousand Philippine-derived forms in Zm so far collected. It is clear, however, that Hiligaynon (Ilongo) Bisayan is undoubtedly the major source of the Philippine-derived element in the Zm lexicon. Tagalog is an important secondary source. These two languages are sufficient to account for the overwhelming bulk of Philippine forms in

Zm. The local contact languages, Cebuano, Samalan, and Taw Sug, have all contributed forms, but their discernible impact has been and continues to be surprisingly small.[12] The major language influencing Zm today is English.

The Tagalog element, especially in the very basic areas of Zm vocabulary, can be attributed to the probable role of this major Philippine language in any early Philippine military pidgin or creole. But what about Hiligaynon Bisayan, a language we have had no occasion to mention when describing past or present language contact in Zamboanga? This is a language spoken in Eastern Panay and Western Negros (see map). Although there are Hiligaynon-speaking immigrants in Zamboanga and elsewhere in Mindanao, nowhere outside of its home area is the language a lingua franca of importance. Presumably Hiligaynon speakers played a major role in the early settlement of Zamboanga, but I have not been able to find any historical documentation of this. We know only that 'Bisayans' participated in many of the Spanish campaigns in Mindanao and Sulu. In any case, Hiligaynon at some time had a profound impact on Zamboangueño that subsequent language contact has not obscured.

Distribution of Philippine-derived Forms
Across Semantic Domains

The situation presented by Zm pronouns where Philippine- and Spanish-derived forms participate as contrasting items in a single semantic domain is repeated over and over in the Zm lexicon. Take common indigenous biota for example. Coconut, bamboo, and ratan are Spanish; bananas, sugar cane, and eggplant are Philippine. Rice is Philippine when growing in the field, Spanish when milled, and Philippine again when cooked. Pigs are Spanish, chickens Philippine. Trees and grass are Spanish; vines are Philippine. Primary forest is Spanish; secondary forest is Philippine. Mature leaves and blossoms are Spanish; young leaves and buds are Philippine. Because of the preponderance of Spanish-derived words in the total lexicon there are, of course, many contrast sets made exclusively of Spanish forms —color terminology for example—but it is extremely difficult to find even two member sets made up exclusively of Philippine forms. Although there is some skewing in the distribution of Philippine forms

across semantic domains—in plant and animal terminology the
Philippine element exceeds 50 percent—it is still fair to say that
Philippine forms in Zm do not sort by semantic domain as one expects of loan words. Nor do they sort by provenience of the objects
they denote. If one were to separate indigenous from introduced
plants, a favorite goal of loan word studies, by the etymologies of
their names in Zm, one would have the Spanish bringing coconuts
(kóko) to the Philippines and discovering chili peppers (katumbal)
there.

At first sight it appears that Spanish and Philippine forms
were distributed through the Zm lexicon by some random device that
produced five Spanish forms to every Philippine form. A possibility,
however, of some pattern to this distribution is suggested by the Zm
pronouns. The distribution of pronouns of Philippine origin coincides
with that of the semantic feature of plurality. Philippine derivation
marks pronoun plurality (among stylistically unmarked forms). Zm
nouns and adjectives are not inflected for plurality, but, following
Greenberg (1966), we can generalize the contrast 'singular-plural' as
a case of the contrast 'unmarked-marked.' Semantic marking appears
in a variety of lexical domains. Among adjectival contrast pairs,
there is a polarity whereby terms such as 'tall,' 'big,' 'far,' 'fast'
are linked as opposed to 'short,' 'little,' 'near,' and 'slow.' The
members of the former set are of positive (unmarked) polarity, the
latter set of negative (marked) polarity.[13] Various criteria have been
given in the literature for sorting out polarity (Greenberg 1966: 90;
Bierwisch 1967; Lamb 1964: 218-23). Osgood (1964) factors out three
dimensions of adjective polarity—activity, potency, and evaluation—
which he feels are universal. If one lists Zm adjectival contrast pairs
in which one member is of Spanish origin and the other member of
Philippine origin, then, where there is a clear case of a marked-
unmarked contrast, the Philippine-derived form will represent the
marked member. Examples are listed in Table 3A. No clear counter-
examples have been found, though there are a number of ambiguous
cases where the direction of polarity is arguable or where it may differ on different dimensions.[14]

Kinship, generation, and growth stage reciprocals also fit
the pattern. Philippine forms designate the younger member of the
pair (Table 3B). I have only one case in which a Spanish and a Phil-

Table 3. Some Zm Contrast Pairs of Contrasting Etymology

A. Adjectives contrasting in magnitude and/or evaluation

<Sp	<Ph		
+	−		
gránde	dyútay	large	small
ʔálto	pandak	tall	short
lihéro	mahínay	fast	slow
kórre	pátaʔ	fast	slow
mapwérso	malúya	strong	weak
ʔárde	ʔamamaluŋ	bright	dim
ʔapretáo	halugaʔ	tight	loose
ʔagúdu	mapurul	sharp	dull
líso	makasap	smooth	rough
sabróso	mataʔbaŋ	tasty	tasteless
dúlse	mapaʔit	sweet	bitter
madúru	mahilaw	ripe	raw
mánso	maʔilap	tame	wild
buníto	ʔumálin	pretty	ugly
límpyo	buliŋ	clean	dirty
kláro	lubug	clear	turbid
deréčo	tikuʔ	straight	bent
balyénte	mahuyaʔ	bold	shy
ʔumílde	hambuk	modest	vain
byého	bátaʔ	old	young
nwébo	dáʔan	new	old

B. Nouns contrasting in generation, age, or sex

<Sp	<Ph		
+	−		
byého/a	bátaʔ	old man/woman	child
lólo/a	ʔapu	grandfather/mother	grandchild
táta/nána	ʔanak	father/mother	son, daughter
ʔóhas	talbus	mature leaf	young leaf
plóres	putut	blossom	bud
soltéro	dalága	bachelor	unmarried girl

ippine form are opposed by sex, but in this case the Philippine form
designates the marked (female) sex (Table 3B).

Extending this argument to taxonomic relations we would, at
first sight, expect that, when Spanish- and Philippine-derived forms
occur at different hierarchical levels, the Philippine form would label
the subordinate (marked) category. Examples conforming to this expectation can be found, but so also can counter-examples. One can
easily find hierarchical series in which Spanish and Philippine forms
alternate. What makes the construction of such series possible is
that the typical situation throughout the lexicon has Philipping forms
contrasting with Spanish forms at the same level. Each successive
contrast set in a taxonomy frequently has both Philippine and Spanish
terms. Given this pattern, Philippine-derived forms cannot consistently mark subordinate relations (Table 4).

Through much of the lexicon, where there is no clear marking or polarity involved within a contrast set, no patterning in the
occurrence of Philippine forms is discernible. Why a roof is Spanish
and a wall Philippine, or why wind and thunder are Spanish, rain and
lightning Philippine, I cannot imagine. But we can make the following
generalization: where a Philippine- and a Spanish-derived form participate in a marked-unmarked relation in the same contrast set, the
Philippine form will designate the marked category: it will signify
lesser magnitude, shorter distance, worse evaluation, female sex,
junior generation, or plurality.

Consider now the distribution of Philippine-derived forms
across speech events, their selection according to style levels. The
crucial data here are those cases of synonyms or near-synonyms in
which one term is Spanish, the other Philippine. Such pairs are not
invariably differentiated by style level, but, when there is a clear
difference, it is the Spanish-derived term that is appropriate to formal situations or which indicates politeness toward the addressee.
The Spanish term is marked for formality, whereas the Philippine
term is the stylistically unmarked, normal conversational form. No
counter-examples have yet been found; however, the investigation of
synonymous pairs has only begun.

Table 4. Partial Taxonomy of Some Zm Meal Constituents
(Philippine-derived Forms Italicized)

---

1. komída 'food'
1.1. kánon 'main dish'
1.1.1. kánon (de arros) 'cooked rice'
1.1.2. mais 'maize'
1.2. ʔúlam 'side dish'
1.2.1. kárne 'meat'
1.2.1.1. manok 'chicken'
1.2.1.1.1. galyina 'hen'
1.2.1.1.2. dumalága 'pullet'
1.2.1.2. pwérko 'pork'
1.2.1.2.1. butakal 'uncastrated boar'
1.2.1.2.2. lečon 'suckling pig'
1.2.2. gulay 'vegetables'
1.2.2.1. prehóles 'string beans'
1.2.2.2. patáni 'lima beans'
1.2.3. peskáo 'fish'
1.2.3.1. tulíŋan 'tuna'
1.2.3.2. kabályas 'mackerel'

In many languages semantic marking may also be used as
stylistic marking. It is quite common that plural (semantically marked)
pronouns are used as second person respect terms in the singular.
Such is the case in Tagalog where, in the second person, kayo contrasts
with ʔikaw in being either semantically marked as plural or stylistically
marked as polite. In the latter case it can be used to address one person. European examples are of course familiar (Brown and Gilman
1960). There is probably no language in which a singular pronoun is
marked for respect in contrast to a plural. The second person pronouns in Zm (Table 2), however, contain an anomaly in this regard.
There are separate three-member sets of second person pronouns,
differentiated by respect, in the singular and in the plural. But the
pattern of differentiation does not match. In the singular, tú is unmarked, ʔuste is marked for respect, and ʔebos may be said to be
marked for lack of respect or intimacy. In the plural, kamo, a Phil-

ippine form, is the stylistically unmarked equivalent of tú, whereas bosótros and ʔustédes are marked for increasing degrees of respect. Given the matching of kamo and tú, it would seem more reasonable if bosótros were the plural equivalent of ʔebos so that respect discriminations would match in the singular and plural. This arrangement, however, would place a Philippine form at a higher respect level than a Spanish form. Given the fact that the marking for pronoun plurality is designated by Philippine provenience, a feature carrying with it stylistic unmarking, then any Spanish plurals added to the set must rank higher in formality.

Structure of Semantic Domains in Zm

To the extent that semantic structures link language with other cultural systems, Zm semantics should parallel that of other Philippine languages more closely than that of Spanish. Nothing like a definitive statement on this problem is possible at this point. Not only are comparable data from the relevant languages lacking, but also the current state of semantic theory—of whatever variety—does not yet make it clear how one goes about describing the semantic structure of a language in anything approaching an exhaustive way. Current theoretical and methodology proposals are backed only by illustrations of semantic relations in some few domains that have proved tractable to analysis by the procedures proposed. I have nothing better to offer here. Limited, and admittedly superficial comparisons of a few domains, however, suggest some tentative generalizations.

The Zm pronouns (Table 1) fulfill the expectation that Zm should exhibit a Philippine semantic structure. Apart from the style differentiations in the second person, Zm pronouns can be matched semantically one-to-one with pronouns in a language like Hiligaynon or Cebuano. A cultural explanation of this matching, however, is jarred by the MBC dialects, which, although their speakers participat in the same culture, fail to make the distinction between exclusive and inclusive that is universal in the Philippines. There are other examples of similar contrasts between Zm and MBC. In distinguishing short of stature (pandak) from short of length (kórto), old of objects (dáʔan) from old of persons (byého), full of containers (lyéno) from

Table 5. Verb Inflection and Negation

A. Zamboangueño

?aykome yo	I will eat
hindi? yo aykome	I will not eat
takome yo	I am (was) eating
hindi? yo takome	I am (was) not eating
yakome yo	I ate
nway yo kome	I did not eat
kome	Eat!
no kome	Don't eat!

$\left.\begin{array}{l}\text{kyére}\\\text{sábe}\\\text{pwéde}\end{array}\right\}$ yo kome   I $\left.\begin{array}{l}\text{want to}\\\text{know how to}\\\text{can}\end{array}\right\}$ eat

no $\left.\begin{array}{l}\text{kyére}\\\text{sábe}\\\text{pwéde}\end{array}\right\}$ yo kome   I $\left.\begin{array}{l}\text{con't want to}\\\text{don't know how to}\\\text{cannot}\end{array}\right\}$ eat

tyéne komída	There is food
nway komída	There is no food

B. Caviteño negation

no yo dikumi	I will not eat
no yo takumi	I am (was) not eating
no yo yakumi	I did not eat
no kumi	Don't eat!
nway kumída	There is no food

---

full of food (busug), negation of completed events (nway) from negation of non-completed events (hindi?),[15] Zm has typical Philippine distinctions lacking in MBC (Table 5). In all of these cases, Zm also has Philippine-derived forms, lacking in MBC, to mark these distinctions. Where Philippine-derived words are lacking in Zm, Philippine semantic distinctions may also be lost. Unlike Philippine languages, for example, Zm represents both 'low' and 'shallow' with one form (bâho). What seems to lend a Philippine-like semantic structure to these domains is not the Philippine culture of the Zamboangueños but the Philippine derivation of much of their lexicon. Comparisons between MBC and Zm suggest that Zm semantic structure in these domains has accommodated to the lexicon rather than the lexicon accommodating to some preexisting semantic structure.

A counter-example to the preceding generalization would be provided by a domain with Spanish-derived forms representing a Philippine-like semantic structure. Unfortunately, good test cases are hard to find. Among domains of easy cross-language comparability, some, such as the terminology of spatial orientation and of color, are exclusively Spanish, but there are no striking contrasts between Philippine and Spanish systems. Zm and Spanish share a three-point system of spatial position deictics ('here,' 'there,' 'elsewhere'); Philippine languages have three or four (with inclusive and exclusive 'here') point systems. In spatial movement deictics, Zm, like Spanish, makes only a two-way contrast ('come' and 'go'), whereas in Philippine languages this set parallels, generally by inflection of the positionals, the three- or four-point distinctions of the positionals. The terminology of time deixis, the universal labeling of 'day-night' units preceding and following the time of the speech event, provides the clearest case of Spanish-derived forms adapted to a Philippine semantic pattern. In Spanish, as in English, the starting point of the system is 'today' (Sp "hoy"), the unit <u>encompassing</u> the time of the speech event. 'Yesterday' is the unit preceding "today"; 'tomorrow' is the unit following 'today.' In all dialects of PCS and in the relevant Philippine languages, there is no 'today' (Sp "hoy" does not occur in PCS). The starting point of time deixis is 'now' (Zm <u>ʔára</u>, MBC <u>ʔagóra</u>). All units preceding and following 'now' have distinctive terms. In Zm, (<u>ʔen</u>)<u>denántes</u> labels the period from the last previous sunrise until 'now'; <u>lwégo</u> labels the period from 'now' until the next sunrise. English 'this afternoon' translates into Zm as <u>lwégo tárde</u> or <u>ʔendenántes tárde</u> depending on whether the time of the speech event (<u>ʔára</u>) is prior to or subsequent to 'this afternoon.' 'Last night' is <u>ʔanóče</u>; 'yesterday' is <u>ʔayer</u>; 'tomorrow' is <u>manyána.</u> The only Philippine-derived term in the system is <u>ʔága</u> 'morning,' removing the ambiguity of Spanish 'mañana.' The orientation of named day-night units (days of the week) is marked by a contrast between genitive definite and locative: <u>del lúnes</u> 'last Monday,' <u>na lúnes</u> 'next Monday.' Compare Hiligaynon <u>saŋ lúnis</u> (gen. def.) 'last Monday,' <u>sa lúnis</u> (loc.) 'next Monday' (Wolff, pers. com.).

All of the domains discussed thus far are of dubious cultural sensitivity. Presumably one can participate in Philippine culture equally well however his particular language structures such domains. In searching for domains of undisputed cultural sensitivity and yet still of cross-cultural comparability, one immediately thinks of kinship terminology, a favorite among anthropologists just because it combines features of sensitivity and comparability. Unfortunately in the structuring of genealogical dimensions, Central Philippine and Spanish systems are practically identical. They both sort kin by generation and by collaterality but ignore sex of linking relatives. Where they differ is in distinguishing sex of kinsmen. Spanish makes such distinctions consistently; Central Philippine languages consistently ignore them outside of the first ascending generation (sometimes sex of spouse is distinguished as well). Despite the presumed greater cultural significance of this domain, the semantic pattern of Zm kinship terminology is much like that of the domains discussed previously. Zm distinguishes sex of relative where it has Spanish-derived terms and fails to do so where it has Philippine-derived terms. The Philippine-derived terms are those for the <u>marked</u> member of lineal reciprocal pairs, i. e. 'child' and 'grandchild.'[16]

All languages spoken by Christian Filipino groups, including PCS, appear to share similarly structured sets of address terms extendable on the basis of sex, age, and assessed status to non-kin, including strangers (cf. Geoghegan 1968). The details of these systems have yet to be worked out. They would undoubtedly provide some very fruitful comparisons. Interestingly, most of the terms used in all of these languages, although varied, derive from Spanish, generally in

Table 6. Rice and Food in the Philippines

	Zamboangueño	Hiligaynon	Tagalog	Phil. Spanish	Phil. English
1	paláy	pálay	pálay	paláy	paláy
2	?arros	bugas	bigas	arroz	rice
3	kánon	kan?un	kánin	morisqueta	food
4	?úlam	sud?an	?úlam	vianda	viand

1, rice plant, unmilled grain. 2, milled rice. 3, cooked rice, main dish. 4, side dish.

phonologically and semantically altered form. A typical example is
manoŋ/manaŋ (<Sp ermano/a) addressed to older siblings and to non-
kin of comparable seniority throughout much of the Christian Philippines. Unlike Philippine kinship terms of reference, these address
sets among Christians consistently distinguish sex of addressee.

When one considers domains of less comparability but of very
clear cultural relevance, such as plant and animal nomenclature, vegetation types, agricultural techniques, and meal constituents, Zm, as
expected, displays Philippine-like semantic structures. Some of
these domains are similarly structured in Philippine English and Philippine Spanish as well (Table 6).

Conclusions

A fundamental problem presented by most creole languages
is that of accounting for the apparently divergent sources of the lexicon on the one hand and the grammatical system on the other. Lexi-
cons themselves rarely show any appreciable mixture and there is no
internal evidence that the lexicon was ever anything other than what
it is today. Zamboangueño provides a special case among creoles
where something has happened to the lexicon. It may not be mixture
and it may not be relexification, but it does seem to me to be a unique
kind of lexical impact, one that differs in many respects from that
ordinarily associated with the acquisition of loan words in situations
of language contact. Consider the Zm data with respect to the following generally accepted assumptions about lexical borrowing (cf. Weinreich 1953: 56-61).

1. High-frequency portions of the lexicon are relatively im-
permeable to borrowing. In Zm, Philippine-derived forms occur
among the pronouns, adverbial particles, conjunctions, negatives, and
derivational affixes. Some 20 words in the Swadesh 200-word list are
of Philippine origin.

2. Loan words are accommodated to existing phonological,
and semantic systems. With Zm one can make the reverse argument
that phonology and semantics have been accommodated to the acquired
lexicon. Zm phonology enables the rendering of both Spanish and Phil-

ippine forms much as they are rendered in their respective source languages. Since it is a combination rather than a simplification of source language phonology, the Zm sound system is difficult to master both for a speaker of a Central Philippine language, who has trouble with initial clusters, palatalized consonants, trilled r's, and five vowels; and for the Spaniard faced with ŋ's, glottal stops, medial clusters, and final consonants.

In semantics we have noted cases where the structure of certain domains parallels that of Philippine languages rather than Spanish. This result is to be expected of a language spoken by native actors in Christian Philippine culture. However, in many of these same domains the semantic structure of the MBC dialects does not exhibit these Philippine features; yet speakers of MBC dialects have been for centuries more fully immersed in the heartland of Christian Philippine culture than the Zamboangueños. Until the present century, Zamboanga was an isolated outpost of Christianity in a Philippine Moslem world. One can, then, propose the following argument: in those domains with a Philippine-like structure in Zm and a Spanish-like structure in MBC, the Zm domain will show Philippine semantic features where it has Philippine-derived words to mark these features. In other words, the more Philippine-like nature of Zm semantics is the product of the adoption of Philippine words and their associated meanings, but these words were not originally adopted in order to make semantic distinctions necessary for participation in Philippine culture.

3. Loan words are adopted to name new concepts; consequently they should sort out by semantic domain. In Zm, on the other hand, Philippine- and Spanish-derived terms typically participate together as contrasting items in a single domain. Basic concepts like 'rain,' 'worry,' 'ugly,' and 'not' have Philippine-derived labels.

4. If the adoption of loans cannot be explained by the need for new labels, then it can be expected that the use of loans from the particular source language confers prestige upon the speaker. In Zm the use of a Philippine form rather than a Spanish-derived alternative never confers prestige. If there is a difference among alternatives in the direction of prestige, politeness, or formality, it is always the Spanish form that ranks higher.

5. Lexical borrowing results from the proximity and interaction of adjacent speech communities. Zm has suffered relatively
little lexical influence from neighboring Philippine languages but a
heavy impact from geographically remote languages, one of which,
Tagalog, has failed to make a corresponding impact on the PCS dialects in the midst of its own territory.

6. Apart from stylistic considerations the etymology of a
linguistic form is irrelevant to its role in a synchronic grammatical
description of the language.[17] In Zm the source of a word is pertinent
to a synchronic description of the language. Being of Philippine provenience is a recognizable and linguistically significant attribute of a
Zm morpheme. It is like an affix that marks the form. Like many
affixes it often has no discernible semantic content, but, when it does
it typically signifies something smaller, closer, less valued, of lesser
generation or sex than its Spanish-derived opposite. Its most widespread meaning seems to be lesser evaluation, a meaning that relates
perhaps to the appropriateness of a Philippine word to less formal
speech situations than its Spanish-derived stylistic alternative. As
an affix, Philippine provenience resembles the affix of morpheme
duplication common in all Philippine languages including Zamboangueño.
Sometimes, as where there is no corresponding non-duplicated form,
duplication signifies little if anything. Generally, however, it denotes
something smaller, less real, more intimate, or more numerous than
the corresponding non-duplicated form. In other words, duplication
marks a form for a range of meanings from diminutive through plurality not unlike that marked by a Philippine form in contrast to a
Spanish form.

NOTES

[1] Current research on Zamboangueño is being supported by
the National Science Foundation. I have been using Zamboangueño and
collecting data on it incidental to work (supported by the National Institute of Mental Health) on other languages in the Zamboanga-Basilan
area since 1962. The arguments of this paper will be documented in
a monographic description of Philippine Creole Spanish now in preparation. I am grateful to the following persons for very helpful comments
on an earlier version of this paper: Harold C. Conklin, Michael For-

man, Dell Hymes, Carol Molony, Keith Whinnom, and John Wolff.
    [2] This label for the language is composed according to principles suggested by Hockett 1958: 424.
    [3] The literature has Zamboangueño on the verge of extinction
with only 1,300 speakers (cf. Taylor 1957: 489; Voegelin 1964: 49).
Their source, Whinnom (1956), must have relied on the 1939 census,
which reported only 1,290 speakers of 'Chabacano' in Zamboanga.
This figure is corrected in the 1948 census to 100,645 with the note:
"The phenomenal increase of the number of persons able to speak
Chabacano is due to the instruction given to census enumerators to
report as able to speak Spanish only those persons who speak the pure
language of Cervantes." Actually it does not require such a lofty
standard to distinguish Zamboangueño from Spanish. The 1960 census
lists 110,376 native speakers of Zamboangueño and 10,628 native
speakers of "Caviteño" (including Ternateño). Another listing based
on the 1960 census gives 126,500 and 13,500 native speakers of Zamboangueño and Caviteño, respectively (Wernstedt and Spencer 1967:
620-21). Zamboanga "City," it should be noted, is a political unit
encompassing 546 square miles, mostly rural.
    [4] The name "Manila Bay Creole" is my own invention. All dialect names ending in -eño, as well as the name "Chabacano" for any
or all dialects of the language, are used locally. I have as yet made
only brief visits to Cavite City and Ternate. Information on these dialects and their speakers presented here must be considered preliminary and subject to correction. I have no firsthand information on
"Davaoeño," a creole or pidgin reportedly once spoken in Davao City,
Mindanao, where Cebuano Bisayan is now the dominant language (cf.
Whinnom 1956).
    [5] 'B&R 36. 237' represents Blair and Robertson (1903-9), vol.
36, p. 237.
    [6] Philippine Ternateños recount a story of the original settlement of their community by 'Márdikas' from Moluccan Ternate that
follows closely the accounts in historical sources (B&R 28.100; 36.
237; 38.167, 177, 203, 220; 42.124, 251, 269; 44.29).
    [7] Mardika, merdeka, merdeheka are Malay variants of a
Sanskrit loan (Skr maharddhika) meaning 'freedom in contrast to servitude' (Wilkinson 1932: 2.134). Tagalog has maharlika? 'aristocratic,'
'high class' from the same source. The etymological meaning of
márdikas is not known in Philippine Ternate today but is given in
seventeenth-century Spanish accounts (see references, note 6).

[8]According to the 1960 census, 95 percent of the residents of the municipality of Ternate speak Tagalog, the lowest percentage for any municipality in Cavite Province.

[9]Identified Samalan loans include terms for Moslem religious practices and Moslem titles, fishing and nautical terms, possibly the word for 'secondary forest' and, from Yakan, a Samalan language of Basilan, the word for 'bandit' or 'pirate.'

[10]I am ignoring Subanun, a peripheral member of the Central Philippine subgroup spoken by pagans in the interior of Zamboanga Peninsula. This language has had no discernible influence on Zamboangueño.

[11]As John Wolff has emphasized to me (personal communication), the dialect variation within Bisayan languages is complex and not fully mapped out. Moreover, forms now diagnostic of particular languages or dialects may be of recent currency (e.g. modern standard Tagalog hindi? 'not' which has replaced an earlier form dili? identical to the current form in modern standard Cebuano (H. C. Conklin, personal communication). Nevertheless, it is clear that the sources of the bulk of the Philippine element in Zm were Bisayan dialects more closely related to modern standard Hiligaynon than to the modern standard Cebuano with which Zm speakers are now in contact.

[12]This data contradicts Whinnom's (1956: 14) conclusion, which accords with local statements about the language, that the sources of the Philippine element in Zamboangueño are Tagalog and Cebuano.

[13]The difference between 'and' and 'but' reflects this polarity. 'And' links adjectives of the same polarity, like 'beautiful and smart,' whereas 'but' links adjectives of opposite polarity like 'beautiful but dumb' (cf. Osgood, cited by D'Andrade and Romney 1964: 240). Logicians usually define 'but' as 'and' plus surprise, but there is nothing surprising about the combination 'beautiful but dumb.'

[14]The apparent discrepancy between the pair nwébo-dá?an 'new-old' and byého-báta? 'old-young' (Table 5A) perhaps reflects the priority of evaluation over other dimensions of polarity. In terms of evaluation nwébo and byého are both positive (unmarked).

[15]The formal distinction of aspect among negatives, together with the use of the word for 'none' to negate completed aspect, is characteristic of Hiligaynon, Cebuano, and many other Philippine languages but not of Tagalog. In phonemic shape, on the other hand, the Zm negative hindi? is identical to the modern standard Tagalog form but differs from Hiligaynon ?indi? and Cebuano dili? (but see note 11).

[16] Zm parental and grandparental terms (Table 5B) are derived from Spanish terms frequently used as terms of address in Philippine languages spoken by Christians. Other Zm kin terms, including terms for step- and god-kin are identical to Spanish with the addition of a low-frequency Philippine form balá?i 'child's spouse's parent.'

[17] Generative phonologists, however, are now proposing features such as

$$\text{Church Slavonic} \begin{bmatrix} + \text{Slavic} \\ - \text{Russian} \end{bmatrix}$$

in the synchronic description of languages such as modern Russian (Chomsky and Halle 2968: 373).

REFERENCES

(Including dictionaries consulted but not cited in the text)

Bierwisch, Manfred. 1967. Some semantic universals of German adjectivals. Foundations of Language 3.1.1-36.

Blair, E. H., and J. A. Robertson, eds. 2903-9. The Philippine Islands. 55 vols. Cleveland: A. H. Clark Co.

Brown, R. W., and A. Gilman. 1960. The pronouns of power and solidarity. In T. A. Sebeok, ed., Style in language, pp. 253-76. Cambridge: MIT Press.

Cassidy, F. G., and R. B. Le Page. 1961. Lexicographical problems of The dictionary of Jamaican English. In Proceedings of the Conference on Creole Language Studies, ed. by R. B. Le Page. Creole Language Studies, 2. London: Macmillan.

Chomsky, Noam, and Morris Halle. 1968. The sound pattern of English. New York: Harper & Row.

Cruz, M., and S. P. Ignashev. 1959. Tagal'sko-Russkii Slovar'. Gosudarstvennoye izdatel'stvo inostrannikh i natsional'nikh slovarei, Moskow.

D'Andrade, R. G., and A. K. Romney. 1964. Summary of participants' discussion. Transcultural Studies in Cognition, AA 66(3), pt. 2, 230-42.

de la Costa, H. 1961. The Jesuits in the Philippines, 1581-1768. Cambridge: Harvard University Press.

Felix de la Encarnacion. 1885. Diccionario Bisaya-Espanol. Tercera Edicion. Aumentada ... por J. Sanchez, Manila [Cebuano].

Geoghegan, William. 1968. Information processing systems in culture
    In Paul Kay, ed., Explorations in mathematical anthropology.
    Cambridge: MIT Press (in press).
Greenberg, Joseph H. 1966. Language Universals. In T. A. Sebeok,
    ed., Current trends in linguistics, vol. III, Theoretical foun-
    dations. The Hague: Mouton.
Hermosisima, T. V., and P. S. Lopez, Jr. 1966. Dictionary Bisayan
    English-Tagalog. Manila: P. B. Ayuda [Cebuano].
Hockett, C. F. 1958. A course in modern linguistics. New York:
    Macmillan.
Jakobson, Roman. 1939. Signe zéro. In Mélanges de linguistique,
    offerts à Charles Bally, pp. 143-52. Geneva: Georg.
_____. 1957. Shifters, verbal categories and the Russian verb.
    Russian Language Project. Cambridge: Harvard University.
Kaufmann, J. n.d. Visayan-English dictionary. Iloilo, La Editorial
    [Hiligaynon and Hiniraya].
Laktaw, Pedro Serrano. 1914. Diccionario Tagalog-Hispano. Manila.
Lamb, Sydney M. 1964. The sememic approach to structural seman-
    tics. American Anthropologist 66.3.57-78, pt. 2.
Montero y Vidal, Jose. 1888. Historia de la pirateria malayomaho-
    metana, vol. 2. Madrid: M. Tello.
Osgood, Charles E. 1964. Semantic differential technique in the study
    of cultures. American Anthropologist 66.3.171-200, pt. 2.
Panganiban, Jose Villa. 1966. Talahuluganang Pilipino-Ingles.
    Kagawaran na Edukasyon, Surian ng Wikang Pambansa.
    Manila: Kawanihan ng Palimbagan [Tagalog dictionary].
Weinreich, U. 1953. Languages in contact. New York: Linguistic
    Circle of New York.
Wernstedt, F. L., and J. E. Spencer. 1967. The Philippine Island
    world: a physical, cultural, and regional geography. Berke-
    ley: University of California Press.
Whinnom, K. 1956. Spanish contact vernaculars in the Philippine
    Islands. Hong Kong: Hong Kong University Press.
Wilkinson, R. J. 1932. A Malay-English dictionary. Mytilene,
    Greece.
Wolff, John. 1967. History of the dialect of the Camotes Islands,
    and the spread of Cebuano Bisayan. Oceanic Linguistics
    7.63-79.

16 | Zamboangueño Verb Expressions

It is the patterns of verb expression that most dramatically set Zamboangueño apart from both its Spanish and its Philippine sources and ally it with other creole languages.[1] Zamboangueño has not "simplified" or "regularized" the complex verbal paradigms of either of its sources; it has abandoned them altogether. Complexity remains, but it lies in patterns of use of negative words, auxiliary verbs, pro-verbs, and adverbial particles rather than in inflectional morphology. The verb itself is morphologically marked. Inflectable morphemes (simple verbs) have a requisite canonical form. All other verbs are derivatives formed by a single prefix, man-.

1. Simple verbs. The vast majority of inflectable morphemes derive historically from the infinitive of Spanish verbs with the loss of the final -r. This etymology gives simple verbs a requisite canonical form; they must end in one of the vowels i, e, or a, and they are unaccented (when uttered in isolation they bear syllable final stress), e.g. pidi 'to request,' kome 'to eat,' mira 'to see.' Although there are some deviations from this pattern among verbs of Spanish origin, the canonical shape of simple verbs constrains the incorporation of forms with verbal meaning from non-Spanish sources. The few simple verbs of non-Spanish origin all conform to the canonical pattern (Table 1). All other forms with verbal meaning, such as ánut 'float,' lúgut 'rub,' aplay 'apply for,' appear in verbal expressions in the same manner as do adjectives and nouns: as derived verbs with man- (man-ánut 'to float') or as complements of simple verbs (ase lúgut 'to rub'). Simple verbs, if suffixed so that they no longer conform to the canonical shape, must undergo the same verbalization: ayuda 'to help,' man-ayuda-han 'to help each other.'

Table 1. Simple Verbs of Non-Spanish Origin:
An Exhaustive List of Known Examples

---

buga   'to drive away animals.' From CP búgaw, presumably by
         analogy with Spanish-derived patterns of the type kebra, v.,
         'to break,' kebráo, adj., 'broken.'

bungka   'to dismantle, to demolish.' cf., Hl, Cb, bungkag

hila   'to drag.' cf. Tg. híla. Contrast Zm hala (Sp) 'to pull.'

luta   'to float.' From CP lutaw.

sangga   'to obstruct.' cf. Tg. sangga.

sunga   'to blow one's nose.' cf., Hl sunga.

tabya   'to scoop with a tábo (coconut shell scooper).' Zm tábo from
         CP tábu. Zm tábo> tabya, presumably by analogy with Span-
         ish-derived patterns of the type táho, n., 'slash,' tahya,
         v., 'to slash.'

Among verbs of Spanish origin there are some exceptions to
the accent pattern. Several simple verbs have special inflectable
accented forms: pude > pwéde, kere > kyére, tene >tyéne (#6, 7).
Spanish doler has yielded the Zamboangueño verb dwéle. One verb,
dále 'to give,' is exceptional in both etymology and accent (< Sp.
darle. The same form appears in Caviteño and Ternateño and underlies Tagalog dali 'to hit'). Several monosyllabic simple verbs are
partially deviant in form: rí 'to laugh' (Sp. reir), kré 'to believe'
(Sp. creer), kái 'to fall' (Sp. caer), wí 'to hear' (Sp. oir). Spanish
monosyllabic verb infinitives (ser, ir, ver) do not provide Zamboangueño simple verbs. Several common polysyllabic Spanish verbs also
have no cognate simple verbs in Zamboangueño: decir, traer, haber.

2. Inflection. In contrast to the complex inflectional paradigms of the Spanish and Philippine verb, Zamboangueño formally
distinguishes only four inflectional categories of general verbs (the

modals, the locative, and the existential have special forms; #6, 7, 8). These categories represent contrasts in tense, aspect, and mode. The inflectional apparatus consists of three prefixes and three negative words. Letting V represent the first verb of a verb expression, the entire array of Zamboangueño inflectional forms can be displayed as follows:

	Affirmative	Negative
Imperative	V	no V
Future	(ay-)V	hindi' (ay-)V
Durative	(ta-)V	hindi' (ta-)V
Punctual	(ya-)V	nway V

The future prefix, ay-, has less formal stylistic variants, ey-, el-; otherwise inflectional forms are invariant. The inflectional prefix ya- is not to be confused with the post-initial adverbial particle ya 'already.' The word no 'don't' is not to be confused with the prefix no- which negates special forms of modals (#6). Both hindi' and nway have uses outside of this paradigm.

   The parentheses enclosing the prefixes in the above display represent the fact that overt marking by prefix of an inflectional category is not grammatically required for each occurrence of that category. The overtly unmarked verb can represent any inflectional category and such representation does not neutralize underlying inflectional distinctions. Neither Spanish nor Philippine languages share this optionality of inflectional marking. The parentheses notation, however, obscures an important fact: in usage the future is rarely marked by prefix, whereas the durative and punctual are rarely unmarked (see Table 2). Thus, formally, the future is like the durative and punctual in being markable, but, in usage, it is most commonly like the imperative in being unmarked. In the negative the contrasts differ. The future and durative share a common negative form, whereas the punctual has a distinct negative, nway, which suppletes the punctual prefix.

   The imperative expresses an underlying command, request, or instruction to an addressee to do what is signified by the verb phrase:

2.1. tendéro, kuhi kon-mígo un móskas
'Bartender, catch me one fly!'

2.2. abla kon-éle pruba lang uste man-rifer na probísyan
del báryo chárter
(IMP)-tell to-him (IMP)-try only you refer to provisiot
of the barrio charter
'Tell him just to try to refer to the provision of the
barrio charter'

Example 2.2 contains an embedded imperative: the speaker is instructing the addressee to instruct someone else. The indirect
addressee is overtly represented by the formal second-person pronoun uste.

Normally pronouns representing the addressee are deleted
in the imperative. Since status and formality considerations constrain second-person pronoun selection, overt use of a pronoun
marks the degree of politeness of the command. Just how it does
this in a given utterance depends on the appropriateness of the pronoun selected to the social relationship between speaker and addressee. The following examples illustrate the use of uste (formal), bos
(intimate), and tu (neutral):

2.3. no uste urbida
'Don't forget' (to a superior: polite)

2.4. no mas bos jó rebata kon-mígo
'Don't grab me anymore Mack!' (to a peer: abrupt)

2.5. no tamen tu kombersa ansína
'And don't talk like that!' (to a peer: mildly abrupt)

If the speaker is including himself within the scope of the
command, the first-plus-second person pronoun, kita 'you and I,' is
used:

2.6. kome ánay kita
'Let's eat first'

2.7. no mas kita toma
      'Let's not drink anymore'

The imperative negative form, no, is a clause initial word
(i. e. not a particle or prefix); post-initial particles and pronouns
obligatorily follow no and precede the imperative verb (e.g. #2.3,
2.4, 2.5, 2.7).

Later (#6) the possibility of relating the imperative to the
special inflectional category of modals will be discussed. This will
be attempted by postulating an underlying imperative modal verb
(IMP) which is deleted in surface structure after it has determined
the position of post-initial adverbs and pronouns, thereby making the
modal negative prefix no- appear as a full word in the negative imperative.

The future represents events which are not imperative, but
which, like imperative events, are unreal: they are predicted, prom-
ised, or hypothetical. Overt marking of the future with ay- is infre-
quent in ordinary conversation. In 2.8 its use seems to add assurance
to a promise:

2.8. hindi' mas yo ay-ase ótro bés
      'I won't do it again'

In 2.9 the time reference of previous sentences in the discourse had
been in the past; the use of ay- marks a shift in reference:

2.9. ay-lyeba bende si tóng el asúkar
      'Tong will take the sugar to sell'

If a future sentence has a second-person subject, the use of ay- marks
the utterance as non-imperative:

2.10. ay-akustrumbra tu syémpre
       'You will get used to it of course'

Occurrences of ay- are more easily found in written texts. (These
examples are retranscribed.)

2.11. <u>ay-keda ma-móskas el di-áton kása</u>
FUT-become ADJ-fly the of-your+my house
'One's house will become full of flies'
(From a primary school reader)

2.12. <u>el yéma ay-keda dúru</u>
'It's the yolk that will become hard'
(From a newspaper column on cooking turtle eggs)

2.13. <u>tene kwidáo pára hindi' ay-machaka</u>
(IMP)-have care that NEG FUT-disintegrate
'Be careful that it doesn't all disintegrate'
(same source as 2.12)

Examples of unmarked future are easily found:

2.14. <u>maskin kai ulan, anda yo</u>
'Even if it rains, I'll go'

2.15. <u>kasa ya yo</u>
'I intend to get married now'

2.16. <u>mata lang kami kon ése pwérko</u>
'We'll just kill that pig'

The contexts of these particular utterances made clear that the unmarked verbs represented the future. The sentences in isolation are
technically ambiguous. Example 2.14 could mean 'Even though it
rained, I went'; 2.15 could mean 'I am married already.' In the same
narrative from which 2.16 was taken, there occurred a similar sentence, this time requiring interpretation as perfective:

2.17. <u>mata ya sila kon ése pwérko</u>
'They had killed the pig already'
(the occurrence of <u>ya</u> 'already' does not rule out a
future interpretation, cf. 2.15)

Although an unmarked verb phrase is technically ambiguous, its normal interpretation, if clearly non-imperative, is future. This fact

is clear from informants' interpretations of such sentences in isolation and is reflected in the frequency patterns discussed below.

Perhaps not unrelated to the relative infrequency of occurrence of ay- is the fact that its pronunciation is variable. Though usually spelled "ay, " the pronunciation /ay/ is considered "old-fashioned" or "rural. " Most speakers currently use /el/ or /ey/. However pronounced, the form of the future prefix is unique to Zamboangueño. Caviteño and Ternateño have di-. The durative and punctual prefixes, ta- and ya-, on the other hand, are invariant in pronunciation and shared with Caviteño and Ternateño.

The durative and punctual contrast with the future in representing events which are real in the sense that they have at least begun at the reference time of the utterance. To be classifiable as punctual, an event must be single, momentary, and completed. If any one of these criteria is not met, the event is classified as durative. Events which are repeated or which go on for a period of time, or which have not been completed are durative. The following examples illustrate the contrast:

2.18. kwándo ya-echa kami na bínta', múcho hénte ta-kompra
       'When we put (the fish) in the boat, many people bought
       (them)'

Putting the fish into the boat was a single act jointly accomplished by several people, whereas the buying was a series of repeated transactions involving several people.

2.19. tyéne dós kláse de wébos de turtúga: el úno akel ke
       ya-akaba ya echa el animal ke ta-engkontra enterráo
       na aréna dónde ya-pone ese wébos el dwényo

       Exist two kind of egg of turtle: the one that which
       PUN-finish already put the animal which DUR-find
       buried at sand where PUN-put that egg the owner

       'There are two kinds of turtle eggs: one is that which
       the animal has finished laying, which are found buried
       in the sand where those eggs were put by their owner'

(In the phrase <u>ya-akaba ya echa</u>, the second <u>ya</u> is not
the punctual prefix, but the post-initial advert meaning 'already')

In example 2.19 (again drawn from our turtle egg recipe), the laying
of eggs by a turtle is construed as a single completed act in contrast
to the finding of eggs on different unspecified occasions by various
unspecified people. Note that the shift of inflection from punctual to
durative and back to punctual helps communicate a shift in clause
subjects: the one who finds (<u>ta-engkontra</u>) the eggs is not the same
as the one who lays (<u>ya-akaba echa, ya-pone</u>) them.

Example 2.20 is durative because, although complete, the
event described is not momentary:

2.20.   <u>antes kel kon lakían ta-trabaha; ta-buta lang urinóla</u>
        'He used to work for Lakian; (he) just emptied urinals'

Example 2.21 is durative because it is not completed:

2.21.   <u>ta-sale ya na aguhéro el raton</u>
        'The rat is coming out of (his) hole now'

The durative and punctual have distinct negation patterns.
With the punctual negative, <u>nway</u>, only the unmarked verb can occur:

2.22.   <u>hindi' man ta-dwéle el kabésa</u>
        'He didn't really have a headache'

2.23.   <u>hindi' yo ta-raska péro ího de púta daw ay-akaba</u>
        <u>di-mío reswélyo</u>
        'I didn't scratch (my pin worms), but—son of a
        whore—it nearly killed me ("like will finish my
        breath")'

2.24.   <u>bwéno nway kon-tígo morde el kulébra</u>
        'It's good the snake didn't bite you'

2.25.   <u>nway man yo man-aksep el maga sén ta-dale le</u>
        'I didn't accept the money he was giving'
        (<u>man-aksep</u> is a derived verb)

Unlike the progressive aspect of English, the Zamboangueño durative can occur with stative verbs. (Statives are agentless verbs such as see, know, hear, in contrast to look, learn, listen, cf. Fillmore 1968: 31). Non-completed or repeated stative events are necesarily durative:

2.26. ta-kré man bos de dányo?
      'Do you believe in sorcery?' (not completed)

2.27. nway múcho hénte ta-mira kon-éle
      'Not many people saw her' (repeated instances of seeing)

Contrast:

2.28. nway kré si Líto
      'Lito didn't believe it'

2.29. ya-mira le kon el uwak ta-bula man-uwak-uwak
      'He saw the crow flying (and) crowing'

A stative event can also be construed as not momentary:

2.30. na di-súyu pensamyénto ta-mira ya le el ichúra di paning
      'In his mind he was already seeing Paning's expression' (Describing a man on his way home to his wife after losing all his money at a cock fight. Is this English gloss ungrammatical?)

Much less commonly than the future, the punctual and durative are represented by unmarked verbs:

2.31. abla el espanyol, larga. larga el téndero
      (PUN)-say the Spaniard, (IMP)-release. (PUN)-release the bartender
      'The Spaniard said, release it. The bartender released it'
      (reference is to the fly caught by the bartender in 2.1)

In quotative use, as in 2.21, <u>abla</u> 'to say' is commonly not overtly marked by prefix.

2.32. <u>espera yo kon-tígo endenántes</u>
       'I was waiting for you earlier today' (durative)

Although in some instances of unmarked verb phrases it may be difficult to interpret the aspect intended—the utterance may be ambiguous in a given context—lack of marking by prefix does not neutralize underlying inflectional distinctions. If a sentence is negated, then a distinction between punctual and durative is obligatorily expressed. Suppose 2.17 is posed as a question:

2.33. <u>mata ya sila kon ése pwérko?</u>

interpretable either as punctual ('Did they already kill that pig?') or durative ('Were they already killing those pigs?', 'Are they killing that pig now?'). If interpreted as punctual, a negative reply must employ <u>nway</u> '(They) did not.' If interpreted as durative, the negative reply must employ <u>hindi</u>' '(They) were not,' '(They) are not.'

The distinctions made by these four inflectional categories can be specified by binary oppositions along three dimensions, here labeled mode, tense, and aspect:

	Mode	Tense	Aspect
Imperative	+imperative	(+future)	(−punctual)
Future	−imperative	+future	(−punctual)
Durative	−imperative	−future	−punctual
Punctual	−imperative	−future	+punctual

One could reverse plus and minus assignments for mode [$\pm$ indicative] and tense [$\pm$ begun], but doing so for aspect would require postulating something like [+durative], defined disjunctively as "repeated or continuing or incomplete." In this formulation, [+punctual] is defined conjunctively as "single and momentary and complete." There are advantages for rule formulation and for interpretation of frequency patterns in aligning the sign values of punctual with those of imperative and future.

The feature values enclosed by parentheses seem to be logically entailed, but are not necessary for minimal contrastive specification. There is some advantage, however, in retaining these redundant features. They provide a basis for explaining the formal similarities in negative selection between the future and durative as well as the usage similarity (lack of prefixation) between the future and the imperative.

Rules for verb prefix and negative marker selection can be formulated using plus feature values as contexts:

1. VP → (Neg)+Pref+Vb
2. Vb → CS
3. CS → [±imperative]
4. [-imperative] → [±future]
5. [-future] → [±punctual]
6. [+imperative] → [+future]
7. [+future] → [-punctual]

8. Neg+Pref → $\left\{ \begin{array}{l} \underline{no} \ / \ \rule{1cm}{0.4pt} \ [+imperative] \\ \underline{nway} \ / \rule{1cm}{0.4pt} \ [+punctual] \\ \underline{hindi'}+Pref \end{array} \right\}$

9. Pref → $\left\{ \begin{array}{ll} \underline{\emptyset} & / \rule{1cm}{0.4pt} \ [+imperative] \\ \underline{ay} & / \rule{1cm}{0.4pt} \ [+future] \\ \underline{ya} & / \rule{1cm}{0.4pt} \ [+punctual] \\ \underline{ta} \end{array} \right\}$

These rules remain incomplete and inadequate in several ways. The constituent structure of VP is not fully specified. No provision is made for modal, existential, and locative verb expressions. More serious is the failure of these rules to account for the differential optionality of verb prefixation. An optional deletion rule of the type

10. Pref → $\emptyset$

does not reveal the fact that the future is commonly unprefixed, whereas the durative and punctual are commonly prefixed, with the punctual occurring unprefixed with a slightly higher frequency than the durative (Table 2).

Table 2. Frequency Count of Inflectional Categories
Represented in 441 Verb Phrases

	Prefixed	Not Prefixed	Total
Imperative		33	33
Future	36	66	102
Punctual	125	26	151
Durative	142	13	155

Note: An effort was made to sample texts representing
a variety of topics and style levels.

It is tempting to turn to the theory of linguistic marking
(Jakobson 1957; Greenberg 1966) to provide a formal way of accounting
for frequency patterns in language. Doing so in this case, however,
leads to a curious paradox. A basic criterion of marked categories
is that they occur with lesser frequency than their unmarked counter-
parts. Greenberg (1966: 46–49) offers data showing that, for languages
in general, the imperative is marked over the non-imperative, and
the future is marked over the non-future. For aspect the data are
less clear but point to the perfective (our "punctual") being marked
over the imperfective. Frequency counts of the occurrence of inflectional categories in Zamboangueño (Table 2) support this interpretation. If we call the underlying marking that corresponds both to general
theory and to Zamboangueño frequencies semantic marking, then we
have a case in which semantic marking is inversely related to overt
marking by inflectional prefix. Semantically marked mode [+impera-
tive] cannot be prefixed. Semantically marked tense [+future], if
[-imperative], can be prefixed, but in usage is much less frequently
prefixed than unmarked tense. Semantically marked aspect, [+punc-
tual], is slightly less often prefixed than the fully semantically
unmarked category, the durative.

3. Derived verbs. The range of verbal expressions is
expanded beyond that provided by the inventory of simple verbs in two
ways: derivation and complementation to a pro-verb. In either case
the non-verb which becomes incorporated into a verbal expression may
be a form with verbal meaning (a "deep structure" verb) which lacks the
requisite canonical form of a simple verb, or it may be a noun or adjecti

Derived verbs are formed by a single affix, man-, which converts non-verbs into inflectable words. (The prefix man- is not to be confused with the post-initial emphatic adverbial particle man.) Table 3 lists examples of verbs derived from forms of Philippine and of Spanish origin. Those of Spanish origin all occur in underived form as nouns or adjectives. The syntactic status of the root morphemes of Philippine origin is more variable. Some (e.g. ánut 'float') occur only as derived verbs or as complements of pro-verbs. Some occur unprefixed as adjectives (e.g. pi'ang 'crippled') or nouns (e.g. tunuk 'thorn,' 'spine'). Others occur as derived verbs or as derived adjectives (e.g. pilit> man-pilit 'to stick,' ma-pilit 'sticky'). Forms that occur both as derived verbs and as complements of the pro-verb ase may contrast in transitivity (#4).

In the imperative, adjectives must appear as surface structure verbs verbalized either by man-:

3.1a. byen hangul pa yo   'I am still very anxious'
3.1b. no mas man-hangul   'Don't be anxious anymore'

or by pro-verbs (#4).

The prefix man- verbalizes forms prefixed by pa- 'pretending to be,' 'becoming,' 'moving in the direction of':

3.2. man-pa-sábe   'pretend to know'
3.3. man-pa-ríko   'pretend to be rich,' 'become rich'
3.4. man-pa-álto   'to act proud,' 'to sit up'
3.5. man-pa-tyéne huya'   'to pretend to have shame'

The mutual plural of simple verbs, formed by -(h)an (#10), must be reverbalized with man-:

3.6a. ta-konose yo kon-éle   'I know her'
3.7b. ya-man-konose-han sila   'They became acquainted with each other'

A final use of man-, and evidence of its productivity in current speech, is to incorporate English words as verbs in Zamboangueño sentences (there are no English-derived simple verbs). See 2.2, 2.25, and the following:

Table 3.   Examples of Derived Verbs

Of Philippine origin:

man-ánut	'to float' (intrans.)
man-uyuk	'to shake' (intrans.)
man-dágit	'(of a bird) to seize prey'
man-gúnit	'to hold with the finger tips'
man-kapa'	'to catch prey (e.g. fish) by hand'
man-kupus	'to shrivel' < kupus (Adj) 'shriveled'
man-kaláwang	'to rust' < kalawang (N) 'rust'
man-lumus	'to drown' (intrans.)
man-pi'ang	'to limp' < pi'ang (Adj) 'lame'
man-pilit	'to stick' (intrans.), cf. ma-pilit 'sticky'
man-panggas	'to plant by dibbling'
man-tabas	'to clear vegetation'
man-tunuk	'to sting, be stung by thorn or spine'
	< tunuk (N) 'thorn or spine'

Of Spanish origin:

man-amígo	'to be friends' < amígo (N)
man-bróma	'to joke' < bróma (N)
man-húnto	'to get together' < húnto (Adj)
man-kalésa	'to ride a horse cart' < kalésa (N)
man-kwénto	'to talk' < kwénto (N)
man-tyángge	'to go to market' < tyángge (N) 'market'

3.8.   <u>taki yo kon sámi ya-man-ebakwet</u>
'I am here at Sammy's evacuated'

3.9.   <u>si kita ta-man-inten ansína, "we have the right"</u>
'If this is what we intend, we have the right'

3.10.   <u>ta-man-enjoy gat kami anóche</u>
'We really had a good time last night'

3.11.   <u>kay ya-man-"breakfast" sila úna "before mass." sábe
uste kósa yo ta-man-"mean"? akel ba antes de kasa,
ya-man-"take advantage" ya el ómbre.</u>

'Because they had breakfast first before mass. You
know what I mean?: when before marriage the man
has already taken advantage (of the girl)'
(From a letter, retranscribed except for English words)

The prefix man- provides a rare opportunity to talk about
morphophonemics. In casual speech the final n undergoes assimilation
to the position of a following non-glottal consonant: man-bróma
/mambróma/, man-kapa' /maŋkapaʔ/, man-uyuk /manʔuyuk/.
These various nasals are taken as manifestations of an underlying n
because /n/ is always acceptable in very deliberate speech and is
what occurs in the position where assimilation is not possible, i.e.
before a glottal stop. (In Philippine languages, nasals assimilate to
/ŋ/ before a glottal stop.) Furthermore, despite the ad hoc nature
of local spelling practices, the prefix is invariably spelled "man."
In combination with perfective and durative prefixes, man- reduces
to N in casual speech: ya-man → yaN, ta-man → taN-. The sequence man-pa regularly reduces by this rule to -mpa-: ta-man-pa-
ríko → /tamparíko/.

The etymology of man- is obscure. Ternateño has a cognate
form, mang-, but it occurs infrequently and then only with suffixed
verbs of Spanish origin. It is not used productively to incorporate
new verbs of non-Spanish origin. Philippine languages have a verb
prefix of similar shape, but it is part of a complex inflectional paradigm and has different morphophonemic properties. Whatever originally suggested its shape, the current form and function of man- appear
to be a Zamboangueño creation.

4. Pro-verbs and cognate objects. Zamboangueño makes
extensive use of a type of verb expression that has been called a
"cognate object construction." "These are constructions in which,
at the very least, there is a high selectivity between a specific V and
an 'object' N, and in which the V + N combination in one language
might well be matched by a V alone in another" (Fillmore 1968: 85).
Within Zamboangueño many forms occur both as cognate objects and
as derived verbs:

4.1a. ta-man-pilit man este pláster
      'This band-aid is really sticking'

4.1b. ase lang pilit kon láway
       'Just stick (it) on with saliva'

4.2a. nway akaba man-panggas el límpyo
       'The cleared (area) was not completely dibbled'

4.2b. poréso ya-ase ya kami ótra bwélta panggas
       'That's why we dibbled (it) again'

Derivation and cognate object constructions are alternate methods of
verbalization.

The simple verbs that occur with cognate objects are pro-
verbs. Table 4 lists common pro-verbs with illustrative cognate
objects. All of these pro-verbs also function as regular simple verbs;
the glosses given the verbs on the list represent their regular meaning. The most general and productive pro-verb is ase 'to do, to make.'
This verb is also a causative (#5) and retains its transitivizing function
when used as a pro-verb; compare 4.1a and 4.2a with 4.1b and 4.2b.

    5. Causatives. Causatives are simple verbs that alter the
underlying case patterns of the noun phrases associated with a verb
expression. They either add an agent or convert a non-agentive noun
phrase to one representing an agent. In either case the new agent
becomes the subject of the sentence. There are three such verbs:
ase 'to do, to make,' manda 'to send,' and dále 'to give.' All three
can be used non-causatively as the main verb of an expression:

    5.1. sábe ba le ase bínta'?
          'Does he know how to make a canoe?'

    5.2. porke gale' tu nway manda kárta
          'Why didn't you apparently send any letters?'

    5.3. ta-dále le agináldo kon el manga syainsyu
          'He gives Christmas presents to the shoeshine boys'

    Used causatively, ase adds an agent to an expression that
otherwise lacks one:

5.4a. <u>ya-kái el wébos</u>
'the egg fell'

5.4b. <u>ase uste kái el wébos úno úno</u>
'Drop the eggs (in the water) one by one'

In 5.4a, the subject of the sentence, 'the egg,' is not an agent but
what experienced falling. In 5.4b, an agent is added which becomes
the subject of the sentence. The verb <u>ase</u> functions as a causative
when in construction with another verb as in 5.4b or with a cognate
object as in 4.2. In traditional terms, <u>ase</u> converts intransitives
into transitives. However, in the case of so-called intransitives
whose subject is an underlying agent, e.g. verbs of motion, <u>ase</u> cannot be used as a causative.

The causative <u>manda</u> adds an agent which in some way causes,
or attempts to cause, some other agent to perform an action; it adds
an additional agent to an expression that already has one. The added
agent becomes the subject of the sentence:

5.5. <u>akel atórni kon-mígo ta-manda entra eskwéla</u>
'That lawyer is sending me to school'

5.6. <u>manda lang kon-éle kompone</u>
'Just have him repair (it)'

5.7. <u>porke hindi' ta-irbi el ágwa? ya-manda ya yo kon rós</u>
<u>ase irbi</u>
'Why isn't the water boiling? I had Rosa boil it'

In 5.7 the subject of <u>irbi</u> is what experiences the boiling, the underlying subject of <u>ase irbi</u> is who does the boiling, and the subject of
<u>manda ase irbi</u> is the one who caused Rosa to do the boiling. In this
manner rather complex verbal expressions can be constructed in
Zamboangueño which are similar in function, if not in form, to some
of the derivational possibilities of verbs in Philippine languages.

Note that with intransitives such as <u>sale</u> 'to exit,' <u>manda,</u>
not <u>ase,</u> is used as a causative if the subject is an agent:

Table 4. Pro-Verbs and Illustrative Cognate Objects

<u>ase</u> 'to do, to make.' All verb expressions formed with <u>ase</u> are transitive. The following is a very small sample of such expressions.

ase ánut	'to set afloat,' cf. man-anut 'to float'
ase ápas	'to chase'
ase baráha	'to deal cards' < baráha, n., 'playing cards'
ase balása	'to shuffle cards' (balása < CP < OldSp /baráša/)
ase bítay	'to hang up'
ase lága'	'to boil food,' cf. irbi 'to be boiling (of water)'
ase lúgut	'to rub'
ase túlak	'to push'
ase úban	'to accompany' < úban, n., 'companion'

<u>keda</u> 'to reside,' 'become.' Verbalizes adjectives.

keda ríko	'to become rich' = one sense of man-pa-ríko

<u>tene</u>, <u>tyéne</u> 'to exist,' 'to have' (see #7)

tene kwidáo	'to be careful'
tene myédo	'to be afraid'
tene óhos	'to have designs on'

<u>echa</u> 'to put'

echa nómbre	'to name'
echa istórya	'to tell a story'
echa timbang	'to balance' (trans.)

<u>dale</u> 'to give'

dale palísa	'to thrash' < palísa, n., thrashing
dale engkwéntro	'to encounter' < engkwéntro, n.

5.8a. <u>ya-sale yo</u> 'I left'

5.8b. <u>si pawlíno ya-manda kon-mígo sale</u>
       'Paulino asked me to leave'

However, if <u>sale</u> has a subject which is not an agent, then <u>ase</u> is used:

Table 4 (continued)

---

pega 'to strike'
    pega salída   'to take a trip'
    pega panggas   'to dibble with haste, ' cf. man-panggas, ase
                        panggas

pasa 'to pass'
    pasa líma   'to file' < líma, n., 'file (tool)'
    pasa trápo   'to wipe' < trápo, n., 'rag'

hila 'to drag'
    hila sagwan   'to paddle' < sagwan, n., 'paddle'

hala 'to pull toward one'
    hala el bóka   'to wipe one's mouth'

kái 'to fall'
    kái ulan   'to rain' < ulan, n., 'rain'

mata 'to kill'
    mata óhos   'to wink' < ohos, n., 'eye'

tira 'to throw, shoot at'
    tira utut   'to fart' < utut, n., 'fart'

tuka 'to touch'
    tuka máno   'to clap'

pone 'to put'
    pone dúda   'to doubt'

5.9a. ya-sale el pregúnta
      'The question came out'

5.9b. bwéno gane' ese mi amígo ya-ase sale de ése
      'It's really good that that friend of mine came out
      with that (question)'

Inanimate agents can be the subject of <u>manda</u>:

> 5.10.   <u>el bunîto rópa lang ta-manda kanîla sinta byen bunita</u>
> <u>mira</u>.
> 'It was just the pretty clothes that made them feel
> very attractive'

The third causative, <u>dále</u>, occurs only with a few specific
verbs and affects underlying case patterns in differing ways.

> 5.11a.   <u>ya-mira yo kon akel dalaga endenántes</u>
> 'I saw that girl earlier today'

> 5.11b.   <u>dále kon-éle mira, ne', dónde el kómfort</u>
> 'Show him, girl, where the rest-room is'

The subject of <u>mira</u> 'to see' is the one who experiences seeing; the
subject of <u>dále mira</u> 'to show' is an agent who causes someone else
to experience seeing. The verb <u>mira</u> can also mean 'to look,' the
seer being construed as an agent. In this sense the appropriate
causative is <u>manda</u>:

> 5.12a.   <u>mira pa-atras</u> 'look back'

> 5.12b.   <u>ya-manda yo mira kon Father Reynolds; no-sábe man</u>
> <u>éle kompone</u>
> 'I had Father Reynolds look at it; he didn't know how
> to fix it at all' (from a letter about a tape-recorder)

The verb <u>dále</u> also modifies the meaning of the events of borrowing,
bathing, giving birth, and encountering:

> 5.13a.   <u>presta</u> 'to borrow'

> 5.13b.   <u>dále presta</u> 'to lend'

In the case of borrowing, <u>dále</u> converts the agent of the action from
the recipient to the donor.

> 5.14a.   <u>banya</u> 'to bathe oneself'

5.14b. dále banya 'to bathe someone else'

with bathing, dále signifies that the agent and the recipient of the
action are not the same individual.

5.15a. nase 'to be born'

5.15b. pari 'to give birth'

5.15c. dále pari 'to attend a birth (as of a midwife)'

with the event of birth, the agentless form (nase) is lexically distinct
from the form whose subject is the agent of birth. Here dále provides an additional agent to assist in the process.

5.16a. ya-man-engkwéntro kon-éle na tyángge
        '(I) encountered her in the market'

5.16b. si pwéde kan-áton dále engkwéntro el hapon
        'If the Japanese can find us'

In 5.16b, dále, functioning as both a pro-verb and a causative, signifies that the encounter, if it occurs, will not be accidental: an agent
is present.

6. Modals. Three types of verb phrases have special inflectional properties: modal, existential, and locative phrase. All of
these phrase types share the property of not occurring in the imperative. Modal phrases are marked by modal verbs which express knowledge, ability, opportunity, desire, need, or obligation. The object
of this expression may be represented in surface structure by sentence,
verb, or noun phrase complements depending on the modal verb employed and the meaning of the expression. When used as auxiliaries
in construction with other verbs, modals appear as the first verb of
a phrase.

Modal verbs have special accented forms derived from the
Spanish third-person present indicative (Table 5). Either the simple
or accented form can appear in any regular inflectional category except the imperative. In addition there is an inflectional category, the

Table 5. Modal Verbs

Accented Form	Simple Verb	
pwéde	pude	'to be able'
kyére	kere	'to want, to like'
tyéne ke	tene ke	'to have to'
kombyéne	kombene*	'to be proper to'
nesesíta		'to be necessary, to need'
débe		'to be obligated to'
sábe		'to know how to, to be able because of knowledge or skill'

*Not recorded.

"neutral," reserved for verb phrases containing an accented form of
a modal. This category permits neutralization of tense and aspect
distinctions in modal phrases. The neutral is morphologically unmarked in the affirmative but has a distinct negative, <u>no-</u>, prefixed to
the modal verb. Unlike the imperative negative, <u>no</u>, the neutral negative is not a full word; post-initial adverbs and pronouns cannot follow
it. Modals used in the neutral will be exemplified first. The tenses
of the English glosses reflect the contexts from which the particular
utterances were drawn.

The modal, <u>sábe</u> 'to know (how),' when used as an auxiliary
verb implies ability because of knowledge or skill:

> 6.1. <u>sábe gale' tu kombersa</u>
> 'So you know how to speak (Zamboangueño)'

> 6.2. <u>no-sábe man éle kompone</u>
> 'He couldn't fix it at all'

With a sentence complement, <u>sábe</u> means either to know a fact (6.3,4)
or to mistakenly believe one knows a fact (6.5):

> 6.3. <u>no-sábe kyen hénte lang ya-regala daw kan-íla un pwérkc</u>
> NEG+NEU-know who person only PUN-give allegedly
> to-them a pig

'(I) don't know who was supposed to have given them
a pig'

6.4. <u>ta-kamina ki kamina yo, no-sábe ya yo dónde ya ginda</u>
'I walked and walked not knowing then where I was
going'

6.5. <u>el gobyérno sábe lyéno man, péro ese nway mas laman</u>
'The government thinks it (a warehouse) is full, but
there is nothing in it anymore'

There is a special negative word <u>nosay</u> which means 'I don't know.'
It is, of course, derived from Spanish <u>no se</u>, but it corresponds in
use to morphemes in Philippine languages which deny knowledge on
the part of the speaker (cf. Tagalog <u>aywan</u>, Cebuano <u>ambut</u>, Yakan
<u>inday</u>). When used with the pronoun <u>kita</u> 'you and I,' the resulting
construction, <u>nosay kita</u>, means something like 'Who knows.'

The modal <u>pwéde</u> expresses ability because of physical circumstances such as one's strength or the lack of external constraints.

6.7. <u>ay, byen alboróto! aki no-pwéde man kita kombersa</u>
'Wow, it's really noisy! We can't talk here' (cf. 6.1)

6.8. <u>no-pwéde gayot rebaha</u>
'One can't even bargain'

6.9. <u>kon-mígo no-pwéde uste abla de ése</u>
'I am not the one who can be told that'

6.10. <u>tendéro, pwéde ba kon-mígo kuhi un namok?</u>
'Bartender, can (you) catch me a mosquito?'

6.11. <u>si ta-man-syort pa, pwede yo kon-tígo dale presta el</u>
<u>pasáhe</u>
'If (you) are still short, I can lend you the fare'

The modal <u>kyére</u> expresses desire with noun phrase or verb complements. It can also express propensity, cf. 6.17.

6.12. no-kyére yo kon-éle
'I don't like him'

6.13. segúro kyére le kon-mígo ase kómo sayd layn
'He probably wants to make me some sort of "side line"

6.14. si kyére yo man-"rewind" pára na ótro láo, no-pwéde
si hindi' kita ayuda bira
'If I want to rewind (the tape) to the other side, it isn't
possible if one doesn't help it turn'

6.15. kósa tu kyére
'What do you want?'

6.16. kyére ba tu kái?
'Do you want to flunk?'

6.17. kyére man ese kái el piríko
'The parrot was about to fall'

The Spanish idiom quiere decir 'to mean' is retained in Zamboangueño
as kyére desir. The form desir does not otherwise occur and there
is no corresponding simple verb.

The modal, kombyéne, expresses appropriateness in much
the sense of English "should."

6.18. no-kombyéne gayot tolera ese
'(One) should not tolerate that at all'

Three modals, nesesíta, tyéne ke, and débe, express varying degrees of necessity: nesesíta is stronger than tyene ke; débe
implies an obligation imposed by someone else. In tyéne ke, the ke
precedes complement as in the corresponding Spanish idiom (other
uses of tyéne are described in #7).

6.19. nesesíta manda polis aki
'It was necessary to call the police here'

6.20. tyéne tu ke man-aplay 'You have to make an application'

6.21. i el sén kon maséda débe yo paga déntro del més máyo
       'And the money from Maceda I must pay back within
       the month of May'

6.22. débe yo ese saka sámer
       'I have to take those (courses) in summer school'

As is apparent from the preceding examples, modal phrases
in the neutral are not constrained by any tense or aspect considerations. Modal phrases, however, can also be inflected for future,
durative, and punctual. Most commonly it is the accented form of
the modal that occurs with an inflectional prefix, but occasionally the
simple form appears. The contrast, if any, between the use of an
inflected simple or accented form remains obscure to me.

6.23. akel el byen sabróso, maskin kyen ay-pwéde traga
       sin resélo
       'That kind is the most delicious, anyone can swallow
       it without reluctance'

6.24. ta-pwéde pa kome chicharon maskin kwánto bílug ya
       lang el dyénte
       'He is still able to eat chicharon no matter how many
       teeth (he has left)'

6.25. si ta-kái ulan, el manga móros hindi' ta-pwéde peska
       'When it rains, the Moslems can't fish'

6.26. ta-ulbida ya ke akel tyémpo ya-pwéde sila kome
       kamanting gitgit, i awra ay-abla ya ke no-pwéde sila
       pasa el día si nway késo de swísa
       DUR-forget already that that time PUN-able they eat
       manioc grated, and now FUT-say already that NEG+
       NEU-able they pass the day if none cheese of Swiss
       'They forget that at that time they had to eat (pwéde
       here conveys the notion of involuntariness) grated
       manioc, and now they will say they cannot go through
       the day without Swiss cheese'

6.27. ya-pwéde ya kita anda wí mísa sin sústo
       'We could then go hear mass without fear'

6.28. nway yo kon-tígo pwéde eskribi
       'I haven't been able to write you'

6.29. hindi' kita pwéde kome pwérko
       'We won't be able to eat pig' (future—note use of hindi'

6.30. hindi' yo ta-sábe
       'I don't know' (cf. no-sábe yo). 'I don't know' (with
       no tense implication)

6.31. nway yo pensa ke el idéa di-uste ay-pude manda kom-
       bense kon tódo
       'I didn't think your idea would convince everyone'

6.32. nway kere kon-mígo
       '(She) didn't like me'

It might be possible to combine what we have called the neutral category of modal verbs with the imperative of general verbs.
The imperative, like the neutral, lacks an inflectional prefix and is
similarly negated (cf. imperative no and neutral no-). Combining thes
two inflectional categories would require postulating a modal verb IMP
which forms imperative verb expressions but which is deleted in surface structure. The fact that modals cannot occur in the imperative
is accounted for by the supposition that the imperative is itself a modal
The surface difference between no and no- is removing by ordering the
post-initial placement rule before the IMP deletion rule. Thus a sentence such as

     no mas bos kome 'Don't eat any more'

would have an underlying form like

     *no-IMP kome mas bos

The post-initial placement rule yields

     *no-IMP mas bos kome

The IMP deletion rule yields the surface sentence

     no mas bos kome

making no- appear as a full word in surface structure. Two difficulties confront this interpretation. First, in the affirmative, post-
initials occur behind the surface verb

> kome pa bos 'Eat some more!'

One would either have to reorder the post-initial placement and deletion rules in the affirmative or not allow post-initial placement after
IMP while allowing it after no-IMP. Another difficulty is that the
inflection of modals shares similarities with that of the existential
and locative (e.g. in having unprefixed accented forms), yet the negative of both the existential and locative is not no but nway, a form
equivalent to the punctual negative!

7. Existential phrases. The existential phrase consists of
the existential verb tene in construction with an indefinite noun phrase.
The verb tene is similar to the modals in its inflectional properties.
It has a special accented form tyéne, which can be inflected but which
also occurs uninflected with neutral tense and aspect signification.
The negative of tyéne is nway. To preserve the parallelism with the
neutral forms of modals, one could state that tyéne becomes -ay in
the context no- . However, the equivalence in form of the negative
existential and the negative punctual is no accident. The negation of
punctual aspect with a form elsewhere meaning 'none' is widespread
in Philippine languages (Tagalog being an exception). Except for its
vestige in nway, the Spanish hay 'there is' has no reflex in Zamboangueño.

The meanings and syntactic properties of tyéne closely parallel those of Philippine existential words, e.g. Tagalog mayro'on,
Cebuano 'adúna, Hiligaynon may'ára'. An existential phrase (tyéne
+ indefinite noun phrase) in construction with an expressed or implicit
locative phrase asserts that some representative of the class denoted
by the indefinite noun phrase exists at the specified locale:

> 7.1. tyéne búngga na buyu'an
>   Exist areca LOC betel container
>   'There is some areca in the betel box'

The corresponding negative asserts that there is no representative
at the specified locale:

7.2. nway búngga lyi
      'There is no areca there'

A sentence containing a definite noun phrase in construction
with an existential phrase asserts possession:

7.3. tyene pa búngga ese byého
      'That old man still has some areca'

The object possessed is indefinite; the possessor is definite. The
corresponding negative is:

7.4. nway mas búngga ese byého
      'That old man has no more areca'

Since noun phrases are freely deleted (pronominalized by Ø if you
prefer) in surface structure, interpretation of existential phrases as
locative or possessive in meaning often requires knowledge of context
outside of the given sentence, Thus

7.5. tyéne ságing EXIST banana
could mean 'I have some bananas' in response to a question such as

7.6. kósa tu tyéne 'What do you have'

With verb phrase complements, existential phrases represent underlying indefinite noun phrases:

7.7. tyéne mundúhin ta-tira kan-áton
      EXIST pirate DUR-shoot at-us
      'Some pirates are shooting at us'

The corresponding sentence with a definite subject would be

7.8. ta-tira kan-áton el mundúhin
      'The pirates are shooting at us'

In such constructions the indefinite noun phrase may be deleted:

7.9. nway ta-tira kan-áton
      NEG+EXIST DUR-shoot at-us
      'No one is shooting at us'

In 7.9 the inflectional prefix signals an existential interpretation of nway; compare

    7.10. nway tira kan-áton
             NEG+PER shoot at-us
             'We weren't shot at'

Unlike the corresponding forms in Philippine languages, the Zamboangueño existential is an inflectable verb. Either tene or tyéne can be inflected, the former apparently preferred in the future. There is also a special past form tenía, which occurs occasionally.

    7.11. el kwarénta i dós tenía yo trés íha
             'In 1942 I had three daughters' (formal style)

    7.12. káda bés ke ta-tene kami beláda, sila amo el ta-bayla
             'Every time we had a (school) program, they were
             the ones who danced'

In constructions where tene acts as a pro-verb (#4), as in 7.12 above, its inflectional possibilities remain the same except that the imperative, with tene, is possible:

    7.13. tyéne yo myédo
             'I'm afraid'

    7.14. no mas tene myédo
             'Don't be afraid any more'

    7.15. el ta-tene yo myédo basi' bira ole' el mundúhin
             The DUR-EXIST I fear perchance (FUT)-turn again the
             pirate
             'What worries me is that the pirates might come back'

The negative of the pro-verb tene remains nway:

    7.16. el raton nway myédo kon el gato
             'The rat does not fear the cat'

There is another pattern of expressing possession involving the use of the particle kon 'with. '

7.17. kon búngga pa ese byého
       'That old man still has some areca'

which has the same meaning as 7.3, tyene pa búngga ese byého. The
difference is syntactic; kon, unlike tyéne, is not a full word and post-
initials, such as pa 'still,' cannot follow it. The negative of kon is
sin:

7.18. sin búngga ya ese byého
       'That old man has no more areca'

Philippine languages, along with full-word existentials, also commonly have existential particles, e.g. Tagalog, Cebuano, Hiligaynon may.
No Philippine language to my knowledge, however, has a negative with
corresponding syntactic properties, cf. Cebuano:

       adúna pa siya y búnga 'He still has some areca'
       may búnga pa siya 'He still has some areca'
       wala' na siya y búnga 'He has no more areca'

in comparison with Zamboangueño:

       tyéne pa le búngga
       kon búngga pa le
       nway mas ele búngga
       sin bungga ya le

Zamboangueño is clearly using Spanish forms according to Philippine
grammatical patterns and can even be said to have filled in a gap in
the Philippine pattern with sin. The particles kon and sin, unlike the
Philippine particles however, cannot be used without definite noun
phrase (possessor) complements.

8. Locative phrases. A locative verb phrase specifies the
location of a definite thing or person. It consists of a deletable locative verb in construction with a locative noun phrase. The resulting
locative phrase takes a definite noun phrase complement:

8.1. (esta) na buyu'an el búngga
      (BE) LOC betel container the areca
      'The areca is in the betel box' (cf. 7.1)

The underlying locative verb, esta, is normally deleted in surface
structure, the locative noun phrase becoming the surface predicate:

8.2. na tyángge pa gale' si ching
       'Ching seems to be still at the market'

esta occasionally occurs in formal or emphatic speech:

8.3. detras di dadong esta syémpre ta-man-hutik-hutik si
       ebanghelína
       'Behind Dadong (Pres. Macapagal), Evangelina (his
       wife) continually stands whispering'

The verb esta, reduced to ta-, must occur when the locative noun
phrase is represented by one of the deictic locatives (a)ki 'here,'
(a)lyi 'there,' (a)lya 'yonder.' The resulting forms are ta-ki, ta-lyi,
and ta-lya, respectively.

8.4. Mira bos, ta-ki el búngga
       'Look, the areca is here'

The negative of esta is nway:

8.5. nway na buyu'an el búngga
       'The areca is not in the betel container'

8.6. nway lyi el búngga
       'The areca is not there' (cf. 7.2)

8.7. sábe yo ta-ki el dwényo péro nway man
       'I thought the owner was here but he is not'

The word nway thus is the negative of the perfective prefix ya-, of
the existential verb tyéne, and of the locative verb esta:

8.8. ya-anda le ⟶ nway le anda
       'He went'   'He didn't go'

8.9. tyéne le kerída ⟶ nway le kerída
       'He has a mistress'   'He doesn't have a mistress'

8.10. ta-ki le → nway le aki
      'He is here' 'He is not here'

The verb esta is not inflectable and has no tense or aspect implications. There is, however, a special form estába to specify former location different from present location:

8.11. antes estába yo na márgos
      'Previously, I was in Margosatubig'

8.12. dónde tu estába
      'Where are you from,' 'Where were you'

8.13. estába yo saka yélo
      'I was (somewhere) getting ice'

8.14. del lúnes estába yo na tyángge ta-kompra arros
      'Last Monday I was at the market buying rice'

The word estába also occurs as an adverb with much the same meaning as antes 'previously':

8.15. ya-tyéne yo kerída estába = ya-tyene yo kerída antes
      'I had a mistress before'

8.16. bungkaw yo estába
      'I was a lazy slob before'

9. Mistaken thinking. There is a common special verb pensába 'to have thought mistakenly' which is uninflectable and unnegatible:

9.1. pensába yo ya-sale le
     'I thought he had left' (but he hadn't)

9.2. pensába yo nway le sale
     'I didn't think he had left' (but he had)

The form pensaría also occurs occasionally with apparently the same meaning. Neither of these forms can be considered part of the paradigm of the verb <u>pensa</u> 'to think (about something), to cogitate,' which is regularly inflected in all categories.

10. Verb derivation. There are three modifications of verb forms which are not part of the inflectional paradigm and which do not alter the form class of the verb. The suffix -<u>(h)an</u> attached to simple verbs or to cognate objects with verbal meaning signifies mutual plural: two or more subjects are simultaneously agents and objects. Simple verbs suffixed by -<u>(h)an</u> are no longer simple verbs in canonical form and must be verbalized by <u>man-</u> (#3) before being inflected:

10.1. <u>ya-man-konosehan sila</u>
'They became acquainted with each other'

10.2. <u>byen borrácho gat kami, poréso ta-man-pelyahan</u>
'We were very drunk; that's why we fought each other'

10.3. <u>ta-ase gale' apásan ese dós jíp</u>
'Those two jeeps seem to be racing each other'

Duplication of a simple verb, the stem of a derived verb, or a cognate object signifies emphatic, repetitive, or continuing action:

10.4. <u>kon tódo el óhos incháo korre-korre na kamíno</u>
'With both eyes swollen, he ran around in the street'

10.5. <u>kyére-kyére kami peska</u>
'We really like to fish'

10.6. <u>básta uwak pírme ta-man-uwak-uwak</u>
'If a crow, always crowing'

10.7. <u>bwéno gayot éle pára ase saláma-saláma kon el maga hénte</u>
'She is very good at treating people as equals'

A more emphatic form of duplication uses -<u>ki</u>- between duplicated forms:

10. 8. ta-kamina-ki-kamina yo, no-sábe ya yo dónde ya-gindǎ
        'I walked and walked without knowing where I was going

10. 9. maskin entéro día ase kita lága'-ki-lága', hindi'
        syémpre ay-keda duru el pelyého
        'Even if we keep boiling (them) all day, the shells will
        never get hard'

NOTE

[1] The research reported here was conducted with the support
of the National Science Foundation. I am grateful to F. Bustamente,
Z. Concepcion, S. Pajarito, S. Reynolds, and the Arabe family of
Zamboanga City for invaluable assistance in the field.

REFERENCES

Fillmore, Charles. 1968. The case for case. Universals in linguis-
    tic theory, ed. by E. Bach and R. Harms, pp. 1-90. New
    York: Holt, Rinehart and Winston.
Greenberg, Joseph H. 1966. Language universals. Current trends
    in linguistics, ed. by T. A. Sebeok. Vol. 3, Theoretical
    foundations, pp. 61-112. The Hague: Mouton.
Jakobson, Roman. 1957. Shifters, verbal categories and the Russian
    verb. Cambridge: Harvard University, Russian Language
    Project.

17 | The Genesis of Kinds of People in the Sulu Archipelago

A universal human preoccupation, by no means restricted to social scientists, is the game of sorting each other out into kinds of people, the game of ascribing and assuming social identities. Not only are the outcomes of this game consequential for all social activities, but also the playing of the game is itself a major social activity. An _ethnic_ identity is, roughly, a social taxon of major scope: one that embraces other social identities, that has salience across a wide range of social situations, and that is construed to be relatively inevitable and immutable. It is a taxon that gives warrant for ascribing and explaining the characteristic behaviors of its members. Anthropologists are in the business of dividing up the world into kinds of people so as best to account for the behavior of people as products of the kind of people they are, as products, as we say, of their "cultures." But everyone else in the world, all the "natives" out there, are in the same business. And just as the best way to do this sorting, the one that reveals the "real" kinds, is problematic and subject to much contention among anthropologists, so it is for natives. This paper examines the game of ethnic classification, with its social functions and consequences, as played by locals and outsiders, including anthropologists, for the last four hundred years in one small corner of the world, the Sulu Archipelago of the southwestern Philippines.[1]

The Sulu Archipelago is a chain of tropical islands and coral reefs extending some 300 miles between northeastern Borneo and the Zamboanga Peninsula of southwestern Mindanao. Lovely as they are, these are not remote and tranquil Pacific isles. Lying astride trade routes, ethnic boundaries, religious cleavages, and political frontiers, the archipelago, named for swirling ocean currents, the _sulug_, has been a vortex drawing local populations into incessant conflict with

each other and with a succession of outside powers.[2] The battle lines
in this long history of strife were not simply laid down by different
kinds of people coming together and clashing because they were different. Individuals and local communities seek allies, those of a kind,
and discern enemies, those of another kind, in their struggles, not
only for military survival, but also for economic gain, self-esteem,
and bare subsistence. In these struggles, ethnic labels, as well as
swords and machine guns, slaves and pesos, dried fish and sea cucum-
bers, have been weapons. The diversity of kinds of people, the ethnic
diversity, now seen in the area has been both a contributor to, and a
product of, local social interactions.

An External View

Whatever one's opinion of the reality of the objects of someone's conceptions, the placing of those objects by someone into a
class of like objects is a conceptual activity, a mental feat. This is
equally true whether the objects being grouped into kinds are rocks,
trees, gods, or people. And it is equally true whether those doing the
grouping are natives or investigators of natives. The various grids of
ethnic diversity imposed on Sulu populations by their own members and
by outsiders, including anthropologists, are conceptual grids. To provide a reference grid, an "objective framework" across which to display these conceptual systems, I will use linguistic relationships
derived from conventional, but by no means uncontroversial, methods
of historical linguistics. By "objective" I mean that the derivation of
these relations is external to the other conceptual systems being described. I do not mean that they are necessarily any more "real" and
any less "interpretive" than other schemes. On the other hand, they
are not arbitrary and their use is not merely heuristic. From these
relationships we can make inferences about historical occurrences
that provide critical input to our understanding of ethnic labeling and
ethnic differentiation in the region.

Apart from Zamboangueño, the Philippine Creole Spanish
spoken by Zamboanga and Basilan Christians, all the languages of the
region are unambiguously related as Western Authronesian languages.
The languages, other than Zamboangueño, spoken by Christians in any
number all belong to a closely related subgroup of Philippine languages

which includes the "Bisayan" languages of the central Philippines, the languages of northeastern Mindanao, and, somewhat more remotely, Tagalog, the language of the Manila area (Zorc 1975, Pallesen 1977). The most common Austronesian language heard among local Christians is Cebuano Bisayan, although Tagalog is finding increasing use as a secondary language. One language spoken by Moslems, Tausug, also belongs to this Central Philippine Group. Even though it shows strong areal convergence with the Samalan languages, Tausug clearly has its closest affiliation with languages now spoken by Christians in northeastern Mindanao (Pallesen 1977). The locally spoken language closest to Tausug is Cebuano Bisayan.

Subanun, the language spoken by Zamboanga pagans, and Magindanao-Maranao, the language of central Mindanao Moslems, are about equidistinct from each other and the languages of the Bisayan group.

The remaining languages of the region stand apart as a separate subgroup of mutually very closely related languages and dialects without close affiliations to any local language outside the group. This subgroup of Samalan languages represents a classic dialect chain extending from northeastern Borneo along the Sulu Archipelago to the southern coast of the Zamboanga Peninsula. A Samalan language is also spoken by a number of widely scattered communities in eastern Indonesia, and there is a Samalan language spoken by Christians on a small island in the midst of the Bisayan-speaking central Philippines (Capul Island off northwestern Samar). This far-flung distribution of a very closely related set of languages, only recently well documented (Pallesen 1977), has important historical implications that challenge both local traditions and published scholarly accounts. What concerns us here, however, is the way in which, within this dialect-chain continuum where language boundaries are difficult to define objectively, ethnic boundaries are drawn and ethnic identities established.

Whereas the evidence for these linguistic relations is independent of local conceptual systems—no one locally, Moslem or Christian, would consider Tausug a "Bisayan" language—the labels for languages in this "objective" framework are necessarily drawn from locally applied ethnolinguistic terms. Only in one case does this practice cause some difficulty. It is necessary to distinguish "Samalan" as a set of languages, established on external evidence, from the internally applied ethnic labels sama, a label applied to themselves by some communities of Samalan speakers, and "Samal" and "Bajao," labels applied (in varying shapes) by outsiders to some peoples who happen to speak Samalan languages. (For this reason I have avoided Pallesen's term "Sama-Bajaw" for what I call here "Samalan.")

It is to concepts of kinds of people that have developed locally in social interactions and social conflicts that we now turn, beginning with a rather gross category instituted by the Spanish, the notion of "Moro."

The "Moros"

My favorite ethnographic map of the Philippines is one published in 1882 by the German scholar Blumentritt. This map has 51 ethnic groups, Pagan, Christian, and Moslem, all numbered, labeled, and carefully colored in. One color, green, covers all the Moslem areas and is labeled simply Die Piratenstämme von Mondanao und Sulu, 'The pirate tribes of Mindanao and Sulu.' This may be ridiculous ethnology, but it is also a graphic portrayal of the actual form of outsiders' views over the past four hundred years of the kinds of peoples in the southern Philippines. This form has received its shape from the warfare between Christian and Moslem that has prevailed in the Philippines since early Spanish times, warfare that has made the enemy appear as a unit, and, indeed, has imposed a unity upon them. To this enemy the Spanish gave the label "Moro," an appellation that had already seen service in their confrontations on the other side of the globe with the Moors of Spain and North Africa. In the Philippines the word "Moro," both in Spanish and in languages spoken by Philippine Christians, quickly became not only a religious label but an ethnic one as well, a label for a social identity to which cultural behaviors, usually unpleasant ones, and even physical features could be ascribed. A Spanish historian in 1888 introduces his two-volume history of "La piratería malayo-mahometana" with a description of the "Moro race" ("Los moros tienen ojos oscuros, rasgados horizontalmente y entornados ... piernas torcidas haci

afuera ... ") and its customs (Montero y Vidal 1888: 85). A Spanish
officer, a veteran of Moro campaigns, writes in 1893 to the Governor
General that "The Moro race is completely antithetic to the Spanish
and will ever be our eternal enemy" (quoted in Saleeby 1908: 386).

The ethnicitization of this antagonistic religious boundary
entailed a conceptualization of Moslem and Christian Filipinos as
kinds of people fundamentally different from each other, a view that
provides a warrant for a search for demarcations of difference—from
psychic antipathy to twisted feet—whose objective justifiability hardly
matters. Such a conceptualization not only serves to erect boundaries, it also works to obscure differences among those construed to
be the same. A Dutch naval officer visiting the Spanish garrison on
Jolo in 1879 complained that the Spanish knew nothing of local languages
and ways of life; they called everyone a "Moro" who was not an "Indio"
—a Christian Filipino ally (van Verschuer 1883: 4). As we shall see,
the Spanish could, and upon occasion did, make further distinctions,
but they also could, and frequently did, rhetorically present the
"Moros" as a solid block of hostile ethnicity.

The Spanish usage of "Moro" was carried over by the Americans, not only the military, who, under Pershing, had their turn at
"Moro wars, " but also by scholars. The American anthropologist
A. L. Kroeber published, in 1909, an ethnographic map of the Philippines which, in the spirit of Blumentritt, distinguishes eight different
kinds of Christians and seventeen different kinds of pagans. The Moslem areas are again colored a uniform green and that color on the map
key is labeled simply "Moro." The first important American scholarly
study of Philippine Moslems (Saleeby 1905) was titled "Studies in Moro
History, Law and Religion. " Use of the word continued into the post-
war period (cf. Kuder 1945), but it has now happily been abandoned in
the scholarly literature, a response not so much to a sense of classificatory inappropriateness as to an awareness of Moslem objections
to its derogatory implications. The use of "Moro, " both as an ethnic
label and as an epithet of abuse, is still, however, very much alive
throughout the Christian Philippines.

One can easily point to distortions in the realities of cultural
and linguistic differentiation caused by the boundaries erected around
the concept of "Moro. " By some measures there is certainly as much

diversity within the boundary as across it. More serious, however, for understanding the region has been the way the notion of "Moro" has obscured the real nature and extent of locally conceived internal ethnic differentiation, a distortion that could lead Kroeber to write, "It is true that the Moro are not wholly uniform, especially on the side of language; but the differences between them have not been primarily ethnic, as in the remainder of the Philippines, but political" (Kroeber 1909: 56). In fact, the worki ngs of internal ethnicity are critical to understanding the Philippine Moslem world. Nevertheless, it is still true that the boundary between Moslem and Christian looks equally formidable from both sides of the fence. And from the Moslem side, as well as the Christian, the boundary gives the appearance of being constructed of ethnic substance. Sulu Moslems, both when identifying themselves as Moslems or when attributing qualities (in this case, usually favorable ones) to themselves as Moslems, use the expression bangsa muslim, bangsa being a term for a kind of social identity with many of the qualities of our fuzzy enough notion of "ethnicity." It includes not only one's religious identity but also one's 'ethnic group' identity (in the sense of being, for example, tausuug, yakan, sama, lannang 'Chinese,' or milikan 'American'), one's hereditary title, if any, and even, in some contexts (at least in Yakan), one's sex. What bangsa never includes are relational identities such as with kin or friends, achieved statuses such as occupation or political office, and temporary matters such as current residence (as opposed to irrevocable provenience). It is those social identities which are construed to be absolute, inherent, and permanent that qualify as bangsa.

        In theory, becoming a Moslem is an achievable status, rather easily achievable in terms of formal requirements. But locally there is no question that being bangsa muslim implies more than having affirmed faith in Islam. It implies a cultural tradition as well, an inherent identity very much a part of the kind of person one is. From the Moslem point of view, across the Moslem-Christian boundary lie the bisayaq, a label that is almost the mirror image of the "Moro." For Sulu Moslems, a bisayaq is any Christian Filipino (but not other Christians; not, for example, Spaniards or Americans). And any Moslem will tell you that the term also means 'slave.' Like "Moro," the term bisayaq is an epithet of abuse, as one will quickly learn if one should ask a Moslem to do a task considered demeaning: "I am no bisayaq" is likely to be the indignant reply. Just as Christians use "Moro" for any language Moslems happen to speak, so Moslems use bisayaq for what is in fact an even greater range of linguistic diversity from the creole Spanish of Zamboanga to a variety of Austronesian languages. Of course, depending on the sophistication of the speaker, further distinctions might be made. Since it is almost impossible for any Moslem to escape some contact with the Philippine Christian world of soldiers, jailors, officials, and, formerly, slaves, the level of sophistication is likely to be higher than among Christians, who, unless they live within, or on the boundary of, the Moslem world, are likely to know of "Moros" only by hearsay. Of course they hear plenty.

Even though they both contain a strong component of ethnic meaning, there remains a critical difference between the outsiders' concept of "Moro" and the Moslem notion of bangsa muslim. The latter concept embraces all Moslems of the world, quite explicitly a superordinate identity that incorporates people of diverse subordinate "ethnic" bangsa. The concept of "Moro," on the other hand, is more of an ethnic or "tribal" notion, a concept of a local kind of people. Most important, it draws a boundary between Philippine Moslems and the Moslems of neighboring Borneo and eastern Indonesia. At first sight this boundary looks like yet another distortion imposed by the warped view of outsiders. There has never been a single "Moro" state. Not only is there no single "Moro" language, or even a "Moro" subgroup of languages; there has never been a single common lingua franca in use among Philippine Moslems.

This last fact, however, is rather curious. Throughout the coastal areas of the rest of island Southeast Asia, forms of Malay have been used as a commercial lingua franca since well before European times (Collins 1975 provides a well-documented discussion). This usage continues today, reinforced by the quite successful establishment of one form of Malay as the standard language of both Malaysia and Indonesia. In Borneo, and in much of coastal Indonesia, Malay is more than a language, it is an identity. To become Moslem, for local populations, is to masok malayu 'become (literally 'enter') Malay.' Yet, even though the use of Malay had clearly penetrated into the Philippines at the time of Spanish contact, and even though parts of north Borneo were once included in the Sulu state, and even

though there are communities of Sulu and Mindanao Moslems in
Borneo, and even though there has always been continuous trade connecting Sulu and Mindanao with the neighboring Malay world, neither
the Malay language nor Malay identity ever took hold in what was to
become the Philippines. In 1779 the fact that a few people of high
rank in Mindanao could speak Malay was a cause for remark by the
Malay-speaking English visitor Forrest (1779: 329). In 1845, a
Dutch officer reports how some Bornean captives of Sulu slavers
managed to escape because they were able to plot openly against
their captors, who spoke no Malay (Gregor 1845: 314). Today, even
though the Malay language has tremendous prestige as a conceptual
object, it has no practical use as a lingua franca among Philippine
Moslems (Frake 1980b). Yet there is no substitute. No local language, and certainly no European language, has the role in Sulu and
Mindanao that Malay has elsewhere.

The adjacency of the boundaries of the outsider's concept of
"Moro" and the local concept of "Malay" cannot be accidental. The
Spanish-induced concept of "Moro," ethnographically fragile as it may
be, has both reflected and created a local reality. Those who become
"Moros" in the eyes of the Spanish thereby came to share a common
fate, a fate that was to have lasting consequences for their lives.
Even though never effectively subjugated as compliant members of a
Philippine state, those Moslems who came under the sphere of Spanish colonial aspirations became sufficiently isolated by that experience
to prevent them, by language or self-conception, from becoming a
part of the adjoining Malay world. The "Moros" became—and remain
today—militant marginals to an encompassing political power, within
its boundaries but outside its laws. And the condition of being outside
the law, of being "outlaws," becomes a cultural attribute of a construed ethnic group. Thus the "Moros" become the "pirate tribes of
Mindanao and Sulu." (For a Sardinian parallel, substituting "bandits"
for "pirates," see Moss 1979.)

"Sea Gypsies"

The first European account of Mindanao and Sulu, that of
Magellan's chronicler Pigafetta (1906, v. 2: 53), notes that off the
tip of Zamboanga Peninsula they passed an island whose people

"make their dwelling in boats and do not live otherwise." Subsequent accounts, down to the present, have sorted out maritime peoples—strand dwellers, boat nomads, and pirates—for special notice and naming. Portuguese voyagers, traveling between Malacca and the Moluccas in the early sixteenth century, also recorded the existence of maritime peoples, pirates and thieves who preyed on shipwrecks, called "celates" and "bajus" (the spelling varies), apparently labels for two different groups (Pires 1944: 147; Jacobs 1971: 168, 196, 343). The first term presumably refers to the various "sea people" (Malay orang laut) of the Malacca Straits (Malay selat). The second term must be the Malay word bajo or bajao, used locally and by outsiders down to the present to label certain maritime peoples of eastern Indonesia, Borneo, and Sulu. This word, its various forms being here represented as "Bajao," has been one of the most persistent and consistently used ethnonyms in island Southeast Asia. It seems never, however, to have been accepted as their label for themselves by any of the people to whom it has been applied.

The English sea captain Thomas Forrest, writing in 1779, recorded the salient characteristics of these maritime folk: "The Badjoo people, called Oran Badjoo, are a kind of itinerant fisherman, said to come originally from Johore, at the east entrance to the Straits of Malacca. They live chiefly in small covered boats, on the coasts of Borneo and Celebes and adjacent islands. Others dwell close to the sea on these islands, their houses being raised on poles, a little distance into the sea, always at the mouths of rivers. They are Mahometans" (Forrest 1779: 372). The apparent significance of the label "Bajao" for those who have used it has been to designate peoples who stand apart by virtue of their mode of life, their extreme maritime orientation, living on, or on the edge of, the sea and deriving the bulk of their livelihood from it. The application of the term has clearly not been grounded on careful linguistic or ethnographic observation either on the part of local neighbors or by Western outsiders. Sopher's (1965) survey of the literature on sea nomads is, through no fault of his own, devoid of useful linguistic information. The use of the term appears to resemble that of many exonyms applied throughout Southeast Asia to the "hill people" of some island or region, labels like "Dayak" of Borneo and "Igorot" of Luzon, each of which has been applied to peoples of diverse linguistic, cultural, and internally perceived ethnic affiliations. It is rather surprising,

then, to learn, as we only recently have, that all these scattered
peoples throughout eastern Indonesia, Borneo, and the Philippines
who have been called "Bajao" by outsiders do in fact have a common
name for themselves, sama, and do in fact speak languages of a single,
distinct subgroup, the Samalan languages. Not all people who call
themselves sama have been called "Bajao," and not all speakers of
Samalan languages call themselves sama, but, so far as I know, all
people called "Bajao" by their neighbors and by Western observers
are Samalan-speaking sama. This usage represents a rather remarkable vindication of an ecologically applied ethnic label.

        Among ethnic labels used in this part of the world, both
"Bajao" and sama stand out in their lack of any transparent meaning
or locality designation; compare, in contrast, orang laut 'sea people'
or tausuug 'people of Jolo.' Of course, semantic opacity does not
protect ethnonyms from imputations of meaningfulness. Speculations
about the origins and motivations of both these words are, given the
limited literature, quite plentiful (cf. Sopher 1965: 158-62; Pelras
1972: 156). It is characteristic of names—personal, place, and
ethnic—that one can ask what they "mean," but the answer does not
really matter. Were I to read convincing evidence that "Navaho"
does not really mean "people," this discovery would in no way affect
which people I, or anyone else, called "Navaho." What matters is
not the answer so much as the effort involved in discerning one. The
lack of transparent semantic motivation can make a name, and the
category it labels, seem less ad hoc, more a permanent part of
reality. To possess distinct internally and externally applied names,
both of which share this property, lends a conceptual unity to the
widely scattered peoples who use and receive these names. It is the
naming practice, more than any social or political coherence, that
constitutes these peoples as an "ethnic group." Since an ethnic
group is presumed, and presumes itself, to have a common origin,
the lack of a clear designation of a locality in an ethnonym suggests
a remote and mysterious provenience appropriate to a wandering people.
It makes of ethnic origins a puzzle, a proper topic for a myth. And the
myth exists, a remarkable one firmly entrenched as history in the
scholarly literature and also in the lore and annals of local states.
It is the myth of Johor origin told to Forrest and reported by many
others over the past several hundred years in Celebes, Borneo, and
Sulu (Sopher 1965: 141-42; Pelras 1972: 157-59; Saleeby 1908: 156-57;

Evans 1952: 48-52). Johor, the site of an important Sultanate since the fall of Malacca to the Portuguese in 1511, is located across from Singapore on the Malacca Straits.

There are differing renditions of this myth, but in all cases the question addressed is: "Where did the sama/Bajao come from?" This question has always been a meaningful one to both the sama and their neighbors. The answer always points to somewhere else, somewhere remote, some place famous. Usually that place is Johor. In south Celebes, Borneo, and Sulu these myths have become part of regional political systems, written down in Bugis and Sulu annals, as accounts of the social positions of the Sama in local systems. (I will use "Sama" for people who call themselves sama and are called "Bajao" or "Samal" by outsiders.) The Sulu myth, recounted by Saleeby (1908: 156-57) as history, brings the Sama from Johor early in the fifteenth century to Sulu where they occupied marginal islands and filled positions in the Sulu social system subordinate to the original inhabitants of Jolo, the Tausug. The Sama, according to Saleeby, thus "remained like strangers or guests in the land until a late date."

This story represents a classic case of a myth whose form has been shaped by social and political motives. As history it is not only false but inverted. The linguistic evidence is now indisputable; the homeland of the original Samalan speech community was in the Philippines, in the eastern Sulu-Zamboanga region. The dispersal of Samalan languages from the Philippines into Borneo and Indonesia clearly took place well before the emergence of Tausug on Jolo and the emergence of Johor as a prominent place in the sixteenth century (Pallesen 1977: 165-76). There may of course be some ultimate connection between Samalan speakers and the maritime peoples of the Malacca Straits, but, apart from the myths, there is as yet no evidence of it. None of the linguistic data available from the Straits, exasperatingly meager for such an easily accessible area, points to Samalan affinities (Pelras 1972; Kähler 1948).

Interestingly, the word "Bajao" does not appear in early Spanish accounts, even though it is freely used by English and Dutch visitors to label Sulu populations. This is further evidence that the Spanish sphere of operations was beyond the range of the common use of Malay. During the first two centuries of Spanish records,

there does frequently appear an ethnic label for maritime people,
"Lutao," which then disappears by the nineteenth century. Descriptions, such as those provided by the Jesuit historian Combés (1897:
28.32) writing in the 1660's, as well as some meager, but telling, bits
of linguistic information (Blair and Robertson 1903-9, v. 40: 285)
reveal that "Lutao" was applied, much as the Malay term "Bajao" in
Borneo and Indonesia, to Samalan-speaking, maritime-oriented
peoples. The fact that the Spanish used a Philippine form—lutaw, as
Combés notes, means 'float' in several central Philippine languages
(but not in Samalan)—indicates that this was a locally used exonym,
perhaps an ad hoc description or a derogatory epithet. There is no
use of the label locally today. The "Lutao" were described as Moslems; they were a kind of "Moro," but a different kind from the
"kings" of Sulu and Mindanao to whom, according to Combés, they
were subject. Although the "Lutao" were, like all Sulu peoples,
liable to being labeled as pirates, they could, in some circumstances,
be seen as less implacably hostile than the hard-core "Moros" of
Jolo. Some were even Christianized. Christian Lutao, who lived in
the neighborhood of the Spanish garrison of Zamboanga, served the
Spanish military both against Moslems and, in at least one case, in
1650, against rebellious Christians in the Bisayan Islands (de la
Costa 1961: 413). These Christian allies were lost forever when the
Spanish temporarily abandoned Zamboanga in 1663. There has been
no comparable category of people since. Other "Lutao" fought
against the Spanish on seaborne raids and in pitched battles alongside
the people of Jolo. In such cases, even the Spanish could convince
themselves that not all "Moros" were alike. During one of the seventeenth-century sieges of the Moslem stronghold on Jolo, the Spanish
commander, Corcuera, negotiating with Lady Baluka, the wife of the
Sulu leader, offered safe conduct to any "Lutaos" and other "allies"
fighting with the "Sulus" (the real people of Jolo). The latter, however, must surrender unconditionally. In such a situation, how did
the Spanish propose to determine, and the Moslems to agree, who
was "just a Lutao" and who was a "real Sulu"? Actually, in this case,
a determination was never necessary: as Lady Baluka protracted the
negotiations (perhaps arguing about the true meaning of ethnicity!),
the bulk of the besieged forces, including their leader, managed to
slip away and escape (de la Costa 1961: 388). It is apparent that Spanish and local concepts of ethnic differentiation of the peoples of Sulu
were mutually informed by social interaction, hostile though it may
have been.

"Notorious Pirates"

"Pirate" is a word which, as we have seen, seems naturally to fall together in European languages with the place name "Sulu." All Sulu inhabitants, all the "Moros" and kinds of "Moros," are subject to this ascription (unless they are not seafarers, in which case they become, like the Yakan of Basilan, "bandits"). The label "pirate," however, carries a saliency, an ethnic load, of its own. To be a pirate is to be somebody.

Through the centuries a number of ethnic labels have emerged that can best be glossed by the phrase invariably attached to them: "the most notorious pirates of Sulu." In the sixteenth and seventeenth centuries, two terms appear in the literature, "Camucones" and "Tidong," to label pirates who were especially fierce and who were not Moslem. These peoples carried on devastating raids throughout the Philippines from home bases in western Sulu and northeastern Borneo. The Spanish apparently considered the Camucones and Tidong to be different groups (cf. Barrantes 1878: 41), but descriptions of them and their fate are indistinguishable. Whoever they were, they were frequently at odds with Sulu Moslems. In the late seventeenth century they were soundly defeated by Spanish and Sulu attacks on their home bases (Barrantes 1878: 294-95; Forrest 1779: 16, 373; de la Costa 1961: 545). After that, these notorious pagan pirates disappear as an ethnic identity. The word "tidong," however, survives as a term for pirate in several central and northern Philippine languages (e.g. Hanunóo and Ilocano) and as an ethnic label in northeastern Borneo for agriculturists speaking languages of the Idaan group (Prentice 1970; Sather 1972). Several "Bajao" groups of Celebes have been reported to use "Tidong" as an ethnonym referring to their alleged but unlocatable homeland (Pelras 1972: 163; Vosmaer 1839; Adrianai 1900).

In the nineteenth century the most notorious pirates of Sulu were Moslems. Their label, assumed by themselves and, for a while, accorded to them by others, was "Balangingi" /ba(l)angingiq/. They were Samalan speakers of northeastern Sulu who claimed the small coral island of Balangingi, between Jolo and Basilan, as their home base and identifying provenience. The notorious exploits of the Balangingi as raiders, slavers, and warriors have been reasonably well chronicled (Barrantes 1878; Montero y Vidal 1888; Geoghegan 1975; Warren 1975; Pallesen 1977). In 1848 the Spanish laid waste to their fortress on Balangingi Island and dispersed the survivors, some as far as Luzon. After that, "Balangingi" slips from the literature as an ethnic identity. They do not appear as a "tribe" in the first American inventories of Philippine groups (cf. Barrows 1904), nor are they listed in Kuder's 1945 discussion of "Moro" groups. Locally, however, the Balangingi still cling to their identity and to the memories of past glory which support it.

Local struggles for identity are, of course, carried on in somewhat different terms. Samalan-speaking communities differentiate themselves as kind of <u>sama</u> by attaching a place name indicating provenience (not necessarily current location) to their ethnonym. Thus a <u>sama ubian</u> is a Sama who identifies his home place as Ubian Island. Outside this practice are the nomadic, sometime boat-dwelling Sama (the people who have been called "Bajao" in the English-language literature on Sulu), who, even though they share a central Sulu dialect, cannot claim a named provenience as part of their ethnonym. (When they do acquire a land base, they may desperately proclaim it. Members of one group who moved ashore near a Mobil Gas storage facility outside Zamboanga City were once heard to identify their <u>bangsa</u> to outsiders as <u>sama mobilgas</u>.) Others, in scorn, often accord nomadic Sama epithets like <u>sama luagan</u> and <u>sama palaqu</u>, terms which do not refer to provenience but to their outcast status and boat-dwelling habits. In their own eyes, however, the sea nomads are <u>sama toqongan</u> 'true Sama' (Pallesen 1977: 398).

There is, thus, a fluid hierarchy of Sama identities with nomadic Sama at the bottom of the scale, barely considered Sama at all by outsiders (reflected in the literature by the distinction between "Samal" and "Bajao"), but themselves desperately clinging to an identity as "true Sama." At the other end of the scale are the people who came to call themselves "Balangingi." They rose to the top of the otherwise ill-defined hierarchy of Sama identities by their military and economic achievements. Once there, they, and those who could claim to be like "them," endeavored to promote themselves as more than a kind of Sama, more than a <u>sama baangingiq</u>, but rather as a kind of people different from ordinary Sama, as Balangingi pure and simple. Sama of northeastern Sulu still frequently identify them-

selves simply as Balangingi or even as a kind of Balangingi, e.g.
baangingiq tagtabun 'Balangingi of Tagtabun Island.' These efforts at
self-identification do not carry very far, however. Neighboring groups,
such as the Tausug and the Samalan-speaking Yakan, lump them together with all the other Sama.

The Balangingi, by virtue of their military exploits, were on
the brink of climbing out of Sama identity, of establishing themselves
as a different kind of people. They did not quite succeed. Being a
'notorious pirate' was not enough. Others, with a lot of work, have
played the game better.

The Yakan

Not all Samalan speakers are oriented to the sea. There are
Samalan agriculturists in northeastern Borneo, in the southern interior of Zamboanga Peninsula, and on Basilan Island at the northeastern
end of the Sulu Archipelago. In spite of their shared deviance from
the norms of Samalan ecological adaptation, these three groups have
not shared similar fates as ethnic identities. The Bornean group is
merged with coastal Samalans, both by outsiders as "Bajao" and by
themselves as sama (Evans 1952). Members of the Zamboanga group,
some 11,000 people who practice swidden agriculture much like their
Subanun-speaking pagan and Moslem neighbors, consider themselves
sama (Pallesen 1977: 394-95). From an outsider's point of view, however, they are practically a non-entity. To my knowledge, apart from
Pallesen, they have never been mentioned in any literature as one of
the "tribes" of Mindanao. Locals, if aware of them at all, are likely
to merge them with Subanun-speaking Moslems in the category "Kalibugan" (literally 'mixed up,' 'half-breed' in several central Philippine
languages), an exonym perhaps best glossed as 'an ecologically anomalous Moslem.' As befits an anomalous category, the "Kalibugan"
have a local reputation as "notorious sorcerers." The only people I
have ever encountered who admit to being "Kalibugan" are Subanun-
speaking Moslems anxious to disassociate themselves from the label
"Subanun" (subanon, subanen, subanqun) locally associated with wine-
drinking, pig-eating pagans. If the Balangingi have been striving to
rise above Sama identity, and, if the sea nomads have been in danger
of sinking below it, the—what do I call them?—"Zamboanga agricultural

Samalans" have almost managed to disappear altogether as an ethnic
identity—which may in fact have been their game.

There can be no doubt about what to call the Basilan Samalan
agriculturists. They are the Yakan. That is what they call themselves,
and that is what everyone else calls them. The name means nothing
else. It has no variants in form. No one ever calls them, or remotely
considers them to be "Sama" even though the Samalan affinity of their
language is readily apparent and readily admitted by the Yakan. The
Yakan, whom Combés (1897) in the 1660's labels Sameacan (presumably from something like sama yakan), have succeeded over the past
several hundred years in completely shedding their Sama identity.
They have worked hard at being different. They have had a fierce
and independent reputation since at least the time Combés recorded
the exploits of the first known Yakan "bandit," a man named Tabaco;
they shun the sea; they take pride in not being able to dance (dancing
is a Sama hallmark); they build distinctive and beautiful concave-
roofed houses; they live in scattered neighborhoods rather than,
Sama style, in tightly clustered villages; they wear unusual and colorful clothes, including, for women, what look like riding breeches
instead of wrap-around skirts. They are noted for many unique customs. The Yakan, in other words, are very ethnic.[3] They have suc-
needed so well at this game that outsiders, including some anthropological investigators, continually speculate about the origins of this
interesting tribe. Among Zamboanga intellectuals there has been a
split among those who favor a Papuan origin and those who favor a
Tibetan origin. I am deemed a failure in these circles because,
after all these years of work with the Yakan, I have never solved the
problem of where the Yakan came from.

Being successfully "ethnic," as the Yakan have, doesn't
come cheap. The Yakan have been able to afford their distinctive
and colorful identity by engaging in relatively prosperous subsistence
and commercial agriculture, by their ability and willingness to fight
off Christian and Tausug encroachment, and by their exploitation of
a strategic position for legal and illegal commerce on the frontiers
of the Moslem and Christian worlds. Their remarkable conceptual
ethnic unity, however, has never really been successfully transformed
into an effective political unity (Frake 1980a). The ultimate escape
from Sama identity was achieved by another people, those of the

island of Jolo, who had the resources to build a semblance of real power over much of the region. These are the people now known as the Tausug.

The Tausug

The widely scattered peoples who call themselves sama have never constituted a political unity, nor have local Sama communities displayed significant political integration as independent entities. Rather, communities of Sama, whether ashore or afloat, typically occupy marginal positions in an encompassing, loosely integrated, commercially based political system of different ethnic identification: Buginese, Ternatean, Malay, or, in Sulu, Tausug. In each case there must be rather strong boundary-maintaining devices preventing the absorption of the Sama into a more prestigeous and powerful identity. The Sulu case is especially problematic. In that archipelago, the Sama are in the majority and their island territories surround the Tausug enclave on the island of Jolo. In such circumstances how did Tausug ethnicity emerge and persist as an identity distinct from and superordinate to the Sama?

Today, within Sulu, Tausug identity is consistently distinguished from that of other Moslems, all of whom are Samalan-speaking. The island of Jolo (Tawsug su(l)ug, Samalan su(l)uk) is not only the Tausug home base and the source of their ethnonym (tausuug 'people of Jolo'), but it is also, by local lore, their undisputed place of origin. No one locally ever speculates about where the Tausug came from. This unproblematic clarity of local conceptions of Tausug ethnicity did not arise out of the nature of things; it has been a social accomplishment of major proportions, one that has successfully fostered a complete inversion of historical fact.

The badge of this nicely labeled identity is the Tausug language, a language which, in spite of having much in common with local Samalan languages, is, nevertheless, very sharply distinct from any of them. It is quite obviously more akin to the Bisayan languages spoken by Christians in the central Philippines. Its closest linguistic affiliations are with languages of northeastern Mindanao, especially the language of Butuan at the mouth of the Agusan River.

Tausug, then, is a language whose speakers are concentrated on one island in the midst of a Samalan sea, a language with little dialect differentiation (in marked contrast to Samalan), and a language whose closest affinities are far from Jolo across areas occupied by more distantly related languages. These simple and indisputable facts, so long ignored by linguistically blind scholars, allow no doubt that it is the Tausug language which is recently intrusive to Sulu, an archipelago that is, in fact, the homeland of Samalan languages.

The language was intrusive, but there is good reason to believe that it was Samalan speakers from Jolo, not outside invaders, who instigated the process that led to the emergence of Tausug identity. Pallesen (1977), in an exhaustive comparative study that focused on Tausug-Samalan convergences, concludes that Tausug emerged from a bilingual community of Samalan-speaking men and Tausug women. He suggests that this bilingual community began in a trading center set up, as one of many in the central Philippines, by traders from, then Samalan-speaking, Jolo. Jolo was a major commercial center in the China trade and the Arab spice trade well before the split of Tausug from northeastern Mindanao languages. As traders returned with families to Jolo, Tausug became established there as well, originally as part of a bilingual speech community. These events, according to Pallesen (pp. 338-75), must have begun around the thirteenth century, several hundred years or so before the coming of Islam to the islands. Increasing commercial prosperity, the coming of Islam, which the Jolo people embraced with more fervor than their neighbors, the war with the Spanish, and, linked with all the rest, the rise of the Sulu Sultanate with the apparatus of hereditary titles, all must have fostered the rise of a separate identity (cf. Brown 1973 for some Bornean parallels). The people of Jolo nailed down their supremacy by becoming a different kind of people from their neighbors. The exclusive adoption of the imported language was the critical instrument in this endeavor. The myth of Johor origin portraying the Sama as recent arrivals in Sulu, as guests and servants of the Tausug, secured Tausug identity in their own eyes, in the eyes of the Sama themselves, and in the eyes of Western observers. At the time of Combés, in the seventeenth century, these processes seem still to have been occurring. At that time "Tausug," or something equivalent like "Joloano," was not a prominent enough identity to merit inclusion in his list of the principal "nations" of Mindanao,

but he did record that the original founders of Jolo came from Butuan.
History had not yet been completely inverted in 1660. (Blair and
Robertson 1903-9, v. 40: 100, 126; for ethnographic description of
the Tausug, see Kiefer 1969.)

The ethnic boundary that arose between Tausug and Sama
helped shape dimensions of ethnic differentiation and ethnic ranking
that were to prevail in local attributions of identity. The Tausug
became associated with the commercial, political, and religious
center of Moslem Sulu; the Sama fell into positions peripheral to this
central place. The Tausug have become predominantly land-oriented
agriculturists; the Sama are thought of as preeminently maritime,
deriving their subsistence from sea and strand. The Tausug see
themselves as warlike, proud, and haughty; the Sama are seen as
more peaceful, tractable, and humble. The Tausug ends of these
dimensions of "central-peripheral," "land-sea," "war-peace" are
the prestigious ends. When Sama become warlike, as did the Balangingi, they become something more than ordinary Sama. When Samalan speakers approach the Tausug ends of the majority of these dimensions, they can become, like the Yakan, something clearly not Sama
at all. At the other extreme of these scales, the further one goes to
sea, the more one wanders from the central places, the meeker one
presents oneself, the lower becomes one's position in the scheme of
things. There, afloat on their houseboats, are the nomadic Sama, in
the eyes of their neighbors, poor, powerless, docile, barely Moslem,
but still, in their own eyes—and in mine—the sama togongan, the
'true Sama.'

NOTES

[1] Data are from the literature cited and from personal field
work among Subanun, Yakan, and Zamboangueños and some field
experience among Sama and Tausug of eastern Sulu and Sama of
north Maluku, Indonesia. The limitations of my own experience are
somewhat mitigated by the vast amount I have learned over the years
from colleagues who have worked in the area, especially Harold
Conklin, James Fox, Robert Fox, William Geoghegan, Thomas
Kiefer, Linda Klug, Carol Molony, Kemp Pallesen, Robert Randall,
and Gerald Rixhon. I am grateful to the Netherlands Institute for

Advanced Study and its helpful staff for providing the opportunity and
facilities for researching and writing this paper.

[2] The form su(l)ug means ocean current in Tausug. It is also
the name of the island of Jolo, known for whirlpool-like tide rips in
its vicinity. In Samalan languages the name of the island, but not
the word for 'current,' is su(l)uk. The Spanish recorded the name
of the island as "Joló" at a time when Spanish "j" represented [š].
After Spanish "j" shifted to [x], locally in all languages [h], a distinction arose between Jolo, the island, and Sulu, the archipelago.

[3] For a description of the maintenance of Yakan identity
beyond Basilan, in the midst of a Sama community, see Molony 1969.

REFERENCES

Adriani, N. 1900. De Talen der Togian-Eilanden. Tijdschrift
        voor Indische Taal-, Land-en Volkenkunde 42: 428-90,
        539-66.
Aernout, W. 1885. Woordenlijst der Tidoengsche Taal. Indische
        Gids. 1: 536.
Barrantes, Vincente. 1878. Guerras piráticas de Filipinas contra
        mindanaos y joloanos. Madrid: M. G. Hernandez.
Barrows, David. 1904. Second Annual Report of the Chief of the
        Ethnological Survey for the Philippine Islands. Report of
        the Philippine Commission, Part 2. Washington, D.C.:
        Annual Reports of the War Department VI, 1903, pp. 769-89.
Blair, E. H., and J. A. Robertson, eds. 1903-9. The Philippine
        Islands. 55 vols. Cleveland: Arthur H. Clark.
Blumentritt, F. 1882. Versuch einer Ethnographie der Philippinen.
        Petermann's Mittheilungen, Erganzungsheft 67. Gotha.
Brown, D. E. 1973. Hereditary rank and ethnic history: an analysis
        of Brunei historiography. Journal of Anthropological
        Research 19: 113-22.
Collins, James T. 1975. Ambonese Malay and creolization theory.
        Department of Linguistics, University of Chicago, ms.
Combés, Francisco. 1897. Historia de Mindanao y Jolo (1667).
        W. E. Retana, ed. Madrid: Viuda de M. Minuesa.
de la Costa, H. S. J. 1961. The Jesuits in the Philippines, 1581-
        1768. Cambridge: Harvard University Press.

Evans, Ivor H. N. 1952. Notes on the Bajaus and other coastal tribes of North Borneo. Journal of the Malayan Branch of the Royal Asiatic Society 25: 48-55.

Forrest, Thomas. 1779. A voyage to New Guinea and the Moluccas from Balambangan. London: G. Scott.

Frake, C. O. 1980a. Kin and supporters among the Yakan. Language and cultural description, essays by Charles O. Frake. Selected and introduced by Anwar Dil. Stanford: Stanford University Press.

_____. 1980b. Languages in Yakan culture. Language and cultural description, essays by Charles O. Frake. Selected and introduced by Anwar Dil. Stanford: Stanford University Press.

Geoghegan, W. 1975. Balangingi. Ethnic groups of insular Southeast Asia. Frank Lebar, ed. Vol. 2, pp. 84-85. New Haven: Human Relations Area Files.

Gregory, F. A. A. 1845. Aanteekeninggen en beschouwingen betrekkelijk de zeeroovers en hunne rooverijen in de Indische Archipel, alsmede aangaande Magindanao en de Soolo Archipel. Tijdschrift voor Nederlands Indië 7.2: 300-337.

Jacobs, Hubert Th. Th., S.J., ed. 1971. A treatise on Moluccas (c. 1544). Probably the preliminary version of António Galvao's lost História das Molucas. Rome: Jesuit Historical Institute.

Kähler, H. 1948. Ethnographische und linguistiche Studien von den Orang Laut der Insel Rangsang. Anthropos.

Kiefer, Thomas M. 1969. Tausug armed conflict: the military activity in a Philippine Moslem society. Research Series No. 7. Department of Anthropology, University of Chicago.

Kroeber, A. L. 1919. Peoples of the Philippines. New York: American Museum.

Kuder, Edward. 1945. The Moros in the Philippines. Far Eastern Quarterly 4: 119-26.

Molony, Carol. 1969. Multilingualism and social behavior in the southern Philippines. Ph.D. dissertation, Stanford University.

Montero y Vidal, Jose. 1888. Historia de la piratería malayo-mahometana en Midanao, Joló y Borneo. 2 vols. Madrid: M. Tello.

Moss, David. 1979. Bandits and boundaries in Sardinia. Man 14: 477-96.

Pallesen, A. Kemp. 1977. Culture contact and language convergence. Ph. D. dissertation, University of California, Berkeley.

Pelras, Christian. 1972. Notes sur quelques populations aquatiques de l'Archipel nusantarian. Archipel 3: 133-68.

Pigafetta, Antonio. 1906. Magellan's voyage around the world. 3 vols. Translated and edited by J. A. Robertson. Cleveland: A. H. Clark Co.

Pires, Tomé. 1944. The Suma Oriental, an account of the East, from the Red Sea to Japan, written in Malacca and India in 1512-1515. Translated by Armando Cortesao. London.

Prentice, D. J. 1970. The linguistic situation in northern Borneo. Pacific Linguistic Studies, S. A. Wurm and D. C. Laycock, eds. Pacific Linguistics, Series C, No. 13.

Saleeby, Najeeb M. 1905. Studies in Moro history, law and religion. Department of the Interior, Ethnological Survey Publications 4.1. Manila.

_____. 1908. The history of Sulu. Bureau of Science, Division of Ethnology Publications 4.2. Manila.

Sather, Clifford. 1972. Tidong. Ethnic groups of insular Southeast Asia. Frank Lebar, ed. Vol. 1, pp. 167-68. New Haven: Human Relations Area Files.

Sopher, D. E. 1965. The sea nomads: a study based on the literature of the maritime boat people of South-East Asia. Memoirs of the National Museum 5. Singapore.

Verschuer, F. H. Van. 1883. De Badjo's. Tijdschrift van het Aardijkskundig Genootschap. 7: 1-7.

Vosmaer, J. N. 1839. Korte beschrijving van de Zuid-Oostelijk schierland van Celebes, in het bijzonder van de Vosmaersbaai of van Kendari, verrijkt met eenige berigten omtrent den stam der Orang Badjos, en meer andere aanteekeningen. Verhandelingen van het Bataviaasch Genootschap van Kunst en Wetenschappen 17.

Wallace, Alfred Russel. 1869. The Malay Archipelago. London: Macmillan.

Warren, James F. 1975. Trade, raid, slave: the socio-economic patterns of the Sulu zone, 1770-1898. Ph. D. dissertation, Australian National University, Canberra.

Zorc, R. David Paul. 1975. The Bisayan dialects of the Philippines: subgrouping and reconstruction. Ph. D. dissertation, Cornell University.

Author's Postscript

A view over the work represented in this collection makes it appear that I have tried my hand at a great variety of topics. But this diversity, like much of the diversity we impute to human endeavors, is, in some measure, an artifact of conventional classifications of what it is we "do." I have "done" medical anthropology, social structure, law, ecology, semantics, discourse, religion, access rituals, Creole languages, and so on. It is a tribute to the editor, Anwar Dil, that he has been able to arrange this assortment of topics in a semblance of order, an order that does reveal, I think, the slim thread of unity that holds the package together. That thread carries a banner labeled "ethnography."

Ethnography is the description of culture. At the same time, given the elusiveness of the locus of culture, it is also a pursuit of it, an endeavor to capture and comprehend something of it. Since my first field work, my orienting goal has not been simply to understand some single, particularly fascinating aspect of culture or some single, particularly representative human carriers of culture, but to understand as well the inordinately difficult task of describing a culture in a way that allows one to have some confidence in a claim to have revealed a bit of reality rather than to have created a bit of fantasy. It is this concern with cultural description as a legitimate and theoretically revealing task in its own right that has led me into attempts to describe a variety of things, as cultural "things" are construed by anthropologists, from skin diseases to religion. It has also led me, from the very beginning of my work, into an intimate involvement with linguistics.

Given a serious concern with cultural description, a major commitment to language and linguistics seems to me to be inevitable.

(In fact, it is not inevitable; there are great ethnographers who show distressingly little interest in language. How they accomplish that lack of interest remains a mystery to me.) The ethnographer confronts language in three ways. First, even the most behavioristic of ethnographers must talk to people sometime; most ethnographers feel they must talk to people a lot. One soon learns that the ability to talk to people and to understand their talk involves much more than producing noises and constructing sentences (although just that part can be incredibly difficult in a new language for many of us). The ethnographer in the field, unlike the linguist in his office, cannot escape the fact that people do not just string words together in an idle game of solitaire. People mean things, intend things, and do things with words. And they accomplish these deeds in concert with other people in social situations. Linguists themselves can be heard to voice such arguments now, but at the time the earliest work represented in this volume was done, meaning—even in the most superficial sense of "What does this word mean?"—was ruled beyond the scope of linguistics. The recognition that people talk to each other came even later. Many linguists still ignore it. Ethnography, then, has not only needed linguistics; it has also had an important contribution to make toward expanding the horizons of that science.

It is not, however, just that the ethnographer must talk to people to get his work done. It is also the case that the ethnographer's work, after all, is to describe what people do. And what people do mostly is talk. Another great mystery in my life has been to understand how social scientists of all breeds have so long been able to ignore this simple fact. Yet it is through talk that people construe their cultural worlds, display and recreate their social orders, plan and critique their activities, and praise and condemn their fellows. Most of the studies here, perhaps especially the Subanun disease and drinking papers and the Yakan law and house-entering papers, reflect attempts to take seriously what it is people happen to be talking about and to take seriously, as well, the social act of talking itself. These efforts have convinced me that good ethnography requires careful listening to—and watching of—people talking to each other in the natural scenes of their social life. We are only beginning to learn how to do that kind of listening and watching in a way that not only yields a finely enough detailed record, but also enables accounts of what people, in their own psychological and cultural worlds, are "doing."

The third way the ethnographer confronts language is perhaps not as inevitable as the other two, but it has, nevertheless, been a major aspect of my own work. This confrontation arises from a conviction that, whatever kind of phenomena "language" and "culture" are, they are phenomena of the same kind. If language is a store of competence or a code book of rules underlying native interpretations of one kind of behavior, then culture must be the same kind of store or book, for there seems to be no natural boundary between the kind of behavior that manifests "language" and that which manifests "culture." If there is a natural boundary, it certainly is not an apparent one. Linguists have fought many wars over its location. It is likely that no linguist will agree with me that there is no boundary, but I am confident that there are no two linguists who will point to the same place when telling me where it is. Certainly the boundary is not between "verbal" and "non-verbal" behavior. Most of what people do, as we have noted, is verbal; and no linguist, no matter how far-reaching, wants to include all that talk within his or her subject. Much of "non-verbal" behavior is an integral part of what people do when talking to each other. One can make a distinction between what people say and what they do (in saying and otherwise), but even that boundary has been crossed by linguists. The import of this argument is that there is nothing essentially invalid, or even analogical, about applying theoretical schemes developed in linguistics to "cultural" material. True enough, attempts to apply linguistic models to cultural fields have had debatable success. But the success of these same models within linguistics has been equally debatable. If linguistic models have sometimes made culture look too rigid, too static, or too homogeneous, they have had the same distorting effects on views of language as well. Here again, the fields of anthropology and linguistics have something to learn from each other.

A very nice, but quite inadvertent, expression of both the difficulty and the vitality of the anthropologist's subject has been made by a Jamaican music group who have taken the name "Culture" and whose advertisements proclaim: CULTURE—HARDER THAN THE REST. The "hardness" of culture can be a source of agony not only for the ethnographer, but also for those who, like inner city teachers and students, must live and work across cultural boundaries. The agonies, both practical and moral, do not arise simply from the unlikeness of other cultures. Anthropology, which trades on explicating the exotic, often obscures this fact. Granted it can tax the anthropologist's ingenuity to make sense of head-hunting, the couvade, asymmetrical circulating connubia, and other "strange customs" (now often called "symbols"). But it is equally hard to understand how we do what we all do all the time: conduct our daily lives. Anthropologists are beginning to discover that it is as hard to study one's "own" culture (if one can find it) as any other. The outcome of ethnography, then, is not to make the strange less strange, but to make the familiar unfamiliar—something to be wondered at and puzzled over. Ethnography, like linguistics and other sciences of the human animal, eventually reveals the essential humanness shared by all of us across the checkerboard of social boundaries that we, being human, have created.

In the world of meanings, where "culture" can be "harder than the rest," it is no compliment to call someone "easy." I would not call my friends in the Philippines, among whom I have done most of my work, easy either. They can be hard just like the rest. But more than most, they have gone out of their way to make it as easy as possible for this ethnographer. Their patience, understanding, and compassion went far beyond what any investigator, who offers little in return, has a right to expect. Since my last field work there, these people, the Subanun, the Yakan, the Zamboangueños, and their neighbors, have suffered immensely in the warfare that has raged across the southwestern Philippines as a consequence of martial law. The ethnographic present of these papers is now past.

Bibliography of Charles O. Frake's Works

1954   Sindangan Subanun word list. Journal of East Asiatic Studies 3. 321-24.

1955   Social organization and shifting cultivation among the Sindangan Subanun. Ph. D. dissertation, Yale University. (Unpublished.)

1956   Malayo-Polynesian land tenure. American Anthropologist 58.170-73. [Reprinted in A. P. Vayda, ed., Peoples and cultures of the Pacific, pp. 150-53. New York: Natural History Press, 1968.]

1957 a.   Post-natal care among the Eastern Subanun. Silliman Journal 4. 207-16.
    b.   Review of Living conditions of plantation workers and peasants on Java, Coolie Budget Commission. American Anthropologist 59.1109-10.
    c.   Sindangan social groups. Philippine Sociological Review 5. 2-11.

1959 a.   Review of The maiden of the Buhong sky, by E. Arsenio Manuel. Journal of American Folklore 72. 364.
    b.   Review of Subsistence agriculture in Melanesia, by Jacques Barrau. American Anthropologist 61. 706-9.

1960 a.   The Eastern Subanun of Mindanao. In G. P. Murdock, ed., Social structure in Southeast Asia, pp. 51-64. Chicago: Aldine. [In this volume, pp. 83-103.]

1960 b. Review of Taro cultivation in Micronesia, ed. by J. de
         Young. Journal of American Folklore 73.344-45.

     c. Review of The use of names by Micronesians, ed. by J. de
         Young. Journal of American Folklore 73.177-78.

1961 a. The diagnosis of disease among the Subanun of Mindanao.
         American Anthropologist 63.113-32. [Reprinted in D. Hymes,
         ed., Language in culture and society. New York: Harper &
         Row, 1964. Reprinted in Stanford Medical Bulletin 1961:
         105-19. Reprinted in Bobbs Merrill Reprint Series A-72.
         Reprinted in D. Landy, ed., Culture, disease, and healing.
         New York: Macmillan, 1977.] [In this volume, pp. 104-31.]

     b. Review of Semantic analysis, by P. Ziff. American Anthro-
         pologist 63.1386-89.

     c. Review of Sociological studies of health and sickness. Jour-
         nal of American Folklore 74.177-78.

     d. Review of The meaning of kinship terms, by F. C. Wallace
         and J. Atkins. International Journal of American Linguis-
         tics 27.166.

1962 a. The ethnographic study of cognitive systems. In T. Gladwin
         and W. Sturtevant, eds., Anthropology and human behavior,
         pp. 72-85. Washington, D.C.: Anthropological Society of
         Washington. [Reprinted in J. A. Fishman, ed., Readings
         in the sociology of language, pp. 434-46. The Hague: Mou-
         ton, 1968. Reprinted in M. Fried, ed., Readings in anthro-
         pology, Vol. II, pp. 401-19. New York: Crowell, 1968.
         Reprinted in R. Manners and D. Kaplan, eds., Theory in
         anthropology, pp. 507-13. Chicago: Aldine, 1968. Reprinted
         in S. Tyler, ed., Cognitive anthropology, pp. 28-40. New
         York: Holt, 1968. Reprinted in J. Spradley, ed., Culture
         and cognition, pp. 191-205. San Francisco: Chandler, 1972.
         Translated as Die Ethnographische Erforschung Kognitiver
         Systeme, Alltagswissen, Interaktion und Gesellschaftliche
         Wirklichkeit. Bd. 2, Arbeitsgruppe Bielefelder Soziologen,
         pp. 323-37. Hamburg: Rowohlt, 2973.] [In this volume,
         pp. 1-17.]

     b. Cultural ecology and ethnography. American Anthropologist
         64.54-59. [Reprinted in R. Murphy, ed., Selected papers
         from the American Anthropologist, 1946-1970, pp. 319-25.

Washington, D.C.: American Anthropological Association,
1976. Reprinted in F. Gamst and E. Norbeck, eds., Ideas
of culture, pp. 270-77. New York: Holt, 1976.] [In this
volume, pp. 18-25.]

c. Review of Linguistic play in its cultural contexts, by H. C.
Conklin. International Journal of American Linguistics
28.66.

d. Review of Linguistic etiquette, by C. Geertz. International
Journal of American Linguistics 28.66-67.

1963 a. Litigation in Lipay: a study in Subanun law. Proceedings
of the Ninth Pacific Science Congress, 1957, Vol. 3, pp.
217-22. Bangkok. [In this volume, pp. 132-43.]

b. The Subanun of Zamboanga: a linguistic survey. Proceedings of the Ninth Pacific Science Congress, 1957, Vol. 3,
pp. 93-94. Bangkok.

1964 a. Discussion of Burling's Cognition and componential analysis.
American Anthropologist 66.28. [Reprinted in S. Tyler, ed.,
Cognitive anthropology, p. 432. New York: Holt, 1968.]

b. Ethno-models of semantic structure. Report to the National
Institute of Mental Health. (Unpublished.)

c. A structural description of Subanun "religious behavior."
In W. Goodenough, ed., Explorations in cultural anthropology:
essays in honor of George Peter Murdock, pp. 111-30. New
York: McGraw-Hill. [Reprinted in W. Lessa and E. Vogt,
eds., Reader in comparative religion, pp. 582-92. 2nd ed.,
1965. Reprinted in S. Tyler, ed., Cognitive anthropology,
pp. 470-86. New York: Holt, 1968.] [In this volume, pp.
144-65.]

d. Notes on queries in ethnography. American Anthropologist
66.132-45. [Reprinted in S. Tyler, ed., Cognitive anthropology, pp. 123-36. New York: Holt, 1968.] [In this volume, pp. 26-44.]

e. How to ask for a drink in Subanun. American Anthropologist
66.127-32. [Reprinted in P. Giglioli, ed., Language and
social context, pp. 87-94. London: Penguin, 1972. Reprinted in J. B. Pride and J. Holmes, eds., Sociolinguistics,
pp. 101-11. London: Penguin, 1972. Reprinted in Warner
Modular Publication 242, 1973. Translated as Como pedir

una bebida en Subanun. Antologia de estudios de etnolinguis-
tica y sociolinguistica, pp. 117-24. Mexico: Universidad
Nacional Autonoma de Mexico, 1974.] [In this volume, pp.
166-73.]

1969   Struck by speech: the Yakan concept of litigation. In L.
          Nader, ed., Law in culture and society, pp. 147-67. Chica-
          go: Aldine. [Reprinted in J. Gumperz and D. Hymes, eds.,
          Directions in sociolinguistics, pp. 106-29. New York: Holt,
          1972. Reprinted in J. Spradley, ed., Culture and cognition,
          pp. 279-301. San Francisco: Chandler, 1972.] [In this vol-
          ume, pp. 175-201.]

1971   Lexical origins and semantic structure in Philippine Creole
          Spanish. In Dell Hymes, ed., Pidginization and creolization
          of languages, pp. 223-42. Cambridge: Cambridge Univer-
          sity Press. [In this volume, pp. 253-76.]

1972 a.   Ethnography. A review prepared for the Committee on
          Social and Cultural Processes, National Institute of Mental
          Health, Washington, D.C. (Unpublished.)
     b.   Review of Philippine minor languages, ed. by L. Reid.
          Journal of Asian Studies 32.750-51.

1973   Manobo. Encyclopedia Britannica. 14th ed., vol. 14, pp.
          800-801. Chicago: William Benton.

1975   How to enter a Yakan house. In M. Sanches and B. Blount,
          eds., Sociocultural dimensions of language use, pp. 25-40.
          New York: Academic Press. [Reprinted in Sulu Studies
          3.87-104 (1974).] [In this volume, pp. 214-32.]

1977   Plying frames can be dangerous: an assessment of methodol-
          ogy in cognitive anthropology. The Quarterly Newsletter of
          the Institute for Comparative Human Development, The
          Rockefeller University, 1.3.1-7. [In this volume, pp. 45-60.]

1980 a.   Interpretations of illness: an ethnographic perspective on
          events and their causes. [In this volume, pp. 61-82.]
     b.   Kin and supporters among the Yakan. [In this volume, pp.
          202-13.]

1980 c. Languages in Yakan culture. [In this volume, pp. 233-52.]

     d. The genesis of kinds of people in the Sulu Archipelago. [In this volume, pp. 311-32.]

     e. Zamboangueño verb expressions. [In this volume, pp. 277-310.]

     f. Author's postscript. [In this volume, pp. 333-36.]